Python Machine Learning Cookbook

Cookbook

Second Edition

Over 100 recipes to progress from smart data analytics to deep learning using real-world datasets

Giuseppe Ciaburro
Prateek Joshi

BIRMINGHAM - MUMBAI

Python Machine Learning Cookbook
Second Edition

Copyright © 2019 Packt Publishing

Commissioning Editor: Sunith Shetty
Acquisition Editor: Devika Battike
Content Development Editor: Nathanya Dias
Technical Editor: Joseph Sunil
Copy Editor: Safis Editing
Project Coordinator: Kirti Pisat
Proofreader: Safis Editing
Indexer: Pratik Shirodkar
Graphics: Jisha Chirayil
Production Coordinator: Arvindkumar Gupta

First published: June 2016
Second edition: March 2019

Production reference: 1290319

Published by Packt Publishing Ltd.
Livery Place
35 Livery Street
Birmingham
B3 2PB, UK.

ISBN 978-1-78980-845-2

www.packtpub.com

`mapt.io`

Mapt is an online digital library that gives you full access to over 5,000 books and videos, as well as industry leading tools to help you plan your personal development and advance your career. For more information, please visit our website.

Why subscribe?

- Spend less time learning and more time coding with practical eBooks and Videos from over 4,000 industry professionals

- Improve your learning with Skill Plans built especially for you

- Get a free eBook or video every month

- Mapt is fully searchable

- Copy and paste, print, and bookmark content

Packt.com

Did you know that Packt offers eBook versions of every book published, with PDF and ePub files available? You can upgrade to the eBook version at `www.packt.com` and as a print book customer, you are entitled to a discount on the eBook copy. Get in touch with us at `customercare@packtpub.com` for more details.

At `www.packt.com`, you can also read a collection of free technical articles, sign up for a range of free newsletters, and receive exclusive discounts and offers on Packt books and eBooks.

Contributors

About the author

Giuseppe Ciaburro holds a PhD in environmental technical physics, along with two master's degrees. His research was focused on machine learning applications in the study of urban sound environments. He works at the Built Environment Control Laboratory at the Università degli Studi della Campania Luigi Vanvitelli, Italy. He has over 15 years' professional experience in programming (Python, R, and MATLAB), first in the field of combustion, and then in acoustics and noise control. He has several publications to his credit.

Prateek Joshi is an artificial intelligence researcher, an author of several books, and a TEDx speaker. He has been featured in Forbes 30 Under 30, CNBC, TechCrunch, Silicon Valley Business Journal, and many more publications. He is the founder of Pluto AI, a venture-funded Silicon Valley start-up building an intelligence platform for water facilities. He graduated from the University of Southern California with a Master's degree specializing in Artificial Intelligence. He has previously worked at NVIDIA and Microsoft Research.

About the reviewer

Greg Walters has been involved with computers and computer programming since 1972. Currently, he is extremely well versed in Visual Basic, Visual Basic .NET, Python, and SQL using MySQL, SQLite, Microsoft SQL Server, Oracle, C++, Delphi, Modula-2, Pascal, C, 80x86 Assembler, COBOL, and Fortran.

He is a programming trainer and has trained numerous people in many pieces of computer software, including MySQL, Open Database Connectivity, Quattro Pro, Corel Draw!, Paradox, Microsoft Word, Excel, DOS, Windows 3.11, Windows for Workgroups, Windows 95, Windows NT, Windows 2000, Windows XP, and Linux.

He is currently retired, and, in his spare time, is a musician and loves to cook, but he is also open to working as a freelancer on various projects.

Packt is searching for authors like you

If you're interested in becoming an author for Packt, please visit `authors.packtpub.com` and apply today. We have worked with thousands of developers and tech professionals, just like you, to help them share their insight with the global tech community. You can make a general application, apply for a specific hot topic that we are recruiting an author for, or submit your own idea.

Table of Contents

Preface

This eagerly anticipated second edition of the popular *Python Machine Learning Cookbook, Second Edition,* will enable you to adopt a fresh approach to dealing with real-world machine learning and deep learning tasks.

With the help of over 100 recipes, you will learn to build powerful machine learning applications using modern libraries from the Python ecosystem. The book will also guide you on how to implement various machine learning algorithms for classification, clustering, and recommendation engines, using a recipe-based approach. With an emphasis on practical solutions, dedicated sections in the book will help you to apply supervised and unsupervised learning techniques to real-world problems. Toward the concluding chapters, you will get to grips with recipes that teach you advanced techniques for fields including reinforcement learning, deep neural networks, and automated machine learning.

By the end of this book, you will be equipped, through real-world examples, with the skills you need to apply machine learning techniques, and will be able to leverage the full capabilities of the Python ecosystem.

Who this book is for

This book is for data scientists, machine learning developers, deep learning enthusiasts, and Python programmers who want to solve real-world challenges using machine learning techniques and algorithms. If you are facing challenges at work and want ready-to-use code solutions to cover key tasks in the machine learning and deep learning domains, then this book is what you need.

What this book covers

Chapter 1, *The Realm of Supervised Learning,* covers various machine learning paradigms that will help you to understand how the field is divided into multiple subgroups. This chapter briefly discuss the differences between supervised and unsupervised learning, along with the concepts of regression, classification, and clustering. We will learn how to preprocess data for machine learning. We will discuss regression analysis in detail and learn how to apply it to a couple of real-world problems, including house price estimation and bicycle demand distribution.

Chapter 2, *Constructing a Classifier*, shows you how to perform data classification using various models. We will discuss techniques including logistic regression and the naïve Bayes model. We will learn how to evaluate the accuracy of classification algorithms. We will discuss the concept of cross-validation and learn how to use it to validate our machine learning model. We will learn about validation curves and how to plot them. We will apply these supervised learning techniques to real-world problems, such as income bracket estimation and activity recognition.

Chapter 3, *Predictive Modeling*, covers the premise of predictive modeling and why it's needed. We will learn about SVMs and understand how they work. We will learn how to use them to classify data. We will discuss the concept of hyperparameters and how they affect the performance of SVMs. We will learn how to use grid search to find the optimal set of hyperparameters. We will discuss how to estimate the confidence measure of the outputs. We will talk about ensemble learning and the various algorithms in this group, such as decision trees and random forests. We will then learn how to apply these techniques to real-world event prediction.

Chapter 4, *Clustering with Unsupervised Learning*, covers the concept of unsupervised learning and what we hope to achieve from it. We will learn how to perform data clustering and how to apply the k-means clustering algorithm to do it. We will visualize the clustering process using sample data. We will discuss mixture models and Gaussian mixture models. We will then apply these techniques to perform market segmentation using customer information.

Chapter 5, *Visualizing Data*, discusses how to visualize data and explains why it's useful for machine learning. We will learn how to use Matplotlib to interact with our data and visualize it using various techniques. We will discuss histograms and how they are useful. We will explore different methods for visualizing data, including line charts, scatter plots, and bubble plots. We will learn how to use heat maps, perform animation, and do 3D plotting.

Chapter 6, *Building Recommendation Engines*, introduces recommendation engines and shows us how to use it for checking movie recommendations. We will construct a k-nearest neighbors classifier to find similar users in our dataset and then generate movie recommendations using a filtering model with TensorFlow.

Chapter 7, *Analyzing Text Data*, shows you how to analyze text data. We will understand various concepts such as the bag-of-words model, tokenization, and stemming. We will learn about the features that can be extracted from text. We will discuss how to build a text classifier. We will then use these techniques to infer the sentiment of a sentence. We will also learn how to automatically identify the topic of an unknown paragraph. We will then move on to evaluating regression and classification models, and then step into recipes that can help us with selecting models.

Chapter 8, *Speech Recognition*, demonstrates how you can work with speech data. We will learn about concepts including windowing and convolution. We will understand how to extract features from speech data. We will learn about hidden Markov models and how to use them to automatically recognize the words being spoken.

Chapter 9, *Dissecting Time Series and Sequential Data*, introduces the concept of structured learning. We will come to understand the various characteristics of time series data. We will learn about conditional random fields and see how to use them for prediction. We will then use this technique to analyze stock market data.

Chapter 10, *Image Content Analysis*, shows how to analyze images. We will learn how to detect keypoints and extract features from images. We will discuss the concept of a *bag of visual words* and see how it applies to image classification. We will learn how to build a visual code book and extract feature vectors for image classification. We will then understand how to use extremely random forests to perform object recognition.

Chapter 11, *Biometric Face Recognition*, shows how to perform face recognition. We will understand the differences between face detection and face recognition. We will talk about dimensionality reduction and how to use PCA to achieve this. We will learn about Fisher Faces and how it can be used for face recognition. We will perform face detection on a live video. We will then use these techniques to identify the person in front of the camera.

Chapter 12, *Reinforcement Learning Techniques*, discusses reinforcement learning techniques and its applications. It also discusses the elements of reinforcement learning setup, approaches to reinforcement learning, and its challenges, along with topics such as Markov decision processes, the exploration-exploitation dilemma, discounted future reward, and Q-learning.

Chapter 13, *Deep Neural Networks*, discusses deep neural networks. We will learn about perceptrons and see how they are used to build neural networks. We will explore the interconnections between multiple layers in a deep neural network. We will discuss how a neural network learns about the training data and builds a model. We will learn about the cost function and backpropagation. We will then use these techniques to perform optical character recognition. We will work with different frameworks for deep learning, including TensorFlow, PyTorch, and Caffe.

Chapter 14, *Unsupervised Representation Learning*, discusses the problem of learning representations for data such as images, videos, and natural language corpuses in an unsupervised manner. We will go through autoencoders and their applications, word embeddings, and t-SNEs. We will also use denoising autoencoders to detect fraudulent transactions using word embeddings. Lastly, we will move on to implementing LDA with the help of various recipes.

Chapter 15, *Automated Machine Learning and Transfer Learning*, discusses recipes based on automated machine learning and transfer learning. We will learn how to work with Auto-WEKA and how to use AutoML to generate machine learning pipelines. We will learn how to work with Auto-Keras and then move on to using MLBox for leak detection. Furthermore, we will learn how to implement transfer learning with the help of multiple recipes.

Chapter 16, *Unlocking Production Issues*, discusses production-related issues. We will go through how a reader can handle unstructured data, along with how we can keep a track of changes in our machine learning models. We will also learn how to optimize a retraining schedule and how to deploy our machine learning models.

To get the most out of this book

A familiarity with Python programming and machine learning concepts will be beneficial.

Download the example code files

You can download the example code files for this book from your account at www.packt.com. If you purchased this book elsewhere, you can visit www.packt.com/support and register to have the files emailed directly to you.

You can download the code files by following these steps:

1. Log in or register at www.packt.com.
2. Select the **SUPPORT** tab.
3. Click on **Code Downloads & Errata**.
4. Enter the name of the book in the **Search** box and follow the onscreen instructions.

Once the file is downloaded, please make sure that you unzip or extract the folder using the latest version of:

- WinRAR/7-Zip for Windows
- Zipeg/iZip/UnRarX for Mac
- 7-Zip/PeaZip for Linux

The code bundle for the book is also hosted on GitHub at `https://github.com/PacktPublishing/Python-Machine-Learning-Cookbook-Second-Edition`. In case there's an update to the code, it will be updated on the existing GitHub repository.

We also have other code bundles from our rich catalog of books and videos available at `https://github.com/PacktPublishing/`. Check them out!

Download the color images

We also provide a PDF file that has color images of the screenshots/diagrams used in this book. You can download it here: `http://www.packtpub.com/sites/default/files/downloads/9781789808452_ColorImages.pdf`.

Conventions used

There are a number of text conventions used throughout this book.

`CodeInText`: Indicates code words in text, database table names, folder names, filenames, file extensions, pathnames, dummy URLs, user input, and Twitter handles. Here is an example: "We will use the `simple_classifier.py` file that is already provided to you as a reference."

A block of code is set as follows:

```
import numpy as np
import matplotlib.pyplot as plt

X = np.array([[3,1], [2,5], [1,8], [6,4], [5,2], [3,5], [4,7],
[4,-1]])
```

When we wish to draw your attention to a particular part of a code block, the relevant lines or items are set in bold:

```
[default]
exten => s,1,Dial(Zap/1|30)
exten => s,2,Voicemail(u100)
exten => s,102,Voicemail(b100)
exten => i,1,Voicemail(s0)
```

Any command-line input or output is written as follows:

```
data = np.array([[3, -1.5, 2, -5.4], [0, 4, -0.3, 2.1], [1, 3.3, -1.9,
-4.3]])
```

Bold: Indicates a new term, an important word, or words that you see onscreen. For example, words in menus or dialog boxes appear in the text like this. Here is an example: "Select **System info** from the **Administration** panel."

Warnings or important notes appear like this.

Tips and tricks appear like this.

Sections

In this book, you will find several headings that appear frequently (*Getting ready, How to do it..., How it works..., There's more...,* and *See also*).

To give clear instructions on how to complete a recipe, use these sections as follows:

Getting ready

This section tells you what to expect in the recipe and describes how to set up any software or any preliminary settings required for the recipe.

How to do it...

This section contains the steps required to follow the recipe.

How it works...

This section usually consists of a detailed explanation of what happened in the previous section.

There's more...

This section consists of additional information about the recipe in order to make you more knowledgeable about the recipe.

See also

This section provides helpful links to other useful information for the recipe.

Get in touch

Feedback from our readers is always welcome.

General feedback: If you have questions about any aspect of this book, mention the book title in the subject of your message and email us at `customercare@packtpub.com`.

Errata: Although we have taken every care to ensure the accuracy of our content, mistakes do happen. If you have found a mistake in this book, we would be grateful if you would report this to us. Please visit `www.packt.com/submit-errata`, selecting your book, clicking on the Errata Submission Form link, and entering the details.

Piracy: If you come across any illegal copies of our works in any form on the Internet, we would be grateful if you would provide us with the location address or website name. Please contact us at `copyright@packt.com` with a link to the material.

If you are interested in becoming an author: If there is a topic that you have expertise in and you are interested in either writing or contributing to a book, please visit `authors.packtpub.com`.

Reviews

Please leave a review. Once you have read and used this book, why not leave a review on the site that you purchased it from? Potential readers can then see and use your unbiased opinion to make purchase decisions, we at Packt can understand what you think about our products, and our authors can see your feedback on their book. Thank you!

For more information about Packt, please visit `packt.com`.

The Realm of Supervised Learning

1

In this chapter, we will cover the following recipes:

- Array creation in Python
- Data preprocessing using mean removal
- Data scaling
- Normalization
- Binarization
- One-hot encoding
- Label encoding
- Building a linear regressor
- Computing regression accuracy
- Achieving model persistence
- Building a ridge regressor
- Building a polynomial regressor
- Estimating housing prices
- Computing the relative importance of features
- Estimating bicycle demand distribution

Technical requirements

We will use various Python packages, such as NumPy, SciPy, scikit-learn, and Matplotlib, during the course of this book to build various things. If you use Windows, it is recommended that you use a SciPy-stack-compatible version of Python. You can check the list of compatible versions at `http://www.scipy.org/install.html`. These distributions come with all the necessary packages already installed. If you use MacOS X or Ubuntu, installing these packages is fairly straightforward. Here are some useful links for installation and documentation:

- NumPy: `https://www.numpy.org/devdocs/user/install.html`.
- SciPy: `http://www.scipy.org/install.html`.
- Scikit-learn: `https://scikit-learn.org/stable/install.html`.
- Matplotlib: `https://matplotlib.org/users/installing.html`.

Make sure that you have these packages installed on your machine before you proceed. In each recipe, we will give a detailed explanation of the functions that we will use in order to make it simple and fast.

Introduction

Machine learning is a multidisciplinary field created at the intersection of, and with synergy between, computer science, statistics, neurobiology, and control theory. It has played a key role in various fields and has radically changed the vision of programming software. For humans, and more generally, for every living being, learning is a form of adaptation of a system to its environment through experience. This adaptation process must lead to improvement without human intervention. To achieve this goal, the system must be able to learn, which means that it must be able to extract useful information on a given problem by examining a series of examples associated with it.

If you are familiar with the basics of machine learning, you will certainly know what supervised learning is all about. To give you a quick refresher, **supervised learning** refers to building a machine learning model that is based on labeled samples. The algorithm generates a function which connects input values to a desired output via of a set of labeled examples, where each data input has its relative output data. This is used to construct predictive models. For example, if we build a system to estimate the price of a house based on various parameters, such as size, locality, and so on, we first need to create a database and label it. We need to tell our algorithm what parameters correspond to what prices. Based on this data, our algorithm will learn how to calculate the price of a house using the input parameters.

Unsupervised learning is in stark contrast to what we just discussed. There is no labeled data available here. The algorithm tries to acquire knowledge from general input without the help of a set of pre-classified examples that are used to build descriptive models. Let's assume that we have a bunch of data points, and we just want to separate them into multiple groups. We don't exactly know what the criteria of separation would be. So, an unsupervised learning algorithm will try to separate the given dataset into a fixed number of groups in the best possible way. We will discuss unsupervised learning in the upcoming chapters.

In the following recipes, we will look at various data preprocessing techniques.

Array creation in Python

Arrays are the essential elements of many programming languages. Arrays are sequential objects that behave very similarly to lists, except that the types of elements contained in them are constrained. The type is specified when the object is created using a single character called **type code**.

Getting ready

In this recipe, we will cover an array creation procedure. We will first create an array using the NumPy library, and then display its structure.

How to do it...

Let's see how to create an array in Python:

1. To start off, import the NumPy library as follows:

```
>> import numpy as np
```

We just imported a necessary package, numpy. This is the fundamental package for scientific computing with Python. It contains, among other things, the following:

- A powerful N-dimensional array object
- Sophisticated broadcasting functions
- Tools for integrating C, C++, and FORTRAN code
- Useful linear algebra, Fourier transform, and random number capabilities

Besides its obvious uses, NumPy is also used as an efficient multidimensional container of generic data. Arbitrary data types can be found. This enables NumPy to integrate with different types of databases.

 Remember, to import a library that is not present in the initial distribution of Python, you must use the `pip install` command followed by the name of the library. This command should be used only once and not every time you run the code.

2. Let's create some sample data. Add the following line to the Python Terminal:

```
>> data = np.array([[3, -1.5, 2, -5.4], [0, 4, -0.3, 2.1], [1, 3.3, -1.9, -4.3]])
```

The `np.array` function creates a NumPy array. A NumPy array is a grid of values, all of the same type, indexed by a tuple of non-negative integers. `rank` and `shape` are essential features of a NumPy array. The `rank` variable is the number of dimensions of the array. The `shape` variable is a tuple of integers that returns the size of the array along each dimension.

3. We display the newly created array with this snippet:

```
>> print(data)
```

The following result is returned:

```
[[ 3.  -1.5  2.   -5.4]
 [ 0.   4.  -0.3  2.1]
 [ 1.   3.3 -1.9 -4.3]]
```

We are now ready to operate on this data.

How it works...

NumPy is an extension package in the Python environment that is fundamental for scientific calculation. This is because it adds to the tools that are already available, the typical features of N-dimensional arrays, element-by-element operations, a massive number of mathematical operations in linear algebra, and the ability to integrate and recall source code written in C, C++, and FORTRAN. In this recipe, we learned how to create an array using the NumPy library.

There's more...

NumPy provides us with various tools for creating an array. For example, to create a one-dimensional array of equidistant values with numbers from 0 to 10, we would use the `arange()` function, as follows:

```
>> NpArray1 = np.arange(10)
>> print(NpArray1)
```

The following result is returned:

```
[0 1 2 3 4 5 6 7 8 9]
```

To create a numeric array from 0 to 50, with a step of 5 (using a predetermined step between successive values), we will write the following code:

```
>> NpArray2 = np.arange(10, 100, 5)
>> print(NpArray2)
```

The following array is printed:

```
[10 15 20 25 30 35 40 45 50 55 60 65 70 75 80 85 90 95]
```

Also, to create a one-dimensional array of 50 numbers between two limit values and that are equidistant in this range, we will use the `linspace()` function:

```
>> NpArray3 = np.linspace(0, 10, 50)
>> print(NpArray3)
```

The following result is returned:

```
[ 0.  0.20408163 0.40816327 0.6122449 0.81632653 1.02040816
 1.2244898 1.42857143 1.63265306 1.83673469 2.04081633 2.24489796
 2.44897959 2.65306122 2.85714286 3.06122449 3.26530612 3.46938776
 3.67346939 3.87755102 4.08163265 4.28571429 4.48979592 4.69387755
 4.89795918 5.10204082 5.30612245 5.51020408 5.71428571 5.91836735
 6.12244898 6.32653061 6.53061224 6.73469388 6.93877551 7.14285714
 7.34693878 7.55102041 7.75510204 7.95918367 8.16326531 8.36734694
 8.57142857 8.7755102 8.97959184 9.18367347 9.3877551 9.59183673
 9.79591837 10. ]
```

These are just some simple samples of NumPy. In the following sections, we will delve deeper into the topic.

See also

- NumPy developer guide (`https://docs.scipy.org/doc/numpy/dev/`).
- NumPy tutorial (`https://docs.scipy.org/doc/numpy/user/quickstart.html`).
- NumPy reference (`https://devdocs.io/numpy~1.12/`).

Data preprocessing using mean removal

In the real world, we usually have to deal with a lot of raw data. This raw data is not readily ingestible by machine learning algorithms. To prepare data for machine learning, we have to preprocess it before we feed it into various algorithms. This is an intensive process that takes plenty of time, almost 80 percent of the entire data analysis process, in some scenarios. However, it is vital for the rest of the data analysis workflow, so it is necessary to learn the best practices of these techniques. Before sending our data to any machine learning algorithm, we need to cross check the quality and accuracy of the data. If we are unable to reach the data stored in Python correctly, or if we can't switch from raw data to something that can be analyzed, we cannot go ahead. Data can be preprocessed in many ways—standardization, scaling, normalization, binarization, and one-hot encoding are some examples of preprocessing techniques. We will address them through simple examples.

Getting ready

Standardization or **mean removal** is a technique that simply centers data by removing the average value of each characteristic, and then scales it by dividing non-constant characteristics by their standard deviation. It's usually beneficial to remove the mean from each feature so that it's centered on zero. This helps us remove bias from features. The formula used to achieve this is the following:

$$x_{scaled} = \frac{x - mean}{sd}$$

Standardization results in the rescaling of features, which in turn represents the properties of a standard normal distribution:

- **mean** = 0
- **sd** = 1

In this formula, **mean** is the mean and **sd** is the standard deviation from the mean.

How to do it...

Let's see how to preprocess data in Python:

1. Let's start by importing the library:

    ```
    >> from sklearn import preprocessing
    ```

    The `sklearn` library is a free software machine learning library for the Python programming language. It features various classification, regression, and clustering algorithms, including **support vector machines** (**SVMs**), random forests, gradient boosting, k-means, and DBSCAN, and is designed to interoperate with the Python numerical and scientific libraries, NumPy and SciPy.

2. To understand the outcome of mean removal on our data, we first visualize the mean and standard deviation of the vector we have just created:

    ```
    >> print("Mean: ",data.mean(axis=0))
    >> print("Standard Deviation: ",data.std(axis=0))
    ```

    The `mean()` function returns the sample arithmetic mean of data, which can be a sequence or an iterator. The `std()` function returns the standard deviation, a measure of the distribution of the array elements. The `axis` parameter specifies the axis along which these functions are computed (0 for columns, and 1 for rows).

    The following results are returned:

    ```
    Mean: [ 1.33333333 1.93333333 -0.06666667 -2.53333333]
    Standard Deviation: [1.24721913 2.44449495 1.60069429 3.30689515]
    ```

3. Now we can proceed with standardization:

```
>> data_standardized = preprocessing.scale(data)
```

The `preprocessing.scale()` function standardizes a dataset along any axis. This method centers the data on the mean and resizes the components in order to have a unit variance.

4. Now we recalculate the mean and standard deviation on the standardized data:

```
>> print("Mean standardized data: ",data_standardized.mean(axis=0))
>> print("Standard Deviation standardized data:
",data_standardized.std(axis=0))
```

The following results are returned:

```
Mean standardized data: [ 5.55111512e-17 -1.11022302e-16
-7.40148683e-17 -7.40148683e-17]
Standard Deviation standardized data: [1. 1. 1. 1.]
```

You can see that the mean is almost 0 and the standard deviation is 1.

How it works...

The `sklearn.preprocessing` package provides several common utility functions and transformer classes to modify the features available in a representation that best suits our needs. In this recipe, the `scale()` function has been used (z-score standardization). In summary, the z-score (also called the standard score) represents the number of standard deviations by which the value of an observation point or data is greater than the mean value of what is observed or measured. Values more than the mean have positive z-scores, while values less than the mean have negative z-scores. The z-score is a quantity without dimensions that is obtained by subtracting the population's mean from a single rough score and then dividing the difference by the standard deviation of the population.

There's more...

Standardization is particularly useful when we do not know the minimum and maximum for data distribution. In this case, it is not possible to use other forms of data transformation. As a result of the transformation, the normalized values do not have a minimum and a fixed maximum. Moreover, this technique is not influenced by the presence of outliers, or at least not the same as other methods.

See also

- Scikit-learn's official documentation of the `sklearn.preprocessing.scale()` function: `https://scikit-learn.org/stable/modules/generated/sklearn.preprocessing.scale.html`.

Data scaling

The values of each feature in a dataset can vary between random values. So, sometimes it is important to scale them so that this becomes a level playing field. Through this statistical procedure, it's possible to compare identical variables belonging to different distributions and different variables.

Remember, it is good practice to rescale data before training a machine learning algorithm. With rescaling, data units are eliminated, allowing you to easily compare data from different locations.

Getting ready

We'll use the **min-max** method (usually called **feature scaling**) to get all of the scaled data in the range [0, 1]. The formula used to achieve this is as follows:

$$x_{scaled} = \frac{x - x_{min}}{x_{max} - x_{min}}$$

To scale features between a given minimum and maximum value—in our case, between 0 and 1—so that the maximum absolute value of each feature is scaled to unit size, the `preprocessing.MinMaxScaler()` function can be used.

How to do it...

Let's see how to scale data in Python:

1. Let's start by defining the `data_scaler` variable:

```
>> data_scaler = preprocessing.MinMaxScaler(feature_range=(0, 1))
```

2. Now we will use the `fit_transform()` method, which fits the data and then transforms it (we will use the same data as in the previous recipe):

```
>> data_scaled = data_scaler.fit_transform(data)
```

A NumPy array of a specific shape is returned. To understand how this function has transformed data, we display the minimum and maximum of each column in the array.

3. First, for the starting data and then for the processed data:

```
>> print("Min: ",data.min(axis=0))
>> print("Max: ",data.max(axis=0))
```

The following results are returned:

```
Min: [ 0. -1.5 -1.9 -5.4]
Max: [3.  4.  2.  2.1]
```

4. Now, let's do the same for the scaled data using the following code:

```
>> print("Min: ",data_scaled.min(axis=0))
>> print("Max: ",data_scaled.max(axis=0))
```

The following results are returned:

```
Min: [0. 0. 0. 0.]
Max: [1. 1. 1. 1.]
```

After scaling, all the feature values range between the specified values.

5. To display the scaled array, we will use the following code:

```
>> print(data_scaled)
```

The output will be displayed as follows:

```
[[ 1.          0.          1.          0.         ]
 [ 0.          1.          0.41025641  1.         ]
 [ 0.33333333  0.87272727  0.          0.14666667]]
```

Now, all the data is included in the same interval.

How it works...

When data has different ranges, the impact on response variables might be higher than the one with a lesser numeric range, which can affect the prediction accuracy. Our goal is to improve predictive accuracy and ensure this doesn't happen. Hence, we may need to scale values under different features so that they fall within a similar range. Through this statistical procedure, it's possible to compare identical variables belonging to different distributions and different variables or variables expressed in different units.

There's more...

Feature scaling consists of limiting the excursion of a set of values within a certain predefined interval. It guarantees that all functionalities have the exact same scale, but does not handle anomalous values well. This is because extreme values become the extremes of the new range of variation. In this way, the actual values are compressed by keeping the distance to the anomalous values.

See also

- Scikit-learn's official documentation of the `sklearn.preprocessing.MinMaxScaler()` function: `https://scikit-learn.org/stable/modules/generated/sklearn.preprocessing.MinMaxScaler.html`.

Normalization

Data normalization is used when you want to adjust the values in the feature vector so that they can be measured on a common scale. One of the most common forms of normalization that is used in machine learning adjusts the values of a feature vector so that they sum up to 1.

Getting ready

To normalize data, the `preprocessing.normalize()` function can be used. This function scales input vectors individually to a unit norm (vector length). Three types of norms are provided, l_1, l_2, or **max**, and they are explained next. If x is the vector of covariates of length n, the normalized vector is $y=x/z$, where z is defined as follows:

$$l1 : z = \sum_{i}^{n} |x_i|$$

$$l2 : z = \sqrt{\sum_{i}^{n} x_i^2}$$

$$max : z = max(x_i)$$

The **norm** is a function that assigns a positive length to each vector belonging to a vector space, except 0.

How to do it...

Let's see how to normalize data in Python:

1. As we said, to normalize data, the `preprocessing.normalize()` function can be used as follows (we will use the same data as in the previous recipe):

```
>> data_normalized = preprocessing.normalize(data, norm='l1',
axis=0)
```

2. To display the normalized array, we will use the following code:

```
>> print(data_normalized)
```

The following output is returned:

```
[[ 0.75 -0.17045455  0.47619048  -0.45762712]
 [ 0.     0.45454545 -0.07142857   0.1779661 ]
 [ 0.25   0.375      -0.45238095  -0.36440678]]
```

This is used a lot to make sure that datasets don't get boosted artificially due to the fundamental nature of their features.

3. As already mentioned, the normalized array along the columns (features) must return a sum equal to 1. Let's check this for each column:

```
>> data_norm_abs = np.abs(data_normalized)
>> print(data_norm_abs.sum(axis=0))
```

In the first line of code, we used the `np.abs()` function to evaluate the absolute value of each element in the array. In the second row of code, we used the `sum()` function to calculate the sum of each column (`axis=0`). The following results are returned:

```
[1. 1. 1. 1.]
```

Therefore, the sum of the absolute value of the elements of each column is equal to 1, so the data is normalized.

How it works...

In this recipe, we normalized the data at our disposal to the unitary norm. Each sample with at least one non-zero component was rescaled independently of other samples so that its norm was equal to one.

There's more...

Scaling inputs to a unit norm is a very common task in text classification and clustering problems.

See also

- Scikit-learn's official documentation of the `sklearn.preprocessing.normalize()` function: `https://scikit-learn.org/stable/modules/generated/sklearn.preprocessing.normalize.html`.

Binarization

Binarization is used when you want to convert a numerical feature vector into a Boolean vector. In the field of digital image processing, image binarization is the process by which a color or grayscale image is transformed into a binary image, that is, an image with only two colors (typically, black and white).

Getting ready

This technique is used for the recognition of objects, shapes, and, specifically, characters. Through binarization, it is possible to distinguish the object of interest from the background on which it is found. Skeletonization is instead an essential and schematic representation of the object, which generally preludes the subsequent real recognition.

How to do it...

Let's see how to binarize data in Python:

1. To binarize data, we will use the `preprocessing.Binarizer()` function as follows (we will use the same data as in the previous recipe):

```
>> data_binarized =
preprocessing.Binarizer(threshold=1.4).transform(data)
```

The `preprocessing.Binarizer()` function binarizes data according to an imposed `threshold`. Values greater than the `threshold` map to 1, while values less than or equal to the `threshold` map to 0. With the default `threshold` of 0, only positive values map to 1. In our case, the `threshold` imposed is `1.4`, so values greater than `1.4` are mapped to 1, while values less than `1.4` are mapped to 0.

2. To display the binarized array, we will use the following code:

```
>> print(data_binarized)
```

The following output is returned:

```
[[ 1.  0.  1.  0.]
 [ 0.  1.  0.  1.]
 [ 0.  1.  0.  0.]]
```

This is a very useful technique that's usually used when we have some prior knowledge of the data.

How it works...

In this recipe, we binarized the data. The fundamental idea of this technique is to draw a fixed demarcation line. It is therefore a matter of finding an appropriate threshold and affirming that all the points of the image whose light intensity is below a certain value belong to the object (background), and all the points with greater intensity belong to the background (object).

There's more...

Binarization is a widespread operation on count data, in which the analyst can decide to consider only the presence or absence of a characteristic rather than a quantified number of occurrences. Otherwise, it can be used as a preprocessing step for estimators that consider random Boolean variables.

See also

- Scikit-learn's official documentation of the `sklearn.preprocessing.Binarizer()` function: `https://scikit-learn.org/stable/modules/generated/sklearn.preprocessing.Binarizer.html`.

One-hot encoding

We often deal with numerical values that are sparse and scattered all over the place. We don't really need to store these values. This is where one-hot encoding comes into the picture. We can think of one-hot encoding as a tool that tightens feature vectors. It looks at each feature and identifies the total number of distinct values. It uses a *one-of-k* scheme to encode values. Each feature in the feature vector is encoded based on this scheme. This helps us to be more efficient in terms of space.

Getting ready

Let's say we are dealing with four-dimensional feature vectors. To encode the *nth* feature in a feature vector, the encoder will go through the *nth* feature in each feature vector and count the number of distinct values. If the number of distinct values is k, it will transform the feature into a k-dimensional vector where only one value is 1 and all other values are 0. Let's take a simple example to understand how this works.

How to do it...

Let's see how to encode data in Python:

1. Let's take an array with four rows (vectors) and three columns (features):

```
>> data = np.array([[1, 1, 2], [0, 2, 3], [1, 0, 1], [0, 1, 0]])
>> print(data)
```

The following result is printed:

```
[[1 1 2]
 [0 2 3]
 [1 0 1]
 [0 1 0]]
```

Let's analyze the values present in each column (feature):

- The first feature has two possible values: 0, 1
- The second feature has three possible values: 0, 1, 2
- The third feature has four possible values: 0, 1, 2, 3

So, overall, the sum of the possible values present in each feature is given by 2 + 3 + 4 = 9. This means that 9 entries are required to uniquely represent any vector. The three features will be represented as follows:

- Feature 1 starts at index 0
- Feature 2 starts at index 2
- Feature 3 starts at index 5

2. To encode categorical integer features as a one-hot numeric array, the `preprocessing.OneHotEncoder()` function can be used as follows:

```
>> encoder = preprocessing.OneHotEncoder()
>> encoder.fit(data)
```

The first row of code sets the encoder, then the `fit()` function fits the `OneHotEncoder` object to a data array.

3. Now we can transform the data array using one-hot encoding. To do this, the `transform()` function will be used as follows:

```
>> encoded_vector = encoder.transform([[1, 2, 3]]).toarray()
```

If you were to print `encoded_vector`, the expected output would be:

```
[[0. 1. 0. 0. 1. 0. 0. 0. 1.]]
```

The result is clear: the first feature (1) has an index of 1, the second feature (3) has an index of 4, and the third feature (3) has an index of 8. As we can verify, only these positions are occupied by a 1; all the other positions have a 0. Remember that Python indexes the positions starting from 0, so the 9 entries will have indexes from 0 to 8.

How it works...

The `preprocessing.OneHotEncoder()` function encodes categorical integer features as a one-hot numeric array. Starting from an array of integers or strings that denotes the values assumed by categorical characteristics (discrete), this function encodes the characteristics using a one-hot coding scheme, returning dummy variables. This creates a binary column for each category and returns a sparse array or a dense array.

There's more...

It often happens that you have to convert categorical data. This is due to the fact that many machine learning algorithms can't work directly with categorical data. To use these methods, it is necessary to first transform categorical data into numerical data. This is required for both input and output variables.

See also

- Scikit-learn's official documentation of the
  `sklearn.preprocessing.OneHotEncoder()` function: `https://scikit-learn.org/stable/modules/generated/sklearn.preprocessing.OneHotEncoder.html`.

Label encoding

In supervised learning, we usually deal with a variety of labels. These can be either numbers or words. If they are numbers, then the algorithm can use them directly. However, labels often need to be in a human-readable form. So, people usually label the training data with words.

Getting ready

Label encoding refers to transforming word labels into a numerical form so that algorithms can understand how to operate on them. Let's take a look at how to do this.

How to do it...

Let's see how to carry out label encoding in Python:

1. Create a new Python file and import the `preprocessing()` package:

   ```
   >> from sklearn import preprocessing
   ```

2. This package contains various functions that are needed for data preprocessing. To encode labels with a value between 0 and `n_classes`-1, the `preprocessing.LabelEncoder()` function can be used. Let's define the label encoder, as follows:

   ```
   >> label_encoder = preprocessing.LabelEncoder()
   ```

3. The `label_encoder` object knows how to understand word labels. Let's create some labels:

   ```
   >> input_classes = ['audi', 'ford', 'audi', 'toyota', 'ford', 'bmw']
   ```

4. We are now ready to encode these labels—first, the `fit()` function is used to fit the label encoder, and then the class mapping encoders are printed:

```
>> label_encoder.fit(input_classes)
>> print("Class mapping: ")
>> for i, item in enumerate(label_encoder.classes_):
...     print(item, "-->", i)
```

5. Run the code, and you will see the following output on your Terminal:

```
Class mapping:
audi --> 0
bmw --> 1
ford --> 2
toyota --> 3
```

6. As shown in the preceding output, the words have been transformed into zero-indexed numbers. Now, when you encounter a set of labels, you can simply transform them, as follows:

```
>> labels = ['toyota', 'ford', 'audi']
>> encoded_labels = label_encoder.transform(labels)
>> print("Labels =", labels)
>> print("Encoded labels =", list(encoded_labels))
```

Here is the output that you'll see on your Terminal:

```
Labels = ['toyota', 'ford', 'audi']
Encoded labels = [3, 2, 0]
```

7. This is way easier than manually maintaining mapping between words and numbers. You can check the correctness by transforming numbers back into word labels:

```
>> encoded_labels = [2, 1, 0, 3, 1]
>> decoded_labels = label_encoder.inverse_transform(encoded_labels)
>> print("Encoded labels =", encoded_labels)
>> print("Decoded labels =", list(decoded_labels))
```

To transform labels back to their original encoding, the `inverse_transform()` function has been applied. Here is the output:

```
Encoded labels = [2, 1, 0, 3, 1]
Decoded labels = ['ford', 'bmw', 'audi', 'toyota', 'bmw']
```

As you can see, the mapping is preserved perfectly.

How it works...

In this recipe, we used the `preprocessing.LabelEncoder()` function to transform word labels into numerical form. To do this, we first set up a series of labels to as many car brands. We then turned these labels into numerical values. Finally, to verify the operation of the procedure, we printed the values corresponding to each class labeled.

There's more...

In the last two recipes, *Label encoding* and *One-hot encoding*, we have seen how to transform data. Both methods are suitable for dealing with categorical data. But what are the pros and cons of the two methodologies? Let's take a look:

- Label encoding can transform categorical data into numeric data, but the imposed ordinality creates problems if the obtained values are submitted to mathematical operations.
- One-hot encoding has the advantage that the result is binary rather than ordinal, and that everything is in an orthogonal vector space. The disadvantage is that for high cardinality, the feature space can explode.

See also

- Scikit-learn's official documentation on the `sklearn.preprocessing.LabelEncoder()` function: https://scikit-learn. org/stable/modules/generated/sklearn.preprocessing.LabelEncoder.html.

Building a linear regressor

Linear regression refers to finding the underlying function with the help of linear combination of input variables. The previous example had an input variable and an output variable. A simple linear regression is easy to understand, but represents the basis of regression techniques. Once these concepts are understood, it will be easier for us to address the other types of regression.

Consider the following diagram:

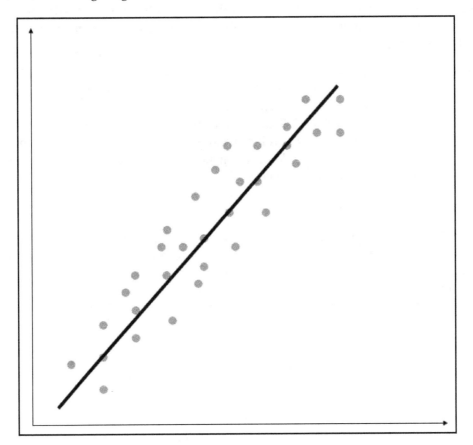

The linear regression method consists of precisely identifying a line that is capable of representing point distribution in a two-dimensional plane, that is, if the points corresponding to the observations are near the line, then the chosen model will be able to describe the link between the variables effectively.

In theory, there are an infinite number of lines that may approximate the observations, while in practice, there is only one mathematical model that optimizes the representation of the data. In the case of a linear mathematical relationship, the observations of the y variable can be obtained by a linear function of the observations of the x variable. For each observation, we will use the following formula:

$$y = \alpha * x + \beta$$

In the preceding formula, x is the explanatory variable and y is the response variable. The α and β parameters, which represent the slope of the line and the intercept with the y-axis respectively, must be estimated based on the observations collected for the two variables included in the model.

The slope, α, is of particular interest, that is, the variation of the mean response for every single increment of the explanatory variable. What about a change in this coefficient? If the slope is positive, the regression line increases from left to right, and if the slope is negative, the line decreases from left to right. When the slope is zero, the explanatory variable has no effect on the value of the response. But it is not just the sign of α that establishes the weight of the relationship between the variables. More generally, its value is also important. In the case of a positive slope, the mean response is higher when the explanatory variable is higher, while in the case of a negative slope, the mean response is lower when the explanatory variable is higher.

The main aim of linear regression is to get the underlying linear model that connects the input variable to the output variable. This in turn reduces the sum of squares of differences between the actual output and the predicted output using a linear function. This method is called **ordinary least squares**. In this method, the coefficients are estimated by determining numerical values that minimize the sum of the squared deviations between the observed responses and the fitted responses, according to the following equation:

$$RSS = \sum_{i=1}^{n}(\alpha * x_i + \beta - y_i)^2$$

This quantity represents the sum of the squares of the distances to each experimental datum (x_i, y_i) from the corresponding point on the straight line.

You might say that there might be a curvy line out there that fits these points better, but linear regression doesn't allow this. The main advantage of linear regression is that it's not complex. If you go into non-linear regression, you may get more accurate models, but they will be slower. As shown in the preceding diagram, the model tries to approximate the input data points using a straight line. Let's see how to build a linear regression model in Python.

Getting ready

Regression is used to find out the relationship between input data and the continuously-valued output data. This is generally represented as real numbers, and our aim is to estimate the core function that calculates the mapping from the input to the output. Let's start with a very simple example. Consider the following mapping between input and output:

```
1 --> 2
3 --> 6
4.3 --> 8.6
7.1 --> 14.2
```

If I ask you to estimate the relationship between the inputs and the outputs, you can easily do this by analyzing the pattern. We can see that the output is twice the input value in each case, so the transformation would be as follows:

$$f(x) = 2x$$

This is a simple function, relating the input values with the output values. However, in the real world, this is usually not the case. Functions in the real world are not so straightforward!

You have been provided with a data file called `VehiclesItaly.txt`. This contains comma-separated lines, where the first element is the input value and the second element is the output value that corresponds to this input value. Our goal is to find the linear regression relation between the vehicle registrations in a state and the population of a state. You should use this as the input argument. As anticipated, the `Registrations` variable contains the number of vehicles registered in Italy and the `Population` variable contains the population of the different regions.

How to do it...

Let's see how to build a linear regressor in Python:

1. Create a file called `regressor.py` and add the following lines:

```
filename = "VehiclesItaly.txt"
X = []
y = []
with open(filename, 'r') as f:
    for line in f.readlines():
        xt, yt = [float(i) for i in line.split(',')]
```

```
X.append(xt)
y.append(yt)
```

We just loaded the input data into X and y, where X refers to the independent variable (explanatory variables) and y refers to the dependent variable (response variable). Inside the loop in the preceding code, we parse each line and split it based on the comma operator. We then convert them into floating point values and save them in X and y.

2. When we build a machine learning model, we need a way to validate our model and check whether it is performing at a satisfactory level. To do this, we need to separate our data into two groups—a training dataset and a testing dataset. The training dataset will be used to build the model, and the testing dataset will be used to see how this trained model performs on unknown data. So, let's go ahead and split this data into training and testing datasets:

```
num_training = int(0.8 * len(X))
num_test = len(X) - num_training

import numpy as np

# Training data
X_train = np.array(X[:num_training]).reshape((num_training,1))
y_train = np.array(y[:num_training])

# Test data
X_test = np.array(X[num_training:]).reshape((num_test,1))
y_test = np.array(y[num_training:])
```

First, we have put aside 80% of the data for the training dataset and the remaining 20% is for the testing dataset. Then, we have built four arrays: X_train, X_test, y_train, and y_test.

3. We are now ready to train the model. Let's create a regressor object, as follows:

```
from sklearn import linear_model

# Create linear regression object
linear_regressor = linear_model.LinearRegression()

# Train the model using the training sets
linear_regressor.fit(X_train, y_train)
```

First, we have imported `linear_model` methods from the `sklearn` library, which are methods used for regression, wherein the target value is expected to be a linear combination of the input variables. Then, we have used the `LinearRegression()` function, which performs ordinary least squares linear regression. Finally, the `fit()` function is used to fit the linear model. Two parameters are passed—training data (`X_train`), and target values (`y_train`).

4. We just trained the linear regressor, based on our training data. The `fit()` method takes the input data and trains the model. To see how it all fits, we have to predict the training data with the model fitted:

```
y_train_pred = linear_regressor.predict(X_train)
```

5. To plot the outputs, we will use the `matplotlib` library as follows:

```
import matplotlib.pyplot as plt
plt.figure()
plt.scatter(X_train, y_train, color='green')
plt.plot(X_train, y_train_pred, color='black', linewidth=4)
plt.title('Training data')
plt.show()
```

When you run this in the Terminal, the following diagram is shown:

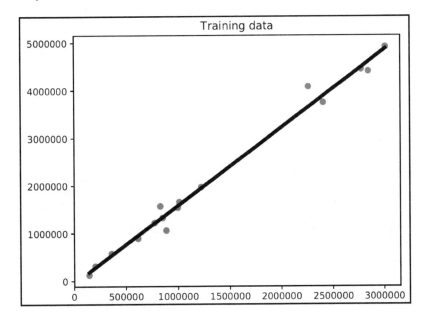

6. In the preceding code, we used the trained model to predict the output for our training data. This wouldn't tell us how the model performs on unknown data, because we are running it on the training data. This just gives us an idea of how the model fits on training data. Looks like it's doing okay, as you can see in the preceding diagram!

7. Let's predict the test dataset output based on this model and plot it, as follows:

```
y_test_pred = linear_regressor.predict(X_test)
plt.figure()
plt.scatter(X_test, y_test, color='green')
plt.plot(X_test, y_test_pred, color='black', linewidth=4)
plt.title('Test data')
plt.show()
```

When you run this in the Terminal, the following output is returned:

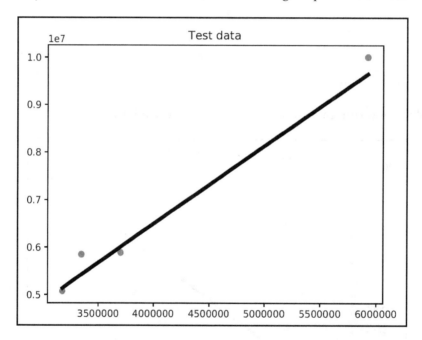

As you might expect, there's a positive association between a state's population and the number of vehicle registrations.

How it works...

In this recipe, we looked for the linear regression relation between the vehicle registrations in a state and the population of a state. To do this we used the `LinearRegression()` function of the `linear_model` method of the `sklearn` library. After constructing the model, we first used the data involved in training the model to visually verify how well the model fits the data. Then, we used the test data to verify the results.

There's more...

The best way to appreciate the results of a simulation is to display those using special charts. In fact, we have already used this technique in this section. I am referring to the chart in which we drew the scatter plot of the distribution with the regression line. In `Chapter 5`, *Visualizing Data*, we will see other plots that will allow us to check the model's hypotheses.

See also

- Scikit-learn's official documentation of the `sklearn.linear_model.LinearRegression()` function: `https://scikit-learn.org/stable/modules/generated/sklearn.linear_model.LinearRegression.html`.
- *Regression Analysis with R*, Giuseppe Ciaburro, Packt Publishing.
- *Linear regression*: `https://en.wikipedia.org/wiki/Linear_regression`.
- *Introduction to Linear Regression*: `http://onlinestatbook.com/2/regression/intro.html`.

Computing regression accuracy

Now that we know how to build a regressor, it's important to understand how to evaluate the quality of a regressor as well. In this context, an error is defined as the difference between the actual value and the value that is predicted by the regressor.

Getting ready

Let's quickly take a look at the metrics that can be used to measure the quality of a regressor. A regressor can be evaluated using many different metrics. There is a module in the scikit-learn library that provides functionalities to compute all the following metrics. This is the sklearn.metrics module, which includes score functions, performance metrics, pairwise metrics, and distance computations.

How to do it...

Let's see how to compute regression accuracy in Python:

1. Now we will use the functions available to evaluate the performance of the linear regression model we developed in the previous recipe:

```
import sklearn.metrics as sm
print("Mean absolute error =", round(sm.mean_absolute_error(y_test,
y_test_pred), 2))
print("Mean squared error =", round(sm.mean_squared_error(y_test,
y_test_pred), 2))
print("Median absolute error =",
round(sm.median_absolute_error(y_test, y_test_pred), 2))
print("Explain variance score =",
round(sm.explained_variance_score(y_test, y_test_pred), 2))
print("R2 score =", round(sm.r2_score(y_test, y_test_pred), 2))
```

The following results are returned:

```
Mean absolute error = 241907.27
Mean squared error = 81974851872.13
Median absolute error = 240861.94
Explain variance score = 0.98
R2 score = 0.98
```

An R2 score near 1 means that the model is able to predict the data very well. Keeping track of every single metric can get tedious, so we pick one or two metrics to evaluate our model. A good practice is to make sure that the mean squared error is low and the explained variance score is high.

How it works...

A regressor can be evaluated using many different metrics, such as the following:

- **Mean absolute error**: This is the average of absolute errors of all the data points in the given dataset.
- **Mean squared error**: This is the average of the squares of the errors of all the data points in the given dataset. It is one of the most popular metrics out there!
- **Median absolute error**: This is the median of all the errors in the given dataset. The main advantage of this metric is that it's robust to outliers. A single bad point in the test dataset wouldn't skew the entire error metric, as opposed to a mean error metric.
- **Explained variance score**: This score measures how well our model can account for the variation in our dataset. A score of 1.0 indicates that our model is perfect.
- **R2 score**: This is pronounced as R-squared, and this score refers to the coefficient of determination. This tells us how well the unknown samples will be predicted by our model. The best possible score is 1.0, but the score can be negative as well.

There's more...

The `sklearn.metrics` module contains a series of simple functions that measure prediction error:

- Functions ending with `_score` return a value to maximize; the higher the better
- Functions ending with `_error` or `_loss` return a value to minimize; the lower the better

See also

- Scikit-learn's official documentation of the `sklearn.metrics` module: `https://scikit-learn.org/stable/modules/classes.html#module-sklearn.metrics`.
- *Regression Analysis with R*, Giuseppe Ciaburro, Packt Publishing.

Achieving model persistence

When we train a model, it would be nice if we could save it as a file so that it can be used later by simply loading it again.

Getting ready

Let's see how to achieve model persistence programmatically. To do this, the `pickle` module can be used. The `pickle` module is used to store Python objects. This module is a part of the standard library with your installation of Python.

How to do it...

Let's see how to achieve model persistence in Python:

1. Add the following lines to the `regressor.py` file:

```
import pickle

output_model_file = "3_model_linear_regr.pkl"

with open(output_model_file, 'wb') as f:
    pickle.dump(linear_regressor, f)
```

2. The regressor object will be saved in the `saved_model.pkl` file. Let's look at how to load it and use it, as follows:

```
with open(output_model_file, 'rb') as f:
    model_linregr = pickle.load(f)

y_test_pred_new = model_linregr.predict(X_test)
print("New mean absolute error =",
round(sm.mean_absolute_error(y_test, y_test_pred_new), 2))
```

The following result is returned:

New mean absolute error = 241907.27

Here, we just loaded the regressor from the file into the `model_linregr` variable. You can compare the preceding result with the earlier result to confirm that it's the same.

How it works...

The `pickle` module transforms an arbitrary Python object into a series of bytes. This process is also called the serialization of the object. The byte stream representing the object can be transmitted or stored, and subsequently rebuilt to create a new object with the same characteristics. The inverse operation is called **unpickling**.

There's more...

In Python, there is also another way to perform serialization, by using the `marshal` module. In general, the `pickle` module is recommended for serializing Python objects. The `marshal` module can be used to support Python `.pyc` files.

See also

- Python's official documentation of the `pickle` module: `https://docs.python. org/3/library/pickle.html`

Building a ridge regressor

One of the main problems of linear regression is that it's sensitive to outliers. During data collection in the real world, it's quite common to wrongly measure output. Linear regression uses ordinary least squares, which tries to minimize the squares of errors. The outliers tend to cause problems because they contribute a lot to the overall error. This tends to disrupt the entire model.

Let's try to deepen our understanding of the concept of outliers: outliers are values that, compared to others, are particularly extreme (values that are clearly distant from the other observations). Outliers are an issue because they might distort data analysis results; more specifically, descriptive statistics and correlations. We need to find these in the data cleaning phase, however, we can also get started on them in the next stage of data analysis. Outliers can be univariate when they have an extreme value for a single variable, or multivariate when they have a unique combination of values for a number of variables. Let's consider the following diagram:

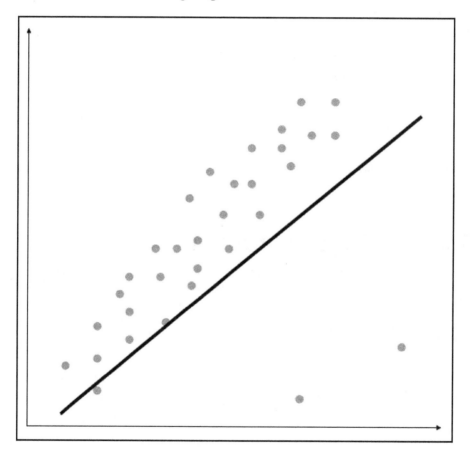

The two points on the bottom right are clearly outliers, but this model is trying to fit all the points. Hence, the overall model tends to be inaccurate. Outliers are the extreme values of a distribution that are characterized by being extremely high or extremely low compared to the rest of the distribution, and thus representing isolated cases with respect to the rest of the distribution. By visual inspection, we can see that the following output is a better model:

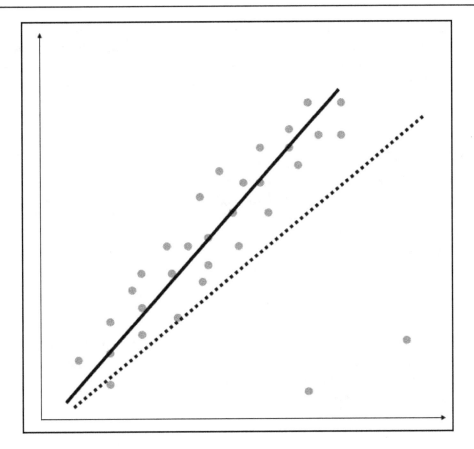

Ordinary least squares considers every single data point when it's building the model. Hence, the actual model ends up looking like the dotted line shown in the preceding graph. We can clearly see that this model is suboptimal.

The `regularization` method involves modifying the performance function, normally selected as the sum of the squares of regression errors on the training set. When a large number of variables are available, the least square estimates of a linear model often have a low bias but a high variance with respect to models with fewer variables. Under these conditions, there is an overfitting problem. To improve precision prediction by allowing greater bias but a small variance, we can use variable selection methods and dimensionality reduction, but these methods may be unattractive for computational burdens in the first case or provide a difficult interpretation in the other case.

Another way to address the problem of overfitting is to modify the estimation method by neglecting the requirement of an unbiased parameter estimator and instead considering the possibility of using a biased estimator, which may have smaller variance. There are several biased estimators, most of which are based on regularization: `Ridge`, `Lasso`, and `ElasticNet` are the most popular methods.

Getting ready

Ridge regression is a regularization method where a penalty is imposed on the size of the coefficients. As we said in the *Building a linear regressor* section, in the ordinary least squares method, the coefficients are estimated by determining numerical values that minimize the sum of the squared deviations between the observed responses and the fitted responses, according to the following equation:

$$RSS = \sum_{i=1}^{n}(y_i - \beta_1 * x_i + \beta_2)^2$$

Ridge regression, in order to estimate the β coefficients, starts from the basic formula of the **residual sum of squares** (**RSS**) and adds the penalty term. λ (≥ 0) is defined as the tuning parameter, which is multiplied by the sum of the β coefficients squared (excluding the intercept) to define the penalty period, as shown in the following equation:

$$\sum_{i=1}^{n}(y_i - \beta_1 * x_i + \beta_2)^2 + \lambda * \beta_1^2 = RSS + \lambda * \beta_1^2$$

It is evident that having $\lambda = 0$ means not having a penalty in the model, that is, we would produce the same estimates as the least squares. On the other hand, having a λ tending toward infinity means having a high penalty effect, which will bring many coefficients close to zero, but will not imply their exclusion from the model. Let's see how to build a ridge regressor in Python.

How to do it...

Let's see how to build a ridge regressor in Python:

1. You can use the data already used in the previous example: *Building a linear regressor* (`VehiclesItaly.txt`). This file contains two values in each line. The first value is the explanatory variable, and the second is the response variable.

2. Add the following lines to `regressor.py`. Let's initialize a ridge regressor with some parameters:

```
from sklearn import linear_model
ridge_regressor = linear_model.Ridge(alpha=0.01,
fit_intercept=True, max_iter=10000)
```

3. The `alpha` parameter controls the complexity. As `alpha` gets closer to 0, the ridge regressor tends to become more like a linear regressor with ordinary least squares. So, if you want to make it robust against outliers, you need to assign a higher value to `alpha`. We considered a value of `0.01`, which is moderate.

4. Let's train this regressor, as follows:

```
ridge_regressor.fit(X_train, y_train)
y_test_pred_ridge = ridge_regressor.predict(X_test)
print( "Mean absolute error =",
round(sm.mean_absolute_error(y_test, y_test_pred_ridge), 2))
print( "Mean squared error =", round(sm.mean_squared_error(y_test,
y_test_pred_ridge), 2))
print( "Median absolute error =",
round(sm.median_absolute_error(y_test, y_test_pred_ridge), 2))
print( "Explain variance score =",
round(sm.explained_variance_score(y_test, y_test_pred_ridge), 2))
print( "R2 score =", round(sm.r2_score(y_test, y_test_pred_ridge),
2))
```

Run this code to view the error metrics. You can build a linear regressor to compare and contrast the results on the same data to see the effect of introducing regularization into the model.

How it works...

Ridge regression is a regularization method where a penalty is imposed on the size of the coefficients. Ridge regression is identical to least squares, barring the fact that ridge coefficients are computed by decreasing a quantity that is somewhat different. In ridge regression, a scale transformation has a substantial effect. Therefore, to avoid obtaining different results depending on the predicted scale of measurement, it is advisable to standardize all predictors before estimating the model. To standardize the variables, we must subtract their means and divide by their standard deviations.

See also

- Scikit-learn's official documentation of the `linear_model.Ridge` function: `https://scikit-learn.org/stable/modules/generated/sklearn.linear_model.Ridge.html`
- *Ridge Regression*, Columbia University: `https://www.mailman.columbia.edu/research/population-health-methods/ridge-regression`
- *Multicollinearity and Other Regression Pitfalls*, The Pennsylvania State University: `https://newonlinecourses.science.psu.edu/stat501/node/343/`

Building a polynomial regressor

One of the main constraints of a linear regression model is the fact that it tries to fit a linear function to the input data. The polynomial regression model overcomes this issue by allowing the function to be a polynomial, thereby increasing the accuracy of the model.

Getting ready

Polynomial models should be applied where the relationship between response and explanatory variables is curvilinear. Sometimes, polynomial models can also be used to model a non-linear relationship in a small range of explanatory variable. A polynomial quadratic (squared) or cubic (cubed) term converts a linear regression model into a polynomial curve. However, since it is the explanatory variable that is squared or cubed and not the beta coefficient, it is still considered as a linear model. This makes it a simple and easy way to model curves, without needing to create big non-linear models. Let's consider the following diagram:

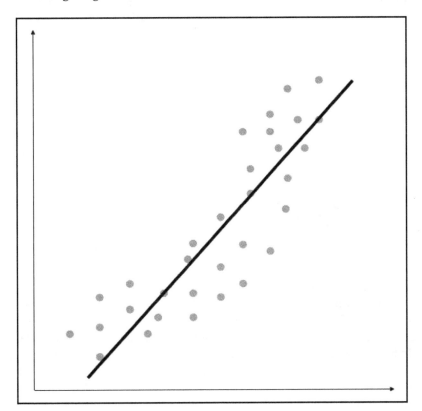

We can see that there is a natural curve to the pattern of data points. This linear model is unable to capture this. Let's see what a polynomial model would look like:

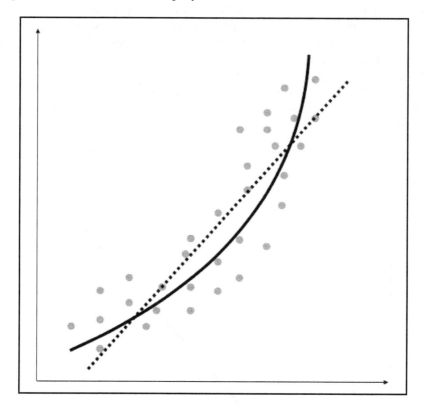

The dotted line represents the linear regression model, and the solid line represents the polynomial regression model. The curviness of this model is controlled by the degree of the polynomial. As the curviness of the model increases, it gets more accurate. However, curviness adds complexity to the model as well, making it slower. This is a trade-off: you have to decide how accurate you want your model to be given the computational constraints.

How to do it...

Let's see how to build a polynomial regressor in Python:

1. In this example, we will only deal with second-degree parabolic regression. Now, we'll show how to model data with a polynomial. We measured the temperature for a few hours of the day. We want to know the temperature trend even at times of the day when we did not measure it. Those times are, however, between the initial time and the final time at which our measurements took place:

```
import numpy as np

Time = np.array([6, 8, 11, 14, 16, 18, 19])
Temp = np.array([4, 7, 10, 12, 11.5, 9, 7])
```

2. Now, we will show the temperature at a few points during the day:

```
import matplotlib.pyplot as plt
plt.figure()
plt.plot(Time, Temp, 'bo')
plt.xlabel("Time")
plt.ylabel("Temp")
plt.title('Temperature versus time')
plt.show()
```

The following graph is produced:

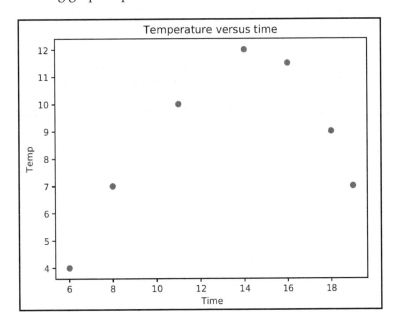

If we analyze the graph, it is possible to note a curvilinear pattern of the data that can be modeled through a second-degree polynomial such as the following equation:

$$Temp = \beta_0 + \beta_1 * Time + \beta_2 * Time^2$$

The unknown coefficients, β_0, β_1, and β_2, are estimated by decreasing the value of the sum of the squares. This is obtained by minimizing the deviations of the data from the model to its lowest value (least squares fit).

3. Let's calculate the polynomial coefficients:

```
beta = np.polyfit(Time, Temp, 2)
```

The `numpy.polyfit()` function returns the coefficients for a polynomial of degree *n* (given by us) that is the best fit for the data. The coefficients returned by the function are in descending powers (highest power first), and their length is *n+1* if *n* is the degree of the polynomial.

4. After creating the model, let's verify that it actually fits our data. To do this, use the model to evaluate the polynomial at uniformly spaced times. To evaluate the model at the specified points, we can use the `poly1d()` function. This function returns the value of a polynomial of degree *n* evaluated at the points provided by us. The input argument is a vector of length *n+1* whose elements are the coefficients in descending powers of the polynomial to be evaluated:

```
p = np.poly1d(beta)
```

As you can see in the upcoming graph, this is close to the output value. If we want it to get closer, we need to increase the degree of the polynomial.

5. Now we can plot the original data and the model on the same plot:

```
xp = np.linspace(6, 19, 100)
plt.figure()
plt.plot(Time, Temp, 'bo', xp, p(xp), '-')
plt.show()
```

The following graph is printed:

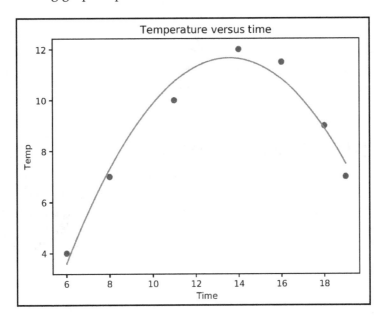

If we analyze the graph, we can see that the curve fits our data sufficiently. This model fits the data to a greater extent than a simple linear regression model. In regression analysis, it's important to keep the order of the model as low as possible. In the first analysis, we keep the model as a first order polynomial. If this is not satisfactory, then a second-order polynomial is tried. The use of higher-order polynomials can lead to incorrect evaluations.

How it works...

Polynomial regression should be used when linear regression is not good enough. With polynomial regression, we approached a model in which some predictors appear in degrees equal to or greater than two to fit the data with a curved line. Polynomial regression is usually used when the relationship between variables looks curved.

There's more...

At what degree of the polynomial must we stop? It depends on the degree of precision we are looking for. The higher the degree of the polynomial, the greater the precision of the model, but the more difficult it is to calculate. In addition, it is necessary to verify the significance of the coefficients that are found, but let's get to it right away.

See also

- Python's official documentation of the `numpy.polyfit()` function (`https://docs.scipy.org/doc/numpy/reference/generated/numpy.polyfit.html`)
- Python's official documentation of the `numpy.poly1d()` function (`https://docs.scipy.org/doc/numpy-1.14.0/reference/generated/numpy.poly1d.html`)

Estimating housing prices

It's time to apply our knowledge to a real-world problem. Let's apply all these principles to estimate house prices. This is one of the most popular examples that is used to understand regression, and it serves as a good entry point. This is intuitive and relatable, hence making it easier to understand the concepts before we perform more complex things in machine learning. We will use a decision tree regressor with AdaBoost to solve this problem.

Getting ready

A decision tree is a tree where each node makes a simple decision that contributes to the final output. The leaf nodes represent the output values, and the branches represent the intermediate decisions that were made, based on input features. **AdaBoost** stands for **adaptive boosting,** and this is a technique that is used to boost the accuracy of the results from another system. This combines the outputs from different versions of the algorithms, called weak learners, using a weighted summation to get the final output. The information that's collected at each stage of the AdaBoost algorithm is fed back into the system so that the learners at the latter stages focus on training samples that are difficult to classify. In this way, it increases the accuracy of the system.

Using AdaBoost, we fit a regressor on the dataset. We compute the error and then fit the regressor on the same dataset again, based on this error estimate. We can think of this as fine-tuning of the regressor until the desired accuracy is achieved. You are given a dataset that contains various parameters that affect the price of a house. Our goal is to estimate the relationship between these parameters and the house price so that we can use this to estimate the price given unknown input parameters.

How to do it...

Let's see how to estimate housing prices in Python:

1. Create a new file called `housing.py` and add the following lines:

```
import numpy as np
from sklearn.tree import DecisionTreeRegressor
from sklearn.ensemble import AdaBoostRegressor
from sklearn import datasets
from sklearn.metrics import mean_squared_error,
explained_variance_score
from sklearn.utils import shuffle
import matplotlib.pyplot as plt
```

2. There is a standard housing dataset that people tend to use to get started with machine learning. You can download it at https://archive.ics.uci.edu/ml/machine-learning-databases/housing/. We will be using a slightly modified version of the dataset, which has been provided along with the code files. The good thing is that `scikit-learn` provides a function to directly load this dataset:

```
housing_data = datasets.load_boston()
```

Each data point has 12 input parameters that affect the price of a house. You can access the input data using `housing_data.data` and the corresponding price using `housing_data.target`. The following attributes are available:

- `crim`: Per capita crime rate by town
- `zn`: Proportion of residential land zoned for lots that are over 25,000 square feet
- `indus`: Proportion of non-retail business acres per town
- `chas`: Charles River dummy variable (= 1 if tract bounds river; 0 otherwise)
- `nox`: Nitric oxides concentration (parts per ten million)
- `rm`: Average number of rooms per dwelling
- `age`: Proportion of owner-occupied units built prior to 1940
- `dis`: Weighted distances to the five Boston employment centers
- `rad`: Index of accessibility to radial highways
- `tax`: Full-value property-tax rate per $10,000
- `ptratio`: Pupil-teacher ratio by town

- lstat: Percent of the lower status of the population
- target: Median value of owner-occupied homes in $1000

Of these, target is the response variable, while the other 12 variables are possible predictors. The goal of this analysis is to fit a regression model that best explains the variation in target.

3. Let's separate this into input and output. To make this independent of the ordering of the data, let's shuffle it as well:

```
X, y = shuffle(housing_data.data, housing_data.target,
random_state=7)
```

The sklearn.utils.shuffle() function shuffles arrays or sparse matrices in a consistent way to do random permutations of collections. Shuffling data reduces variance and makes sure that the patterns remain general and less overfitted. The random_state parameter controls how we shuffle data so that we can have reproducible results.

4. Let's divide the data into training and testing. We'll allocate 80% for training and 20% for testing:

```
num_training = int(0.8 * len(X))
X_train, y_train = X[:num_training], y[:num_training]
X_test, y_test = X[num_training:], y[num_training:]
```

Remember, machine learning algorithms, train models by using a finite set of training data. In the training phase, the model is evaluated based on its predictions of the training set. But the goal of the algorithm is to produce a model that predicts previously unseen observations, in other words, one that is able to generalize the problem by starting from known data and unknown data. For this reason, the data is divided into two datasets: training and test. The training set is used to train the model, while the test set is used to verify the ability of the system to generalize.

5. We are now ready to fit a decision tree regression model. Let's pick a tree with a maximum depth of 4, which means that we are not letting the tree become arbitrarily deep:

```
dt_regressor = DecisionTreeRegressor(max_depth=4)
dt_regressor.fit(X_train, y_train)
```

The DecisionTreeRegressor function has been used to build a decision tree regressor.

6. Let's also fit the decision tree regression model with AdaBoost:

```
ab_regressor =
AdaBoostRegressor(DecisionTreeRegressor(max_depth=4),
n_estimators=400, random_state=7)
ab_regressor.fit(X_train, y_train)
```

The `AdaBoostRegressor` function has been used to compare the results and see how AdaBoost really boosts the performance of a decision tree regressor.

7. Let's evaluate the performance of the decision tree regressor:

```
y_pred_dt = dt_regressor.predict(X_test)
mse = mean_squared_error(y_test, y_pred_dt)
evs = explained_variance_score(y_test, y_pred_dt)
print("#### Decision Tree performance ####")
print("Mean squared error =", round(mse, 2))
print("Explained variance score =", round(evs, 2))
```

First, we used the `predict()` function to predict the response variable based on the test data. Next, we calculated mean squared error and explained variance. `Mean squared error` is the average of the squared difference between actual and predicted values across all data points in the input. The `explained variance` is an indicator that, in the form of proportion, indicates how much variability of our data is explained by the model in question.

8. Now, let's evaluate the performance of AdaBoost:

```
y_pred_ab = ab_regressor.predict(X_test)
mse = mean_squared_error(y_test, y_pred_ab)
evs = explained_variance_score(y_test, y_pred_ab)
print("#### AdaBoost performance ####")
print("Mean squared error =", round(mse, 2))
print("Explained variance score =", round(evs, 2))
```

Here is the output on the Terminal:

```
#### Decision Tree performance ####
Mean squared error = 14.79
Explained variance score = 0.82

#### AdaBoost performance ####
Mean squared error = 7.54
Explained variance score = 0.91
```

The error is lower and the variance score is closer to 1 when we use AdaBoost, as shown in the preceding output.

How it works...

`DecisionTreeRegressor` builds a decision tree regressor. Decision trees are used to predict a response or class y, from several input variables; $x1, x2,...,xn$. If y is a continuous response, it's called a regression tree, if y is categorical, it's called a classification tree. The algorithm is based on the following procedure: We see the value of the input x_i at each node of the tree, and based on the answer, we continue to the left or to the right branch. When we reach a leaf, we will find the prediction. In regression trees, we try to divide the data space into tiny parts, where we can equip a simple different model on each of them. The non-leaf part of the tree is just the way to find out which model we will use for predicting it.

A regression tree is formed by a series of nodes that split the root branch into two child branches. Such subdivision continues to cascade. Each new branch, then, can go in another node, or remain a leaf with the predicted value.

There's more...

An AdaBoost regressor is a meta-estimator that starts by equipping a regressor on the actual dataset and adding additional copies of the regressor on the same dataset, but where the weights of instances are adjusted according to the error of the current prediction. As such, consecutive regressors look at difficult cases. This will help us compare the results and see how AdaBoost really boosts the performance of a decision tree regressor.

See also

- Scikit-learn's official documentation of the `DecisionTreeRegressor` function (https://scikit-learn.org/stable/modules/generated/sklearn.tree.DecisionTreeRegressor.html)
- Scikit-learn's official documentation of the `AdaBoostRegressor` function (https://scikit-learn.org/stable/modules/generated/sklearn.ensemble.AdaBoostRegressor.html)

Computing the relative importance of features

Are all features equally important? In this case, we used 13 input features, and they all contributed to the model. However, an important question here is, *How do we know which features are more important?* Obviously, not all features contribute equally to the output. In case we want to discard some of them later, we need to know which features are less important. We have this functionality available in scikit-learn.

Getting ready

Let's calculate the relative importance of the features. Feature importance provides a measure that indicates the value of each feature in the construction of the model. The more an attribute is used to build the model, the greater its relative importance. This importance is explicitly calculated for each attribute in the dataset, allowing you to classify and compare attributes to each other. Feature importance is an attribute contained in the model (feature_importances_).

How to do it...

Let's see how to compute the relative importance of features:

1. Let's see how to extract this. Add the following lines to housing.py:

```
DTFImp= dt_regressor.feature_importances_
DTFImp= 100.0 * (DTFImp / max(DTFImp))
index_sorted = np.flipud(np.argsort(DTFImp))
pos = np.arange(index_sorted.shape[0]) + 0.5
```

The regressor object has a callable feature_importances_ method that gives us the relative importance of each feature. To compare the results, the importance values have been normalized. Then, we ordered the index values and turned them upside down so that they are arranged in descending order of importance. Finally, for display purposes, the location of the labels on the *x*-axis has been centered.

2. To visualize the results, we will plot the bar graph:

```
plt.figure()
plt.bar(pos, DTFImp[index_sorted], align='center')
plt.xticks(pos, housing_data.feature_names[index_sorted])
plt.ylabel('Relative Importance')
plt.title("Decision Tree regressor")
plt.show()
```

3. We just take the values from the feature_importances_ method and scale them so that they range between 0 and 100. Let's see what we will get for a decision tree-based regressor in the following output:

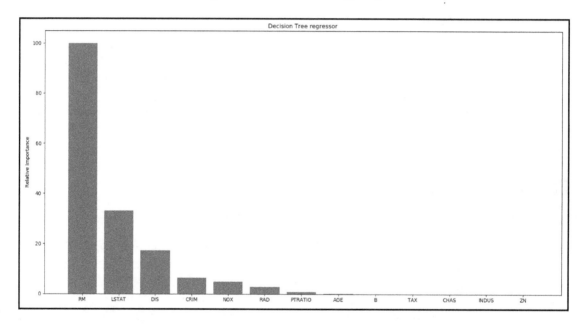

So, the decision tree regressor says that the most important feature is RM.

4. Now, we carry out a similar procedure for the AdaBoost model:

```
ABFImp= ab_regressor.feature_importances_
ABFImp= 100.0 * (ABFImp / max(ABFImp))
index_sorted = np.flipud(np.argsort(ABFImp))
pos = np.arange(index_sorted.shape[0]) + 0.5
```

5. To visualize the results, we will plot the bar graph:

```
plt.figure()
plt.bar(pos, ABFImp[index_sorted], align='center')
plt.xticks(pos, housing_data.feature_names[index_sorted])
plt.ylabel('Relative Importance')
plt.title("AdaBoost regressor")
plt.show()
```

Let's take a look at what AdaBoost has to say in the following output:

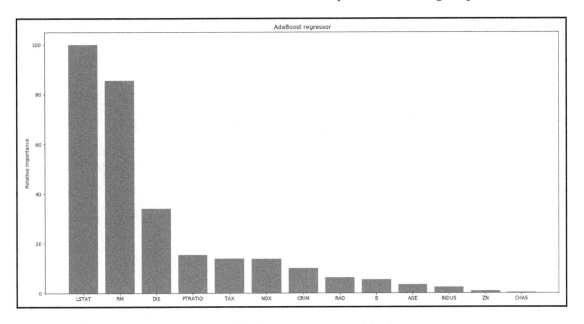

According to AdaBoost, the most important feature is LSTAT. In reality, if you build various regressors on this data, you will see that the most important feature is in fact LSTAT. This shows the advantage of using AdaBoost with a decision tree-based regressor.

How it works...

Feature importance provides a measure that indicates the value of each feature in the construction of a model. The more an attribute is used to build a model, the greater its relative importance. In this recipe, the `feature_importances_` attribute was used to extract the relative importance of the features from the model.

There's more...

Relative importance returns the utility of each characteristic in the construction of decision trees. The more an attribute is used to make predictions with decision trees, the greater its relative importance. This importance is explicitly calculated for each attribute in the dataset, allowing you to classify and compare attributes to each other.

See also

- Scikit-learn's official documentation of the `DecisionTreeRegressor` function: `https://scikit-learn.org/stable/modules/generated/sklearn.tree.DecisionTreeRegressor.html`

Estimating bicycle demand distribution

Let's use a different regression method to solve the bicycle demand distribution problem. We will use the random forest regressor to estimate the output values. A random forest is a collection of decision trees. This basically uses a set of decision trees that are built using various subsets of the dataset, and then it uses averaging to improve the overall performance.

Getting ready

We will use the `bike_day.csv` file that is provided to you. This is also available at `https://archive.ics.uci.edu/ml/datasets/Bike+Sharing+Dataset`. There are 16 columns in this dataset. The first two columns correspond to the serial number and the actual date, so we won't use them for our analysis. The last three columns correspond to different types of outputs. The last column is just the sum of the values in the fourteenth and fifteenth columns, so we can leave those two out when we build our model. Let's go ahead and see how to do this in Python. We will analyze the code line by line to understand each step.

How to do it...

Let's see how to estimate bicycle demand distribution:

1. We first need to import a couple of new packages, as follows:

```
import csv
import numpy as np
```

2. We are processing a CSV file, so the CSV package for useful in handling these files. Let's import the data into the Python environment:

```
filename="bike_day.csv"
file_reader = csv.reader(open(filename, 'r'), delimiter=',')
X, y = [], []
for row in file_reader:
    X.append(row[2:13])
    y.append(row[-1])
```

This piece of code just read all the data from the CSV file. The `csv.reader()` function returns a `reader` object, which will iterate over lines in the given CSV file. Each row read from the CSV file is returned as a list of strings. So, two lists are returned: X and y. We have separated the data from the output values and returned them. Now we will extract feature names:

```
feature_names = np.array(X[0])
```

The feature names are useful when we display them on a graph. So, we have to remove the first row from X and y because they are feature names:

```
X=np.array(X[1:]).astype(np.float32)
y=np.array(y[1:]).astype(np.float32)
```

We have also converted the two lists into two arrays.

3. Let's shuffle these two arrays to make them independent of the order in which the data is arranged in the file:

```
from sklearn.utils import shuffle
X, y = shuffle(X, y, random_state=7)
```

4. As we did earlier, we need to separate the data into training and testing data. This time, let's use 90% of the data for training and the remaining 10% for testing:

```
num_training = int(0.9 * len(X))
X_train, y_train = X[:num_training], y[:num_training]
X_test, y_test = X[num_training:], y[num_training:]
```

5. Let's go ahead and train the regressor:

```
from sklearn.ensemble import RandomForestRegressor
rf_regressor = RandomForestRegressor(n_estimators=1000,
max_depth=10, min_samples_split=2)
rf_regressor.fit(X_train, y_train)
```

The RandomForestRegressor() function builds a random forest regressor. Here, n_estimators refers to the number of estimators, which is the number of decision trees that we want to use in our random forest. The max_depth parameter refers to the maximum depth of each tree, and the min_samples_split parameter refers to the number of data samples that are needed to split a node in the tree.

6. Let's evaluate the performance of the random forest regressor:

```
y_pred = rf_regressor.predict(X_test)
from sklearn.metrics import mean_squared_error,
explained_variance_score
mse = mean_squared_error(y_test, y_pred)
evs = explained_variance_score(y_test, y_pred)
print( "#### Random Forest regressor performance ####")
print("Mean squared error =", round(mse, 2))
print("Explained variance score =", round(evs, 2))
```

The following results are returned:

```
#### Random Forest regressor performance ####
Mean squared error = 357864.36
Explained variance score = 0.89
```

7. Let's extract the relative importance of the features:

```
RFFImp= rf_regressor.feature_importances_
RFFImp= 100.0 * (RFFImp / max(RFFImp))
index_sorted = np.flipud(np.argsort(RFFImp))
pos = np.arange(index_sorted.shape[0]) + 0.5
```

To visualize the results, we will plot a bar graph:

```
import matplotlib.pyplot as plt
plt.figure()
plt.bar(pos, RFFImp[index_sorted], align='center')
plt.xticks(pos, feature_names[index_sorted])
plt.ylabel('Relative Importance')
plt.title("Random Forest regressor")
plt.show()
```

The following output is plotted:

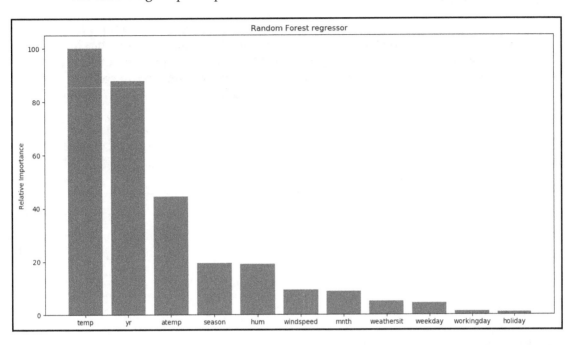

Looks like the temperature is the most important factor controlling bicycle rentals.

How it works...

A random forest is a special regressor formed of a set of simple regressors (decision trees), represented as independent and identically distributed random vectors, where each one chooses the mean prediction of the individual trees. This type of structure has made significant improvements in regression accuracy and falls within the sphere of ensemble learning. Each tree within a random forest is constructed and trained from a random subset of the data in the training set. The trees therefore do not use the complete set, and the best attribute is no longer selected for each node, but the best attribute is selected from a set of randomly selected attributes.

Randomness is a factor that then becomes part of the construction of regressors and aims to increase their diversity and thus reduce correlation. The final result returned by the random forest is nothing but the average of the numerical result returned by the different trees in the case of a regression, or the class returned by the largest number of trees if the random forest algorithm was used to perform classification.

There's more...

Let's see what happens when you include the fourteenth and fifteenth columns in the dataset. In the feature importance graph, every feature other than these two has to go to zero. The reason is that the output can be obtained by simply summing up the fourteenth and fifteenth columns, so the algorithm doesn't need any other features to compute the output. Make the following change inside the `for` loop (the rest of the code remains unchanged):

```
X.append(row[2:15])
```

If you plot the feature importance graph now, you will see the following:

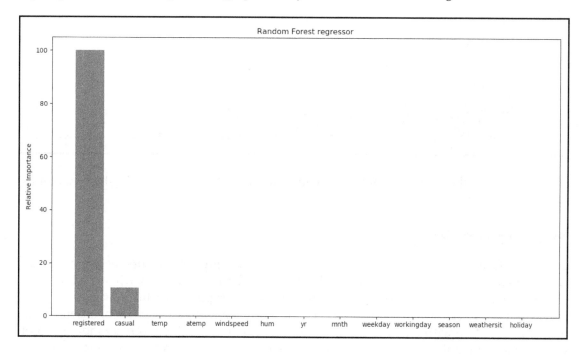

As expected, it says that only these two features are important. This makes sense intuitively because the final output is a simple summation of these two features. So, there is a direct relationship between these two variables and the output value. Hence, the regressor says that it doesn't need any other variable to predict the output. This is an extremely useful tool to eliminate redundant variables in your dataset. But this is not the only difference from the previous model. If we analyze the model's performance, we can see a substantial improvement:

```
#### Random Forest regressor performance ####
Mean squared error = 22552.26
Explained variance score = 0.99
```

We therefore have 99% of the variance explained: a very good result.

There is another file, called `bike_hour.csv`, that contains data about how the bicycles are shared hourly. We need to consider columns 3 to 14, so let's make this change in the code (the rest of the code remains unchanged):

```
filename="bike_hour.csv"
file_reader = csv.reader(open(filename, 'r'), delimiter=',')
X, y = [], []
for row in file_reader:
    X.append(row[2:14])
    y.append(row[-1])
```

If you run the new code, you will see the performance of the regressor displayed, as follows:

```
#### Random Forest regressor performance ####
Mean squared error = 2613.86
Explained variance score = 0.92
```

The feature importance graph will look like the following:

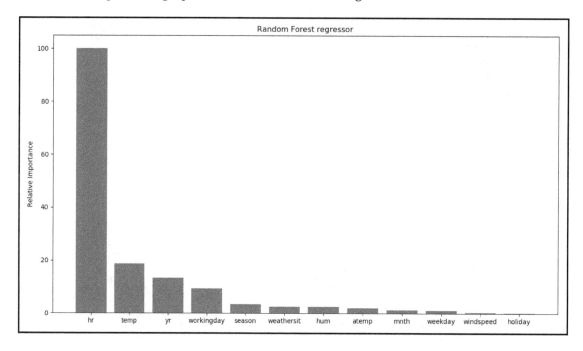

This shows that the hour of the day is the most important feature, which makes sense intuitively if you think about it! The next important feature is temperature, which is consistent with our earlier analysis.

See also

- Scikit-learn's official documentation of the `RandomForestRegressor` function: `https://scikit-learn.org/stable/modules/generated/sklearn.ensemble.RandomForestRegressor.html`

Constructing a Classifier

2

In this chapter, we will cover the following recipes:

- Building a simple classifier
- Building a logistic regression classifier
- Building a Naive Bayes classifier
- Splitting a dataset for training and testing
- Evaluating accuracy using cross-validation
- Visualizing a confusion matrix
- Extracting a performance report
- Evaluating cars based on their characteristics
- Extracting validation curves
- Extracting learning curves
- Estimating a income bracket
- Predicting the quality of wine
- Newsgroup trending topics classification

Technical requirements

To work on the recipes in this chapter, you need the following files (available on GitHub):

- `simple_classifier.py`
- `logistic_regression.py`
- `naive_bayes.py`
- `data_multivar.txt`
- `splitting_dataset.py`
- `confusion_matrix.py`
- `performance_report.py`

- `car.py`
- `car.data.txt`
- `income.py`
- `adult.data.txt`
- `wine.quality.py`
- `wine.txt`
- `post.classification`

Introduction

In the field of machine learning, **classification** refers to the process of using the characteristics of data to separate it into a certain number of classes. This is different than regression, which we discussed in `Chapter 1`, *The Realm of Supervised Learning*, where the output is a real number. A supervised learning classifier builds a model using labeled training data and then uses this model to classify unknown data.

A classifier can be any algorithm that implements classification. In simple cases, a classifier can be a straightforward mathematical function. In more real-world cases, a classifier can take very complex forms. In the course of study, we will see that classification can be either binary, where we separate data into two classes, or it can be multi-class, where we separate data into more than two classes. The mathematical techniques that are devised to deal with classification problems tend to deal with two classes, so we extend them in different ways to deal with multi-class problems as well.

Evaluating the accuracy of a classifier is vital for machine learning. What we need to know is, how we can use the available data, and get a glimpse of how the model performs in the real world. In this chapter, we will look at recipes that deal with all these things.

Building a simple classifier

A **classifier** is a system with some characteristics that allow you to identify the class of the sample examined. In different classification methods, groups are called **classes**. The goal of a classifier is to establish the classification criterion to maximize performance. The performance of a classifier is measured by evaluating the capacity for generalization. **Generalization** means attributing the correct class to each new experimental observation. The way in which these classes are identified discriminates between the different methods that are available.

Getting ready

Classifiers identify the class of a new objective, based on knowledge that's been extracted from a series of samples (a dataset). Starting from a dataset, a classifier extracts a model, which is then used to classify new instances.

How to do it...

Let's see how to build a simple classifier using some training data:

1. We will use the `simple_classifier.py` file, already provided to you as a reference. To start, we import the `numpy` and `matplotlib.pyplot` packages, as we did in Chapter 1, *The Realm of Supervised Learning*, and then we create some sample data:

```
import numpy as np
import matplotlib.pyplot as plt

X = np.array([[3,1], [2,5], [1,8], [6,4], [5,2], [3,5], [4,7],
[4,-1]])
```

2. Let's assign some labels to these points:

```
y = [0, 1, 1, 0, 0, 1, 1, 0]
```

3. As we have only two classes, the `y` list contains 0's and 1's. In general, if you have N classes, then the values in `y` will range from 0 to *N-1*. Let's separate the data into classes based on the labels:

```
class_0 = np.array([X[i] for i in range(len(X)) if y[i]==0])
class_1 = np.array([X[i] for i in range(len(X)) if y[i]==1])
```

4. To get an idea about our data, let's plot it, as follows:

```
plt.figure()
plt.scatter(class_0[:,0], class_0[:,1], color='black', marker='s')
plt.scatter(class_1[:,0], class_1[:,1], color='black', marker='x')
plt.show()
```

This is a **scatterplot**, where we use squares and crosses to plot the points. In this context, the `marker` parameter specifies the shape you want to use. We use squares to denote points in `class_0` and crosses to denote points in `class_1`. If you run this code, you will see the following output:

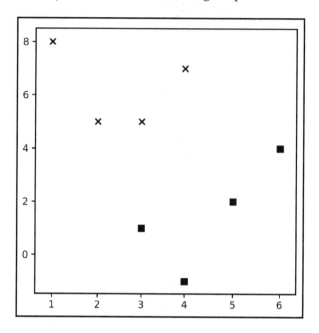

5. In the preceding two lines, we just use the mapping between X and y to create two lists. If you were asked to inspect the datapoints visually and draw a separating line, what would you do? You would simply draw a line in between them. Let's go ahead and do this:

```
line_x = range(10)
line_y = line_x
```

6. We just created a line with the mathematical equation $y = x$. Let's plot it, as follows:

```
plt.figure()
plt.scatter(class_0[:,0], class_0[:,1], color='black', marker='s')
plt.scatter(class_1[:,0], class_1[:,1], color='black', marker='x')
plt.plot(line_x, line_y, color='black', linewidth=3)
plt.show()
```

7. If you run this code, you should see the following output:

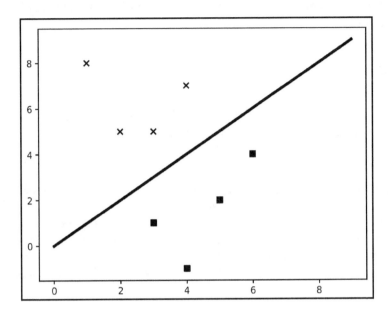

The preceding shows how that construction of a separation line between the two classes was simple. In this simple example, this operation was easy, but in many cases, building a line of separation between two classes can be very difficult.

How it works...

In this recipe, we showed how simple it is to build a classifier. We started from a series of identifying pairs of as many points on a plane (x, y). We therefore assigned a class to each of these points (0,1) so as to divide them into two groups. To understand the spatial arrangement of these points, we visualized them by associating a different marker to each class. Finally, to divide the two groups, we have drew the line of the $y = x$ equation.

There's more...

We built a simple classifier using the following rule—the input point (a, b) belongs to class_0 if a is greater than or equal to b; otherwise, it belongs to class_1. If you inspect the points one by one, you will see that this is, in fact, true. That's it! You just built a linear classifier that can classify unknown data. It's a linear classifier because the separating line is a straight line. If it's a curve, then it becomes a *nonlinear* classifier.

This formation worked well, because there were a limited number of points, and we could visually inspect them. What if there were thousands of points? How would we generalize this process? Let's discuss that in the next recipe.

See also

- The official documentation of the NumPy library (http://www.numpy.org/)
- The official documentation of the Matplotlib library (https://matplotlib.org/)

Building a logistic regression classifier

Despite the word *regression* being present in the name, logistic regression is actually used for classification purposes. Given a set of datapoints, our goal is to build a model that can draw linear boundaries between our classes. It extracts these boundaries by solving a set of equations derived from the training data. In this recipe, we will build a logistic regression classifier.

Getting ready

Logistic regression is a non-linear regression model used when the dependent variable is dichotomous. The purpose is to establish the probability with which an observation can generate one or the other value of the dependent variable; it can also be used to classify observations, according to their characteristics, into two categories.

How to do it...

Let's see how to build a logistic regression classifier:

1. Let's see how to do this in Python. We will use the logistic_regression.py file, provided to you as a reference. Assuming that you imported the necessary packages, let's create some sample data, along with training labels:

```
import numpy as np
from sklearn import linear_model
import matplotlib.pyplot as plt
X = np.array([[4, 7], [3.5, 8], [3.1, 6.2], [0.5, 1], [1, 2], [1.2,
1.9], [6, 2], [5.7, 1.5], [5.4, 2.2]])
y = np.array([0, 0, 0, 1, 1, 1, 2, 2, 2])
```

Here, we assume that we have three classes (0, 1, and 2).

2. Let's initialize the logistic regression classifier:

```
classifier = linear_model.LogisticRegression(solver='lbfgs', C=100)
```

There are a number of input parameters that can be specified for the preceding function, but a couple of important ones are `solver` and C. The `solver` parameter specifies the type of `solver` that the algorithm will use to solve the system of equations. The C parameter controls the regularization strength. A lower value indicates higher regularization strength.

3. Let's train the classifier:

```
classifier.fit(X, y)
```

4. Let's draw datapoints and boundaries. To do this, first, we need to define ranges to plot the diagram, as follows:

```
x_min, x_max = min(X[:, 0]) - 1.0, max(X[:, 0]) + 1.0
y_min, y_max = min(X[:, 1]) - 1.0, max(X[:, 1]) + 1.0
```

The preceding values indicate the range of values that we want to use in our figure. The values usually range from the minimum value to the maximum value present in our data. We add some buffers, such as 1.0, to the preceding lines, for clarity.

5. In order to plot the boundaries, we need to evaluate the function across a grid of points and plot it. Let's go ahead and define the grid:

```
# denotes the step size that will be used in the mesh grid
step_size = 0.01

# define the mesh grid
x_values, y_values = np.meshgrid(np.arange(x_min, x_max,
step_size), np.arange(y_min, y_max, step_size))
```

The `x_values` and `y_values` variables contain the grid of points where the function will be evaluated.

6. Let's compute the output of the classifier for all these points:

```
# compute the classifier output
mesh_output = classifier.predict(np.c_[x_values.ravel(),
y_values.ravel()])
```

```
# reshape the array
mesh_output = mesh_output.reshape(x_values.shape)
```

7. Let's plot the boundaries using colored regions:

```
# Plot the output using a colored plot
plt.figure()

# choose a color scheme you can find all the options
# here:
http://matplotlib.org/examples/color/colormaps_reference.html
plt.pcolormesh(x_values, y_values, mesh_output, cmap=plt.cm.gray)
```

This is basically a 3D plotter that takes the 2D points and the associated values to draw different regions using a color scheme.

8. Let's overlay the training points on the plot:

```
# Overlay the training points on the plot
plt.scatter(X[:, 0], X[:, 1], c=y, s=80, edgecolors='black',
linewidth=1, cmap=plt.cm.Paired)

# specify the boundaries of the figure
plt.xlim(x_values.min(), x_values.max())
plt.ylim(y_values.min(), y_values.max())

# specify the ticks on the X and Y axes
plt.xticks((np.arange(int(min(X[:, 0])-1), int(max(X[:, 0])+1),
1.0)))
plt.yticks((np.arange(int(min(X[:, 1])-1), int(max(X[:, 1])+1),
1.0)))

plt.show()
```

Here, plt.scatter plots the points on the 2D graph. X[:, 0] specifies that we should take all the values along the 0 axis (the *x* axis in our case), and X[:, 1] specifies axis 1 (the *y* axis). The c=y parameter indicates the color sequence. We use the target labels to map to colors using cmap. Basically, we want different colors that are based on the target labels. Hence, we use y as the mapping. The limits of the display figure are set using plt.xlim and plt.ylim. In order to mark the axes with values, we need to use plt.xticks and plt.yticks. These functions mark the axes with values so that it's easier for us to see where the points are located. In the preceding code, we want the ticks to lie between the minimum and maximum values with a buffer of one unit. Also, we want these ticks to be integers. So, we use the int() function to round off the values.

9. If you run this code, you should see the following output:

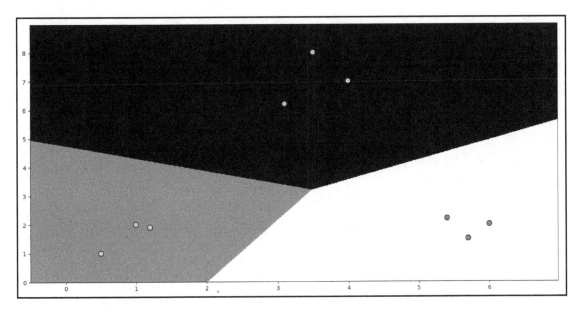

10. Let's see how the C parameter affects our model. The C parameter indicates the penalty for misclassification. If we set it to 1.0, we will get the following:

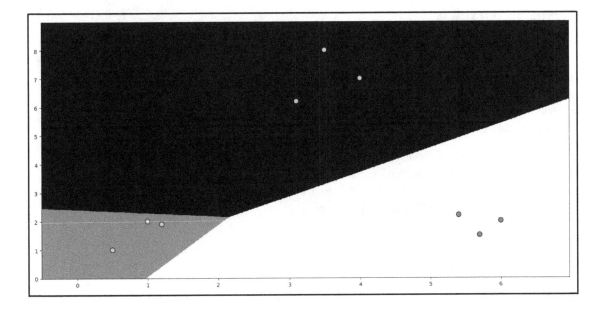

11. If we set `c` to `10000`, we get the following:

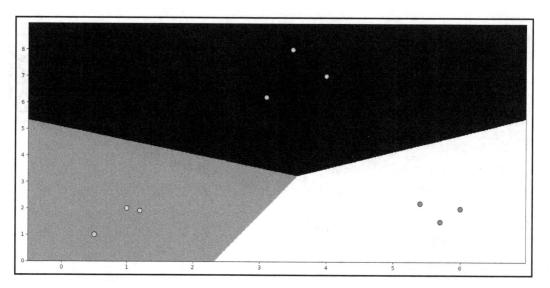

As we increase `c`, there is a higher penalty for misclassification. Hence, the boundaries become more optimized.

How it works...

Logistic regression is a classification method within the family of supervised learning algorithms. Using statistical methods, logistic regression allows us to generate a result that, in fact, represents a probability that a given input value belongs to a given class. In binomial logistic regression problems, the probability that output belongs to a class will be *P*, whereas the probability of it belonging to another class will be *1-P* (where *P* is a number between 0 and 1 because it expresses probability).

Logistic regression uses the logistic function to determine the classification of input values. Also called the **sigmoid** function, the logistic function is an S-shaped curve that can take any number of of a real value and map it to a value between 0 and 1, extremes excluded. It can be described by the following equation:

$$F(x) = \frac{1}{1 + e^{-(\beta_0 + \beta_1 * x)}}$$

This function transforms the real values into numbers between 0 and 1.

There's more...

To obtain the logistic regression equation expressed in probabilistic terms, we need to include the probabilities in the logistic regression equation:

$$P(x) = \frac{e^{-(\beta_0 + \beta_1 * x)}}{1 + e^{-(\beta_0 + \beta_1 * x)}}$$

Recalling that the e function is the opposite of the natural logarithm (ln), we can write:

$$\frac{P(x)}{1 - P(x)} = \beta_0 + \beta_1 * x$$

This function is called a **logit** function. The logit function, on the other hand, allows us to associate the probabilities (therefore, a value included between 0 and 1) to the whole range of real numbers. It is a link function and represents the inverse of the logistic function.

See also

- *Logit Models for Binary Data*, Princeton University: https://data.princeton.edu/
- *Regression Analysis with R*, Giuseppe Ciaburro, Packt Publishing
- wws509/notes/c3.pdf
- Matplotlib color scheme options: https://matplotlib.org/examples/color/colormaps_reference.html

Building a Naive Bayes classifier

A classifier solves the problem of identifying sub-populations of individuals with certain features in a larger set, with the possible use of a subset of individuals known as a priori (a training set). A Naive Bayes classifier is a supervised learning classifier that uses Bayes' theorem to build the model. In this recipe, we will build a Naive Bayes classifier.

Getting ready

The underlying principle of a Bayesian classifier is that some individuals belong to a class of interest with a given probability based on some observations. This probability is based on the assumption that the characteristics observed can be either dependent or independent from one another; in this second case, the Bayesian classifier is called Naive because it assumes that the presence or absence of a particular characteristic in a given class of interest is not related to the presence or absence of other characteristics, greatly simplifying the calculation. Let's go ahead and build a Naive Bayes classifier.

How to do it...

Let's see how to build a Naive Bayes classifier:

1. We will use naive_bayes.py, provided to you as a reference. Let's import some libraries:

```
import numpy as np
import matplotlib.pyplot as plt
from sklearn.naive_bayes import GaussianNB
```

2. You were provided with a data_multivar.txt file. This contains data that we will use here. This contains comma-separated numerical data in each line. Let's load the data from this file:

```
input_file = 'data_multivar.txt'
X = []
y = []
with open(input_file, 'r') as f:
    for line in f.readlines():
        data = [float(x) for x in line.split(',')]
        X.append(data[:-1])
        y.append(data[-1])
X = np.array(X)
y = np.array(y)
```

We have now loaded the input data into X and the labels into y. There are four labels: 0, 1, 2, and 3.

3. Let's build the Naive Bayes classifier:

```
classifier_gaussiannb = GaussianNB()
classifier_gaussiannb.fit(X, y)
y_pred = classifier_gaussiannb.predict(X)
```

The `gauusiannb` function specifies the Gaussian Naive Bayes model.

4. Let's compute the `accuracy` measure of the classifier:

```
accuracy = 100.0 * (y == y_pred).sum() / X.shape[0]
print("Accuracy of the classifier =", round(accuracy, 2), "%")
```

The following accuracy is returned:

Accuracy of the classifier = 99.5 %

5. Let's plot the data and the boundaries. We will use the procedure followed in the previous recipe, *Building a logistic regression classifier*:

```
x_min, x_max = min(X[:, 0]) - 1.0, max(X[:, 0]) + 1.0
y_min, y_max = min(X[:, 1]) - 1.0, max(X[:, 1]) + 1.0

# denotes the step size that will be used in the mesh grid
step_size = 0.01

# define the mesh grid
x_values, y_values = np.meshgrid(np.arange(x_min, x_max,
step_size), np.arange(y_min, y_max, step_size))

# compute the classifier output
mesh_output = classifier_gaussiannb.predict(np.c_[x_values.ravel(),
y_values.ravel()])

# reshape the array
mesh_output = mesh_output.reshape(x_values.shape)

# Plot the output using a colored plot
plt.figure()

# choose a color scheme
plt.pcolormesh(x_values, y_values, mesh_output, cmap=plt.cm.gray)

# Overlay the training points on the plot
plt.scatter(X[:, 0], X[:, 1], c=y, s=80, edgecolors='black',
linewidth=1, cmap=plt.cm.Paired)

# specify the boundaries of the figure
plt.xlim(x_values.min(), x_values.max())
plt.ylim(y_values.min(), y_values.max())

# specify the ticks on the X and Y axes
plt.xticks((np.arange(int(min(X[:, 0])-1), int(max(X[:, 0])+1),
1.0)))
```

```
plt.yticks((np.arange(int(min(X[:, 1])-1), int(max(X[:, 1])+1),
1.0)))

plt.show()
```

You should see the following:

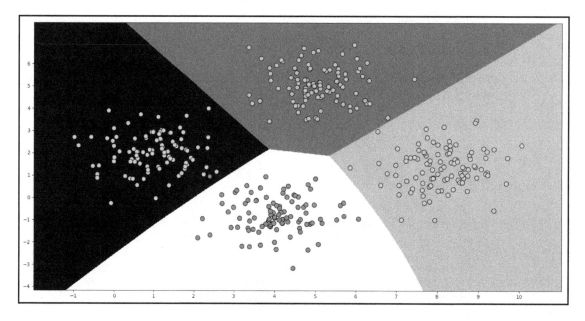

There is no restriction on the boundaries to be linear here. In the preceding recipe, *Building a logistic regression classifier*, we used up all the data for training. A good practice in machine learning is to have non-overlapping data for training and testing. Ideally, we need some unused data for testing so that we can get an accurate estimate of how the model performs on unknown data. There is a provision in `scikit-learn` that handles this very well, as shown in the next recipe.

How it works...

A **Bayesian classifier** is a classifier based on the application of Bayes' theorem. This classifier requires the knowledge of a priori and conditional probabilities related to the problem; quantities that, in general, are not known but are typically estimable. If reliable estimates of the probabilities involved in the theorem can be obtained, the Bayesian classifier is generally reliable and potentially compact.

The probability that a given event (E) occurs, is the ratio between the number (s) of favorable cases of the event itself and the total number (n) of the possible cases, provided all the considered cases are equally probable. This can be better represented using the following formula:

$$P = P(E) = \frac{number\ of\ favorable\ cases}{total\ number\ of\ the\ possible\ cases} = \frac{s}{n}$$

Given two events, A and B, if the two events are independent (the occurrence of one does not affect the probability of the other), the joint probability of the event is equal to the product of the probabilities of A and B:

$$P(A \cap B) = P(A) \times P(B)$$

If the two events are dependent (that is, the occurrence of one affects the probability of the other), then the same rule may apply, provided $P(B \mid A)$ is the probability of event A given that event B has occurred. This condition introduces conditional probability, which we are going to dive into now:

$$P(A \cap B) = P(A) \times P(B|A)$$

The probability that event A occurs, calculated on the condition that event B occurred, is called **conditional probability**, and is indicated by $P(A \mid B)$. It is calculated using the following formula:

$$P(B|A) = \frac{P(A \cap B)}{P(A)}$$

Let A and B be two dependent events, as we stated that the joint probability between them is calculated using the following formula:

$$P(A \cap B) = P(A) \times P(B|A)$$

Or, similarly, we can use the following formula:

$$P(A \cap B) = P(B) \times P(A|B)$$

By looking at the two formulas, we see that they have the first equal member. This shows that even the second members are equal, so the following equation can be written:

$$P(A) \times P(B|A) = P(B) \times P(A|B)$$

By solving these equations for conditional probability, we get the following:

$$P(B|A) = \frac{P(B) \times P(A|B)}{P(A)}$$

The proposed formulas represent the mathematical statement of Bayes' theorem. The use of one or the other depends on what we are looking for.

There's more...

In 1763, an article by Reverend Thomas Bayes was published in England; the article became famous for its implications. According to the article, making predictions about a phenomenon depends not only on the observations that the scientist obtains from his experiments, but also on what he himself thinks and understands of the phenomenon studied, even before proceeding to the experiment itself. These premises were developed in the 1900s by distinguished scholars, such as Bruno de Finetti (*La prévision: ses lois logiques, ses sources subjectives*, 1937), L J Savage (*The Fondations of statistics Reconsidered*, 1959), and others.

See also

- *Keras 2.x Projects*, Giuseppe Ciaburro, Packt Publishing.
- *Bayes' Theorem*, Stanford Encyclopedia of Philosophy: `https://plato.stanford.edu/entries/bayes-theorem/`
- The official documentation of the `sklearn.naive_bayes.GaussianNB` function: `https://scikit-learn.org/stable/modules/generated/sklearn.naive_bayes.GaussianNB.html`

Splitting a dataset for training and testing

Let's see how to split our data properly into training and testing datasets. As we said in `Chapter 1`, *The Realm of Supervised Learning*, in the *Building a linear regressor* recipe, when we build a machine learning model, we need a way to validate our model to check whether it is performing at a satisfactory level. To do this, we need to separate our data into two groups—a **training** dataset and a **testing** dataset. The training dataset will be used to build the model, and the testing dataset will be used to see how this trained model performs on unknown data.

In this recipe, we will learn how to split the dataset for training and testing phases.

Getting ready

The fundamental objective of a model based on machine learning is to make accurate predictions. Before using a model to make predictions, it is necessary to evaluate the predictive performance of the model. To estimate the quality of a model's predictions, it is necessary to use data that you have never seen before. Training a predictive model and testing it on the same data is a methodological error: a model that simply classifies the labels of samples it has just seen would have a high score but would not be able to predict the new data class. Under these conditions, the generalization capacity of the model would be less.

How to do it...

Let's see how to split the dataset:

1. The first part of the recipe is similar to the previous recipe, *Building a Naive Bayes classifier* (load the `Splitting_dataset.py` file):

```
import numpy as np
import matplotlib.pyplot as plt
from sklearn.naive_bayes import GaussianNB

input_file = 'data_multivar.txt'

X = []
y = []
with open(input_file, 'r') as f:
    for line in f.readlines():
        data = [float(x) for x in line.split(',')]
        X.append(data[:-1])
        y.append(data[-1])

X = np.array(X)
y = np.array(y)

#Splitting the dataset for training and testing
from sklearn import model_selection
X_train, X_test, y_train, y_test =
model_selection.train_test_split(X, y, test_size=0.25,
random_state=5)
```

```
#Building the classifier
classifier_gaussiannb_new = GaussianNB()
classifier_gaussiannb_new.fit(X_train, y_train)
```

Here, we allocated 25% of the data for testing, as specified by the `test_size` parameter. The remaining 75% of the data will be used for training.

2. Let's evaluate the classifier on the test data:

```
y_test_pred = classifier_gaussiannb_new.predict(X_test)
```

3. Let's compute the `accuracy` measure of the classifier:

```
accuracy = 100.0 * (y_test == y_test_pred).sum() / X_test.shape[0]
print("Accuracy of the classifier =", round(accuracy, 2), "%")
```

The following result is printed:

Accuracy of the classifier = 98.0 %

4. Let's plot the datapoints and the boundaries on the test data:

```
#Plot a classifier
#Define the data
X= X_test
y=y_test

# define ranges to plot the figure
x_min, x_max = min(X[:, 0]) - 1.0, max(X[:, 0]) + 1.0
y_min, y_max = min(X[:, 1]) - 1.0, max(X[:, 1]) + 1.0

# denotes the step size that will be used in the mesh grid
step_size = 0.01

# define the mesh grid
x_values, y_values = np.meshgrid(np.arange(x_min, x_max,
step_size), np.arange(y_min, y_max, step_size))

# compute the classifier output
mesh_output =
classifier_gaussiannb_new.predict(np.c_[x_values.ravel(),
y_values.ravel()])

# reshape the array
mesh_output = mesh_output.reshape(x_values.shape)

# Plot the output using a colored plot
plt.figure()
```

```
# choose a color scheme
plt.pcolormesh(x_values, y_values, mesh_output, cmap=plt.cm.gray)

# Overlay the training points on the plot
plt.scatter(X[:, 0], X[:, 1], c=y, s=80, edgecolors='black',
linewidth=1, cmap=plt.cm.Paired)

# specify the boundaries of the figure
plt.xlim(x_values.min(), x_values.max())
plt.ylim(y_values.min(), y_values.max())

# specify the ticks on the X and Y axes
plt.xticks((np.arange(int(min(X[:, 0])-1), int(max(X[:, 0])+1),
1.0)))
plt.yticks((np.arange(int(min(X[:, 1])-1), int(max(X[:, 1])+1),
1.0)))

plt.show()
```

5. You should see the following:

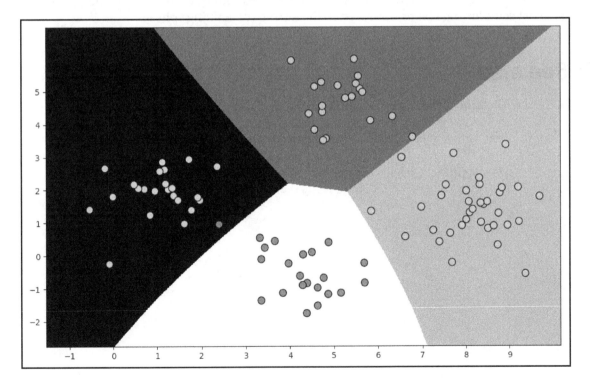

How it works...

In this recipe, we split the data using the `train_test_split()` function of the `scikit-learn` library. This function splits arrays or matrices into random train and testing subsets. Random division of input data into data sources for training and testing ensures that data distribution is similar for training and testing data sources. You choose this option when it is not necessary to preserve the order of the input data.

There's more...

The performance estimate depends on the data used. Therefore, simply dividing data randomly into a training and a testing set does not guarantee that the results are statistically significant. The repetition of the evaluation on different random divisions and the calculation of the performance in terms of the average and standard deviation of the individual evaluations creates a more reliable estimate.

However, even the repetition of evaluations on different random divisions could prevent the most complex data being classified in the testing (or training) phase.

See also

- The official documentation of the `sklearn.model_selection.train_test_split` function: https://scikit-learn.org/stable/modules/generated/sklearn.model_selection.train_test_split.html
- *Data Splitting*, Charles University: https://www.mff.cuni.cz/veda/konference/wds/proc/pdf10/WDS10_105_i1_Reitermanova.pdf

Evaluating accuracy using cross-validation metrics

Cross-validation is an important concept in machine learning. In the previous recipe, we split the data into training and testing datasets. However, in order to make it more robust, we need to repeat this process with different subsets. If we just fine-tune it for a particular subset, we may end up overfitting the model. **Overfitting** refers to a situation where we fine-tune a model to a dataset too much and it fails to perform well on unknown data. We want our machine learning model to perform well on unknown data. In this recipe, we will learn how to evaluate model accuracy using cross-validation metrics.

Getting ready...

When we are dealing with machine learning models, we usually care about three things—precision, recall, and F1 score. We can get the required performance metric using parameter scoring. **Precision** refers to the number of items that are correctly classified as a percentage of the overall number of items in the list. **Recall** refers to the number of items that are retrieved as a percentage of the overall number of items in the training list.

How to do it...

Let's see how to evaluate model accuracy using cross-validation metrics:

1. We will use the classifier just used in the *Building a Naive Bayes* classifier recipe (load the `naive_bayes.py` file). We will start with the `accuracy` measure:

```
from sklearn import model_selection
num_validations = 5
accuracy = model_selection.cross_val_score(classifier_gaussiannb,
        X, y, scoring='accuracy', cv=num_validations)
print "Accuracy: " + str(round(100*accuracy.mean(), 2)) + "%"
```

2. We will use the preceding function to compute `precision`, `recall`, and the F1 score as well:

```
f1 = model_selection.cross_val_score(classifier_gaussiannb,
 X, y, scoring='f1_weighted', cv=num_validations)
print "F1: " + str(round(100*f1.mean(), 2)) + "%"
precision = model_selection.cross_val_score(classifier_gaussiannb,
 X, y, scoring='precision_weighted', cv=num_validations)
print "Precision: " + str(round(100*precision.mean(), 2)) + "%"
```

```
recall = model_selection.cross_val_score(classifier_gaussiannb,
 X, y, scoring='recall_weighted', cv=num_validations)
print "Recall: " + str(round(100*recall.mean(), 2)) + "%"
```

How it works...

Let's consider a test dataset containing 100 items, out of which 82 are of interest to us. Now, we want our classifier to identify these 82 items for us. Our classifier picks out 73 items as the items of interest. Out of these 73 items, only 65 are actually items of interest, and the remaining 8 are misclassified. We can compute precision in the following way:

- The number of correct identifications = 65
- The total number of identifications = 73
- Precision = 65 / 73 = 89.04%

To compute recall, we use the following:

- The total number of items of interest in the dataset = 82
- The number of items retrieved correctly = 65
- Recall = 65 / 82 = 79.26%

A good machine learning model needs to have good precision and good recall simultaneously. It's easy to get one of them to 100%, but the other metric suffers! We need to keep both metrics high at the same time. To quantify this, we use an F1 score, which is a combination of precision and recall. This is actually the harmonic mean of precision and recall:

$$F_{1score} = \frac{2 * precision * recall}{precision + recall}$$

In the preceding case, the F1 score will be as follows:

$$F_{1score} = \frac{2 * 0.89 * 0.79}{0.89 + 0.79} = 0.8370$$

There's more...

In cross-validation, all available data is used, in groups of a fixed size, alternatively as a testing and as a training set. Therefore, each pattern is either classified (at least once) or used for training. The performances obtained depend, however, on the particular division. Therefore, it may be useful to repeat cross-validation several times in order to become independent of the particular division.

See also

- The official documentation of the `sklearn.model_selection.cross_val_score` function: `https://scikit-learn.org/stable/modules/generated/sklearn.model_selection.cross_val_score.html#sklearn.model_selection.cross_val_score`

- *Cross-validation* (from scikit-learn's official documentation): `http://ogrisel.github.io/scikit-learn.org/sklearn-tutorial/modules/cross_validation.html`

Visualizing a confusion matrix

A **confusion matrix** is a table that we use to understand the performance of a classification model. This helps us understand how we classify testing data into different classes. When we want to fine-tune our algorithms, we need to understand how data gets misclassified before we make these changes. Some classes are worse than others, and the confusion matrix will help us understand this. Let's look at the following:

	Predicted class 0	Predicted class 1	Predicted class 2
True class 0	45	4	3
True class 1	11	56	2
True class 2	5	6	49

In the preceding diagram, we can see how we categorize data into different classes. Ideally, we want all the non-diagonal elements to be 0. This would indicate perfect classification! Let's consider class 0. Overall, 52 items actually belong to class 0. We get 52 if we sum up the numbers in the first row. Now, 45 of these items are being predicted correctly, but our classifier says that 4 of them belong to class 1 and three of them belong to class 2. We can apply the same analysis to the remaining 2 rows as well. An interesting thing to note is that 11 items from class 1 are misclassified as class 0. This constitutes around 16% of the datapoints in this class. This is an insight that we can use to optimize our model.

Getting ready

A confusion matrix identifies the nature of the classification errors, as our classification results are compared to real data. In this matrix, the diagonal cells show the number of cases that were correctly classified; all the others cells show the misclassified cases.

How to do it...

Let's see how to visualize the confusion matrix:

1. We will use the `confusion_matrix.py` file that we already provided to you as a reference. Let's see how to extract the confusion matrix from our data:

```
import numpy as np
import matplotlib.pyplot as plt
from sklearn.metrics import confusion_matrix
```

   We use some sample data here. We have 4 classes with values ranging from 0 to 3. We have predicted labels as well. We use the `confusion_matrix` method to extract the confusion matrix and plot it.

2. Let's go ahead and define this function:

```
# Show confusion matrix
def plot_confusion_matrix(confusion_mat):
    plt.imshow(confusion_mat, interpolation='nearest',
cmap=plt.cm.Paired)
    plt.title('Confusion matrix')
    plt.colorbar()
    tick_marks = np.arange(4)
    plt.xticks(tick_marks, tick_marks)
    plt.yticks(tick_marks, tick_marks)
    plt.ylabel('True label')
```

```
plt.xlabel('Predicted label')
plt.show()
```

We use the imshow function to plot the confusion matrix. Everything else in the function is straightforward! We just set the title, color bar, ticks, and the labels using the relevant functions. The tick_marks argument range from 0 to 3 because we have 4 distinct labels in our dataset. The np.arange function gives us this numpy array.

3. Let's define the data (real and predicted) and then we will call the confusion_matrix function:

```
y_true = [1, 0, 0, 2, 1, 0, 3, 3, 3]
y_pred = [1, 1, 0, 2, 1, 0, 1, 3, 3]
confusion_mat = confusion_matrix(y_true, y_pred)
plot_confusion_matrix(confusion_mat)
```

4. If you run the preceding code, you will see the following:

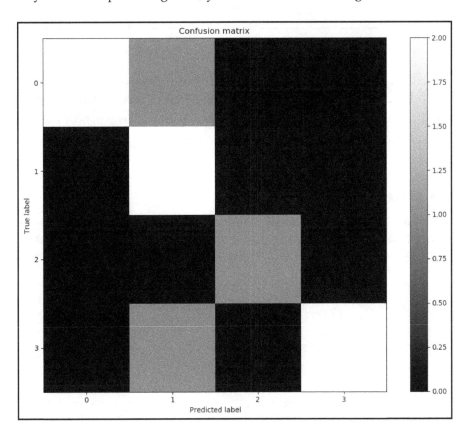

The diagonal colors are strong, and we want them to be strong. The black color indicates zero. There are a couple of gray squares in the non-diagonal spaces, which indicate misclassification. For example, when the real label is 0, the predicted label is 1, as we can see in the first row. In fact, all the misclassifications belong to class 1 in the sense that the second column contains 3 rows that are non-zero. It's easy to see this from the matrix.

How it works...

A confusion matrix displays information about the actual and predicted classifications made by a model. The performance of such systems is evaluated with the help of data in the matrix.

The following table shows the confusion matrix for a two-class classifier:

	PREDICTED POSITIVE	PREDICTED NEGATIVE
Actual TRUE	TP	FN
Actual FALSE	FP	TN

The entries in the confusion matrix have the following meanings:

- TP is the number of correct predictions that an instance is positive
- FN is the number of incorrect predictions that an instance is negative
- FP is the number of incorrect predictions that an instance is positive
- TN is the number of correct predictions that an instance is negative

There's more...

The confusion matrix shows us the performance of an algorithm. Each row returns the instances in an actual class, while each column returns the instances in an expected class. The term *confusion matrix* results from the fact that it makes it easy to see whether the system is confusing two classes.

See also

- The official documentation of the `sklearn.metrics.confusion_matrix()` function: `https://scikit-learn.org/stable/modules/generated/sklearn.metrics.confusion_matrix.html`
- *Confusion Matrix*, University of Notre Dame: `https://www3.nd.edu/~busiforc/Confusion_Matrix.html`

Extracting a performance report

In the *Evaluating accuracy using cross-validation metrics* recipe, we calculated some metrics to measure the accuracy of the model. Let's remember its meaning. The accuracy returns the percentage of correct classifications. Precision returns the percentage of positive classifications that are correct. Recall (sensitivity) returns the percentage of positive elements of the testing set that have been classified as positive. Finally, in F1, both the precision and the recall are used to compute the score. In this recipe, we will learn how to extract a performance report.

Getting ready

We also have a function in `scikit-learn` that can directly print the precision, recall, and F1 scores for us. Let's see how to do this.

How to do it...

Let's see how to extract a performance report:

1. Add the following lines to a new Python file (load the `performance_report.py` file):

```
from sklearn.metrics import classification_report
y_true = [1, 0, 0, 2, 1, 0, 3, 3, 3]
y_pred = [1, 1, 0, 2, 1, 0, 1, 3, 3]
target_names = ['Class-0', 'Class-1', 'Class-2', 'Class-3']
print(classification_report(y_true, y_pred,
target_names=target_names))
```

2. If you run this code, you will see the following on your Terminal:

	precision	recall	f1-score	support
Class-0	1.00	0.67	0.80	3
Class-1	0.50	1.00	0.67	2
Class-2	1.00	1.00	1.00	1
Class-3	1.00	0.67	0.80	3
avg / total	0.89	0.78	0.79	9

Instead of computing these metrics separately, you can directly use the preceding function to extract those statistics from your model.

How it works...

In this recipe, we used the `classification_report ()` function of the scikit-learn library to extract a performance report. This function builds a text report showing the main classification metrics. A text summary of the precision, recall, and the F1 score for each class is returned. Referring to the terms introduced in the confusion matrix addressed in the previous recipe, these metrics are calculated as follows:

- The precision is the ratio tp / (tp + fp), where tp is the number of true positives and fp the number of false positives. The precision is the ability of the classifier to not label a sample that is negative as positive.
- The recall is the ratio tp / (tp + fn), where tp is the number of true positives and fn the number of false negatives. The recall is the ability of the classifier to find the positive samples.
- The F1 score is said to be a weighted harmonic mean of the precision and recall, where an F-beta score reaches its peak value at 1 and its lowest score at 0.

There's more...

The reported averages include the **micro average** (averaging the total true positives, false negatives, and false positives), the **macro average** (averaging the unweighted mean per label), the **weighted average** (averaging the support-weighted mean per label), and the **sample average** (only for multilabel classification).

See also

- The official documentation of the
  `sklearn.metrics.classification_report()` function: `https://scikit-learn.org/stable/modules/generated/sklearn.metrics.classification_report.html`

Evaluating cars based on their characteristics

In this recipe, let's see how we can apply classification techniques to a real-world problem. We will use a dataset that contains some details about cars, such as number of doors, boot space, maintenance costs, and so on. Our goal is to determine the quality of the car. For the purposes of classification, quality can take four values: unacceptable, acceptable, good, or very good.

Getting ready

You can download the dataset at `https://archive.ics.uci.edu/ml/datasets/Car+Evaluation`.

You need to treat each value in the dataset as a string. We consider six attributes in the dataset. Here are the attributes along with the possible values they can take:

- `buying`: These will be `vhigh`, `high`, `med`, and `low`.
- `maint`: These will be `vhigh`, `high`, `med`, and `low`.
- `doors`: These will be 2, 3, 4, 5, and `more`.
- `persons`: These will be 2, 4, and `more`.
- `lug_boot`: These will be `small`, `med`, and `big`.
- `safety`: These will be `low`, `med`, and `high`.

Given that each line contains strings, we need to assume that all the features are strings and design a classifier. In the previous chapter, we used random forests to build a regressor. In this recipe, we will use random forests as a classifier.

How to do it...

Let's see how to evaluate cars based on their characteristics:

1. We will use the `car.py` file that we already provided to you as reference. Let's go ahead and import a couple of packages:

```
from sklearn import preprocessing
from sklearn.ensemble import RandomForestClassifier
```

2. Let's load the dataset:

```
input_file = 'car.data.txt'
# Reading the data
X = []
count = 0
with open(input_file, 'r') as f:
    for line in f.readlines():
        data = line[:-1].split(',')
        X.append(data)
X = np.array(X)
```

Each line contains a comma-separated list of words. Therefore, we parse the input file, split each line, and then append the list to the main data. We ignore the last character on each line because it's a newline character. Python packages only work with numerical data, so we need to transform these attributes into something that those packages will understand.

3. In the previous chapter, we discussed label encoding. That is what we will use here to convert strings to numbers:

```
# Convert string data to numerical data
label_encoder = []
X_encoded = np.empty(X.shape)
for i,item in enumerate(X[0]):
    label_encoder.append(preprocessing.LabelEncoder())
    X_encoded[:, i] = label_encoder[-1].fit_transform(X[:, i])
X = X_encoded[:, :-1].astype(int)
y = X_encoded[:, -1].astype(int)
```

As each attribute can take a limited number of values, we can use the label encoder to transform them into numbers. We need to use different label encoders for each attribute. For example, the `lug_boot` attribute can take three distinct values, and we need a label encoder that knows how to encode this attribute. The last value on each line is the class, so we assign it to the *y* variable.

4. Let's train the classifier:

```
# Build a Random Forest classifier
params = {'n_estimators': 200, 'max_depth': 8, 'random_state': 7}
classifier = RandomForestClassifier(**params)
classifier.fit(X, y)
```

You can play around with the `n_estimators` and `max_depth` parameters to see how they affect classification accuracy. We will actually do this soon in a standardized way.

5. Let's perform cross-validation:

```
# Cross validation
from sklearn import model_selection

accuracy = model_selection.cross_val_score(classifier,
        X, y, scoring='accuracy', cv=3)
print("Accuracy of the classifier: " +
str(round(100*accuracy.mean(), 2)) + "%")
```

Once we train the classifier, we need to see how it performs. We use three-fold cross-validation to calculate the accuracy here. The following result is returned:

Accuracy of the classifier: 78.19%

6. One of the main goals of building a classifier is to use it on isolated and unknown data instances. Let's use a single datapoint and see how we can use this classifier to categorize it:

```
# Testing encoding on single data instance
input_data = ['high', 'low', '2', 'more', 'med', 'high']
input_data_encoded = [-1] * len(input_data)
for i,item in enumerate(input_data):
    input_data_encoded[i] =
int(label_encoder[i].transform([input_data[i]]))
input_data_encoded = np.array(input_data_encoded)
```

The first step was to convert that data into numerical data. We need to use the label encoders that we used during training because we want it to be consistent. If there are unknown values in the input datapoint, the label encoder will complain because it doesn't know how to handle that data. For example, if you change the first value in the list from `high` to `abcd`, then the label encoder won't work because it doesn't know how to interpret this string. This acts like an error check to see whether the input datapoint is valid.

7. We are now ready to predict the output class for this datapoint:

```
# Predict and print output for a particular datapoint
output_class = classifier.predict([input_data_encoded])
print("Output class:",
label_encoder[-1].inverse_transform(output_class)[0])
```

We use the `predict()` method to estimate the output class. If we output the encoded output label, it won't mean anything to us. Therefore, we use the `inverse_transform` method to convert this label back to its original form and print out the output class. The following result is returned:

```
Output class: acc
```

How it works...

The **random forest** was developed by Leo Breiman (University of California, Berkeley, USA) based on the use of classification trees. He has extended the classification tree technique by integrating it into a Monte Carlo simulation procedure and named it **random forest**. It is based on the creation of a large set of tree classifiers, each of which is proposed to classify a single instance, wherein some features have been evaluated. Comparing the classification proposals provided by each tree in the forest shows the class to which to attribute the request: it is the one that received the most votes.

There's more...

Random forest has three adjustment parameters: the number of trees, the minimum amplitude of the terminal nodes, and the number of variables sampled in each node. The absence of overfitting makes the first two parameters important only from a computational point of view.

See also

- The official documentation of the
  `sklearn.ensemble.RandomForestClassifier()` function: `https://scikit-learn.org/stable/modules/generated/sklearn.ensemble.RandomForestClassifier.html`
- *Random Forests* by Leo Breiman and Adele Cutler (from the University of California, Berkeley): `https://www.stat.berkeley.edu/~breiman/RandomForests/cc_home.htm`

Extracting validation curves

We used random forests to build a classifier in the previous recipe, *Evaluating cars based on their characteristics*, but we don't exactly know how to define the parameters. In our case, we dealt with two parameters: `n_estimators` and `max_depth`. They are called **hyperparameters**, and the performance of the classifier depends on them. It would be nice to see how the performance gets affected as we change the hyperparameters. This is where validation curves come into the picture.

Getting ready

Validation curves help us understand how each hyperparameter influences the training score. Basically, all other parameters are kept constant and we vary the hyperparameter of interest according to our range. We will then be able to visualize how this affects the score.

How to do it...

Let's see how to extract validation curves:

1. Add the following code to the same Python file as in the previous recipe, *Evaluating cars based on their characteristics*:

```
# Validation curves
import matplotlib.pyplot as plt
from sklearn.model_selection import validation_curve

classifier = RandomForestClassifier(max_depth=4, random_state=7)

parameter_grid = np.linspace(25, 200, 8).astype(int)
```

```
train_scores, validation_scores = validation_curve(classifier, X,
y, "n_estimators", parameter_grid, cv=5)
print("##### VALIDATION CURVES #####")
print("\nParam: n_estimators\nTraining scores:\n", train_scores)
print("\nParam: n_estimators\nValidation scores:\n",
validation_scores)
```

In this case, we defined the classifier by fixing the `max_depth` parameter. We want to estimate the optimal number of estimators to use, and so have defined our search space using `parameter_grid`. It is going to extract training and validation scores by iterating from 25 to 200 in 8 steps.

2. If you run it, you will see the following on your Terminal:

```
##### VALIDATION CURVES #####

Param: n_estimators
Training scores:
[[0.80680174 0.80824891 0.80752533 0.80463097 0.81358382]
 [0.79522431 0.80535456 0.81041968 0.8089725  0.81069364]
 [0.80101302 0.80680174 0.81114327 0.81476122 0.8150289 ]
 [0.8024602  0.80535456 0.81186686 0.80752533 0.80346821]
 [0.80028944 0.80463097 0.81114327 0.80824891 0.81069364]
 [0.80390738 0.80535456 0.81041968 0.80969609 0.81647399]
 [0.80390738 0.80463097 0.81114327 0.81476122 0.81719653]
 [0.80390738 0.80607815 0.81114327 0.81403763 0.81647399]]

Param: n_estimators
Validation scores:
[[0.71098266 0.76589595 0.72543353 0.76300578 0.75290698]
 [0.71098266 0.75433526 0.71965318 0.75722543 0.74127907]
 [0.71098266 0.72254335 0.71965318 0.75722543 0.74418605]
 [0.71098266 0.71387283 0.71965318 0.75722543 0.72674419]
 [0.71098266 0.74277457 0.71965318 0.75722543 0.74127907]
 [0.71098266 0.74277457 0.71965318 0.75722543 0.74127907]
 [0.71098266 0.74566474 0.71965318 0.75722543 0.74418605]
 [0.71098266 0.75144509 0.71965318 0.75722543 0.74127907]]
```

3. Let's plot it:

```
# Plot the curve
plt.figure()
plt.plot(parameter_grid, 100*np.average(train_scores, axis=1),
color='black')
plt.title('Training curve')
plt.xlabel('Number of estimators')
plt.ylabel('Accuracy')
plt.show()
```

4. Here is what you'll get:

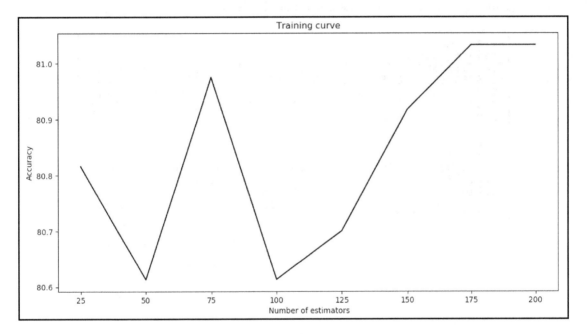

5. Let's do the same for the `max_depth` parameter:

```
classifier = RandomForestClassifier(n_estimators=20,
random_state=7)
parameter_grid = np.linspace(2, 10, 5).astype(int)
train_scores, valid_scores = validation_curve(classifier, X, y,
        "max_depth", parameter_grid, cv=5)
print("\nParam: max_depth\nTraining scores:\n", train_scores)
print("\nParam: max_depth\nValidation scores:\n",
validation_scores)
```

We fixed the `n_estimators` parameter at 20 to see how the performance varies with `max_depth`. Here is the output on the Terminal:

```
Param: max_depth
Training scores:
[[0.71852388 0.70043415 0.70043415 0.70043415 0.69942197]
 [0.80607815 0.80535456 0.80752533 0.79450072 0.81069364]
 [0.90665702 0.91027496 0.92836469 0.89797395 0.90679191]
 [0.97467438 0.96743849 0.96888567 0.97829233 0.96820809]
 [0.99421129 0.99710564 0.99782923 0.99855282 0.99277457]]

Param: max_depth
Validation scores:
[[0.71098266 0.76589595 0.72543353 0.76300578 0.75290698]
 [0.71098266 0.75433526 0.71965318 0.75722543 0.74127907]
 [0.71098266 0.72254335 0.71965318 0.75722543 0.74418605]
 [0.71098266 0.71387283 0.71965318 0.75722543 0.72674419]
 [0.71098266 0.74277457 0.71965318 0.75722543 0.74127907]
 [0.71098266 0.74277457 0.71965318 0.75722543 0.74127907]
 [0.71098266 0.74566474 0.71965318 0.75722543 0.74418605]
 [0.71098266 0.75144509 0.71965318 0.75722543 0.74127907]]
```

6. Let's plot it:

```
# Plot the curve
plt.figure()
plt.plot(parameter_grid, 100*np.average(train_scores, axis=1),
color='black')
plt.title('Validation curve')
plt.xlabel('Maximum depth of the tree')
plt.ylabel('Accuracy')
plt.show()
```

7. If you run this code, you will get the following:

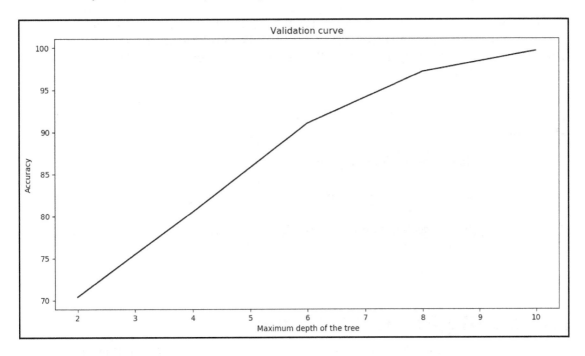

How it works...

In this recipe, we used the `validation_curve` function of the scikit-learn library to plot the validation curve. This function determines training and test scores for varying parameter values and computes scores for an estimator with different values of a specified parameter.

There's more...

Choosing an estimator's hyperparameters is a fundamental procedure for setting up a model. Among the available procedures, grid search is one of the most used. This procedure selects the hyperparameter with the maximum score on a validation set or a multiple validation set.

See also

- The official documentation of the `sklearn.model_selection.validation_curve()` function: `https://scikit-learn.org/stable/modules/generated/sklearn.model_selection.validation_curve.html`
- *Validation curves: plotting scores to evaluate models* (from scikit-learn's official documentation): `https://scikit-learn.org/stable/modules/learning_curve.html`

Extracting learning curves

Learning curves help us understand how the size of our training dataset influences the machine learning model. This is very useful when you have to deal with computational constraints. Let's go ahead and plot learning curves by varying the size of our training dataset.

Getting ready

A learning curve shows the validation and training score of an estimator for varying numbers of training samples.

How to do it...

Let's see how to extract learning curves:

1. Add the following code to the same Python file as in the previous recipe, *Extracting validation curves*:

```
from sklearn.model_selection import validation_curve

classifier = RandomForestClassifier(random_state=7)

parameter_grid = np.array([200, 500, 800, 1100])
train_scores, validation_scores = validation_curve(classifier, X,
y, "n_estimators", parameter_grid, cv=5)
print("\n##### LEARNING CURVES #####")
print("\nTraining scores:\n", train_scores)
print("\nValidation scores:\n", validation_scores)
```

We want to evaluate the performance metrics using training datasets of 200, 500, 800, and 1,100 samples. We use five-fold cross-validation, as specified by the cv parameter in the validation_curve method.

2. If you run this code, you will get the following output on the Terminal:

```
##### LEARNING CURVES #####

Training scores:
[[1.          1.          1.          1.          1.         ]
 [1.          1.          0.998       0.998       0.998      ]
 [0.99875     0.9975      0.99875     0.99875     0.99875    ]
 [0.99818182  0.99545455  0.99909091  0.99818182  0.99818182]]

Validation scores:
[[0.69942197 0.69942197 0.69942197 0.69942197 0.70348837]
 [0.74855491 0.65028902 0.76878613 0.76589595 0.70348837]
 [0.70520231 0.78612717 0.52312139 0.76878613 0.77034884]
 [0.65028902 0.75433526 0.65317919 0.75433526 0.76744186]]
```

3. Let's plot it:

```
# Plot the curve
plt.figure()
plt.plot(parameter_grid, 100*np.average(train_scores, axis=1),
color='black')
plt.title('Learning curve')
plt.xlabel('Number of training samples')
plt.ylabel('Accuracy')
plt.show()
```

4. Here is the output:

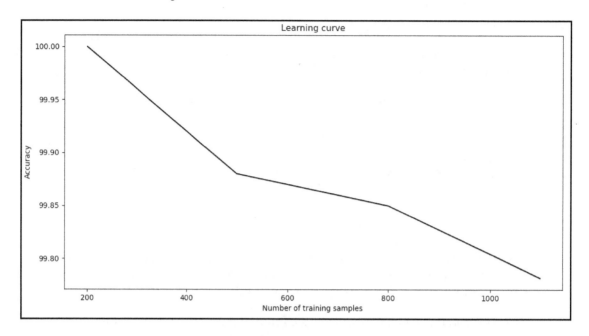

Although smaller training sets seem to give better accuracy, they are prone to overfitting. If we choose a bigger training dataset, it consumes more resources. Therefore, we need to make a trade-off here to pick the right size for the training dataset.

How it works...

In this recipe, we used the `validation_curve` function of the scikit-learn library to plot the learning curve. This function determines cross-validated training and testing scores for different training set sizes.

There's more...

A learning curve allows us to check whether the addition of training data leads to a benefit. It also allows us to estimate the contribution deriving from variance error and bias error. If the validation score and the training score converge with the size of the training set too low, we will not benefit from further training data.

See also

- The official documentation of the
  `sklearn.model_selection.validation_curve` function: `https://scikit-learn.org/stable/modules/generated/sklearn.model_selection.validation_curve.html`
- *Learning curve* (from scikit-learn's official documentation): `https://scikit-learn.org/stable/modules/learning_curve.html`

Estimating the income bracket

We will build a classifier to estimate the income bracket of a person based on 14 attributes. The possible output classes are higher than 50,000 or lower than or equal to 50,000. There is a slight twist in this dataset, in the sense that each datapoint is a mixture of numbers and strings. Numerical data is valuable, and we cannot use a label encoder in these situations. We need to design a system that can deal with numerical and non-numerical data at the same time.

Getting ready

We will use the census income dataset available at `https://archive.ics.uci.edu/ml/datasets/Census+Income`.

The dataset has the following characteristics:

- Number of instances: 48,842
- Number of attributes: 14

The following is a list of attributes:

- Age: continuous
- Workclass: text
- fnlwgt: continuous
- Education: text
- Education-num: continuous
- Marital-status: text
- Occupation: text
- Relationship: text

- Race: text
- Sex: female or male
- Capital-gain: continuous
- Capital-loss: continuous
- Hours-per-week: continuous
- Native-country: text

How to do it...

Let's see how to estimate the income bracket:

1. We will use the `income.py` file, already provided to you as a reference. We will use a Naive Bayes classifier to achieve this. Let's import a couple of packages:

```
import numpy as np
from sklearn import preprocessing
from sklearn.naive_bayes import GaussianNB
```

2. Let's load the dataset:

```
input_file = 'adult.data.txt'
# Reading the data
X = []
y = []
count_lessthan50k = 0
count_morethan50k = 0
num_images_threshold = 10000
```

3. We will use 20,000 datapoints from the datasets—10,000 for each class to avoid class imbalance. During training, if you use many datapoints that belong to a single class, the classifier tends to get biased toward that class. Therefore, it's better to use the same number of datapoints for each class:

```
with open(input_file, 'r') as f:
    for line in f.readlines():
        if '?' in line:
            continue
        data = line[:-1].split(', ')
        if data[-1] == '<=50K' and count_lessthan50k <
num_images_threshold:
            X.append(data)
            count_lessthan50k = count_lessthan50k + 1
        elif data[-1] == '>50K' and count_morethan50k <
num_images_threshold:
```

```
            X.append(data)
            count_morethan50k = count_morethan50k + 1
        if count_lessthan50k >= num_images_threshold and
count_morethan50k >= num_images_threshold:
            break
X = np.array(X)
```

It's a comma-separated file again. We just loaded the data in the X variable just as before.

4. We need to convert string attributes to numerical data while leaving out the original numerical data:

```
# Convert string data to numerical data
label_encoder = []
X_encoded = np.empty(X.shape)
for i,item in enumerate(X[0]):
    if item.isdigit():
        X_encoded[:, i] = X[:, i]
    else:
        label_encoder.append(preprocessing.LabelEncoder())
        X_encoded[:, i] = label_encoder[-1].fit_transform(X[:, i])
X = X_encoded[:, :-1].astype(int)
y = X_encoded[:, -1].astype(int)
```

The isdigit() function helps us to identify numerical data. We converted string data to numerical data and stored all the label encoders in a list so that we can use it when we want to classify unknown data.

5. Let's train the classifier:

```
# Build a classifier
classifier_gaussiannb = GaussianNB()
classifier_gaussiannb.fit(X, y)
```

6. Let's split the data into training and testing to extract performance metrics:

```
# Cross validation
from sklearn import model_selection
X_train, X_test, y_train, y_test =
model_selection.train_test_split(X, y, test_size=0.25,
random_state=5)
classifier_gaussiannb = GaussianNB()
classifier_gaussiannb.fit(X_train, y_train)
y_test_pred = classifier_gaussiannb.predict(X_test)
```

7. Let's extract performance metrics:

```
# compute F1 score of the classifier
f1 = model_selection.cross_val_score(classifier_gaussiannb,
        X, y, scoring='f1_weighted', cv=5)
print("F1 score: " + str(round(100*f1.mean(), 2)) + "%")
```

The following result is returned:

F1 score: 75.9%

8. Let's see how to classify a single datapoint. We need to convert the datapoint into something that our classifier can understand:

```
# Testing encoding on single data instance
input_data = ['39', 'State-gov', '77516', 'Bachelors', '13',
'Never-married', 'Adm-clerical', 'Not-in-family', 'White', 'Male',
'2174', '0', '40', 'United-States']
count = 0
input_data_encoded = [-1] * len(input_data)
for i,item in enumerate(input_data):
    if item.isdigit():
        input_data_encoded[i] = int([input_data[i]])
    else:
        input_data_encoded[i] =
int(label_encoder[count].transform([input_data[i]]))
        count = count + 1
input_data_encoded = np.array(input_data_encoded)
```

9. We are now ready to classify it:

```
# Predict and print output for a particular datapoint
output_class = classifier_gaussiannb.predict([input_data_encoded])
print(label_encoder[-1].inverse_transform(output_class)[0])
```

Just as before, we use the `predict` method to get the `output` class and the `inverse_transform` method to convert this label back to its original form to print it out on the Terminal. The following result is returned:

<=50K

How it works...

The underlying principle of a Bayesian classifier is that some individuals belong to a class of interest with a given probability based on some observations. This probability is based on the assumption that the characteristics observed can be dependent or independent from one another; in the second case, the Bayesian classifier is called *naive* because it assumes that the presence or absence of a particular characteristic in a given class of interest is not related to the presence or absence of other characteristics, greatly simplifying the calculation. Let's go ahead and build a Naive Bayes classifier.

There's more...

The concept of Bayes applied to classification is very intuitive: if I look at a particular measurable feature, I can estimate the probability that this feature represents a certain class after the observation.

See also

- The official documentation of
  the `sklearn.naive_bayes.GaussianNB` function: `https://scikit-learn.org/stable/modules/generated/sklearn.naive_bayes.GaussianNB.html`

Predicting the quality of wine

In this recipe, we will predict the quality of wine based on the chemical properties of wines grown. The code uses a wine dataset, which contains a DataFrame with 177 rows and 13 columns; the first column contains the class labels. This data is obtained from the chemical analyses of wines grown in the same region in Italy (Piemonte) but derived from three different cultivars—namely, the Nebbiolo, Barberas, and Grignolino grapes. The wine from the Nebbiolo grape is called Barolo.

Getting ready

The data consists of the amounts of several constituents found in each of the three types of wines, as well as some spectroscopic variables. The attributes are as follows:

- Alcohol
- Malic acid
- Ash
- Alcalinity of ash
- Magnesium
- Total phenols
- Flavanoids
- Nonflavanoid phenols
- Proanthocyanins
- Color intensity
- Hue
- OD280/OD315 of diluted wines
- Proline

The first column of the DataFrame contains the class which indicates one of three types of wine as (0, 1, or 2).

How to do it...

Let's see how to predict the quality of wine:

1. We will use the `wine.quality.py` file, already provided to you as a reference. We start, as always, by importing the NumPy library and loading the data (`wine.txt`):

```
import numpy as np
input_file = 'wine.txt'
X = []
y = []
with open(input_file, 'r') as f:
  for line in f.readlines():
      data = [float(x) for x in line.split(',')]
      X.append(data[1:])
      y.append(data[0])
X = np.array(X)
y = np.array(y)
```

Two arrays are returned: X (input data), and y (target).

2. Now we need to separate our data into two groups: a training dataset and a testing dataset. The training dataset will be used to build the model, and the testing dataset will be used to see how this trained model performs on unknown data:

```
from sklearn import model_selection
X_train, X_test, y_train, y_test =
model_selection.train_test_split(X, y, test_size=0.25,
random_state=5)
```

Four arrays are returned: X_train, X_test, y_train, and y_test. This data will be used to train and validate the model.

3. Let's train the classifier:

```
from sklearn.tree import DecisionTreeClassifier

classifier_DecisionTree = DecisionTreeClassifier()
classifier_DecisionTree.fit(X_train, y_train)
```

To train the model, a decision tree algorithm has been used. A decision tree algorithm is based on a non-parametric supervised learning method used for classification and regression. The aim is to build a model that predicts the value of a target variable using decision rules inferred from the data features.

4. Now it's time to the compute accuracy of the classifier:

```
y_test_pred = classifier_DecisionTree.predict(X_test)

accuracy = 100.0 * (y_test == y_test_pred).sum() / X_test.shape[0]
print("Accuracy of the classifier =", round(accuracy, 2), "%")
```

The following result is returned:

Accuracy of the classifier = 91.11 %

5. Finally, a confusion matrix will be calculated to compute the model performance:

```
from sklearn.metrics import confusion_matrix

confusion_mat = confusion_matrix(y_test, y_test_pred)
print(confusion_mat)
```

The following result is returned:

```
[[17  2  0]
 [ 1 12  1]
 [ 0  0 12]]
```

Values not present on the diagonals represent classification errors. So, only four errors were committed by the classifier.

How it works...

In this recipe, the quality of wine based on the chemical properties of wines grown was predicted. To do this, a decision tree algorithm was used. A decision tree shows graphically the choices made or proposed. It does not happen so often that things are so clear that the choice between two solutions is immediate. Often, a decision is determined by a series of cascading conditions. Representing this concept with tables and numbers is difficult. In fact, even if a table represents a phenomenon, it may confuse the reader because the justification for the choice is not obvious.

There's more...

A tree structure allows us to extract the information with clear legibility by highlighting the branch we have inserted to determine the choice or evaluation. Decision tree technology is useful for identifying a strategy or pursuing a goal by creating a model with probable results. The decision tree graph immediately orients the reading of the result. A plot is much more eloquent than a table full of numbers. The human mind prefers to see a solution first and then go back to understand a justification of the solution, instead of a series of algebraic descriptions, percentages, and data to describe a result.

See also

- The official documentation of the
  `sklearn.tree.DecisionTreeClassifier()` function: `https://scikit-learn.org/stable/modules/generated/sklearn.tree.DecisionTreeClassifier.html#sklearn.tree.DecisionTreeClassifier`

- *Decision Trees* (from the University of Hildesheim, Germany): `https://www.ismll.uni-hildesheim.de/lehre/ml-06w/skript/ml-4up-04-decisiontrees.pdf`
- *Decision Trees* (from scikit-learn's official documentation): `https://scikit-learn.org/stable/modules/tree.html#tree`

Newsgroup trending topics classification

Newsgroups are discussion groups on many issues and are made available by news-servers, located all over the world, which collect messages from clients and transmit them, on the one hand, to all their users and, on the other, to other news-servers connected to the network. The success of this technology is due to user interaction in discussions. Everyone has to respect the rules of the group.

Getting ready

In this recipe, we will build a classifier that will allow us to classify the membership of a topic into a particular discussion group. This operation will be useful to verify whether the topic is relevant to the discussion group. We will use the data contained in the 20 newsgroups dataset, available at the following URL: `http://qwone.com/~jason/20Newsgroups/`.

This is a collection of about 20,000 newsgroup documents, divided into 20 different newsgroups. Originally collected by Ken Lang, and published in *Newsweeder paper: Learning to filter netnews,* the dataset is particularly useful for dealing with text classification problems.

How to do it...

In this recipe, we will learn how to perform newsgroup trending topics classification:

1. We will use the `post.classification.py` file, already provided to you as a reference. We start importing the dataset as follows:

   ```
   from sklearn.datasets import fetch_20newsgroups
   ```

This dataset is contained in the `sklearn.datasets` library; in this way, it will be very easy for us to recover the data. As anticipated, the dataset contains posts related to 20 newsgroups. We will limit our analysis to only the following two newsgroups:

```
NewsClass = ['rec.sport.baseball', 'rec.sport.hockey']
```

2. Download the data:

```
DataTrain = fetch_20newsgroups(subset='train',categories=NewsClass,
shuffle=True, random_state=42)
```

3. The data has two attributes: `data` and `target`. Obviously, `data` represents the input and `target` is the output. Let's check which newsgroups have been selected:

```
print(DataTrain.target_names)
```

The following results are printed:

['rec.sport.baseball', 'rec.sport.hockey']

4. Let's check the shape:

```
print(len(DataTrain.data))
print(len(DataTrain.target))
```

The following results are returned:

1197
1197

5. To extract features from texts, we will use the `CountVectorizer()` function as follows:

```
from sklearn.feature_extraction.text import CountVectorizer

CountVect = CountVectorizer()
XTrainCounts = CountVect.fit_transform(DataTrain.data)
print(XTrainCounts.shape)
```

The following result is returned:

(1197, 18571)

In this way, we have made a count of the occurrences of words.

6. Now let's divide the number of occurrences of each word in a document by the total number of words in the document:

```
from sklearn.feature_extraction.text import TfidfTransformer

TfTransformer = TfidfTransformer(use_idf=False).fit(XTrainCounts)
XTrainNew = TfTransformer.transform(XTrainCounts)
TfidfTransformer = TfidfTransformer()
XTrainNewidf = TfidfTransformer.fit_transform(XTrainCounts)
```

7. Now we can build the classifier:

```
from sklearn.naive_bayes import MultinomialNB

NBMultiClassifier = MultinomialNB().fit(XTrainNewidf,
DataTrain.target)
```

8. Finally, we will compute the accuracy of the classifier:

```
NewsClassPred = NBMultiClassifier.predict(XTrainNewidf)

accuracy = 100.0 * (DataTrain.target == NewsClassPred).sum() /
XTrainNewidf.shape[0]
print("Accuracy of the classifier =", round(accuracy, 2), "%")
```

The following result is returned:

```
Accuracy of the classifier = 99.67 %
```

How it works...

In this recipe, we built a classifier to classify the membership of a topic into a particular discussion group. To extract features from the text, a **tokenization** procedure was needed. In the tokenization phase, within each single sentence, atomic elements called **tokens** are identified; based on the token identified, it's possible to carry out an analysis and evaluation of the sentence itself. Once the characteristics of the text had been extracted, a classifier based on the multinomial Naive Bayes algorithm was constructed.

There's more...

The Naive Bayes multinomial algorithm is used for text and images when features represent the frequency of words (textual or visual) in a document.

See also

- The official documentation of the *Dataset loading utilities*: `https://scikit-learn.org/stable/datasets/index.html`
- The official documentation of the `sklearn.feature_extraction.text.CountVectorizer()` function: `https://scikit-learn.org/stable/modules/generated/sklearn.feature_extraction.text.CountVectorizer.html`
- The official documentation of the `sklearn.feature_extraction.text.TfidfTransformer()` function: `https://scikit-learn.org/stable/modules/generated/sklearn.feature_extraction.text.TfidfTransformer.html`
- The official documentation of the `sklearn.naive_bayes.MultinomialNB()` function: `https://scikit-learn.org/stable/modules/generated/sklearn.naive_bayes.MultinomialNB.html`

Predictive Modeling 3

In this chapter, we will cover the following recipes:

- Building a linear classifier using **support vector machines** (**SVMs**)
- Building a nonlinear classifier using SVMs
- Tackling class imbalance
- Extracting confidence measurements
- Finding optimal hyperparameters
- Building an event predictor
- Estimating traffic
- Simplifying a machine learning workflow using TensorFlow
- Implementing the stacking method

Technical requirements

To address the recipes in this chapter, you need the following files (available on GitHub):

- svm.py
- data_multivar.txt
- svm_imbalance.py
- data_multivar_imbalance.txt
- svm_confidence.py
- perform_grid_search.py
- building_event_binary.txt
- building_event_multiclass.txt
- event.py

- `traffic_data.txt`
- `traffic.py`
- `IrisTensorflow.py`
- `stacking.py`

Introduction

Predictive modeling is probably one of the most exciting fields in data analytics. It has gained a lot of attention in recent years due to massive amounts of data being available in many different verticals. It is very commonly used in areas concerning data mining to forecast future trends.

Predictive modeling is an analysis technique that is used to predict the future behavior of a system. It is a collection of algorithms that can identify the relationship between independent input variables and the target responses. We create a mathematical model, based on observations, and then use this model to estimate what's going to happen in the future.

In predictive modeling, we need to collect data with known responses to train our model. Once we create this model, we validate it using some metrics, and then use it to predict future values. We can use many different types of algorithms to create a predictive model. In this chapter, we will use SVMs to build linear and nonlinear models.

A predictive model is built using a number of features that are likely to influence the behavior of the system. For example, to estimate weather conditions, we may use various types of data, such as temperature, barometric pressure, precipitation, and other atmospheric processes. Similarly, when we deal with other types of systems, we need to decide what factors are likely to influence its behavior and include them as part of the feature vector before training our model.

Building a linear classifier using SVMs

SVMs are supervised learning models that we can use to create classifiers and regressors. An SVM solves a system of mathematical equations and finds the best separating boundary between two sets of points. Let's see how to build a linear classifier using an SVM.

Getting ready

Let's visualize our data to understand the problem at hand. We will use the `svm.py` file for this. Before we build the SVM, let's understand our data. We will use the `data_multivar.txt` file that's already provided to you. Let's see how to to visualize the data:

1. Create a new Python file and add the following lines to it (the full code is in the `svm.py` file which has already been provided to you):

```python
import numpy as np
import matplotlib.pyplot as plt

import utilities

# Load input data
input_file = 'data_multivar.txt'
X, y = utilities.load_data(input_file)
```

2. We just imported a couple of packages and named the input file. Let's look at the `load_data()` method:

```python
# Load multivar data in the input file
def load_data(input_file):
    X = []
    y = []
    with open(input_file, 'r') as f:
        for line in f.readlines():
            data = [float(x) for x in line.split(',')]
            X.append(data[:-1])
            y.append(data[-1])

    X = np.array(X)
    y = np.array(y)

    return X, y
```

3. We need to separate the data into classes, as follows:

```python
class_0 = np.array([X[i] for i in range(len(X)) if y[i]==0])
class_1 = np.array([X[i] for i in range(len(X)) if y[i]==1])
```

4. Now that we have separated the data, let's plot it:

```
plt.figure()
plt.scatter(class_0[:,0], class_0[:,1], facecolors='black',
edgecolors='black', marker='s')
plt.scatter(class_1[:,0], class_1[:,1], facecolors='None',
edgecolors='black', marker='s')
plt.title('Input data')
plt.show()
```

If you run this code, you will see the following:

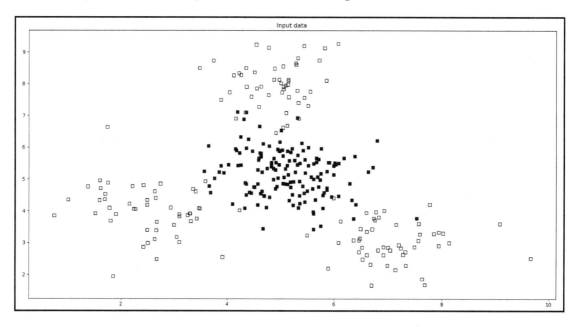

The preceding consists of two types of points—**solid squares** and **empty squares**. In machine learning lingo, we say that our data consists of two classes. Our goal is to build a model that can separate the solid squares from the empty squares.

How to do it...

In this recipe, we will learn how to build a linear classifier using SVMs:

1. We need to split our dataset into training and testing datasets. Add the following lines to the same Python file:

```
# Train test split and SVM training
```

```
from sklearn import cross_validation
from sklearn.svm import SVC

X_train, X_test, y_train, y_test =
cross_validation.train_test_split(X, y, test_size=0.25,
random_state=5)
```

2. Let's initialize the SVM object using a `linear` kernel. Add the following lines to the file:

```
params = {'kernel': 'linear'}
classifier = SVC(**params, gamma='auto')
```

3. We are now ready to train the linear SVM classifier:

```
classifier.fit(X_train, y_train)
```

4. We can now see how the classifier performs:

```
utilities.plot_classifier(classifier, X_train, y_train, 'Training
dataset')
plt.show()
```

If you run this code, you will get the following:

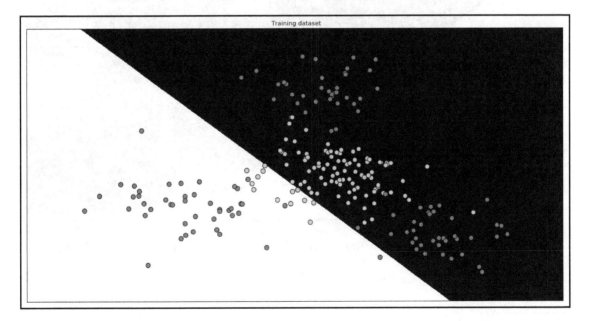

The `plot_classifier` function is the same as we discussed in Chapter 1, *The Realm of Supervised Learning*. It has a couple of minor additions.

You can check out the `utilities.py` file already provided to you for more details.

5. Let's see how this performs on the test dataset. Add the following lines to the `svm.py` file:

```
y_test_pred = classifier.predict(X_test)
utilities.plot_classifier(classifier, X_test, y_test, 'Test
dataset')
plt.show()
```

If you run this code, you will see the following output:

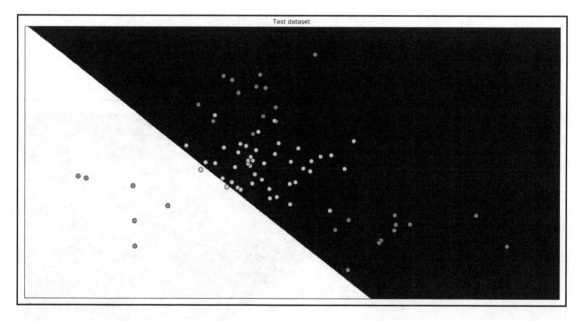

As you can see, the classifier boundaries on the input data are clearly identified.

6. Let's compute the accuracy for the training set. Add the following lines to the same file:

```
from sklearn.metrics import classification_report

target_names = ['Class-' + str(int(i)) for i in set(y)]
print("\n" + "#"*30)
print("\nClassifier performance on training dataset\n")
print(classification_report(y_train, classifier.predict(X_train),
target_names=target_names))
print("#"*30 + "\n")
```

If you run this code, you will see the following on your Terminal:

```
Classifier performance on training dataset

                precision    recall  f1-score   support

    Class-0          0.55      0.88      0.68       105
    Class-1          0.78      0.38      0.51       120

avg / total          0.67      0.61      0.59       225
```

7. Finally, let's see the classification report for the testing dataset:

```
print("#"*30)
print("\nClassification report on test dataset\n")
print(classification_report(y_test, y_test_pred,
target_names=target_names))
print("#"*30 + "\n")
```

8. If you run this code, you will see the following on the Terminal:

```
Classification report on test dataset

                precision    recall  f1-score   support

    Class-0          0.64      0.96      0.77        45
    Class-1          0.75      0.20      0.32        30

avg / total          0.69      0.65      0.59        75
```

From the output screenshot where we visualized the data, we can see that the solid squares are completely surrounded by empty squares. This means that the data is not linearly separable. We cannot draw a nice straight line to separate the two sets of points! Hence, we need a nonlinear classifier to separate these datapoints.

How it works...

SVMs are a set of supervised learning methods that can be used for both classification and regression. Given two classes of linearly separable multidimensional patterns, among all the possible separating hyperplanes, the SVM algorithm determines the one able to separate the classes with the greatest possible margin. The margin is the minimum distance of the points in the two classes in the training set from the hyperplane identified.

Maximization of the margin is linked to generalization. If the training set patterns are classified with a large margin, you can hope that even test-set patterns close to the boundary between the classes are managed correctly. In the following, you can see three lines (**l1, l2,** and **l3**). Line **l1** does not separate the two classes, line **l2** separates them, but with a small margin, while line **l3** maximizes the distance between the two classes:

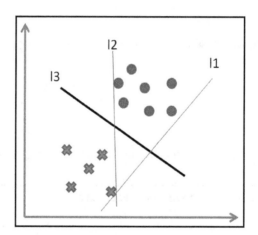

SVMs can be used to separate classes that cannot be separated with a linear classifier. Object coordinates are mapped into a space called a **feature space** using non-linear functions, called **characteristic functions**. This space is highly multidimensional, in which the two classes can be separated with a linear classifier. So, the initial space is remapped in the new space, at which point the classifier is identified and then returned to the initial space.

There's more...

SVMs constitute a class of learning machines recently introduced in the literature. SVMs derive from concepts concerning the statistical theory of learning and present theoretical generalization properties. The theory that governs the functioning mechanisms of SVMs was introduced by Vapnik in 1965 (statistical learning theory), and was more recently perfected, in 1995, by Vapnik himself, and others. SVMs are one of the most widely used tools for pattern classification. Instead of estimating the probability densities of classes, Vapnik suggests directly solving the problem of interest, that is, to determine the decisional surfaces between the classes (classification boundaries).

See also

- Refer to the official documentation of the `sklearn.svm.SVC()` function: `https://scikit-learn.org/stable/modules/generated/sklearn.svm.SVC.html`
- Refer to *Support Vector Machine Tutorial* (from Columbia University): `http://www.cs.columbia.edu/~kathy/cs4701/documents/jason_svm_tutorial.pdf`
- Refer to *Support Vector Machines* - Lecture notes (by Andrew Ng from Stanford University): `http://cs229.stanford.edu/notes/cs229-notes3.pdf`
- *Tutorial on Support Vector Machine* (from Washington State University): `https://course.ccs.neu.edu/cs5100f11/resources/jakkula.pdf`
- *SVM Tutorial*: `http://web.mit.edu/zoya/www/SVM.pdf`

Building a nonlinear classifier using SVMs

An SVM provides a variety of options to build a nonlinear classifier. We need to build a nonlinear classifier using various kernels. In this recipe, let's consider two cases here. When we want to represent a curvy boundary between two sets of points, we can either do this using a polynomial function or a radial basis function.

Getting ready

In this recipe, we will use the same file used in the previous recipe, *Building a linear classifier using SVMs*, but in this case, we will use a different kernel to deal with a markedly nonlinear problem.

How to do it...

Let's see how to build a nonlinear classifier using SVMs:

1. For the first case, let's use a polynomial kernel to build a nonlinear classifier. In the same Python file (svm.py), search for the following line:

```
params = {'kernel': 'linear'}
```

Replace this line with the following:

```
params = {'kernel': 'poly', 'degree': 3}
```

This means that we use a polynomial function with degree as 3. If we increase the degree, this means we allow the polynomial to be curvier. However, curviness comes at a cost, in the sense that it will take more time to train because it's more computationally expensive.

2. If you run this code now, you will get the following:

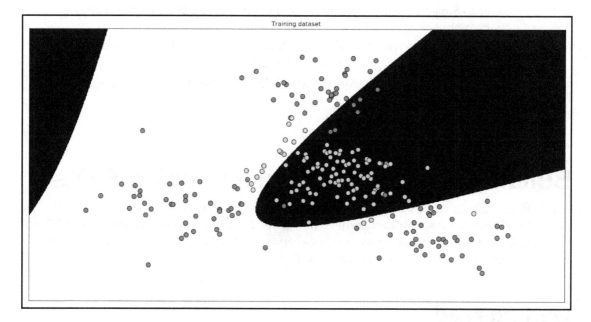

3. You will also see the following classification report printed on your Terminal:

```
Classifier performance on training dataset

                precision    recall  f1-score    support

    Class-0          0.92      0.84      0.88        105
    Class-1          0.87      0.93      0.90        120

avg / total          0.89      0.89      0.89        225
```

4. We can also use a radial basis function kernel to build a nonlinear classifier. In the same Python file, search for the following line:

```
params = {'kernel': 'poly', 'degree': 3}
```

5. Replace this line with the following one:

```
params = {'kernel': 'rbf'}
```

6. If you run this code now, you will get the following:

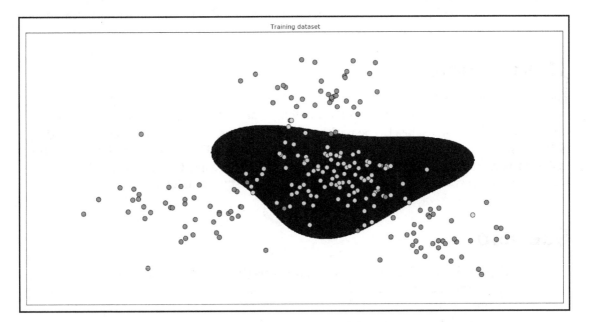

Training dataset

7. You will also see the following classification report printed on your Terminal:

```
Classifier performance on training dataset

              precision    recall  f1-score   support

     Class-0       0.95      0.98      0.97       105
     Class-1       0.98      0.96      0.97       120

  avg / total      0.97      0.97      0.97       225
```

How it works...

In this recipe, we have used an SVM classifier to find the best separating boundary between a dataset of points by solving a system of mathematical equations. To address a nonlinear problem, we used Kernel methods. Kernel methods are thus named for Kernel functions, which are used to operate in the feature space without calculating data coordinates in space, but rather by calculating the internal product between images of all copies of data in the function space. The calculation of the internal product is often computationally cheaper than the explicit calculation of the coordinates. This method is called the **Kernel stratagem**.

There's more...

The main point of the SVM is that a generic problem can always be solved as long as you carefully choose the kernel and all its parameters—for example, going to make a total overfitting of the input dataset. The problem with this method is that it scales quite badly with the size of the dataset, as it is classically attributed to a D2 factor, even if, in this sense, faster implementations can be obtained by optimizing this aspect. The problem is identifying the best kernel and providing it with the best parameters.

See also

- *Support Vector Machines and Kernel Methods* (from Carnegie Mellon's School of Computer Science): https://www.cs.cmu.edu/~ggordon/SVMs/new-svms-and-kernels.pdf
- *Support Vector Machines and Kernel Methods* (from the Department of Computer Science, National Taiwan University): https://www.csie.ntu.edu.tw/~cjlin/talks/postech.pdf

Tackling class imbalance

Until now, we dealt with problems where we had a similar number of datapoints in all our classes. In the real world, we might not be able to get data in such an orderly fashion. Sometimes, the number of datapoints in one class is a lot more than the number of datapoints in other classes. If this happens, then the classifier tends to get biased. The boundary won't reflect the true nature of your data, just because there is a big difference in the number of datapoints between the two classes. Therefore, it is important to account for this discrepancy and neutralize it so that our classifier remains impartial.

Getting ready

In this recipe, we will use a new dataset, named `data_multivar_imbalance.txt`, in which there are three values for each line; the first two represent the coordinates of the point, the third, the class to which the point belongs. Our aim is, once again, to build a classifier, but this time, we will have to face a data-balancing problem.

How to do it...

Let's see how to tackle class imbalance:

1. Let's import the libraries:

```
import numpy as np
import matplotlib.pyplot as plt
from sklearn.svm import SVC
import utilities
```

2. Let's load the data (`data_multivar_imbalance.txt`):

```
input_file = 'data_multivar_imbalance.txt'
X, y = utilities.load_data(input_file)
```

3. Let's visualize the data. The code for visualization is exactly the same as it was in the previous recipe. You can also find it in the file named `svm_imbalance.py`, already provided to you:

```
# Separate the data into classes based on 'y'
class_0 = np.array([X[i] for i in range(len(X)) if y[i]==0])
class_1 = np.array([X[i] for i in range(len(X)) if y[i]==1])
# Plot the input data
plt.figure()
```

```
plt.scatter(class_0[:,0], class_0[:,1], facecolors='black',
edgecolors='black', marker='s')
plt.scatter(class_1[:,0], class_1[:,1], facecolors='None',
edgecolors='black', marker='s')
plt.title('Input data')
plt.show()
```

4. If you run it, you will see the following:

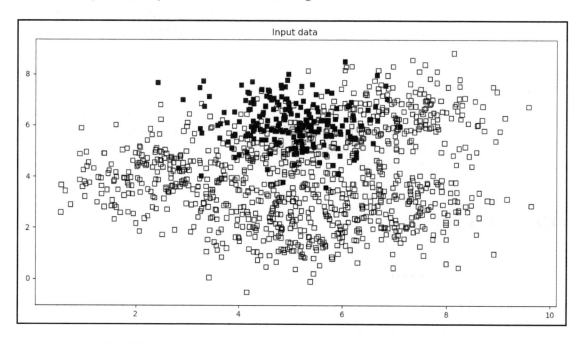

5. Let's build an SVM with a linear kernel. The code is the same as it was in the previous recipe, *Building a nonlinear classifier using SVMs*:

```
from sklearn import model_selection
X_train, X_test, y_train, y_test =
model_selection.train_test_split(X, y, test_size=0.25,
random_state=5)
params = {'kernel': 'linear'}
classifier = SVC(**params, gamma='auto')
classifier.fit(X_train, y_train)
utilities.plot_classifier(classifier, X_train, y_train, 'Training
dataset')
plt.show()
```

6. Let's print a classification report:

```
from sklearn.metrics import classification_report
target_names = ['Class-' + str(int(i)) for i in set(y)]
print("\n" + "#"*30)
print("\nClassifier performance on training dataset\n")
print(classification_report(y_train, classifier.predict(X_train),
target_names=target_names))
print("#"*30 + "\n")
print("#"*30)
print("\nClassification report on test dataset\n")
print(classification_report(y_test, y_test_pred,
target_names=target_names))
print("#"*30 + "\n")
```

7. If you run it, you will see the following:

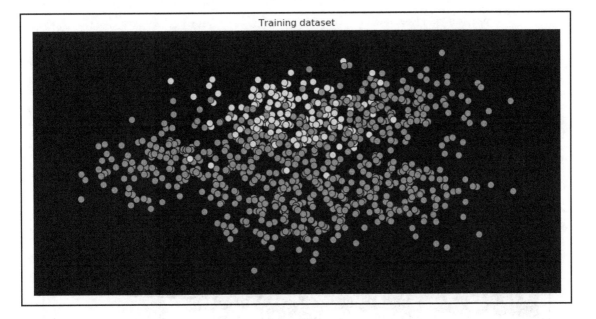

8. You might wonder why there's no boundary here! Well, this is because the classifier is unable to separate the two classes at all, resulting in 0% accuracy for Class-0. You will also see a classification report printed on your Terminal, as shown in the following screenshot:

```
Classifier performance on training dataset

                precision    recall  f1-score   support

      Class-0        0.00      0.00      0.00       158
      Class-1        0.82      1.00      0.90       742

  avg / total        0.68      0.82      0.75       900
```

9. As we expected, Class-0 has 0% precision, so let's go ahead and fix this! In the Python file, search for the following line:

```
params = {'kernel': 'linear'}
```

10. Replace the preceding line with the following:

```
params = {'kernel': 'linear', 'class_weight': 'balanced'}
```

11. The class_weight parameter will count the number of datapoints in each class to adjust the weights so that the imbalance doesn't adversely affect the performance.

12. You will get the following output once you run this code:

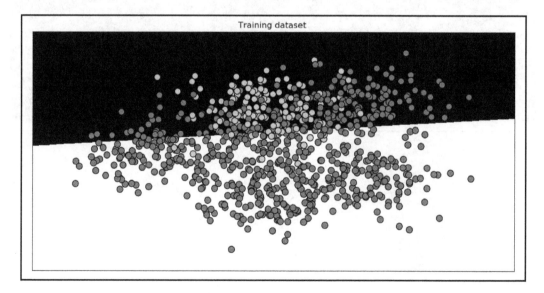

13. Let's look at the classification report:

```
Classifier performance on training dataset

             precision    recall  f1-score   support

   Class-0        0.39      0.91      0.54       158
   Class-1        0.97      0.69      0.81       742

avg / total        0.87      0.73      0.76       900
```

14. As we can see, `Class-0` is now detected with nonzero percentage accuracy.

How it works...

In this recipe, we have used a SVM classifier to find the best separating boundary between a dataset of points. To address a data-balancing problem, we once again used the linear Kernel method, but we implemented a `class_weight` keyword in the `fit` method. The `class_weight` variable is a dictionary in the form `{class_label: value}`, where `value` is a floating-point number greater than 0 that modifies the C parameter of the class (`class_label`), setting it with a new value, obtained by multiplying the old C value with that specified in the value attribute (C * *value*).

There's more...

C is a hyperparameter that determines the penalty for the incorrect classification of an observation. So, we used a weight for the classes to manage unbalanced classes. In this way, we will assign a new value of C to the classes, defined as follows:

$$C_i = C \times w_i$$

Where $\underline{C}$ is the penalty, w_i is a weight inversely proportional to class i's frequency, and C_i is the C value for class *i*. This method suggests increasing the penalty to classify the less represented classes so as to prevent them from being outclassed by the most represented class.

In the `scikit-learn` library, when using SVC, we can set the values for C_i automatically by setting `class_weight='balanced'`.

See also

- *Support Vector Machines*—official documentation of the `scikit-learn` library: `https://scikit-learn.org/stable/modules/svm.html`

Extracting confidence measurements

It would be nice to know the confidence with which we classify unknown data. When a new datapoint is classified into a known category, we can train the SVM to compute the confidence level of that output as well. A *confidence level* refers to the probability that the value of a parameter falls within a specified range of values.

Getting ready

In this recipe, we will use an SVM classifier to find the best separating boundary between a dataset of points. In addition, we will also perform a measure of the confidence level of the results obtained.

How to do it...

Let's see how to extract confidence measurements:

1. The full code is given in the `svm_confidence.py` file, already provided to you. We will discuss the code of the recipe here. Let's define some input data:

```
import numpy as np
import matplotlib.pyplot as plt
from sklearn.svm import SVC
import utilities

# Load input data
input_file = 'data_multivar.txt'
X, y = utilities.load_data(input_file)
```

2. At this point, we split the data for training and testing, and then we will build the classifier:

```
from sklearn import model_selection
X_train, X_test, y_train, y_test =
model_selection.train_test_split(X, y, test_size=0.25,
```

```
random_state=5)
params = {'kernel': 'rbf'}
classifier = SVC(**params, gamma='auto')
classifier.fit(X_train, y_train)
```

3. Define the input datapoint:

```
input_datapoints = np.array([[2, 1.5], [8, 9], [4.8, 5.2], [4, 4],
[2.5, 7], [7.6, 2], [5.4, 5.9]])
```

4. Let's measure the distance from the boundary:

```
print("Distance from the boundary:")
for i in input_datapoints:
    print(i, '-->', classifier.decision_function([i])[0])
```

5. You will see the following printed on your Terminal:

```
Distance from the boundary:
[2.  1.5] --> 0.9248968828198472
[8. 9.]   --> 0.6422390024622062
[4.8 5.2] --> -2.035417667930382
[4. 4.]   --> -0.07623172174998727
[2.5 7. ] --> 0.7345593292517577
[7.6 2. ] --> 1.0982437814537895
[5.4 5.9] --> -1.2114549553124778
```

6. The distance from the boundary gives us some information about the datapoint, but it doesn't exactly tell us how confident the classifier is about the output tag. To do this, we need **Platt scaling**. This is a method that converts the distance measure into a probability measure between classes. Let's go ahead and train an SVM using Platt scaling:

```
# Confidence measure
params = {'kernel': 'rbf', 'probability': True}
classifier = SVC(**params, gamma='auto')
```

The `probability` parameter tells the SVM that it should train to compute the probabilities as well.

7. Let's train the classifier:

```
classifier.fit(X_train, y_train)
```

8. Let's compute the confidence measurements for these input datapoints:

```
print("Confidence measure:")
for i in input_datapoints:
    print(i, '-->', classifier.predict_proba([i])[0])
```

The `predict_proba` function measures the confidence value.

9. You will see the following on your Terminal:

```
Confidence measure:
[2.   1.5] --> [0.04971101 0.95028899]
[8. 9.]    --> [0.10789695 0.89210305]
[4.8 5.2] --> [0.99707139 0.00292861]
[4. 4.]    --> [0.50519174 0.49480826]
[2.5 7. ] --> [0.08421437 0.91578563]
[7.6 2. ] --> [0.03034752 0.96965248]
[5.4 5.9] --> [0.96642513 0.03357487]
```

10. Let's see where the points are with respect to the boundary:

```
utilities.plot_classifier(classifier, input_datapoints,
[0]*len(input_datapoints), 'Input datapoints', 'True')
```

11. If you run this, you will get the following:

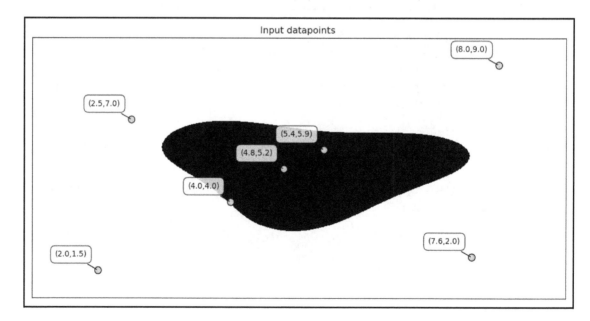

How it works...

In this recipe, we built a classifier based on SVM. Once the classifier was obtained, we used a set of points to measure the distance of those points from the boundary and then measured the confidence levels for each of those points. When estimating a parameter, the simple identification of a single value is often not sufficient. It is therefore advisable to accompany the estimate of a parameter with a plausible range of values for that parameter, which is defined as the confidence interval. It is therefore associated with a cumulative probability value that indirectly, in terms of probability, characterizes its amplitude with respect to the maximum values assumed by the random variable that measures the probability that the random event described by that variable in question falls into this interval and is equal to this area graphically, subtended by the probability distribution curve of the random variable in that specific interval.

There's more...

The confidence interval measures the reliability of a statistic, such as an opinion poll. For example, if 40% of the sample interviewed declare to choose a certain product, it can be inferred with a level of confidence of 99% that a percentage between 30 and 50 of the total consumer population will be expressed in favor of that product. From the same sample interviewed, with a 90% confidence interval, it can be assumed that the percentage of opinions favorable to that product is now between 37% and 43%.

See also

- Refer to the official documentation of
  the `sklearn.svm.SVC.decision_` function: `https://scikit-learn.org/stable/modules/generated/sklearn.svm.SVC.html#sklearn.svm.SVC.decision_function`
- Refer to *Probabilistic Outputs for Support Vector Machines and Comparisons to Regularized Likelihood Methods*: `https://www.researchgate.net/publication/2594015_Probabilistic_Outputs_for_Support_Vector_Machines_and_Comparisons_to_Regularized_Likelihood_Methods`

Finding optimal hyperparameters

As discussed in the previous chapter, hyperparameters are important for determining the performance of a classifier. Let's see how to extract optimal hyperparameters for SVMs.

Getting ready

In machine learning algorithms, various parameters are obtained during the learning process. In contrast, hyperparameters are set before the learning process begins. Given these hyperparameters, the training algorithm learns the parameters from the data. In this recipe, we will extract hyperparameters for a model based on an SVM algorithm using the grid search method.

How to do it...

Let's see how to find optimal hyperparameters:

1. The full code is given in the `perform_grid_search.py` file that's already provided to you. We start importing the libraries:

```
from sklearn import svm
from sklearn import model_selection
from sklearn.model_selection import GridSearchCV
from sklearn.metrics import classification_report
import pandas as pd
import utilities
```

2. Then, we load the data:

```
input_file = 'data_multivar.txt'
X, y = utilities.load_data(input_file)
```

3. We split the data into a train and test dataset:

```
X_train, X_test, y_train, y_test =
model_selection.train_test_split(X, y, test_size=0.25,
random_state=5)
```

4. Now, we will use cross-validation here, which we covered in the previous recipes. Once you load the data and split it into training and testing datasets, add the following to the file:

```
# Set the parameters by cross-validation
parameter_grid = {"C": [1, 10, 50, 600],
                   'kernel':['linear','poly','rbf'],
                   "gamma": [0.01, 0.001],
                   'degree': [2, 3]}
```

5. Let's define the metrics that we want to use:

```
metrics = ['precision']
```

6. Let's start the search for optimal hyperparameters for each of the metrics:

```
for metric in metrics:

    print("#### Grid Searching optimal hyperparameters for",
metric)
    classifier = GridSearchCV(svm.SVC(C=1),
            parameter_grid,
cv=5,scoring=metric,return_train_score=True)

    classifier.fit(X_train, y_train)
```

7. Let's look at the scores:

```
    print("Scores across the parameter grid:")
    GridSCVResults = pd.DataFrame(classifier.cv_results_)
    for i in range(0,len(GridSCVResults)):
        print(GridSCVResults.params[i], '-->',
round(GridSCVResults.mean_test_score[i],3))
```

8. Let's print the best parameter set:

```
    print("Highest scoring parameter set:",
classifier.best_params_)
```

9. If you run this code, you will see the following on your Terminal:

```
#### Grid Searching optimal hyperparameters for precision
Scores across the parameter grid:
{'C': 1, 'degree': 2, 'gamma': 0.01, 'kernel': 'linear'} --> 0.676
{'C': 1, 'degree': 2, 'gamma': 0.01, 'kernel': 'poly'} --> 0.527
{'C': 1, 'degree': 2, 'gamma': 0.01, 'kernel': 'rbf'} --> 0.98
{'C': 1, 'degree': 2, 'gamma': 0.001, 'kernel': 'linear'} --> 0.676
{'C': 1, 'degree': 2, 'gamma': 0.001, 'kernel': 'poly'} --> 0.533
```

```
. . .
. . .
{'C': 600, 'degree': 2, 'gamma': 0.001, 'kernel': 'linear'} -->
0.676
{'C': 600, 'degree': 2, 'gamma': 0.001, 'kernel': 'poly'} --> 0.9
{'C': 600, 'degree': 2, 'gamma': 0.001, 'kernel': 'rbf'} --> 0.983
{'C': 600, 'degree': 3, 'gamma': 0.01, 'kernel': 'linear'} -->
0.676
{'C': 600, 'degree': 3, 'gamma': 0.01, 'kernel': 'poly'} --> 0.884
{'C': 600, 'degree': 3, 'gamma': 0.01, 'kernel': 'rbf'} --> 0.967
{'C': 600, 'degree': 3, 'gamma': 0.001, 'kernel': 'linear'} -->
0.676
{'C': 600, 'degree': 3, 'gamma': 0.001, 'kernel': 'poly'} --> 0.533
{'C': 600, 'degree': 3, 'gamma': 0.001, 'kernel': 'rbf'} --> 0.983
Highest scoring parameter set: {'C': 10, 'degree': 2, 'gamma':
0.01, 'kernel': 'rbf'}
```

10. As we can see in the preceding output, it searches for all the optimal hyperparameters. In this case, the hyperparameters are the type of `kernel`, the C value, and `gamma`. It will try out various combinations of these parameters to find the best parameters. Let's test it out on the testing dataset:

```
y_true, y_pred = y_test, classifier.predict(X_test)
print("Full performance report:\n")
print(classification_report(y_true, y_pred))
```

11. If you run this code, you will see the following on your Terminal:

```
Full performance report:

             precision    recall  f1-score   support

        0.0       0.92      0.98      0.95        45
        1.0       0.96      0.87      0.91        30

avg / total       0.94      0.93      0.93        75
```

12. We have previously said that there are different techniques for optimizing hyperparameters. We'll apply the `RandomizedSearchCV` method. To do this, just use the same data and change the classifier. To the code just seen, we add a further section:

```
# Perform a randomized search on hyper parameters
from sklearn.model_selection import RandomizedSearchCV
parameter_rand = {'C': [1, 10, 50, 600],
                  'kernel':['linear','poly','rbf'],
                  'gamma': [0.01, 0.001],
```

```
                         'degree': [2, 3]}
metrics = ['precision']
for metric in metrics:
    print("#### Randomized Searching optimal hyperparameters for",
metric)
    classifier = RandomizedSearchCV(svm.SVC(C=1),
            param_distributions=parameter_rand,n_iter=30,
            cv=5,return_train_score=True)
    classifier.fit(X_train, y_train)
    print("Scores across the parameter grid:")
    RandSCVResults = pd.DataFrame(classifier.cv_results_)
    for i in range(0,len(RandSCVResults)):
        print(RandSCVResults.params[i], '-->',
                round(RandSCVResults.mean_test_score[i]
```

13. If you run this code, you will see the following on your Terminal:

```
#### Randomized Searching optimal hyperparameters for precision
Scores across the parameter grid:
{'kernel': 'rbf', 'gamma': 0.001, 'degree': 2, 'C': 50} --> 0.671
{'kernel': 'rbf', 'gamma': 0.01, 'degree': 3, 'C': 600} --> 0.951
{'kernel': 'linear', 'gamma': 0.01, 'degree': 3, 'C': 50} --> 0.591
{'kernel': 'poly', 'gamma': 0.01, 'degree': 2, 'C': 10} --> 0.804
...
...
{'kernel': 'rbf', 'gamma': 0.01, 'degree': 3, 'C': 10} --> 0.92
{'kernel': 'poly', 'gamma': 0.001, 'degree': 3, 'C': 600} --> 0.533
{'kernel': 'linear', 'gamma': 0.001, 'degree': 2, 'C': 10} -->
0.591
{'kernel': 'poly', 'gamma': 0.01, 'degree': 3, 'C': 50} --> 0.853
{'kernel': 'linear', 'gamma': 0.001, 'degree': 2, 'C': 600} -->
0.591
{'kernel': 'poly', 'gamma': 0.01, 'degree': 3, 'C': 10} --> 0.844
Highest scoring parameter set: {'kernel': 'rbf', 'gamma': 0.01,
'degree': 3, 'C': 600}
```

14. Let's test it out on the testing dataset:

```
print("Highest scoring parameter set:", classifier.best_params_)
y_true, y_pred = y_test, classifier.predict(X_test)
print("Full performance report:\n")
print(classification_report(y_true, y_pred))
```

15. The following results are returned:

```
Full performance report:
                precision    recall   f1-score    support

        0.0         0.98       0.91       0.94         45
        1.0         0.88       0.97       0.92         30

avg / total         0.94       0.93       0.93         75|
```

How it works...

In the previous recipe, *Building a nonlinear classifier using SVMs*, we repeatedly modified the kernel of the SVM algorithm to obtain an improvement in the classification of data. On the basis of the hyperparameter definition given at the beginning of the recipe, it is clear that the kernel represents a hyperparameter. In this recipe, we randomly set the value for this hyperparameter and checked the results to find out which value determines the best performance. However, a random selection of algorithm parameters may be inadequate.

Furthermore, it is difficult to compare the performance of different algorithms by setting the parameters randomly, because an algorithm can perform better than another with a different set of parameters. And if the parameters are changed, the algorithm may have worse results than the other algorithms.

As a result, the random selection of parameter values is not the best approach we can take to find the best performance for our model. On the contrary, it would be advisable to develop an algorithm that automatically finds the best parameters for a particular model. There are several methods for searching for hyperparameters, such as the following: grid search, randomized search, and Bayesian optimization.

The grid search algorithm

The **grid search** algorithm does this by automatically looking for the set of hyperparameters that detracts from the best performance of the model.

The `sklearn.model_selection.GridSearchCV()` function performs an exhaustive search over specified parameter values for an estimator. **Exhaustive search** (also named direct search, or brute force) is a comprehensive examination of all possibilities, and therefore represents an efficient solution method in which every possibility is tested to determine whether it is the solution.

The randomized search algorithm

Unlike the `GridSearchCV` method, not all parameter values are tested in this method, but the parameter settings are sampled in a fixed number. The parameter settings that are tested are set through the `n_iter` attribute. Sampling without replacement is performed if the parameters are presented as a list. If at least one parameter is supplied as a distribution, substitution sampling is used.

The Bayesian optimization algorithm

The aim of a Bayesian hyperparameter optimizer is to construct a probability model of the objective function and use it to select the hyperparameters that work best for use in the real objective function. Bayesian statistics allow us to foresee not only a value, but a distribution, and this is the success of this methodology.

The Bayesian method, when compared with the two methods already dealt with (grid search and random search), stores the results of the past evaluation, which it uses to form a probabilistic model that associates the hyperparameters with a probability of a score on the objective function.

This model is called a **surrogate** of the objective function and is much easier to optimize than the objective function itself. This result is obtained by following this procedure:

1. A surrogate probability model of the objective function is constructed.
2. The hyperparameters that give the best results on the surrogate are searched.
3. These hyperparameters are applied to the real objective function.
4. The surrogate model is updated by incorporating the new results.
5. Repeat steps 2–4 until you reach the pre-established iterations or the maximum time.

In this way, the surrogate probability model is updated after each evaluation of the objective function. To use a Bayesian hyperparameter optimizer, several libraries are available: `scikit-optimize`, `spearmint`, and `SMAC3`.

There's more...

Commonly, hyperparameters are all those values that can be freely set by the user, and that are generally optimized, maximizing the accuracy on the validation data with appropriate research. Even the choice of a technique rather than another can be seen as a categorical hyperparameter, which has as many values as the methods we can choose from.

See also

- The official documentation of
  the `sklearn.model_selection.GridSearchCV()`
  function: `https://scikit-learn.org/stable/modules/generated/sklearn.model_selection.GridSearchCV.html#sklearn.model_selection.GridSearchCV`
- *Hyperparameter optimization* (from Wikipedia): `https://en.wikipedia.org/wiki/Hyperparameter_optimization`
- *Spearmint Bayesian optimization* (from GitHub): `https://github.com/HIPS/Spearmint`
- The SMAC3 official documentation: `https://automl.github.io/SMAC3/stable/`
- *A Tutorial on Bayesian Optimization for Machine Learning* (from the School of Engineering and Applied Sciences, Harvard University): `https://www.iro.umontreal.ca/~bengioy/cifar/NCAP2014-summerschool/slides/Ryan_adams_140814_bayesopt_ncap.pdf`

Building an event predictor

Let's apply all of this knowledge from this chapter to a real-world problem. We will build an SVM to predict the number of people going in and out of a building. The dataset is available at
`https://archive.ics.uci.edu/ml/datasets/CalIt2+Building+People+Counts`. We will use a slightly modified version of this dataset so that it's easier to analyze. The modified data is available in the `building_event_binary.txt` and
the `building_event_multiclass.txt` files that are already provided to you. In this recipe, we will learn how to build an event predictor.

Getting ready

Let's understand the data format before we start building the model. Each line in `building_event_binary.txt` consists of six comma-separated strings. The ordering of these six strings is as follows:

- Day
- Date
- Time
- The number of people going out of the building
- The number of people coming into the building
- **The output indicating whether or not it's an event**

The first five strings form the input data, and our task is to predict whether or not an event is going on in the building.

Each line in `building_event_multiclass.txt` consists of six comma-separated strings. This is more granular than the previous file, in the sense that the output is the exact type of event going on in the building. The ordering of these six strings is as follows:

- Day
- Date
- Time
- The number of people going out of the building
- The number of people coming into the building
- **The output indicating the type of event**

The first five strings form the input data, and our task is to predict what type of event is going on in the building.

How to do it...

Let's see how to build an event predictor:

1. We will use `event.py` that's already provided to you for reference. Create a new Python file, and add the following lines:

```
import numpy as np
from sklearn import preprocessing
from sklearn.svm import SVC
```

```
input_file = 'building_event_binary.txt'

# Reading the data
X = []
count = 0
with open(input_file, 'r') as f:
    for line in f.readlines():
        data = line[:-1].split(',')
        X.append([data[0]] + data[2:])

X = np.array(X)
```

We just loaded all the data into X.

2. Let's convert the data into numerical form:

```
# Convert string data to numerical data
label_encoder = []
X_encoded = np.empty(X.shape)
for i,item in enumerate(X[0]):
    if item.isdigit():
        X_encoded[:, i] = X[:, i]
    else:
        label_encoder.append(preprocessing.LabelEncoder())
        X_encoded[:, i] = label_encoder[-1].fit_transform(X[:, i])

X = X_encoded[:, :-1].astype(int)
y = X_encoded[:, -1].astype(int)
```

3. Let's train the SVM using the radial basis function, Platt scaling, and class balancing:

```
# Build SVM
params = {'kernel': 'rbf', 'probability': True, 'class_weight':
'balanced'}
classifier = SVC(**params, gamma='auto')
classifier.fit(X, y)
```

4. We are now ready to perform cross-validation:

```
from sklearn import model_selection

accuracy = model_selection.cross_val_score(classifier,
        X, y, scoring='accuracy', cv=3)
print("Accuracy of the classifier: " +
str(round(100*accuracy.mean(), 2)) + "%")
```

5. Let's test our SVM on a new datapoint:

```
# Testing encoding on single data instance
input_data = ['Tuesday', '12:30:00','21','23']
input_data_encoded = [-1] * len(input_data)
count = 0

for i,item in enumerate(input_data):
    if item.isdigit():
        input_data_encoded[i] = int(input_data[i])
    else:
        input_data_encoded[i] =
int(label_encoder[count].transform([input_data[i]]))
        count = count + 1

input_data_encoded = np.array(input_data_encoded)

# Predict and print(output for a particular datapoint
output_class = classifier.predict([input_data_encoded])
print("Output class:",
label_encoder[-1].inverse_transform(output_class)[0])
```

6. If you run this code, you will see the following output on your Terminal:

```
Accuracy of the classifier: 93.95%
Output class: noevent
```

7. If you use the `building_event_multiclass.txt` file as the input data file instead of `building_event_binary.txt`, you will see the following output on your Terminal:

```
Accuracy of the classifier: 65.33%
Output class: eventA
```

How it works...

In this recipe, we used data obtained from observations of people who flowed in and out of a building during 15 weeks, and at 48 time intervals per day. We therefore built a classifier able to predict the presence of an event such as a conference in the building, which determines an increase in the number of people present in the building for that period of time.

There's more...

Later in the recipe, we used the same classifier on a different database to also predict the type of event that is held within the building.

See also

- The official documentation of the `sklearn.svm.SVC()` function: `https://scikit-learn.org/stable/modules/generated/sklearn.svm.SVC.html`
- The official documentation of the `sklearn.model_selection.cross_validate()` function: `https://scikit-learn.org/stable/modules/generated/sklearn.model_selection.cross_validate.html#sklearn.model_selection.cross_validate`

Estimating traffic

An interesting application of SVMs is to predict traffic, based on related data. In the previous recipe, we used an SVM as a classifier. In this recipe, we will use an SVM as a regressor to estimate the traffic.

Getting ready

We will use the dataset available at `https://archive.ics.uci.edu/ml/datasets/Dodgers+Loop+Sensor`. This is a dataset that counts the number of cars passing by during baseball games at the Los Angeles Dodgers home stadium. We will use a slightly modified form of that dataset so that it's easier to analyze. You can use the `traffic_data.txt` file, already provided to you. Each line in this file contains comma-separated strings formatted in the following manner:

- Day
- Time
- The opponent team
- Whether or not a baseball game is going on
- The number of cars passing by

How to do it...

Let's see how to estimate traffic:

1. Let's see how to build an SVM regressor. We will use `traffic.py` that's already provided to you as a reference. Create a new Python file, and add the following lines:

```
# SVM regressor to estimate traffic

import numpy as np
from sklearn import preprocessing
from sklearn.svm import SVR

input_file = 'traffic_data.txt'

# Reading the data
X = []
count = 0
with open(input_file, 'r') as f:
    for line in f.readlines():
        data = line[:-1].split(',')
        X.append(data)

X = np.array(X)
```

We loaded all the input data into X.

2. Let's encode this data:

```
# Convert string data to numerical data
label_encoder = []
X_encoded = np.empty(X.shape)
for i,item in enumerate(X[0]):
    if item.isdigit():
        X_encoded[:, i] = X[:, i]
    else:
        label_encoder.append(preprocessing.LabelEncoder())
        X_encoded[:, i] = label_encoder[-1].fit_transform(X[:, i])

X = X_encoded[:, :-1].astype(int)
y = X_encoded[:, -1].astype(int)
```

3. Let's build and train the SVM regressor using the radial basis function:

```
# Build SVR
params = {'kernel': 'rbf', 'C': 10.0, 'epsilon': 0.2}
regressor = SVR(**params)
regressor.fit(X, y)
```

In the preceding lines, the C parameter specifies the penalty for misclassification and epsilon specifies the limit within which no penalty is applied.

4. Let's perform cross-validation to check the performance of the regressor:

```
# Cross validation
import sklearn.metrics as sm

y_pred = regressor.predict(X)
print("Mean absolute error =", round(sm.mean_absolute_error(y,
y_pred), 2))
```

5. Let's test it on a datapoint:

```
# Testing encoding on single data instance
input_data = ['Tuesday', '13:35', 'San Francisco', 'yes']
input_data_encoded = [-1] * len(input_data)
count = 0
for i, item in enumerate(input_data):
    if item.isdigit():
        input_data_encoded[i] = int(input_data[i])
    else:
        input_data_encoded[i] =
int(label_encoder[count].transform([input_data[i]]))
        count = count + 1

input_data_encoded = np.array(input_data_encoded)

# Predict and print output for a particular datapoint
print("Predicted traffic:",
int(regressor.predict([input_data_encoded])[0]))
```

6. If you run this code, you will see the following printed on your Terminal:

```
Mean absolute error = 4.08
Predicted traffic: 29
```

How it works...

In this recipe, we used data collected by a sensor on the 101 North Highway in Los Angeles, near the stadium where the Dodgers play. This position is sufficiently close to the stadium to detect the increase in traffic that occurs during a match.

The observations were made over 25 weeks, over 288 time intervals per day (every 5 minutes). We built a regressor based on the SVM algorithm to predict the presence of a baseball game at the Dodgers stadium. In particular, we can estimate the number of cars that pass that position on the basis of the value assumed by the following predictors: day, time, the opponent team, and whether or not a baseball game is going on.

There's more...

Support vector regression (**SVR**) is based on the same principles as SVMs. In fact, SVR is adapted from SVMs, where the dependent variable is numeric rather than categorical. One of the main advantages of using SVR is that it is a nonparametric technique.

See also

- The official documentation of
  the `sklearn.metrics.mean_absolute_error()` function: `https://scikit-learn.org/stable/modules/generated/sklearn.metrics.mean_absolute_error.html`
- *Linear Regression and Support Vector Regression* (from the University of Adelaide): `https://cs.adelaide.edu.au/~chhshen/teaching/ML_SVR.pdf`

Simplifying machine learning workflow using TensorFlow

TensorFlow is an open source numerical calculation library. The library was created by Google programmers. It provides all the tools necessary to build deep learning models and offers developers a black-box interface to program.

Getting ready

In this recipe, we will introduce the TensorFlow framework, using a simple neural network to classify the `iris` species. We will use the `iris` dataset, which has 50 samples from the following species:

- Iris setosa
- Iris virginica
- Iris versicolor

Four features are measured from each sample, namely the length and the width of the sepals and petals, in centimeters.

The following variables are contained:

- Sepal length in cm
- Sepal width in cm
- Petal length in cm
- Petal width in cm
- Class: `setosa`, `versicolor`, or `virginica`

How to do it...

Let's see how to simplify machine learning workflow using TensorFlow:

1. We start, as always, by importing the libraries:

```
from sklearn import datasets
from sklearn import model_selection
import tensorflow as tf
```

The first two libraries are imported only to load and split the data. The third library loads the `tensorflow` library.

2. Load the `iris` dataset:

```
iris = datasets.load_iris()
```

3. Load and split the features and classes:

```
x_train, x_test, y_train, y_test =
model_selection.train_test_split(iris.data,
iris.target,
test_size=0.7,
random_state=1)
```

The data is split into 70% for training and 30% for testing.
The random_state=1 parameter is the seed used by the random number
generator.

4. Now we will build a simple neural network with one hidden layer and 10 nodes:

```
feature_columns =
tf.contrib.learn.infer_real_valued_columns_from_input(x_train)
classifier_tf =
tf.contrib.learn.DNNClassifier(feature_columns=feature_columns,
                                             hidden_units=[10],
                                             n_classes=3)
```

5. Then we fit the network:

```
classifier_tf.fit(x_train, y_train, steps=5000)
```

6. We will then make the predictions:

```
predictions = list(classifier_tf.predict(x_test, as_iterable=True))
```

7. Finally, we will calculate the accuracy metric of the model:

```
n_items = y_test.size
accuracy = (y_test == predictions).sum() / n_items
print("Accuracy :", accuracy)
```

The following result is returned:

```
Accuracy : 0.9333333333333333
```

How it works...

In this recipe, we used the tensorflow library to build a simple neural network to
classify iris species from four features measured. In this way, we saw how simple it is to
implement a model based on a machine learning algorithm using the tensorflow
library. This topic, and on deep neural networks in general, will be analyzed in detail in
Chapter 13, *Deep Neural Networks*.

There's more...

TensorFlow provides native APIs in Python, C, C++, Java, Go, and Rust. The third-party APIs available are in C#, R, and Scala. Since October 2017, it has integrated eager execution functionality which allows the immediate execution of the operations referred to by Python.

See also

- The official documentation of the `tensorflow` library: `https://www.tensorflow.org/tutorials`
- *Tensorflow for Deep Learning Research* (from Stanford University): `http://web.stanford.edu/class/cs20si/`

Implementing a stacking method

A combination of different approaches leads to better results: this statement works in different aspects of our life and also adapts to algorithms based on machine learning. Stacking is the process of combining various machine learning algorithms. This technique is due to David H. Wolpert, an American mathematician, physicist, and computer scientist.

In this recipe, we will learn how to implement a stacking method.

Getting ready

We will use the `heamy` library to stack the two models that we just used in the previous recipes. The `heamy` library is a set of useful tools for competitive data science.

How to do it...

Let's see how to implement a stacking method:

1. We start by importing the libraries:

```
from heamy.dataset import Dataset
from heamy.estimator import Regressor
from heamy.pipeline import ModelsPipeline
```

```
from sklearn.datasets import load_boston
from sklearn.model_selection import train_test_split
from sklearn.ensemble import RandomForestRegressor
from sklearn.linear_model import LinearRegression
from sklearn.metrics import mean_absolute_error
```

1. Load the `boston` dataset, already used in `Chapter 1`, *The Realm of Supervised Learning*, for the *Estimating housing prices* recipe:

```
data = load_boston()
```

3. Split the data:

```
X, y = data['data'], data['target']
X_train, X_test, y_train, y_test = train_test_split(X, y,
test_size=0.1, random_state=2)
```

4. Let's create the dataset:

```
Data = Dataset(X_train,y_train,X_test)
```

5. Now we can build the two models that we will use in the stacking procedure:

```
RfModel = Regressor(dataset=Data, estimator=RandomForestRegressor,
parameters={'n_estimators': 50},name='rf')
LRModel = Regressor(dataset=Data, estimator=LinearRegression,
parameters={'normalize': True},name='lr')
```

6. It's time to stack these models:

```
Pipeline = ModelsPipeline(RfModel,LRModel)
StackModel = Pipeline.stack(k=10,seed=2)
```

7. Now we will train a `LinearRegression` model on stacked data:

```
Stacker = Regressor(dataset=StackModel, estimator=LinearRegression)
```

8. Finally, we will calculate the results to validate the model:

```
Results = Stacker.predict()
Results = Stacker.validate(k=10,scorer=mean_absolute_error)
```

How it works...

Stacked generalization works by deducing the biases of the classifier/regressor relative to a supplied learning dataset. This deduction works by generalizing into a second space whose inputs are the hypotheses of the original generalizers and whose output is the correct hypothesis. When used with multiple generators, stacked generalization is an alternative to cross-validation.

There's more...

Stacking tries to exploit the advantages of each algorithm by ignoring or correcting their disadvantages. It can be seen as a mechanism that corrects errors in your algorithms. Another library to perform a stacking procedure is StackNet.

StackNet is a framework implemented in Java based on Wolpert's stacked generalization on multiple levels to improve accuracy in machine learning predictive problems. The StackNet model functions as a neural network in which the transfer function takes the form of any supervised machine learning algorithm.

See also

- The official documentation of the `heamy` library: `https://heamy.readthedocs.io/en/latest/index.html`
- The official documentation of the `StackNet` framework: `https://github.com/kaz-Anova/StackNet`
- *Stacked Generalization* by David H. Wolpert: `http://www.machine-learning.martinsewell.com/ensembles/stacking/Wolpert1992.pdf`

Clustering with Unsupervised Learning

4

In this chapter, we will cover the following recipes:

- Clustering data using the k-means algorithm
- Compressing an image using vector quantization
- Grouping data using agglomerative clustering
- Evaluating the performance of clustering algorithms
- Estimating the number of clusters using the **Density-Based Spatial Clustering of Applications with Noise (DBSCAN)** algorithm
- Finding patterns in stock market data
- Building a customer segmentation model
- Using autoencoders to reconstruct handwritten digit images

Technical requirements

To address the recipes in this chapter, you will need the following files (which are available on GitHub):

- `kmeans.py`
- `data_multivar.txt`
- `vector_quantization.py`
- `flower_image.jpg`
- `agglomerative.py`
- `performance.py`
- `data_perf.txt`
- `estimate_clusters.py`

- stock_market.py
- symbol_map.json
- stock_market_data.xlsx
- customer_segmentation.py
- wholesale.csv
- AutoencMnist.py

Introduction

Unsupervised learning is a paradigm in machine learning where we build models without relying on labeled training data. Up to this point, we have dealt with data that was labeled in some way. This means that learning algorithms can look at this data and learn to categorize it them based on labels. In the world of unsupervised learning, we don't have this opportunity! These algorithms are used when we want to find subgroups within datasets using a similarity metric.

In unsupervised learning, information from the database is automatically extracted. All this takes place without prior knowledge of the content to be analyzed. In unsupervised learning, there is no information on the classes that the examples belong to, or on the output corresponding to a given input. We want a model that can discover interesting properties, such as groups with similar characteristics, which happens in **clustering**. An example of the application of these algorithms is a search engine. These applications are able to create a list of links related to our search, starting from one or more keywords.

These algorithms work by comparing data and looking for similarities or differences. The validity of these algorithms depends on the usefulness of the information they can extract from the database. Available data only concerns the set of features that describe each example.

One of the most common methods is clustering. You will have heard this term being used quite frequently; we mainly use it for data analysis when we want to find clusters in our data. These clusters are usually found by using a certain kind of similarity measure, such as the Euclidean distance. Unsupervised learning is used extensively in many fields, such as data mining, medical imaging, stock market analysis, computer vision, and market segmentation.

Clustering data using the k-means algorithm

The k-means algorithm is one of the most popular clustering algorithms. This algorithm is used to divide the input data into *k* subgroups using various attributes of the data. Grouping is achieved using an optimization technique where we try to minimize the sum of squares of distances between the datapoints and the corresponding centroid of the cluster.

Getting ready

In this recipe, we will use the k-means algorithm to group the data into four clusters identified by the relative centroid. We will also be able to trace the boundaries to identify the areas of relevance of each cluster.

How to do it...

Let's see how to perform a clustering data analysis using the k-means algorithm:

1. The full code for this recipe is given in the kmeans.py file that has already been provided to you. Now let's take a look at how it's built. Create a new Python file, and import the following packages:

```
import numpy as np
import matplotlib.pyplot as plt
from sklearn.cluster import KMeans
```

2. Now let's load the input data and define the number of clusters. We will use the data_multivar.txt file that has already been provided to you:

```
input_file = ('data_multivar.txt')
# Load data
x = []
with open(input_file, 'r') as f:
    for line in f.readlines():
        data = [float(i) for i in line.split(',')]
        x.append(data)

data = np.array(x)
num_clusters = 4
```

3. We need to see what the input data looks like. Let's go ahead and add the following lines of code to the Python file:

```python
plt.figure()
plt.scatter(data[:,0], data[:,1], marker='o',
        facecolors='none', edgecolors='k', s=30)
x_min, x_max = min(data[:, 0]) - 1, max(data[:, 0]) + 1
y_min, y_max = min(data[:, 1]) - 1, max(data[:, 1]) + 1
plt.title('Input data')
plt.xlim(x_min, x_max)
plt.ylim(y_min, y_max)
plt.xticks(())
plt.yticks(())
```

If you run this code, you will get the following output:

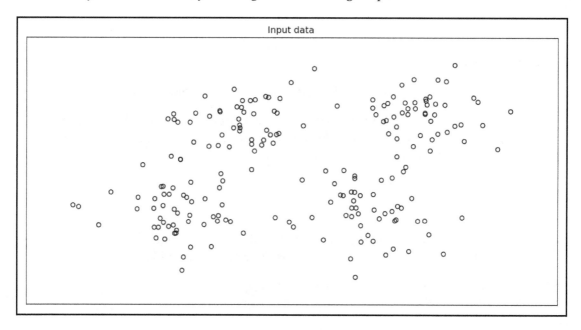

4. We are now ready to train the model. Let's initialize the kmeans object and train it:

```python
kmeans = KMeans(init='k-means++', n_clusters=num_clusters,
n_init=10)
kmeans.fit(data)
```

5. Now that the data is trained, we need to visualize the boundaries. Let's go ahead and add the following lines of code to the Python file:

```
# Step size of the mesh
step_size = 0.01

# Plot the boundaries
x_min, x_max = min(data[:, 0]) - 1, max(data[:, 0]) + 1
y_min, y_max = min(data[:, 1]) - 1, max(data[:, 1]) + 1
x_values, y_values = np.meshgrid(np.arange(x_min, x_max,
step_size), np.arange(y_min, y_max, step_size))

# Predict labels for all points in the mesh
predicted_labels = kmeans.predict(np.c_[x_values.ravel(),
y_values.ravel()])
```

6. We just evaluated the model across a grid of points. Let's plot these results to view the boundaries:

```
# Plot the results
predicted_labels = predicted_labels.reshape(x_values.shape)
plt.figure()
plt.clf()
plt.imshow(predicted_labels, interpolation='nearest',
        extent=(x_values.min(), x_values.max(), y_values.min(),
y_values.max()),
        cmap=plt.cm.Paired,
        aspect='auto', origin='lower')

plt.scatter(data[:,0], data[:,1], marker='o',
        facecolors='none', edgecolors='k', s=30)
```

7. Now let's overlay `centroids` on top of it:

```
centroids = kmeans.cluster_centers_
plt.scatter(centroids[:,0], centroids[:,1], marker='o', s=200,
linewidths=3,
        color='k', zorder=10, facecolors='black')
x_min, x_max = min(data[:, 0]) - 1, max(data[:, 0]) + 1
y_min, y_max = min(data[:, 1]) - 1, max(data[:, 1]) + 1
plt.title('Centoids and boundaries obtained using KMeans')
plt.xlim(x_min, x_max)
plt.ylim(y_min, y_max)
plt.xticks(())
plt.yticks(())
plt.show()
```

If you run this code, you should see the following output:

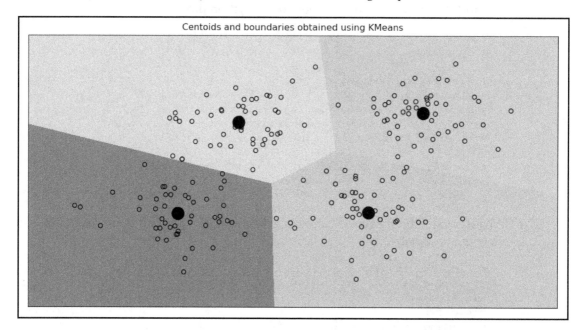

The four centroids and their boundaries are sufficiently highlighted.

How it works...

K-means was developed by James MacQueen, who, in 1967, designed it for the purpose of dividing groups of objects into *k* partitions based on their attributes. It is a variation of the **expectation-maximization** (**EM**) algorithm, whose objective is to determine the groups of k data generated by Gaussian distributions. The difference between the two algorithms lies in the Euclidean distance calculation method. In k-means, it is assumed that the attributes of the object can be represented as vectors, and thus form a vector space. The goal is to minimize the total intra-cluster variance (or standard deviation). Each cluster is identified by a centroid.

The algorithm follows an iterative procedure, as follows:

1. Choose the number of k clusters
2. Initially, create k partitions and assign each entry partition either randomly, or by using some heuristic information
3. Calculate the centroid of each group
4. Calculate the distance between each observation and each cluster centroid
5. Then, construct a new partition by associating each entry point with the cluster whose centroid is closer to it
6. The centroid for new clusters is recalculated
7. Repeat steps 4 to 6 until the algorithm converges

There's more...

The purpose of the algorithm is to locate k centroids, one for each cluster. The position of each centroid is of particular importance as different positions cause different results. The best choice is to put them as far apart as possible from each other. When this is done, you must associate each object with the nearest centroid. In this way, we will get a first grouping. After finishing the first cycle, we go to the next one by recalculating the new k centroids as the cluster's barycenter using the previous one. Once you locate these new k centroids, you need to make a new connection between the same dataset and the new closest centroid. At the end of these operations, a new cycle is performed. Due to this cycle, we can note that the k centroids change their position step by step until they are modified. So, the centroid no longer moves.

See also

- Refer to the official documentation of the `sklearn.cluster.KMeans` function: `https://scikit-learn.org/stable/modules/generated/sklearn.cluster.KMeans.html#sklearn.cluster.KMeans.fit`
- Refer to *MATLAB for Machine Learning*, Giuseppe Ciaburro, Packt Publishing
- Refer to *K Means* (from Stanford University): `http://stanford.edu/~cpiech/cs221/handouts/kmeans.html`
- Refer to *K-means and Hierarchical Clustering* (by Andrew Moore): `https://www.autonlab.org/tutorials/kmeans.html`

Compressing an image using vector quantization

One of the main applications of k-means clustering is **vector quantization**. Simply speaking, vector quantization is the *N*-dimensional version of rounding off. When we deal with one-dimensional data, such as numbers, we use the rounding-off technique to reduce the memory needed to store that value. For example, instead of storing 23.73473572, we just store 23.73 if we want to be accurate up to the second decimal place. Or, we can just store 24 if we don't care about decimal places. It depends on our needs and the trade-off that we are willing to make.

Similarly, when we extend this concept to *N*-dimensional data, it becomes vector quantization. Of course, there are more nuances to it! Vector quantization is popularly used in image compression where we store each pixel using fewer bits than the original image to achieve compression.

Getting ready

In this recipe, we will use a sample image and then we will compress the image further by reducing the number of bits.

How to do it...

Let's see how to compress an image using vector quantization:

1. The full code for this recipe is given in the `vector_quantization.py` file that has already been provided to you. Let's take a look at how it's built. We'll start by importing the required packages. Create a new Python file, and add the following lines:

```
import argparse

import numpy as np
from scipy import misc
from sklearn import cluster
import matplotlib.pyplot as plt
```

2. Let's create a function to parse the input arguments. We will be able to pass the image and the number of bits per pixel as input arguments:

```
def build_arg_parser():
    parser = argparse.ArgumentParser(description='Compress the
input image \
            using clustering')
    parser.add_argument("--input-file", dest="input_file",
required=True,
            help="Input image")
    parser.add_argument("--num-bits", dest="num_bits",
required=False,
            type=int, help="Number of bits used to represent each
pixel")
    return parser
```

3. Let's create a function to compress the input image:

```
def compress_image(img, num_clusters):
    # Convert input image into (num_samples, num_features)
    # array to run kmeans clustering algorithm
    X = img.reshape((-1, 1))

    # Run kmeans on input data
    kmeans = cluster.KMeans(n_clusters=num_clusters, n_init=4,
random_state=5)
    kmeans.fit(X)
    centroids = kmeans.cluster_centers_.squeeze()
    labels = kmeans.labels_

    # Assign each value to the nearest centroid and
    # reshape it to the original image shape
    input_image_compressed = np.choose(labels,
centroids).reshape(img.shape)

    return input_image_compressed
```

4. Once we compress the image, we need to see how it affects the quality. Let's define a function to plot the output image:

```
def plot_image(img, title):
    vmin = img.min()
    vmax = img.max()
    plt.figure()
    plt.title(title)
    plt.imshow(img, cmap=plt.cm.gray, vmin=vmin, vmax=vmax)
```

5. We are now ready to use all these functions. Let's define the main function that takes the input arguments, processes them, and extracts the output image:

```
if __name__=='__main__':
    args = build_arg_parser().parse_args()
    input_file = args.input_file
    num_bits = args.num_bits

    if not 1 <= num_bits <= 8:
        raise TypeError('Number of bits should be between 1 and 8')

    num_clusters = np.power(2, num_bits)

    # Print compression rate
    compression_rate = round(100 * (8.0 - args.num_bits) / 8.0, 2)
    print("The size of the image will be reduced by a factor of",
8.0/args.num_bits)
    print("Compression rate = " + str(compression_rate) + "%")
```

6. Let's load the input image:

```
# Load input image
input_image = misc.imread(input_file, True).astype(np.uint8)

# original image
plot_image(input_image, 'Original image')
```

7. Now, let's compress this image using the input argument:

```
# compressed image
input_image_compressed = compress_image(input_image, num_clusters)
plot_image(input_image_compressed, 'Compressed image; compression rate
= '
        + str(compression_rate) + '%')

plt.show()
```

8. We are now ready to run the code; run the following command on your Terminal:

```
$ python vector_quantization.py --input-file flower_image.jpg --num-bits 4
```

The following results are returned:

```
The size of the image will be reduced by a factor of 2.0
Compression rate = 50.0%
```

The input image looks like the following:

You should get a compressed image as the output:

9. Let's compress the image further by reducing the number of bits to 2. Run the following command on your Terminal:

```
$ python vector_quantization.py --input-file flower_image.jpg --num-bits 2
```

The following results are returned:

```
The size of the image will be reduced by a factor of 4.0
Compression rate = 75.0%
```

You should get the following compressed image as the output:

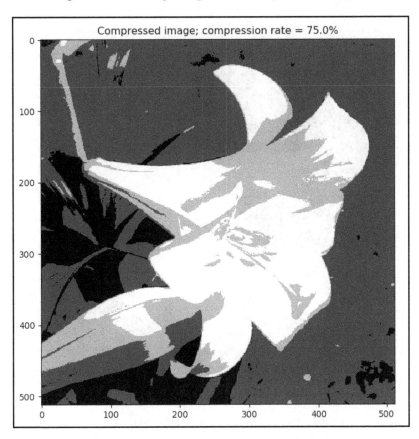

10. If you reduce the number of bits to 1, you can see that it will become a binary image with black and white as the only two colors. Run the following command:

```
$ python vector_quantization.py --input-file flower_image.jpg --num-bits 1
```

The following results are returned:

```
The size of the image will be reduced by a factor of 8.0
Compression rate = 87.5%
```

You will get the following output:

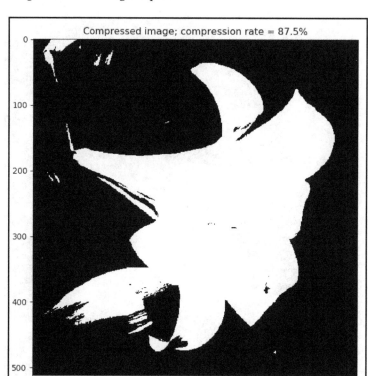

We have seen how, by compressing the image further, the quality of the image has undergone considerable downsizing.

How it works...

Vector quantization is an algorithm used for signal compression, image coding, and speech. We use geometric criteria (the Euclidean distance) to find clusters. It is, therefore, an example of unsupervised training. It is a technique that allows the modeling of probability density functions through the distribution of prototype vectors. Vector quantization divides a large set of points (vectors) into clusters by using a similar number of points closer to them. Each cluster is illustrated by its centroid point (as in k-means).

There's more...

The vector quantization algorithm can be used to divide a dataset into a number of clusters. The algorithm is based on the calculation of the Euclidean distance for the allocation of the samples to the cluster, to which it belongs. The algorithm consists of the following steps:

1. At the beginning, all the vectors are assigned to the same cluster, whose centroid is calculated as the mean value of all the vectors.
2. For each centroid, a perturbation is introduced that generates two new cluster centers. The old representative is discarded.
3. Each carrier is reassigned to one of the new clusters according to the minimum distance criterion.
4. The new representatives are calculated as the average value of the vectors assigned to each cluster. These will be the new centers of the cluster.
5. If the end criterion is met, the algorithm terminates. If not, return to step 2.

See also

- Refer to the official documentation of the `sklearn.cluster.KMeans` function: `https://scikit-learn.org/stable/modules/generated/sklearn.cluster.KMeans.html#sklearn.cluster.KMeans.fit`
- Refer to *Image Compression Using Vector Quantization Algorithms: A Review*: `https://pdfs.semanticscholar.org/24d2/db6db81f1000b74246d22641e83390fb1065.pdf`
- Refer to the *Argparse Tutorial*: `https://docs.python.org/2/howto/argparse.html`
- Refer to the official documentation of the `scipy.misc.imread` function: `https://docs.scipy.org/doc/scipy/reference/generated/scipy.misc.imread.html`

Grouping data using agglomerative clustering

Before we talk about agglomerative clustering, we need to understand **hierarchical clustering**. Hierarchical clustering refers to a set of clustering algorithms that creates tree-like clusters by consecutively splitting or merging them, and they are represented using a tree. Hierarchical clustering algorithms can be either bottom-up or top-down. Now, what does this mean? In bottom-up algorithms, each datapoint is treated as a separate cluster with a single object. These clusters are then successively merged until all the clusters are merged into a single giant cluster. This is called **agglomerative clustering**. On the other hand, top-down algorithms start with a giant cluster and successively split these clusters until individual datapoints are reached.

Getting ready

In hierarchical clustering, we construct clusters by partitioning the instances recursively using a top-down or bottom-up fashion. We can divide these methods as follows:

- **Agglomerative algorithm** (bottom-up): Here, we obtain the solution from individual statistical units. At each iteration, we aggregate the most closely-related statistical units and the procedure ends when a single cluster is formed.
- **Divisive algorithm** (top-down): Here, all units are in the same class and the unit that is not similar to others is added to a new cluster for each subsequent iteration.

Both methods result in a dendrogram. This represents a nested group of objects, and the similarity levels at which the groups change. By cutting the dendrogram at the desired similarity level, we can get a clustering of data objects. The merging or division of clusters is performed using a similarity measure, which optimizes a criterion.

How to do it...

Let's see how to group data using agglomerative clustering:

1. The full code for this recipe is given in the `agglomerative.py` file that's provided to you. Now let's look at how it's built. Create a new Python file, and import the necessary packages:

```
import numpy as np
import matplotlib.pyplot as plt
from sklearn.cluster import AgglomerativeClustering
from sklearn.neighbors import kneighbors_graph
```

2. Let's define the function that we need to perform agglomerative clustering:

```
def perform_clustering(X, connectivity, title, num_clusters=3,
linkage='ward'):
    plt.figure()
    model = AgglomerativeClustering(linkage=linkage,
                    connectivity=connectivity,
n_clusters=num_clusters)
    model.fit(X)
```

3. Let's extract the labels and specify the shapes of the markers for the graph:

```
# extract labels
labels = model.labels_

# specify marker shapes for different clusters
markers = '.vx'
```

4. Iterate through the datapoints and plot them accordingly using different markers:

```
for i, marker in zip(range(num_clusters), markers):
    # plot the points belong to the current cluster
    plt.scatter(X[labels==i, 0], X[labels==i, 1], s=50,
                marker=marker, color='k', facecolors='none')

    plt.title(title)
```

5. In order to demonstrate the advantage of agglomerative clustering, we need to run it on datapoints that are linked spatially, but also located close to each other in space. We want the linked datapoints to belong to the same cluster, as opposed to datapoints that are just spatially close to each other. Let's, now define a function to get a set of datapoints on a spiral:

```
def get_spiral(t, noise_amplitude=0.5):
    r = t
    x = r * np.cos(t)
    y = r * np.sin(t)

    return add_noise(x, y, noise_amplitude)
```

6. In the previous function, we added some noise to the curve because it adds some uncertainty. Let's define this function:

```
def add_noise(x, y, amplitude):
    X = np.concatenate((x, y))
    X += amplitude * np.random.randn(2, X.shape[1])
    return X.T
```

7. Now let's define another function to get datapoints located on a rose curve:

```
def get_rose(t, noise_amplitude=0.02):
    # Equation for "rose" (or rhodonea curve); if k is odd, then
    # the curve will have k petals, else it will have 2k petals
    k = 5
    r = np.cos(k*t) + 0.25
    x = r * np.cos(t)
    y = r * np.sin(t)

    return add_noise(x, y, noise_amplitude)
```

8. Just to add more variety, let's also define a hypotrochoid function:

```
def get_hypotrochoid(t, noise_amplitude=0):
    a, b, h = 10.0, 2.0, 4.0
    x = (a - b) * np.cos(t) + h * np.cos((a - b) / b * t)
    y = (a - b) * np.sin(t) - h * np.sin((a - b) / b * t)

    return add_noise(x, y, 0)
```

9. We are now ready to define the main function:

```
if __name__=='__main__':
    # Generate sample data
    n_samples = 500
    np.random.seed(2)
    t = 2.5 * np.pi * (1 + 2 * np.random.rand(1, n_samples))
    X = get_spiral(t)

    # No connectivity
    connectivity = None
    perform_clustering(X, connectivity, 'No connectivity')

    # Create K-Neighbors graph
    connectivity = kneighbors_graph(X, 10, include_self=False)
    perform_clustering(X, connectivity, 'K-Neighbors connectivity')

    plt.show()
```

If you run this code, you will get the following output if we don't use any connectivity:

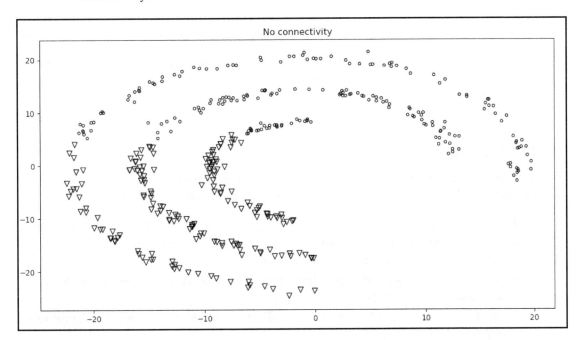

The second output diagram looks like the following:

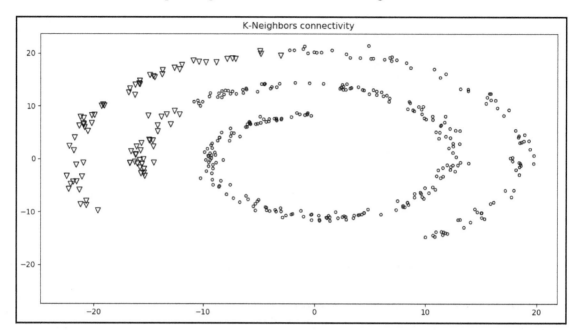

As you can see, using the connectivity feature enables us to group the datapoints that are linked to each other as opposed to clustering them, based on their spatial locations.

How it works...

In agglomerative clustering, each observation begins in its cluster and the clusters are subsequently combined. The strategies for joining the clusters are as follows:

- Ward clustering minimizes the sum of squared differences within all the clusters.
- Maximum or complete linkage is used to minimize the maximum distance between observations of pairs of clusters.
- Average linkage is used to minimize the average of the distances between all observations of pairs of clusters.
- Single linkage is used to minimize the distance between the closest observations of pairs of clusters.

There's more...

To decide what clusters must be combined, it is necessary to define a measure of dissimilarity between the clusters. In most hierarchical clustering methods, specific metrics are used to quantify the distance between two pairs of elements, and a linking criterion that defines the dissimilarity of two sets of elements (clusters) as a function of the distance between pairs of elements in the two sets.

These common metrics are as follows:

- The Euclidean distance
- The Manhattan distance
- The uniform rule
- The Mahalanobis distance, which corrects data by different scales and correlations in variables
- The angle between the two vectors
- The Hamming distance, which measures the minimum number of substitutions required to change one member into another

See also

- Refer to the official documentation of the `sklearn.cluster.AgglomerativeClustering` function: `https://scikit-learn.org/stable/modules/generated/sklearn.cluster.AgglomerativeClustering.html`
- Refer to *Hierarchical agglomerative clustering* (from Stanford University): `https://nlp.stanford.edu/IR-book/html/htmledition/hierarchical-agglomerative-clustering-1.html`

Evaluating the performance of clustering algorithms

So far, we have built different clustering algorithms, but haven't measured their performance. In supervised learning, the predicted values with the original labels are compared to calculate their accuracy. In contrast, in unsupervised learning, we have no labels, so we need to find a way to measure the performance of our algorithms.

Getting ready

A good way to measure a clustering algorithm is by seeing how well the clusters are separated. Are the clusters well separated? Are the datapoints in a cluster that is tight enough? We need a metric that can quantify this behavior. We will use a metric called the **silhouette coefficient** score. This score is defined for each datapoint; this coefficient is defined as follows:

$$score = \frac{x - y}{max(x, y)}$$

Here, x is the average distance between the current datapoint and all the other datapoints in the same cluster, and y is the average distance between the current datapoint and all the datapoints in the next nearest cluster.

How to do it...

Let's see how to evaluate the performance of clustering algorithms:

1. The full code for this recipe is given in the `performance.py` file that has already been provided to you. Now let's look at how it's built. Create a new Python file, and import the following packages:

```
import numpy as np
import matplotlib.pyplot as plt
from sklearn import metrics
from sklearn.cluster import KMeans
```

2. Let's load the input data from the `data_perf.txt` file that has already been provided to you:

```
input_file = ('data_perf.txt')

x = []
with open(input_file, 'r') as f:
    for line in f.readlines():
        data = [float(i) for i in line.split(',')]
        x.append(data)

data = np.array(x)
```

3. In order to determine the optimal number of clusters, let's iterate through a range of values and see where it peaks:

```
scores = []
range_values = np.arange(2, 10)

for i in range_values:
    # Train the model
    kmeans = KMeans(init='k-means++', n_clusters=i, n_init=10)
    kmeans.fit(data)
    score = metrics.silhouette_score(data, kmeans.labels_,
                metric='euclidean', sample_size=len(data))

    print("Number of clusters =", i)
    print("Silhouette score =", score)
    scores.append(score)
```

4. Now let's plot the graph to see where it peaked:

```
# Plot scores
plt.figure()
plt.bar(range_values, scores, width=0.6, color='k', align='center')
plt.title('Silhouette score vs number of clusters')

# Plot data
plt.figure()
plt.scatter(data[:,0], data[:,1], color='k', s=30, marker='o',
facecolors='none')
x_min, x_max = min(data[:, 0]) - 1, max(data[:, 0]) + 1
y_min, y_max = min(data[:, 1]) - 1, max(data[:, 1]) + 1
plt.title('Input data')
plt.xlim(x_min, x_max)
plt.ylim(y_min, y_max)
plt.xticks(())
plt.yticks(())

plt.show()
```

5. If you run this code, you will get the following output on the Terminal:

```
Number of clusters = 2
Silhouette score = 0.5290397175472954
Number of clusters = 3
Silhouette score = 0.5572466391184153
Number of clusters = 4
Silhouette score = 0.5832757517829593
Number of clusters = 5
Silhouette score = 0.6582796909760834
Number of clusters = 6
Silhouette score = 0.5991736976396735
Number of clusters = 7
Silhouette score = 0.5194660249299737
Number of clusters = 8
Silhouette score = 0.44937089046511863
Number of clusters = 9
Silhouette score = 0.3998899991555578
```

The bar graph looks like the following:

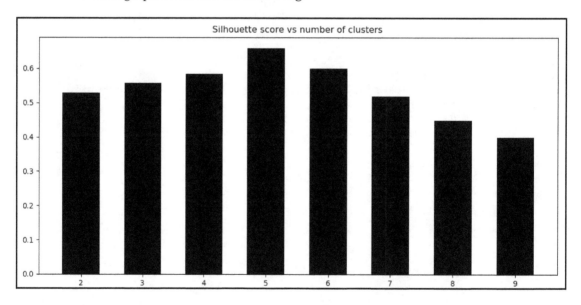

As with these scores, the best configuration is five clusters. Let's see what the data actually looks like:

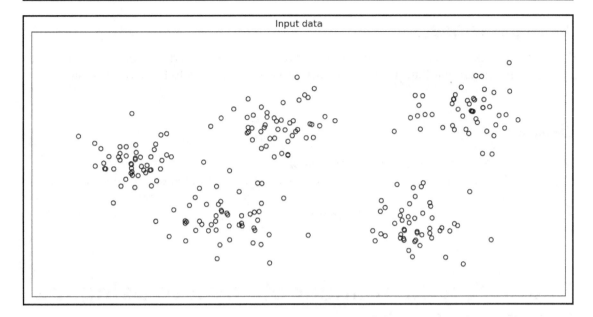

We can visually confirm that the data, in fact, has five clusters. We just took the example of a small dataset that contains five distinct clusters. This method becomes very useful when you are dealing with a huge dataset that contains high-dimensional data that cannot be visualized easily.

How it works...

The `sklearn.metrics.silhouette_score` function computes the mean silhouette coefficient of all the samples. For each sample, two distances are calculated: the mean intra-cluster distance (x), and the mean nearest-cluster distance (y). The silhouette coefficient for a sample is given by the following equation:

$$score = \frac{x - y}{max(x, y)}$$

Essentially, **y** is the distance between a sample and the nearest cluster that does not include the sample.

There's more...

The best value is 1, and the worst value is -1. 0 represents clusters that overlap, while values of less than 0 mean that that particular sample has been attached to the wrong cluster.

See also

- Refer to the official documentation of
  the `sklearn.metrics.silhouette_score` function: `https://scikit-learn.org/stable/modules/generated/sklearn.metrics.silhouette_score.html`
- Refer to *Silhouette* (from Wikipedia):`https://en.wikipedia.org/wiki/Silhouette_(clustering)`

Estimating the number of clusters using the DBSCAN algorithm

When we discussed the k-means algorithm, we saw that we had to give the number of clusters as one of the input parameters. In the real world, we won't have this information available. We can definitely sweep the parameter space to find out the optimal number of clusters using the silhouette coefficient score, but this will be an expensive process! A method that returns the number of clusters in our data will be an excellent solution to the problem. DBSCAN does just that for us.

Getting ready

In this recipe, we will perform a DBSCAN analysis using the `sklearn.cluster.DBSCAN` function. We will use the same data that we used in the previous *Evaluating the performance of clustering algorithms* (`data_perf.txt`) recipe, to compare the two methods used.

How to do it...

Let's see how to automatically estimate the number of clusters using the DBSCAN algorithm:

1. The full code for this recipe is given in the `estimate_clusters.py` file that has already been provided to you. Now let's look at how it's built. Create a new Python file, and import the necessary packages:

```
from itertools import cycle
import numpy as np
from sklearn.cluster import DBSCAN
from sklearn import metrics
import matplotlib.pyplot as plt
```

2. Load the input data from the `data_perf.txt` file. This is the same file that we used in the previous recipe, which will help us to compare the methods on the same dataset:

```
# Load data
input_file = ('data_perf.txt')

x = []
with open(input_file, 'r') as f:
    for line in f.readlines():
        data = [float(i) for i in line.split(',')]
        x.append(data)

X = np.array(x)
```

3. We need to find the best parameter, so let's initialize a few variables:

```
# Find the best epsilon
eps_grid = np.linspace(0.3, 1.2, num=10)
silhouette_scores = []
eps_best = eps_grid[0]
silhouette_score_max = -1
model_best = None
labels_best = None
```

4. Let's sweep the parameter space:

```
for eps in eps_grid:
    # Train DBSCAN clustering model
    model = DBSCAN(eps=eps, min_samples=5).fit(X)

    # Extract labels
    labels = model.labels_
```

5. For each iteration, we need to extract the performance metric:

```
    # Extract performance metric
    silhouette_score = round(metrics.silhouette_score(X, labels),
4)
    silhouette_scores.append(silhouette_score)

    print("Epsilon:", eps, " --> silhouette score:",
silhouette_score)
```

6. We need to store the best score and its associated epsilon value:

```
    if silhouette_score > silhouette_score_max:
        silhouette_score_max = silhouette_score
        eps_best = eps
        model_best = model
        labels_best = labels
```

7. Let's now plot the bar graph, as follows:

```
# Plot silhouette scores vs epsilon
plt.figure()
plt.bar(eps_grid, silhouette_scores, width=0.05, color='k',
align='center')
plt.title('Silhouette score vs epsilon')

# Best params
print("Best epsilon =", eps_best)
```

8. Let's store the best models and labels:

```
# Associated model and labels for best epsilon
model = model_best
labels = labels_best
```

9. Some datapoints may remain unassigned. We need to identify them, as follows:

```
# Check for unassigned datapoints in the labels
offset = 0
if -1 in labels:
    offset = 1
```

10. Extract the number of clusters, as follows:

```
# Number of clusters in the data
num_clusters = len(set(labels)) - offset

print("Estimated number of clusters =", num_clusters)
```

11. We need to extract all the core samples, as follows:

```
# Extracts the core samples from the trained model
mask_core = np.zeros(labels.shape, dtype=np.bool)
mask_core[model.core_sample_indices_] = True
```

12. Let's visualize the resultant clusters. We will start by extracting the set of unique labels and specifying different markers:

```
# Plot resultant clusters
plt.figure()
labels_uniq = set(labels)
markers = cycle('vo^s<>')
```

13. Now let's iterate through the clusters and plot the datapoints using different markers:

```
for cur_label, marker in zip(labels_uniq, markers):
    # Use black dots for unassigned datapoints
    if cur_label == -1:
        marker = '.'

    # Create mask for the current label
    cur_mask = (labels == cur_label)

    cur_data = X[cur_mask & mask_core]
    plt.scatter(cur_data[:, 0], cur_data[:, 1], marker=marker,
            edgecolors='black', s=96, facecolors='none')
    cur_data = X[cur_mask & ~mask_core]
    plt.scatter(cur_data[:, 0], cur_data[:, 1], marker=marker,
            edgecolors='black', s=32)
plt.title('Data separated into clusters')
plt.show()
```

14. If you run this code, you will get the following output on your Terminal:

```
Epsilon: 0.3 --> silhouette score: 0.1287
Epsilon: 0.39999999999999997 --> silhouette score: 0.3594
Epsilon: 0.5 --> silhouette score: 0.5134
Epsilon: 0.6 --> silhouette score: 0.6165
Epsilon: 0.7 --> silhouette score: 0.6322
Epsilon: 0.7999999999999999 --> silhouette score: 0.6366
Epsilon: 0.8999999999999999 --> silhouette score: 0.5142
Epsilon: 1.0 --> silhouette score: 0.5629
Epsilon: 1.0999999999999999 --> silhouette score: 0.5629
Epsilon: 1.2 --> silhouette score: 0.5629
Best epsilon = 0.7999999999999999
Estimated number of clusters = 5
```

This will produce the following bar graph:

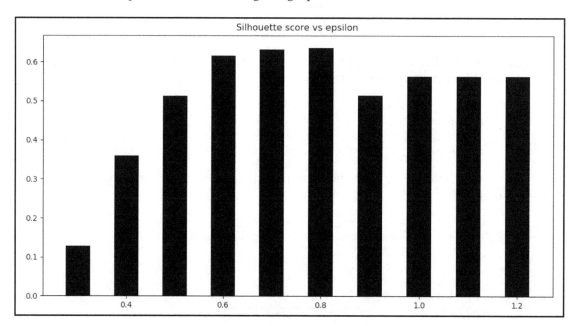

Let's take a look at the labeled datapoints, along with unassigned datapoints marked by solid points in the following output:

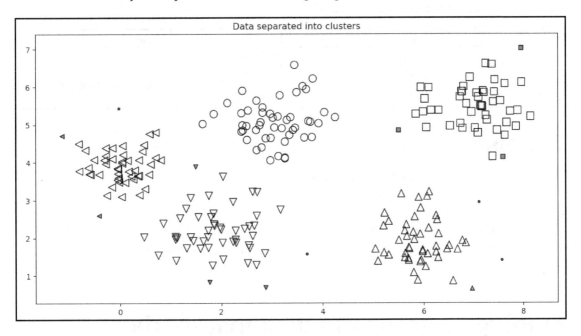

How it works...

DBSCAN works by treating datapoints as groups of dense clusters. If a point belongs to a cluster, then there should be a lot of other points that belong to the same cluster. One of the parameters that we can control is the maximum distance of this point from other points. This is called **epsilon**. No two points in a given cluster should be further away than epsilon. One of the main advantages of this method is that it can deal with outliers. If there are some points located alone in a low-density area, DBSCAN will detect these points as outliers as opposed to forcing them into a cluster.

There's more...

DBSCAN presents the following pros and cons:

Pros	Cons
• It does not require to know the number of a priori clusters. • It can find clusters of arbitrary forms. • It requires only two parameters.	• The quality of clustering depends on its distance measurement. • It is not able to classify datasets with large differences in density.

See also

- Refer to the official documentation of the `sklearn.cluster.DBSCAN` function: `https://scikit-learn.org/stable/modules/generated/sklearn.cluster.DBSCAN.html`
- Refer to *DBSCAN* (from Wikipedia):`https://en.wikipedia.org/wiki/DBSCAN`
- Refer to *Density-based Methods* (from the University at Buffalo): `https://cse.buffalo.edu/~jing/cse601/fa12/materials/clustering_density.pdf`

Finding patterns in stock market data

Let's see how we can use unsupervised learning for stock market analysis. Since we don't know how many clusters there are, we'll use an algorithm called **affinity propagation** (**AP**) on the cluster. It tries to find a representative datapoint for each cluster in our data, along with measures of similarity between pairs of datapoints, and considers all our datapoints as potential representatives, also called **exemplars**, of their respective clusters.

Getting ready

In this recipe, we will analyze the stock market variations of companies over a specified duration. Our goal is to then find out what companies behave similarly in terms of their quotes over time.

How to do it...

Let's see how to find patterns in stock market data:

1. The full code for this recipe is given in the `stock_market.py` file that has already been provided to you. Now let's look at how it's built. Create a new Python file, and import the following packages:

   ```
   import json
   import sys
   import pandas as pd

   import numpy as np
   from sklearn import covariance, cluster
   ```

2. We need a file that contains all the symbols and the associated names. This information is located in the `symbol_map.json` file provided to you. Let's load this, as follows:

   ```
   # Input symbol file
   symbol_file = 'symbol_map.json'
   ```

3. Let's read the data from the `symbol_map.json` file:

   ```
   # Load the symbol map
   with open(symbol_file, 'r') as f:
       symbol_dict = json.loads(f.read())

   symbols, names = np.array(list(symbol_dict.items())).T
   ```

4. Now let's load the data. We will use an Excel file (`stock_market_data.xlsx`); this is a multisheet file, one for each symbol:

   ```
   quotes = []

   excel_file = 'stock_market_data.xlsx'

   for symbol in symbols:
       print('Quote history for %r' % symbol, file=sys.stderr)
       quotes.append(pd.read_excel(excel_file, symbol))
   ```

5. As we need some feature points for analysis, we will use the difference between the opening and closing quotes every day to analyze the data:

   ```
   # Extract opening and closing quotes
   opening_quotes = np.array([quote.open for quote in
   quotes]).astype(np.float)
   ```

```
closing_quotes = np.array([quote.close for quote in
quotes]).astype(np.float)

# The daily fluctuations of the quotes
delta_quotes = closing_quotes - opening_quotes
```

7. Let's build a graph model:

```
# Build a graph model from the correlations
edge_model = covariance.GraphicalLassoCV(cv=3)
```

8. We need to standardize the data before we use it:

```
# Standardize the data
X = delta_quotes.copy().T
X /= X.std(axis=0)
```

9. Now let's train the model using this data:

```
# Train the model
with np.errstate(invalid='ignore'):
    edge_model.fit(X)
```

10. We are now ready to build the clustering model, as follows:

```
# Build clustering model using affinity propagation
_, labels = cluster.affinity_propagation(edge_model.covariance_)
num_labels = labels.max()

# Print the results of clustering
for i in range(num_labels + 1):
    print "Cluster", i+1, "-->", ', '.join(names[labels == i])
```

11. If you run this code, you will get the following output on the Terminal:

```
Cluster 1 --> Apple, Amazon, Yahoo
Cluster 2 --> AIG, American express, Bank of America, DuPont de
Nemours, General Dynamics, General Electrics, Goldman Sachs,
GlaxoSmithKline, Home Depot, Kellogg
Cluster 3 --> Boeing, Canon, Caterpillar, Ford, Honda
Cluster 4 --> Colgate-Palmolive, Kimberly-Clark
Cluster 5 --> Cisco, Dell, HP, IBM
Cluster 6 --> Comcast, Cablevision
Cluster 7 --> CVS
Cluster 8 --> ConocoPhillips, Chevron
```

Eight clusters are identified. From an initial analysis, we can see that the grouped companies seem to treat the same products: IT, banks, engineering, detergents, and computers.

How it works...

AP is a clustering algorithm based on the concept of passing messages between points (item). Unlike clustering algorithms such as k-means, AP does not require the cluster number to be defined a priori. AP searches for representative members (exemplars) of the set of inputs, which are, in fact, representative of the individual clusters.

The central point of the AP algorithm is the identification of a subset of exemplars. In the input, a matrix of similarity is taken between pairs of data. The data exchanges real values as messages until suitable specimens emerge, and consequently, good clusters are obtained.

There's more...

To perform AP clustering, the `sklearn.cluster.affinity_propagation()` function was used. In the case of training samples with similar similarities and preferences, the assignment of cluster centers and labels depends on preference. If the preference is less than the similarities, a single cluster center and a 0 label for each sample will be returned. Otherwise, each training sample becomes its cluster center and a unique mark is assigned.

See also

- Refer to the official documentation of
  the `sklearn.cluster.affinity_propagation()` function: `https://scikit-learn.org/stable/modules/generated/sklearn.cluster.affinity_propagation.html`
- Refer to *AFFINITY PROPAGATION: CLUSTERING DATA BY PASSING MESSAGES* (from Toronto University): `http://www.cs.columbia.edu/~delbert/docs/DDueck-thesis_small.pdf`.

Building a customer segmentation model

One of the main applications of unsupervised learning is market segmentation. This is when we don't have labeled data available all the time, but it's important to segment the market so that people can target individual groups. This is very useful in advertising, inventory management, implementing strategies for distribution, and mass media. Let's go ahead and apply unsupervised learning to one such use case to see how it can be useful.

Getting ready

We will be dealing with a wholesale vendor and his customers. We will be using the data available at https://archive.ics.uci.edu/ml/datasets/Wholesale+customers. The spreadsheet contains data regarding the consumption of different types of items by their customers and our goal is to find clusters so that they can optimize their sales and distribution strategy.

How to do it...

Let's see how to build a customer segmentation model:

1. The full code for this recipe is given in the customer_segmentation.py file that has already been provided to you. Now let's look at how it's built. Create a new Python file, and import the following packages:

```
import csv
import numpy as np
from sklearn.cluster import MeanShift, estimate_bandwidth
import matplotlib.pyplot as plt
```

2. Let's load the input data from the wholesale.csv file that's already provided to you:

```
# Load data from input file
input_file = 'wholesale.csv'
file_reader = csv.reader(open(input_file, 'rt'), delimiter=',')
X = []
for count, row in enumerate(file_reader):
    if not count:
        names = row[2:]
        continue

    X.append([float(x) for x in row[2:]])
```

```
# Input data as numpy array
X = np.array(X)
```

3. Let's build a mean shift model:

```
# Estimating the bandwidth
bandwidth = estimate_bandwidth(X, quantile=0.8, n_samples=len(X))

# Compute clustering with MeanShift
meanshift_estimator = MeanShift(bandwidth=bandwidth,
bin_seeding=True)
meanshift_estimator.fit(X)
labels = meanshift_estimator.labels_
centroids = meanshift_estimator.cluster_centers_
num_clusters = len(np.unique(labels))

print("Number of clusters in input data =", num_clusters)
```

4. Let's print the centroids of clusters that we obtained, as follows:

```
print("Centroids of clusters:")
print('\t'.join([name[:3] for name in names]))
for centroid in centroids:
    print('\t'.join([str(int(x)) for x in centroid]))
```

5. Let's visualize a couple of features to get a sense of the output:

```
# Visualizing data

centroids_milk_groceries = centroids[:, 1:3]

# Plot the nodes using the coordinates of our
centroids_milk_groceries
plt.figure()
plt.scatter(centroids_milk_groceries[:,0],
centroids_milk_groceries[:,1],
        s=100, edgecolors='k', facecolors='none')

offset = 0.2
plt.xlim(centroids_milk_groceries[:,0].min() - offset *
centroids_milk_groceries[:,0].ptp(),
        centroids_milk_groceries[:,0].max() + offset *
centroids_milk_groceries[:,0].ptp(),)
plt.ylim(centroids_milk_groceries[:,1].min() - offset *
centroids_milk_groceries[:,1].ptp(),
        centroids_milk_groceries[:,1].max() + offset *
centroids_milk_groceries[:,1].ptp())
```

```
plt.title('Centroids of clusters for milk and groceries')
plt.show()
```

6. If you run this code, you will get the following output on the Terminal:

Fre	Mil	Gro	Fro	Det	Del
9632	4671	6593	2570	2296	1248
40204	46314	57584	5518	25436	4241
16117	46197	92780	1026	40827	2944
22925	73498	32114	987	20070	903
112151	29627	18148	16745	4948	8550
36847	43950	20170	36534	239	47943
32717	16784	13626	60869	1272	5609
8565	4980	67298	131	38102	1215

Number of clusters in input data = 8
Centroids of clusters:

You will get the following output that depicts the centroids for the features, *milk* and *groceries*, where milk is on the *x* axis and groceries is on the *y* axis:

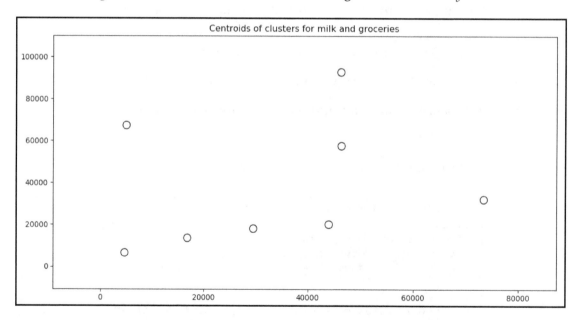

In this output, the eight centroids of the identified clusters are clearly represented.

How it works...

In this recipe, we have faced a clustering problem by using the mean shift algorithm. It is a clustering type that assigns datapoints to clusters in an iterative manner by moving points to the mode. The mode is the value that appears most frequently.

The algorithm assigns iteratively each data point to the centroid of the nearest cluster. The centroid of the nearest cluster is determined by where most of the neighboring points are located. Thus, at each iteration, each data point approaches the point where the greatest number of points is located, which is, or will lead to, the cluster center. When the algorithm stops, each point is assigned to a cluster. Unlike the k-means algorithm, the mean shift algorithm is not required in advance to specify the number of clusters; this is determined automatically by the algorithm. The mean shift algorithm is widely used in the field of image processing and artificial vision.

There's more...

To perform the mean shift clustering, a `sklearn.cluster.MeanShift()` function was used. This function carries out a mean shift clustering using a flat kernel. The mean shift clustering allows us to identify point aggregates in a uniform density of samples. Candidates for the centroids are updated with the average of points within a given region. These points are then filtered in a postprocessing phase to eliminate possible duplicates to form the final set of centroids.

See also

- Refer to the official documentation of the `sklearn.cluster.MeanShift()` function: `https://scikit-learn.org/stable/modules/generated/sklearn.cluster.MeanShift.html#sklearn-cluster-meanshift`
- Refer to *Mean Shift: A Robust Approach Toward Feature Space Analysis* (by Dorin Comaniciu , Peter Meer): `https://courses.csail.mit.edu/6.869/handouts/PAMIMeanshift.pdf`

Using autoencoders to reconstruct handwritten digit images

An autoencoder is a neural network whose purpose is to code its input into small dimensions, and for the result that is obtained to be able to reconstruct the input itself. Autoencoders are made up by the union of the following two subnets: encoder and decoder. A loss function is added to these functions and it is calculated as the distance between the amount of information loss between the compressed representation of the data and the decompressed representation. The encoder and the decoder will be differentiable with respect to the distance function, so the parameters of the encoding and decoding functions can be optimized to minimize the loss of reconstruction, using the gradient stochastic.

Getting ready

Handwriting recognition (HWR) is widely used in modern technology. The written text image can be taken offline from a piece of paper by optical scanning (**optical character recognition, OCR**), or intelligent word recognition. Calligraphy recognition shows the ability of a computer to receive and interpret input that can be understood by hand from sources such as paper documents, touchscreens, photographs, and other devices. HWR consists of various techniques that generally require OCR. However, a complete script recognition system also manages formatting, carries out correct character segmentation, and finds the most plausible words.

The **Modified National Institute of Standards and Technology (MNIST)** is a large database of handwritten digits. It has a set of 70,000 examples of data. It is a subset of MNIST's larger dataset. The digits are of 28 x 28 pixel resolution and are stored in a matrix of 70,000 rows and 785 columns; 784 columns form each pixel value from the 28 x 28 matrix, and one value is the actual digit. The digits have been size-normalized and centered in a fixed-size image.

How to do it...

Let's see how to build autoencoders to reconstruct handwritten digit images:

1. The full code for this recipe is given in the `AutoencMnist.py` file that has already been provided to you. Let's look at how it's built. Create a new Python file, and import the following package:

   ```
   from keras.datasets import mnist
   ```

2. To import the MNIST dataset, the following code must be used:

   ```
   (XTrain, YTrain), (XTest, YTest) = mnist.load_data()

   print('XTrain shape = ',XTrain.shape)
   print('XTest shape = ',XTest.shape)
   print('YTrain shape = ',YTrain.shape)
   print('YTest shape = ',YTest.shape)
   ```

3. After importing the dataset, we have printed the shape of the data, and the following results are returned:

   ```
   XTrain shape = (60000, 28, 28)
   XTest shape = (10000, 28, 28)
   YTrain shape = (60000,)
   YTest shape = (10000,)
   ```

4. The 70,000 items in the database were divided into 60,000 items for training, and 10,000 items for testing. The data output is represented by integers in the range 0 to 9. Let's check it as follows:

   ```
   import numpy as np
   print('YTrain values = ',np.unique(YTrain))
   print('YTest values = ',np.unique(YTest))
   ```

5. The following results are printed:

```
YTrain values = [0 1 2 3 4 5 6 7 8 9]
YTest values = [0 1 2 3 4 5 6 7 8 9]
```

6. It may be useful to analyze the distribution of the two values in the available arrays. To start, we count the number of occurrences:

```
unique, counts = np.unique(YTrain, return_counts=True)
print('YTrain distribution = ',dict(zip(unique, counts)))
unique, counts = np.unique(YTest, return_counts=True)
print('YTrain distribution = ',dict(zip(unique, counts)))
```

7. The following results are returned:

```
YTrain distribution = {0: 5923, 1: 6742, 2: 5958, 3: 6131, 4: 5842,
5: 5421, 6: 5918, 7: 6265, 8: 5851, 9: 5949}
YTrain distribution = {0: 980, 1: 1135, 2: 1032, 3: 1010, 4: 982,
5: 892, 6: 958, 7: 1028, 8: 974, 9: 1009}
```

8. We can also see it in a graph, as follows:

```
import matplotlib.pyplot as plt
plt.figure(1)
plt.subplot(121)
plt.hist(YTrain, alpha=0.8, ec='black')
plt.xlabel("Classes")
plt.ylabel("Number of occurrences")
plt.title("YTrain data")

plt.subplot(122)
plt.hist(YTest, alpha=0.8, ec='black')
plt.xlabel("Classes")
plt.ylabel("Number of occurrences")
plt.title("YTest data")
plt.show()
```

9. To compare the results obtained on both output datasets (YTrain and YTest), two histograms were traced and displayed side by side, as shown in the following output:

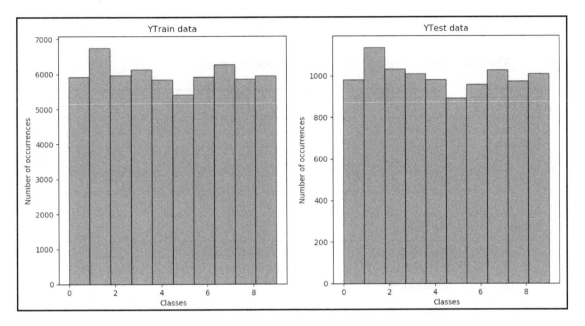

10. From the analysis of the previous output, we can see that in both datasets, the 10 digits are represented in the same proportions. In fact, the bars seem to have the same dimensions, even if the vertical axis has different ranges.

11. Now, we have to normalize all values between 0 and 1:

```
XTrain = XTrain.astype('float32') / 255
XTest = XTest.astype('float32') / 255
```

12. To reduce the dimensionality, we will flatten the 28 x 28 images into vectors of size 784:

```
XTrain = XTrain.reshape((len(XTrain), np.prod(XTrain.shape[1:])))
XTest = XTest.reshape((len(XTest), np.prod(XTest.shape[1:])))
```

13. Now, we will build the model using the Keras functional API. Let's start importing the libraries:

```
from keras.layers import Input
from keras.layers import Dense
from keras.models import Model
```

14. Then, we can build the Keras model, as follows:

```
InputModel = Input(shape=(784,))
EncodedLayer = Dense(32, activation='relu')(InputModel)
```

```
DecodedLayer = Dense(784, activation='sigmoid')(EncodedLayer)
AutoencoderModel = Model(InputModel, DecodedLayer)
AutoencoderModel.summary()
```

The following output shows the model architecture:

Layer (type)	Output Shape	Param #
input_1 (InputLayer)	(None, 784)	0
dense_1 (Dense)	(None, 32)	25120
dense_2 (Dense)	(None, 784)	25872

```
Total params: 50,992
Trainable params: 50,992
Non-trainable params: 0
```

15. So, we have to configure the model for training. To do this, we will use the `compile` method, as follows:

```
AutoencoderModel.compile(optimizer='adadelta',
loss='binary_crossentropy')
```

16. At this point, we can train the model, as follows:

```
history = AutoencoderModel.fit(XTrain, XTrain,
batch_size=256,
epochs=100,
shuffle=True,
validation_data=(XTest, XTest))
```

17. Our model is now ready, so we can use it to rebuild the handwritten digits automatically. To do this, we will use the `predict()` method:

```
DecodedDigits = AutoencoderModel.predict(XTest)
```

18. We have now finished; the model has been trained and will later be used to make predictions. So, we can just print the starting handwritten digits and those that were reconstructed from our model. Of course, we will do it only for some of the 60,000 digits contained in the dataset. In fact, we will limit ourselves to displaying the first five; we will also use the `matplotlib` library in this case:

```
n=5
plt.figure(figsize=(20, 4))
for i in range(n):
  ax = plt.subplot(2, n, i + 1)
```

```
plt.imshow(XTest[i+10].reshape(28, 28))
plt.gray()
ax.get_xaxis().set_visible(False)
ax.get_yaxis().set_visible(False)
ax = plt.subplot(2, n, i + 1 + n)
plt.imshow(DecodedDigits[i+10].reshape(28, 28))
plt.gray()
ax.get_xaxis().set_visible(False)
ax.get_yaxis().set_visible(False)
plt.show()
```

The results are shown in the following output:

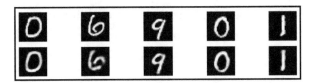

As you can see in the preceding output, the result is very close to the original, meaning that the model works well.

How it works...

An autoencoder is a neural network whose purpose is to code its input into small dimensions and the result obtained so as to be able to reconstruct the input itself. Autoencoders are made up of a union of the following two subnets.

First, we have an encoder that calculates the following function:

$$z = \phi(x)$$

Given an x input, the encoder encodes it in a z variable, which is also called a latent variable. z usually has much smaller dimensions than x.

Second, we have a decoder that calculates the following function:

$$x' = \psi(z)$$

Since z is the code of x produced by the encoder, the decoder must decode it so that x' is similar to x. The training of autoencoders is intended to minimize the mean squared error between the input and the result.

There's more...

Keras is a Python library that provides a simple and clean way to create a range of deep learning models. The Keras code was released under the MIT license. Keras has been structured based on austerity and simplicity, and it provides a programming model without ornaments to maximize readability. It allows neural networks to be expressed in a very modular way, considering models as a sequence or a single graph.

See also

- Refer to the official documentation of the Keras library: `https://keras.io/`
- Refer to *Keras 2.x Projects*, Giuseppe Ciaburro, Packt Publishing.

5
Visualizing Data

In this chapter, we will cover the following recipes:

- Plotting three-dimensional scatter plots
- Plotting bubble plots
- Animating bubble plots
- Drawing pie charts
- Plotting date-formatted time series data
- Plotting histograms
- Visualizing heat maps
- Animating dynamic signals
- Working with the Seaborn library

Technical requirements

To address the recipes in this chapter, you will need the following files (available on GitHub):

- `scatter_3d.py`
- `bubble_plot.py`
- `dynamic_bubble_plot.py`
- `pie_chart.py`
- `time_series.py`
- `aapl.csv`
- `histogram.py`
- `heatmap.py`
- `moving_wave_variable.py`
- `seaborn.boxplot.py`

An introduction to data visualization

Data visualization is an important pillar of machine learning. It helps us to formulate the right strategies to understand data. The visual representation of data assists helps us choose the right algorithms. One of the main goals of data visualization is to communicate clearly by using graphs and charts.

We encounter numerical data all the time in the real world. We want to encode this numerical data by using graphs, lines, dots, bars, and so on, to visually display the information contained in those numbers. This makes complex distributions of data more understandable and usable. The process is used in a variety of situations, including comparative analysis, tracking growth, market distribution, public opinion polls, and much more.

We use different charts to show patterns or relationships between variables. We use histograms to display the distribution of data. We use tables when we want to look up a specific measurement. In this chapter, we will look at various scenarios and discuss what visualizations we can use in those situations.

Plotting three-dimensional scatter plots

The relationships between quantitative variables can be represented by using a scatter plot. A version of this graph is represented by the three-dimensional scatter plots that are used to show the relationships between three variables.

Getting ready

In this recipe, you will learn how to plot three-dimensional scatter plots and visualize them in three dimensions.

How to do it...

Let's look at how to plot three-dimensional scatter plots:

1. Create a new Python file and import the following packages (the full code is in the `scatter_3d.py` file that's already provided to you):

   ```
   import numpy as np
   import matplotlib.pyplot as plt
   ```

2. Create the empty figure, as follows:

   ```
   # Create the figure
   fig = plt.figure()
   ax = fig.add_subplot(111, projection='3d')
   ```

3. Define the number of values that we should generate:

   ```
   # Define the number of values
   n = 250
   ```

4. Create a `lambda` function to generate the values in a given range:

   ```
   # Create a lambda function to generate the random values in the
   given range
   f = lambda minval, maxval, n: minval + (maxval - minval) *
   np.random.rand(n)
   ```

5. Generate the x, y, and z values using the `lambda` function:

   ```
   # Generate the values
   x_vals = f(15, 41, n) y_vals = f(-10, 70, n)
   z_vals = f(-52, -37, n)
   ```

6. Plot these values, as follows:

   ```
   # Plot the values
   ax.scatter(x_vals, y_vals, z_vals, c='k', marker='o')
   ax.set_xlabel('X axis')
   ax.set_ylabel('Y axis')
   ax.set_zlabel('Z axis')

   plt.show()
   ```

If you run the preceding code, you will see the following output:

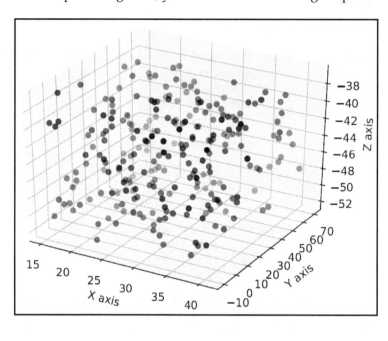

How it works...

The scatter plot helps us to understand whether there is a statistical association between two quantitative characters. If as one variable increases, the other tends to decrease, we have a discordant association. If as one variable increases, the other tends to increase, we have a concordant association. If one changes and the other tends to not change, we have no association. To analyze this trend, the disposition of markers is analyzed. If the markers are close to forming a straight line in any direction in the three-dimensional space of the graph, the correlation between the corresponding variables is high. If the markers are equally distributed in the graph, the correlation is low, or zero.

There's more...

Three-dimensional scatter plots are used to show the relationship between three variables. A fourth variable can be added by matching the color or size of the markers, adding another variable to the plot.

See also

- Refer to the official documentation of Matplotlib at `https://matplotlib.org/gallery/mplot3d/scatter3d.html`.
- Refer to *Visualize Your Data: Scatter Plots* (from the University of Illinois) at `http://guides.library.illinois.edu/visualize-your-data/scatter-plots`.

Plotting bubble plots

A **bubble plot** is a type of chart in which each represented entity is defined in terms of three distinct numerical parameters. The first two parameters are used as values of the two Cartesian axes, while the third is used to find the radius of the bubble. Bubble plots are used to describe relationships in various scientific fields.

Getting ready

Let's look at how to plot bubble plots. The size of each circle in a two-dimensional bubble plot represents the amplitude of that particular point.

How to do it...

Let's look at how to plot bubble plots:

1. Create a new Python file and import the following packages (the full code is in the `bubble_plot.py` file that's already been provided to you):

```
import numpy as np
import matplotlib.pyplot as plt
```

2. Define the number of values that we should generate:

```
# Define the number of values
num_vals = 40
```

3. Generate random values for x and y:

```
# Generate random values
x = np.random.rand(num_vals)
y = np.random.rand(num_vals)
```

4. Define the area value for each point in the bubble plot:

```
# Define area for each bubble
# Max radius is set to a specified value
max_radius = 25
area = np.pi * (max_radius * np.random.rand(num_vals)) ** 2
```

5. Define the colors:

```
# Generate colors
colors = np.random.rand(num_vals)
```

6. Plot these values:

```
# Plot the points
plt.scatter(x, y, s=area, c=colors, alpha=1.0)

plt.show()
```

If you run this code, you will see the following output:

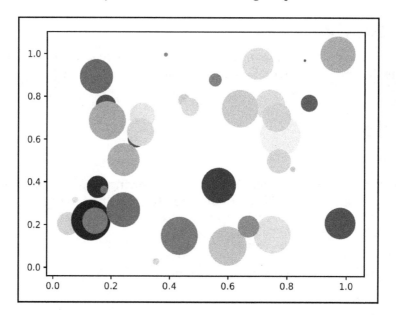

How it works...

The variables that were shown previously can be compared to each other based on their sizes and their positions relative to the numeric axis. In fact, the x and y axis of a bubble chart are numerical scales, so the position in which data is represented describes two numerical values, while the area of the drawing depends on the value of the third parameter.

When drawing a bubble chart, it is necessary to pay attention to the fact that the area of a circle is proportional to the square of the radius, so if the radius is determined proportionally to the third value, the result will disproportionately emphasize the third value. To have a correctly weighed scale, the radius must be chosen in proportion to the square root of the third value. This error is commonly committed when drawing bubble charts.

There's more...

A bubble plot can be considered a variation of a scatter plot, where points are replaced with bubbles. This type of chart can be used instead of a scatter plot if the data has three series, each of which contains a set of data.

See also

- Refer to the official documentation of Matplotlib at `https://matplotlib.org/api/_as_gen/matplotlib.pyplot.scatter.html`.
- Refer to the `pyplot` tutorial at `https://matplotlib.org/users/pyplot_tutorial.html`.

Animating bubble plots

An animating bubble plot is a bubble plot in motion. It allows for the efficient and interactive visualization of correlations through time. It is particularly useful, as it allows us to visualize how the correlations between variables change over time efficiently and interactively.

Getting ready

Let's look at how to animate a bubble plot. This will be useful when you want to visualize data that's transient and dynamic.

How to do it...

Let's look at how to animate bubble plots:

1. Create a new Python file and import the following packages (the full code is in the `dynamic_bubble_plot.py` file that's already been provided to you):

```
import numpy as np
import matplotlib.pyplot as plt
from matplotlib.animation import FuncAnimation
```

2. Let's define a `tracker` function that will dynamically update the bubble plot:

```
def tracker(cur_num):
    # Get the current index
    cur_index = cur_num % num_points
```

3. Define the color:

```
# Set the color of the datapoints
datapoints['color'][:, 3] = 1.0
```

4. Update the size of the circles:

```
# Update the size of the circles
datapoints['size'] += datapoints['growth']
```

5. Update the position of the oldest data point in the set:

```
# Update the position of the oldest datapoint
datapoints['position'][cur_index] = np.random.uniform(0, 1, 2)
datapoints['size'][cur_index] = 7
datapoints['color'][cur_index] = (0, 0, 0, 1)
datapoints['growth'][cur_index] = np.random.uniform(40, 150)
```

6. Update the parameters of the scatter plot:

```
# Update the parameters of the scatter plot
scatter_plot.set_edgecolors(datapoints['color'])
scatter_plot.set_sizes(datapoints['size'])
scatter_plot.set_offsets(datapoints['position'])
```

7. Define the `main` function and create an empty figure:

```
if __name__=='__main__':
    # Create a figure
    fig = plt.figure(figsize=(9, 7), facecolor=(0,0.9,0.9))
    ax = fig.add_axes([0, 0, 1, 1], frameon=False)
    ax.set_xlim(0, 1), ax.set_xticks([])
    ax.set_ylim(0, 1), ax.set_yticks([])
```

8. Define the number of points that will be on the plot at any given point in time:

```
    # Create and initialize the datapoints in random positions
    # and with random growth rates.
    num_points = 20
```

9. Define the `datapoints` by using random values:

```
    datapoints = np.zeros(num_points, dtype=[('position', float, 2),
              ('size', float, 1), ('growth', float, 1), ('color', float, 4)])
    datapoints['position'] = np.random.uniform(0, 1, (num_points, 2))
    datapoints['growth'] = np.random.uniform(40, 150, num_points)
```

10. Create the scatter plot that will be updated in every frame:

```
    # Construct the scatter plot that will be updated every frame
    scatter_plot = ax.scatter(datapoints['position'][:, 0],
datapoints['position'][:, 1],
                      s=datapoints['size'], lw=0.7,
edgecolors=datapoints['color'],
                      facecolors='none')
```

11. Start the animation by using the `tracker` function:

```
    # Start the animation using the 'tracker' function
    animation = FuncAnimation(fig, tracker, interval=10)

    plt.show()
```

If you run this code, you will see the following output:

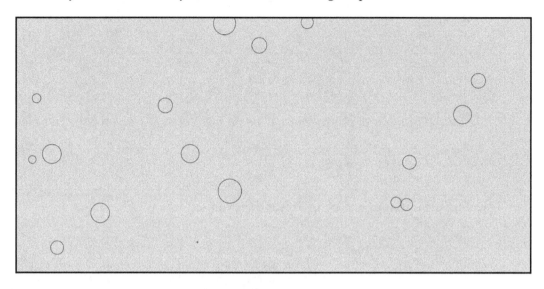

How it works...

In this recipe, we simply used a series of bubble plots with values that change over time to build an animation. To do this, we started with the construction of a function that updates the parameters of these graphs. Then, we defined the code that traces the bubble plot with the current parameters. Finally, we used the `FuncAnimation()` function to create animations from the individual bubble plots.

There's more...

The `FuncAnimation()` function of Matplotlib creates an animation by repeatedly calling a specific function.

See also

- Refer to the official documentation of Matplotlib at `https://matplotlib.org/api/_as_gen/matplotlib.animation.FuncAnimation.html`.
- Refer to the Matplotlib animation at `https://matplotlib.org/api/animation_api.html`.

Drawing pie charts

The circular diagram, often referred to as a pie chart, is a method used in descriptive statistics for graphical representations of quantitative variables measured on classes of categories (nominal values), in order to avoid establishing, even unintentionally, an order that does not exist in the categories.

Getting ready

Let's look at how to draw pie charts. This will be useful when you want to visualize the percentages of a set of labels in a group.

How to do it...

Let's look at how to draw pie charts, as follows:

1. Create a new Python file and import the following package (the full code is in the `pie_chart.py` file that's already been provided to you):

   ```
   import matplotlib.pyplot as plt
   ```

2. Define the labels and values:

   ```
   # Labels and corresponding values in counter clockwise direction
   data = {'Apple': 26,
           'Mango': 17,
           'Pineapple': 21,
           'Banana': 29,
           'Strawberry': 11}
   ```

3. Define the colors for visualization:

   ```
   # List of corresponding colors
   colors = ['orange', 'lightgreen', 'lightblue', 'gold', 'cyan']
   ```

4. Define a variable to highlight a section of the pie chart by separating it from the rest. If you don't want to highlight any sections, set all of the values to 0:

   ```
   # Needed if we want to highlight a section
   explode = (0, 0, 0, 0, 0)
   ```

5. Plot the pie chart. Note that if you are using Python 3, you should use `list(data.values())` in the following function call:

```
# Plot the pie chart
plt.pie(data.values(), explode=explode, labels=data.keys(),
        colors=colors, autopct='%1.1f%%', shadow=False,
startangle=90)

# Aspect ratio of the pie chart, 'equal' indicates tht we
# want it to be a circle
plt.axis('equal')

plt.show()
```

If you run this code, you will see the following output:

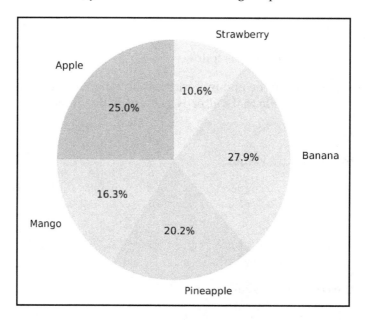

7. If you change the explode array to (0, 0.2, 0, 0, 0), it will highlight the Mango section. You will see the following output:

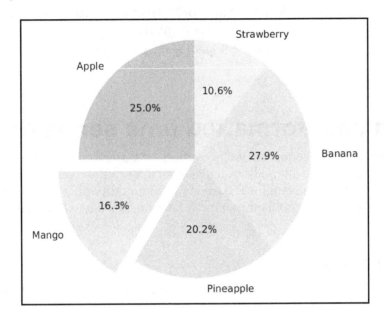

How it works...

A pie chart is constructed by dividing a circle into slices whose angular amplitudes are proportional to the frequency classes. The areas identified by the slices are proportional to the frequencies. To make the diagram clearer, the various slices are filled with different colors.

There's more...

The pie chart is useful for displaying the market shares of products and brands, or the percentages taken by political parties in elections. The chart does not work with large percentage differences or with too many elements, as this would make the pie too jagged.

See also

- Refer to the official documentation of Matplotlib at `https://matplotlib.org/api/_as_gen/matplotlib.pyplot.pie.html`.
- Refer to the pie chart (from Wikipedia) at `https://en.wikipedia.org/wiki/Pie_chart`.

Plotting date-formatted time series data

A **time series** constitutes a sequence of observations of a phenomenon, carried out in consecutive instants or time intervals. Usually, even if it's not necessary, they are evenly spaced out or are of the same length. The trends of commodity prices, stock market indices, government bonds spread, and unemployment rates are just a few examples of times series.

Getting ready

Let's look at how to plot time series data by using date formatting. This will be useful in visualizing stock data over time.

How to do it...

Let's look at how to plot date-formatted time series data, as follows:

1. Create a new Python file and import the following packages (the full code is in the `time_series.py` file that's already been provided to you):

```
import numpy
import matplotlib.pyplot as plt
from matplotlib.mlab import csv2rec
from matplotlib.ticker import Formatter
```

2. Define a function to format the dates. The __init__ function sets the class variables:

```
# Define a class for formatting
class DataFormatter(Formatter):
    def __init__(self, dates, date_format='%Y-%m-%d'):
        self.dates = dates
        self.date_format = date_format
```

3. Extract the value at any given time and return it in the following format:

```
# Extract the value at time t at position 'position'
def __call__(self, t, position=0):
    index = int(round(t))
    if index >= len(self.dates) or index < 0:
        return ''

    return self.dates[index].strftime(self.date_format)
```

4. Define the `main` function. We'll use the Apple stock quotes CSV file that was already provided to you (`aapl.csv`). Load the CSV file:

```
# Load csv file into numpy record array
data = csv2rec('aapl.csv')
```

5. Extract a subset of these values in order to plot them:

```
# Take a subset for plotting
data = data[-70:]
```

6. Create the `formatter` object and initialize it with the dates:

```
# Create the date formatter object
formatter = DataFormatter(data.date)
```

7. Define the *x* and *y* axes:

```
# X axis
x_vals = numpy.arange(len(data))

# Y axis values are the closing stock quotes
y_vals = data.close
```

8. Plot the data:

```
# Plot data
fig, ax = plt.subplots()
ax.xaxis.set_major_formatter(formatter)
ax.plot(x_vals, y_vals, 'o-')
fig.autofmt_xdate()
plt.show()
```

If you run this code, you will see the following output:

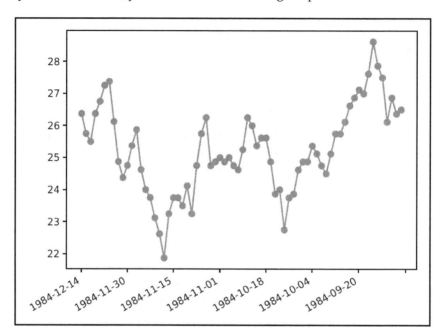

How it works...

In this recipe, we have plotted time series data by using date formatting. We started by defining a class for formatting the date. We extracted the value at time *t* at a specific position. Then, we loaded a CSV file into a NumPy record array. So, we took a subset for plotting and we created the date `formatter` object. Finally, we set the *x* and *y* axes and plotted the data.

There's more...

Visualization is fundamental in the analysis of time series. Viewing raw data can provide tools for identifying temporal structures, such as trends, cycles, and seasonality. However, the formatting of the dates represents an operation that you must learn to process, in order to obtain a correct visualization of the axes.

See also

- Refer to *Time Series Basics* (from Pennsylvania State University) at `https://newonlinecourses.science.psu.edu/stat510/node/41/`.

Plotting histograms

A **histogram** is a reproduction of numerical distributions that shows the shape of a distribution. It consists of adjacent rectangles (bins) whose bases are aligned on an axis and are equipped with a unit of measure.

For more information, refer to the book *MATLAB for Machine Learning* by Giuseppe Ciaburro.

Getting ready

We'll look at how to plot histograms in this recipe. We'll compare two sets of data and build a comparative histogram.

How to do it...

Let's look at how to plot histograms, as follows:

1. Create a new Python file and import the following packages (the full code is in the `histogram.py` file that's already been provided to you):

```
import numpy as np
import matplotlib.pyplot as plt
```

2. We'll compare the production quantities of apples and oranges in this recipe. Let's define some values:

```
# Input data
apples = [30, 25, 22, 36, 21, 29]
oranges = [24, 33, 19, 27, 35, 20]

# Number of groups
num_groups = len(apples)
```

3. Create the figure and define its parameters:

```
# Create the figure
fig, ax = plt.subplots()

# Define the X axis
indices = np.arange(num_groups)

# Width and opacity of histogram bars
bar_width = 0.4
opacity = 0.6
```

4. Plot the histogram:

```
# Plot the values
hist_apples = plt.bar(indices, apples, bar_width,
        alpha=opacity, color='g', label='Apples')

hist_oranges = plt.bar(indices + bar_width, oranges, bar_width,
        alpha=opacity, color='b', label='Oranges')
```

5. Set the parameters of the plot:

```
plt.xlabel('Month')
plt.ylabel('Production quantity')
plt.title('Comparing apples and oranges')
plt.xticks(indices + bar_width, ('Jan', 'Feb', 'Mar', 'Apr', 'May',
'Jun'))
plt.ylim([0, 45])
plt.legend()
plt.tight_layout()

plt.show()
```

If you run this code, you will see the following output:

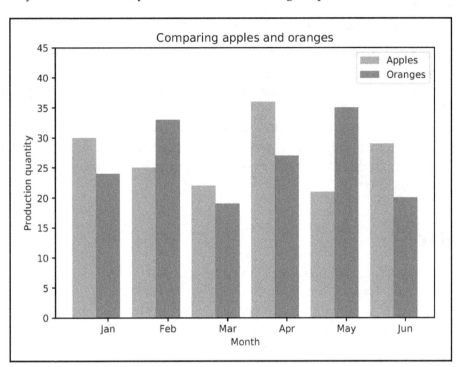

How it works...

The histogram is a particular Cartesian diagram that has discrete values on the abscissas and a magnitude on the ordinates, represented by the height of a column, which we call a bin. In physics, histograms allow us to study the results of an experiment, since they provide us with a graphic indication of how the counts or frequencies are distributed, according to the discrete values taken into consideration.

To build a histogram, perform the following steps:

1. First of all, you have to decide the number of tests.
2. Then, you must choose the binning, that is, the division of the domain of the variable on the abscissas, in intervals. You must therefore define the number of intervals, where the jth bin will have a predetermined width.
3. Finally, you must count the occurrences to associate with the individual bins.

There's more...

A histogram is most useful under the following circumstances:

- The data to be represented are of the numeric type.
- You want to visualize the form of the data distribution, in order to see whether it is normal and analyze whether a process can (or cannot) meet the requirements imposed.
- You want to determine whether the output of two or more processes is different.
- You want to quickly communicate data distributions.
- You want to check whether a change has occurred in a process over a certain period of time.

See also

- Refer to *Histograms* (from the University of Leicester) at `https://www2.le.ac.uk/offices/ld/resources/numerical-data/histograms`.
- Refer to the official documentation of Matplotlib at `https://matplotlib.org/api/_as_gen/matplotlib.pyplot.bar.html`.

Visualizing heat maps

The **heat map** is a graph where the individual values contained in a matrix are represented through gradations of colors. Both fractal maps and tree maps often use the same color-coding systems to represent the hierarchy of a variable. For example, if we measure the number of clicks on a web page or the areas where the mouse pointer passes the most often, we will obtain a heat map with certain areas highlighted by warm colors, that is, those that most attract our attention.

Getting ready

We'll look at how to visualize heat maps in this recipe. This is a pictorial representation of data, where two groups are associated point by point. The individual values that are contained in a matrix are represented as color values in the plot.

How to do it...

Let's look at how to visualize heat maps:

1. Create a new Python file and import the following packages (the full code is in the `heatmap.py` file that's been provided to you):

```
import numpy as np
import matplotlib.pyplot as plt
```

2. Define the two groups:

```
# Define the two groups
group1 = ['France', 'Italy', 'Spain', 'Portugal', 'Germany']
group2 = ['Japan', 'China', 'Brazil', 'Russia', 'Australia']
```

3. Generate a random two-dimensional matrix:

```
# Generate some random values
data = np.random.rand(5, 5)
```

4. Create a figure:

```
# Create a figure
fig, ax = plt.subplots()
```

5. Create a heat map:

```
# Create the heat map
heatmap = ax.pcolor(data, cmap=plt.cm.gray)
```

6. Plot these values:

```
# Add major ticks at the middle of each cell
ax.set_xticks(np.arange(data.shape[0]) + 0.5, minor=False)
ax.set_yticks(np.arange(data.shape[1]) + 0.5, minor=False)

# Make it look like a table
ax.invert_yaxis()
ax.xaxis.tick_top()

# Add tick labels
ax.set_xticklabels(group2, minor=False)
ax.set_yticklabels(group1, minor=False)

plt.show()
```

If you run this code, you will see the following output:

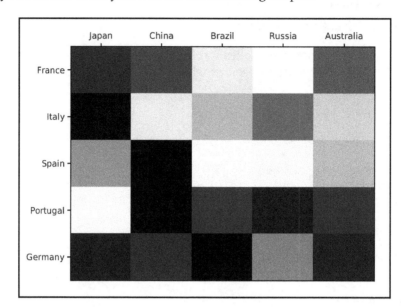

How it works...

We already stated that a heat map is a type of graphical representation of data, where the values are expressed through a different color range. Its representation usually includes the following:

- **Warm colors**: Red, orange, and yellow, in the areas of greatest interest
- **Cold colors**: Green or blue, for the areas with worse results

Generally, heat maps require a large sample of data, and their main objective is to obtain useful data on the trend of a particular variable. This means of analysis allows us to evaluate the distribution of the variable of interest in the analyzed area. In this way, the concentration of warm colors in particular areas will highlight the areas in which the variable assumes the highest values.

There's more...

The creator of heat maps was Cormac Kinney, who, in the mid-1990s, developed this solution to provide stock market operators with an extremely quick tool for gathering a variety of financial data.

See also

- Refer to *Creating Annotated Heatmaps* (from the official documentation of Matplotlib) at `https://matplotlib.org/gallery/images_contours_and_fields/image_annotated_heatmap.html`.
- Refer to the official documentation of Matplotlib at `https://matplotlib.org/api/_as_gen/matplotlib.pyplot.pcolor.html`.

Animating dynamic signals

When we visualize real-time signals, it's nice to look at how the waveform builds up. A **dynamic system** is a mathematical model that represents an object with a finite number of degrees of freedom that evolves over time, according to a deterministic law. A dynamic system is identified by a vector in the phase space, which is, the space of the system states, where **state** is a term that indicates the set of physical quantities, called **state variables** that characterize the dynamics of the system.

Getting ready

In this recipe, we will look at how to animate dynamic signals and visualize them as they are encountered in real time.

How to do it...

Let's look at how to animate dynamic signals, as follows:

1. Create a new Python file and import the following packages (the full code is in the `moving_wave_variable.py` file that's already been provided to you):

```
import numpy as np
import matplotlib.pyplot as plt
import matplotlib.animation as animation
```

2. Create a function to generate a damping sinusoid signal:

```
# Generate the signal
def generate_data(length=2500, t=0, step_size=0.05):
    for count in range(length):
        t += step_size
```

```
        signal = np.sin(2*np.pi*t)
        damper = np.exp(-t/8.0)
        yield t, signal * damper
```

3. Define an `initializer` function to initialize the parameters of the plot:

```
# Initializer function
def initializer():
    peak_val = 1.0
    buffer_val = 0.1
```

4. Set these parameters, as follows:

```
        ax.set_ylim(-peak_val * (1 + buffer_val), peak_val * (1 +
    buffer_val))
        ax.set_xlim(0, 10)
        del x_vals[:]
        del y_vals[:]
        line.set_data(x_vals, y_vals)
        return line
```

5. Define a function to draw the values:

```
def draw(data):
    # update the data
    t, signal = data
    x_vals.append(t)
    y_vals.append(signal)
    x_min, x_max = ax.get_xlim()
```

6. If the values go past the current *x* axis limits, then update and extend the graph:

```
if t >= x_max:
    ax.set_xlim(x_min, 2 * x_max)
    ax.figure.canvas.draw()

line.set_data(x_vals, y_vals)

return line
```

7. Define the `main` function:

```
if __name__=='__main__':
    # Create the figure
    fig, ax = plt.subplots()
    ax.grid()
```

8. Extract the line:

```
# Extract the line
line, = ax.plot([], [], lw=1.5)
```

9. Create the variables and initialize them to empty lists:

```
# Create the variables
x_vals, y_vals = [], []
```

10. Define and start the animation by using the `animator` object:

```
# Define the animator object
animator = animation.FuncAnimation(fig, draw, generate_data,
        blit=False, interval=10, repeat=False, init_func=initializer)
```

```
plt.show()
```

If you run this code, you will see the following output:

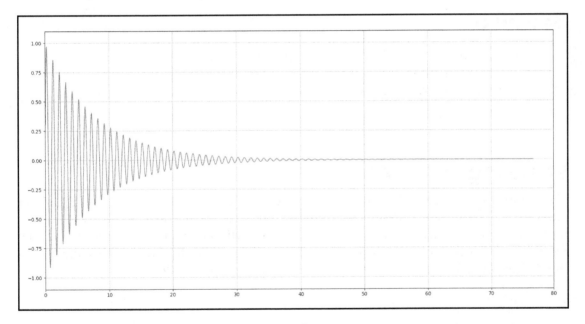

How it works...

In this recipe, we animated dynamic signals and visualized them as they are encountered in real time. To do this, a damped sine wave was used. When we go on a seesaw, we know that after the initial push, it oscillates for a while and then stops. The seesaw is an example of a pendulum, whose motion is represented by a damped sine wave. A **damped sine wave** is a sinusoidal function whose amplitude approaches zero as time increases.

There's more...

Sinusoidal waves are used to describe many oscillating phenomena. When a sine wave is muted, each successive peak decreases with time. The most common form of damping is exponential damping, in which the outer envelope of the subsequent peaks is an exponential decay curve.

See also

- Refer to the official documentation of Matplotlib at `https://matplotlib.org/api/_as_gen/matplotlib.animation.FuncAnimation.html`.
- Refer to Matplotlib animation at `https://matplotlib.org/api/animation_api.html`.

Working with the Seaborn library

A **box plot**, also called a **whiskers chart**, is a graph that uses simple dispersion and position indexes to describe the distribution of a sample. A box plot can be depicted either horizontally or vertically, by means of a rectangular partition divided by two segments. The rectangle (box) is delimited by the first quartile (the 25th percentile) and the third quartile (the 75th percentile), and is divided by the median (the 50th percentile).

Getting ready

In this recipe, we will draw a box plot to show the distribution of the predictors contained in the Boston dataset, which we already used in the *Estimating housing prices* recipe in Chapter 1, *The Realm of Supervised Learning*.

How to do it...

Let's look at how to work with the seaborn library, as follows:

1. Create a new Python file and import the following packages (the full code is in the seaborn.boxplot.py file that's already been provided to you):

```
import pandas as pd
from sklearn import datasets
import seaborn as sns
```

2. Load the dataset contained in the sklearn.datasets library:

```
boston = datasets.load_boston()
```

3. Convert the data into a pandas DataFrame:

```
BostonDF = pd.DataFrame(boston.data, columns=boston.feature_names)
```

4. Extract the first 12 features as predictors:

```
Predictors = BostonDF[BostonDF.columns[0:12]]
```

5. Draw the box plot by using the seaborn library:

```
sns.set(style="ticks")
sns.boxplot(data = Predictors)
```

Let's look at the results in the following output:

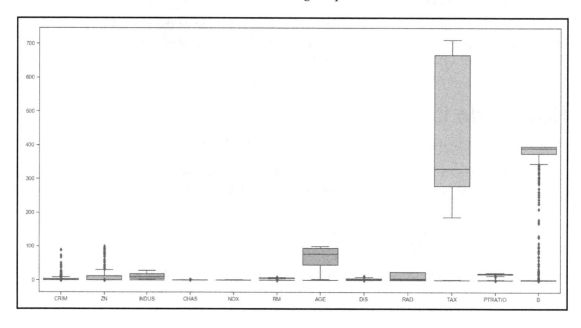

We can see that the predictors have different ranges of values. This makes the chart difficult to read; the variability for some predictors is not highlighted. In these cases, it is necessary to scale the data.

6. Import the `sklearn.preprocessing.MinMaxScaler` library and scale the data, as follows:

```
from sklearn.preprocessing import MinMaxScaler

scaler = MinMaxScaler()
DataScaled = scaler.fit_transform(Predictors)
```

6. Now, we draw a box plot again to see the difference:

```
sns.set(style="ticks")
sns.boxplot(data = DataScaled)
```

The results are shown in the following screenshot:

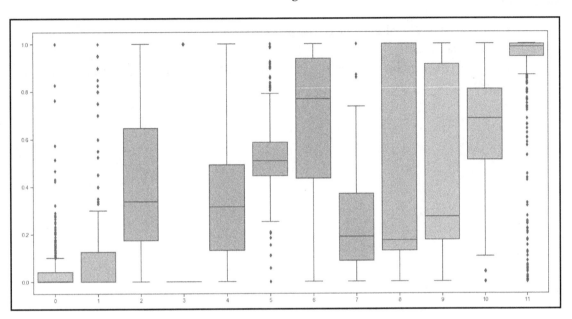

In this case, we can see that the data is between 0-1. In this way, the variability of the data is recognizable for all of the predictors.

How it works...

The Seaborn library is a data visualization library that's based on Matplotlib. It is useful for drawing attractive and informative statistical graphics, and is closely integrated with Pandas data structures. Seaborn offers many features that can help us with the visual analysis of a data source.

These features can be seen at `http://seaborn.pydata.org/introduction.html`.

There's more...

In a box plot, the segments outside of the box (the whiskers) represent the minimum and maximum of the sample. In this way, the four equally populated ranges, delineated by quartiles, are graphically represented.

See also

- Refer to the official website of the Seaborn library at `https://seaborn.pydata.org/index.html`.
- Refer to the official Seaborn tutorial at `https://seaborn.pydata.org/tutorial.html`.

6
Building Recommendation Engines

In this chapter, we will cover the following recipes:

- Building function compositions for data processing
- Building machine learning pipelines
- Finding the nearest neighbors
- Constructing a k-nearest neighbors classifier
- Constructing a k-nearest neighbors regressor
- Computing the Euclidean distance score
- Computing the Pearson correlation score
- Finding similar users in the dataset
- Generating movie recommendations
- Implementing ranking algorithms
- Building a filtering model using TensorFlow

Technical requirements

To address the recipes in this chapter, you will need the following files (which are available on GitHub):

- function_composition.py
- pipeline.py

- `knn.py`
- `nn_classification.py`
- `nn_regression.py`
- `euclidean_score.py`
- `pearson_score.py`
- `find_similar_users.py`
- `movie_recommendations.py`
- `LambdaMARTModel.py`
- `train.txt`
- `vali.txt`
- `test.txt`
- `TensorFilter.py`

Introducing the recommendation engine

A recommendation engine is a model that can predict what a user may be interested in. When we apply this to the context of movies, for example, this becomes a movie recommendation engine. We filter items in our database by predicting how the current user might rate them. This helps us in connecting the user to the right content in our dataset. Why is this relevant? If you have a massive catalog, then the user may or may not find all the content that is relevant to them. By recommending the right content, you increase consumption. Companies such as Netflix heavily rely on recommendations to keep the user engaged.

Recommendation engines usually produce a set of recommendations using either collaborative filtering or content-based filtering. The difference between the two approaches is in the way that the recommendations are mined. Collaborative filtering builds a model from the past behavior of the current user, as well as ratings given by other users. We then use this model to predict what this user might be interested in. Content-based filtering, on the other hand, uses the characteristics of the item itself in order to recommend more items to the user. The similarity between items is the main driving force here. In this chapter, we will focus on collaborative filtering.

Building function compositions for data processing

One of the major parts of any machine learning system is the data processing pipeline. Before data is fed into the machine learning algorithm for training, we need to process it in different ways to make it suitable for that algorithm. Having a robust data processing pipeline goes a long way in building an accurate and scalable machine learning system. There are a lot of basic functionalities available, and data processing pipelines usually consist of a combination of these. Instead of calling these functions in a nested or loopy way, it's better to use the functional programming paradigm to build the combination.

Getting ready

Let's take a look at how to combine these basic functions to form a reusable function composition. In this recipe, we will create three basic functions and look at how to compose a pipeline.

How to do it...

Let's take a look at how to build function compositions for data processing:

1. Create a new Python file and add the following line (the full code is in the `function_composition.py` file that's already provided for you):

   ```
   import numpy as np
   from functools import reduce
   ```

2. Let's define a function to add 3 to each element of the array:

   ```
   def add3(input_array):
       return map(lambda x: x+3, input_array)
   ```

3. Now, let's define a second function to multiply 2 with each element of the array:

   ```
   def mul2(input_array): return map(lambda x: x*2, input_array)
   ```

4. Now, let's now define a third function to subtract 5 from each element of the array:

   ```
   def sub5(input_array):
       return map(lambda x: x-5, input_array)
   ```

5. Let's define a function composer that takes functions as input arguments and returns a composed function. This composed function is basically a function that applies all the input functions in a sequence:

```
def function_composer(*args):
    return reduce(lambda f, g: lambda x: f(g(x)), args)
```

We use the `reduce` function to combine all the input functions by successively applying the functions in a sequence.

6. We are now ready to play with this function composer. Let's define some data and a sequence of operations:

```
if __name__=='__main__':
    arr = np.array([2,5,4,7])

    print("Operation: add3(mul2(sub5(arr)))")
```

7. If we use the regular method, we apply this successively, as follows:

```
arr1 = add3(arr)
arr2 = mul2(arr1)
arr3 = sub5(arr2)
print("Output using the lengthy way:", list(arr3))
```

8. Now, let's use the function composer to achieve the same thing in a single line:

```
func_composed = function_composer(sub5, mul2, add3)
    print("Output using function composition:",
list(func_composed(arr)))
```

9. We can do the same thing in a single line with the previous method as well, but the notation becomes very nested and unreadable. Also, it is not reusable; you will have to write the whole thing again if you want to reuse this sequence of operations:

```
    print("Operation: sub5(add3(mul2(sub5(mul2(arr)))))\nOutput:",
\
            list(function_composer(mul2, sub5, mul2, add3,
sub5)(arr)))
```

10. If you run this code, you will get the following output on the Terminal:

```
Operation: add3(mul2(sub5(arr)))
Output using the lengthy way: [5, 11, 9, 15]
Output using function composition: [5, 11, 9, 15]
Operation: sub5(add3(mul2(sub5(mul2(arr)))))
Output: [-10, 2, -2, 10]
```

How it works...

In this recipe, we have created three basic functions and have learned how to compose a pipeline. To do this, the reduce() function was used. This function accepts a function and a sequence and returns a single value.

The reduce () function calculates the return value, as follows:

- To start, the function calculates the result by using the first two elements of the sequence.
- Next, the function uses the result obtained in the previous step and the next value in the sequence.
- This process is repeated until the end of the sequence.

There's more...

The three basic functions used at the beginning of the recipe make use of the map() function. This function is used to apply a function on all the elements of a specific value. As a result, a map object is returned; this object is an iterator, so we can iterate over its elements. To print this object, we have converted the map object to sequence objects as a list.

See also

- Refer to Python's official documentation of the map() function: https://docs.python.org/3/library/functions.html#map
- Refer to Python's official documentation of the reduce() function: https://docs.python.org/3/library/functools.html?highlight=reduce#functools.reduce

Building machine learning pipelines

The `scikit-learn` library is used to build machine learning pipelines. When we define the functions, the library will build a composed object that makes the data go through the entire pipeline. This pipeline can include functions, such as preprocessing, feature selection, supervised learning, and unsupervised learning.

Getting ready

In this recipe, we will be building a pipeline to take the input feature vector, select the top *k* features, and then classify them using a random forest classifier.

How to do it...

Let's take a look at how to build machine learning pipelines:

1. Create a new Python file and import the following packages (the full code is in the `pipeline.py` file that's already provided for you):

```
from sklearn.datasets import samples_generator
from sklearn.ensemble import RandomForestClassifier
from sklearn.feature_selection import SelectKBest, f_regression
from sklearn.pipeline import Pipeline
```

2. Let's generate some sample data to play with, as follows:

```
# generate sample data
X, y = samples_generator.make_classification(
        n_informative=4, n_features=20, n_redundant=0,
random_state=5)
```

This line generated 20 dimensional feature vectors because this is the default value. You can change it using the `n_features` parameter in the previous line.

3. Our first step of the pipeline is to select the *k* best features before the datapoint is used further. In this case, let's set k to 10:

```
# Feature selector
selector_k_best = SelectKBest(f_regression, k=10)
```

4. The next step is to use a random forest classifier method to classify the data:

```
# Random forest classifier
classifier = RandomForestClassifier(n_estimators=50, max_depth=4)
```

5. We are now ready to build the pipeline. The `Pipeline()` method allows us to use predefined objects to build the pipeline:

```
# Build the machine learning pipeline
pipeline_classifier = Pipeline([('selector', selector_k_best),
('rf', classifier)])
```

We can also assign names to the blocks in our pipeline. In the preceding line, we'll assign the `selector` name to our feature selector, and `rf` to our random forest classifier. You are free to use any other random names here!

6. We can also update these parameters as we go along. We can set the parameters using the names that we assigned in the previous step. For example, if we want to set `k` to 6 in the feature selector and set `n_estimators` to 25 in the random forest classifier, we can do so as demonstrated in the following code. Note that these are the variable names given in the previous step:

```
pipeline_classifier.set_params(selector__k=6,
        rf__n_estimators=25)
```

7. Let's go ahead and train the classifier:

```
# Training the classifier
pipeline_classifier.fit(X, y)
```

8. Let's now predict the output for the training data, as follows:

```
# Predict the output prediction = pipeline_classifier.predict(X)
print("Predictions:\n", prediction)
```

9. Now, let's estimate the performance of this classifier, as follows:

```
# Print score
print("Score:", pipeline_classifier.score(X, y))
```

10. We can also see which features will get selected, so let's go ahead and print them:

```
# Print the selected features chosen by the selector
features_status =
pipeline_classifier.named_steps['selector'].get_support()
selected_features = [] for count, item in
enumerate(features_status): if item:
```

```
selected_features.append(count) print("Selected features (0-
indexed):", ', '.join([str(x) for x in selected_features]))
```

11. If you run this code, you will get the following output on your Terminal:

```
Predictions:
[1 1 0 1 0 0 0 0 1 1 1 1 0 1 1 0 0 1 0 0 0 0 0 1 0 1 0 0 1 1 0 0 0
1 0 0 1
 1 1 1 1 1 1 1 0 0 1 1 0 1 1 0 1 0 1 1 0 0 0 1 1 1 0 0 1 0 0 0 1
1 0 0 1
 1 1 0 0 0 1 0 1 0 1 0 0 1 1 1 0 1 0 1 1 1 0 1 1 0 1]
Score: 0.95
Selected features (0-indexed): 0, 5, 9, 10, 11, 15
```

How it works...

The advantage of selecting the *k* best features is that we will be able to work with low-dimensional data. This is helpful in reducing the computational complexity. The way in which we select the *k* best features is based on univariate feature selection. This performs univariate statistical tests and then extracts the top performing features from the feature vector. Univariate statistical tests refer to analysis techniques where a single variable is involved.

There's more...

Once these tests are performed, each feature in the feature vector is assigned a score. Based on these scores, we select the top *k* features. We do this as a preprocessing step in our classifier pipeline. Once we extract the top *k* features, a k-dimensional feature vector is formed, and we use it as the input training data for the random forest classifier.

See also

- Refer to the official documentation of the `sklearn.ensemble.RandomForestClassifier()` function: https://scikit-learn.org/stable/modules/generated/sklearn.ensemble.RandomForestClassifier.html
- Refer to the official documentation of the `sklearn.feature_selection.SelectKBest()` function: https://scikit-learn.org/stable/modules/generated/sklearn.feature_selection.SelectKBest.html

- Refer to the official documentation of the `sklearn.pipeline.Pipeline()` function: `https://scikit-learn.org/stable/modules/generated/sklearn.pipeline.Pipeline.html`
- Refer to the official documentation of the `sklearn.feature_selection.f_regression()` function: `https://scikit-learn.org/stable/modules/generated/sklearn.feature_selection.f_regression.html`

Finding the nearest neighbors

The nearest neighbors model refers to a general class of algorithms that aim to make a decision based on the number of nearest neighbors in the training dataset. The nearest neighbors method consists of finding a predefined number of training samples that are close to the distance from the new point and predicting the label. The number of samples can be user defined, consistent, or differ from each other – it depends on the local density of points. The distance can be calculated with any metric measure – the standard Euclidean distance is the most common choice. Neighbor-based methods simply remember all training data.

Getting ready

In this recipe, we will find the nearest neighbors using a series of points on a Cartesian plane.

How to do it...

Let's see how to find the nearest neighbors, as follows:

1. Create a new Python file and import the following packages (the full code is in the `knn.py` file that's already provided for you):

   ```
   import numpy as np
   import matplotlib.pyplot as plt
   from sklearn.neighbors import NearestNeighbors
   ```

2. Let's create some sample two-dimensional data:

   ```
   # Input data
   X = np.array([[1, 1], [1, 3], [2, 2], [2.5, 5], [3, 1],
           [4, 2], [2, 3.5], [3, 3], [3.5, 4]])
   ```

3. Our goal is to find the three closest neighbors to any given point, so let's define this parameter:

```
# Number of neighbors we want to find
num_neighbors = 3
```

4. Let's define a random datapoint that's not present in the input data:

```
# Input point
input_point = [2.6, 1.7]
```

5. We need to see what this data looks like; let's plot it, as follows:

```
# Plot datapoints
plt.figure()
plt.scatter(X[:,0], X[:,1], marker='o', s=25, color='k')
```

6. In order to find the nearest neighbors, we need to define the `NearestNeighbors` object with the right parameters and train it on the input data:

```
# Build nearest neighbors model
knn = NearestNeighbors(n_neighbors=num_neighbors,
algorithm='ball_tree').fit(X)
```

7. We can now find the `distances` parameter of the input point to all the points in the input data:

```
distances, indices = knn.kneighbors(input_point)
```

8. We can print k nearest neighbors, as follows:

```
# Print the 'k' nearest neighbors
print("k nearest neighbors")
for rank, index in enumerate(indices[0][:num_neighbors]):
    print(str(rank+1) + " -->", X[index])
```

The `indices` array is already sorted, so we just need to parse it and print the datapoints.

9. Now, let's plot the input datapoint and highlight the k-nearest neighbors:

```
# Plot the nearest neighbors
plt.figure()
plt.scatter(X[:,0], X[:,1], marker='o', s=25, color='k')
plt.scatter(X[indices][0][:][:,0], X[indices][0][:][:,1],
        marker='o', s=150, color='k', facecolors='none')
plt.scatter(input_point[0], input_point[1],
        marker='x', s=150, color='k', facecolors='none')

plt.show()
```

10. If you run this code, you will get the following output on your Terminal:

```
k nearest neighbors
1 --> [2. 2.]
2 --> [3. 1.]
3 --> [3. 3.]
```

Here is the plot of the input datapoints:

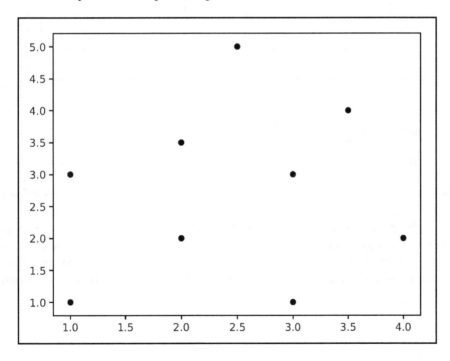

The second output diagram depicts the location of the test datapoint and the three nearest neighbors, as shown in the following screenshot:

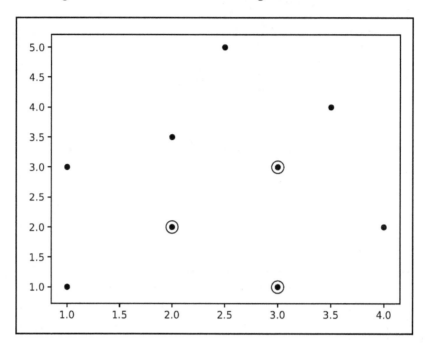

How it works...

In this recipe, we looked for the nearest neighbors by using a series of points on a Cartesian plane. To do this, the space is partitioned into regions based on the positions and characteristics of the training objects. This can be considered as the training set for the algorithm even if it is not explicitly required by the initial conditions. To calculate the distance, the objects are represented through position vectors in a multidimensional space. Finally, a point is assigned to a class if it is the most frequent of the k examples closest to the object under examination. The proximity is measured by the distance between points. Neighbors are taken from a set of objects for which the correct classification is known.

There's more...

To build the nearest neighbors model, the `BallTree` algorithm was used. `BallTree` is a data structure that organizes points in a multidimensional space. The algorithm gets its name because it partitions datapoints into a nested set of hyperspheres, known as **balls**. It's useful for a number of applications, most notably, the nearest neighbor search.

See also

- Refer to the official documentation of
  the `sklearn.neighbors.NearestNeighbors()` function: `https://scikit-learn.org/stable/modules/generated/sklearn.neighbors.NearestNeighbors.html`
- Refer to the official documentation of the `sklearn.neighbors.BallTree()` function: `https://scikit-learn.org/stable/modules/generated/sklearn.neighbors.BallTree.html#sklearn.neighbors.BallTree`
- Refer to *Nearest Neighbors* (from Texas A&M University College of Engineering): `https://www.nada.kth.se/~stefanc/DATORSEENDE_AK/l8.pdf`

Constructing a k-nearest neighbors classifier

The k-nearest neighbors algorithm is an algorithm that uses k-nearest neighbors in the training dataset to find the category of an unknown object. When we want to find the class that an unknown point belongs to, we find the k-nearest neighbors and take a majority vote.

Getting ready

In this recipe, we will create a k-nearest neighbors classifier starting from the input data that contains a series of points arranged on a Cartesian plane that shows a grouping within three areas.

How to do it...

Let's take a look at how to build a k-nearest neighbors classifier:

1. Create a new Python file and import the following packages (the full code is in the nn_classification.py file that's already provided for you):

```
import numpy as np
import matplotlib.pyplot as plt
import matplotlib.cm as cm
from sklearn import neighbors, datasets

from utilities import load_data
```

2. We will use the data_nn_classifier.txt file for input data. Let's load this input data:

```
# Load input data
input_file = 'data_nn_classifier.txt'
data = load_data(input_file)
X, y = data[:,:-1], data[:,-1].astype(np.int)
```

The first two columns contain input data, and the last column contains the labels. Hence, we separated them into X and y, as shown in the preceding code.

3. Now, let's visualize the input data, as follows:

```
# Plot input data
plt.figure()
plt.title('Input datapoints')
markers = '^sov<>hp'
mapper = np.array([markers[i] for i in y])
for i in range(X.shape[0]):
    plt.scatter(X[i, 0], X[i, 1], marker=mapper[i],
            s=50, edgecolors='black', facecolors='none')
```

We iterate through all the datapoints and use the appropriate markers to separate the classes.

4. In order to build the classifier, we need to specify the number of nearest neighbors that we want to consider. Let's define this parameter:

```
# Number of nearest neighbors to consider
num_neighbors = 10
```

5. In order to visualize the boundaries, we need to define a grid and evaluate the classifier on that grid. Let's define the step size:

```
# step size of the grid
h = 0.01
```

6. We are now ready to build the k-nearest neighbors classifier. Let's define this and train it, as follows:

```
# Create a K-Neighbours Classifier model and train it
classifier = neighbors.KNeighborsClassifier(num_neighbors,
weights='distance')
classifier.fit(X, y)
```

7. We need to create a mesh to plot the boundaries. Let's define this, as follows:

```
# Create the mesh to plot the boundaries
x_min, x_max = X[:, 0].min() - 1, X[:, 0].max() + 1
y_min, y_max = X[:, 1].min() - 1, X[:, 1].max() + 1
x_grid, y_grid = np.meshgrid(np.arange(x_min, x_max, h),
np.arange(y_min, y_max, h))
```

8. Now, let's evaluate the `classifier` output for all the points:

```
# Compute the outputs for all the points on the mesh
predicted_values = classifier.predict(np.c_[x_grid.ravel(),
y_grid.ravel()])
```

9. Let's plot it, as follows:

```
# Put the computed results on the map
predicted_values = predicted_values.reshape(x_grid.shape)
plt.figure()
plt.pcolormesh(x_grid, y_grid, predicted_values, cmap=cm.Pastel1)
```

10. Now that we have plotted the color mesh, let's overlay the training datapoints to see where they lie in relation to the boundaries:

```
# Overlay the training points on the map
for i in range(X.shape[0]):
    plt.scatter(X[i, 0], X[i, 1], marker=mapper[i],
            s=50, edgecolors='black', facecolors='none')

plt.xlim(x_grid.min(), x_grid.max())
plt.ylim(y_grid.min(), y_grid.max())
plt.title('k nearest neighbors classifier boundaries')
```

11. Now, we can consider a test datapoint and see whether the classifier performs correctly. Let's define it and plot it, as follows:

```
# Test input datapoint
test_datapoint = [4.5, 3.6]
plt.figure()
plt.title('Test datapoint')
for i in range(X.shape[0]):
    plt.scatter(X[i, 0], X[i, 1], marker=mapper[i],
            s=50, edgecolors='black', facecolors='none')

plt.scatter(test_datapoint[0], test_datapoint[1], marker='x',
        linewidth=3, s=200, facecolors='black')
```

12. We need to extract the k-nearest neighbors classifier using the following model:

```
# Extract k nearest neighbors
dist, indices = classifier.kneighbors(test_datapoint)
```

13. Let's plot the k-nearest neighbors classifier and highlight it:

```
# Plot k nearest neighbors
plt.figure()
plt.title('k nearest neighbors')

for i in indices:
    plt.scatter(X[i, 0], X[i, 1], marker='o',
            linewidth=3, s=100, facecolors='black')

plt.scatter(test_datapoint[0], test_datapoint[1], marker='x',
        linewidth=3, s=200, facecolors='black')

for i in range(X.shape[0]):
    plt.scatter(X[i, 0], X[i, 1], marker=mapper[i],
            s=50, edgecolors='black', facecolors='none')

plt.show()
```

14. Now, let's print the `classifier` output on the Terminal:

```
print("Predicted output:", classifier.predict(test_datapoint)[0])
```

The following result is printed:

```
Predicted output: 2
```

Furthermore, a series of diagrams are shown. The first output diagram depicts the distribution of the input datapoints:

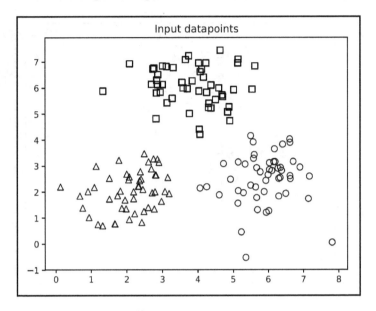

The second output diagram depicts the boundaries obtained using the `k-nearest neighbors` classifier:

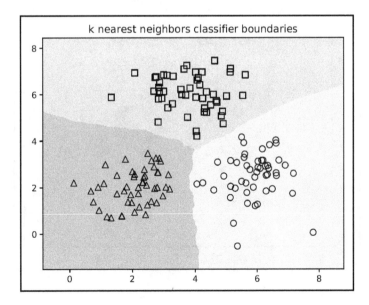

The third output diagram depicts the location of the test datapoint:

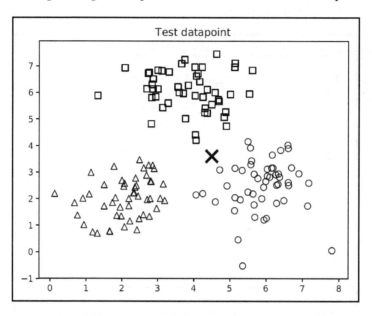

The fourth output diagram depicts the location of the 10 nearest neighbors:

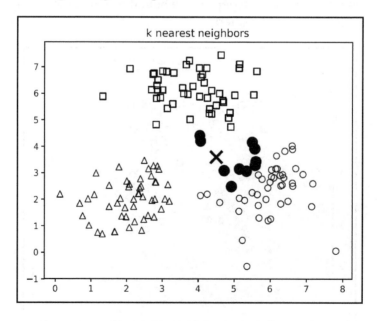

How it works...

The k-nearest neighbors classifier stores all the available datapoints and classifies new datapoints based on a similarity metric. This similarity metric usually appears in the form of a distance function. This algorithm is a nonparametric technique, which means that it doesn't need to find out any underlying parameters before formulation. All we need to do is select a value of k that works for us.

Once we find out the k-nearest neighbors classifier, we take a majority vote. A new datapoint is classified by this majority vote of the k-nearest neighbors classifier. This datapoint is assigned to the class that is most common among its k-nearest neighbors. If we set the value of k to 1, then this simply becomes a case of a nearest neighbor classifier where we just assign the datapoint to the class of its nearest neighbor in the training dataset.

There's more...

The k-nearest neighbor algorithm is based on the concept of classifying an unknown sample by considering the class of k samples closest to the training set. The new sample will be assigned to the class that most of the k nearest samples belong to. The choice of k is, therefore, very important for the sample to be assigned to the correct class. If k is too small, the classification may be sensitive to noise; if k is too large, the classification may be computationally expensive, and the neighborhood may include samples belonging to other classes.

See also

- Refer to *kNN classifiers* (from the Faculty of Humanities, University of Amsterdam): `http://www.fon.hum.uva.nl/praat/manual/kNN_classifiers_1__What_is_a_kNN_classifier_.html`
- Refer to the official documentation of the `sklearn.neighbors()` module: `https://scikit-learn.org/stable/modules/classes.html#module-sklearn.neighbors`
- Refer to *Nearest neighbor methods* (from New York University): `http://people.csail.mit.edu/dsontag/courses/ml13/slides/lecture11.pdf`
- Refer to the official documentation of the `sklearn.neighbors.KNeighborsClassifier()` function: `https://scikit-learn.org/stable/modules/generated/sklearn.neighbors.KNeighborsClassifier.html`

Constructing a k-nearest neighbors regressor

We learned how to use the k-nearest neighbors algorithm to build a classifier. The good thing is that we can also use this algorithm as a regressor. The object's output is represented by its property value, which is the average of the values of its k-nearest neighbors.

Getting ready

In this recipe, we will see how to use the k-nearest neighbors algorithm to build a regressor.

How to do it...

Let's take a look at how to build a k-nearest neighbors regressor:

1. Create a new Python file and import the following packages (the full code is in the nn_regression.py file that's already provided for you):

```
import numpy as np
import matplotlib.pyplot as plt
from sklearn import neighbors
```

2. Let's generate some sample Gaussian-distributed data:

```
# Generate sample data
amplitude = 10
num_points = 100
X = amplitude * np.random.rand(num_points, 1) - 0.5 * amplitude
```

3. We need to add some noise to the data to introduce some randomness into it. The goal of adding noise is to see whether our algorithm can get past it and still function in a robust way:

```
# Compute target and add noise
y = np.sinc(X).ravel()
y += 0.2 * (0.5 - np.random.rand(y.size))
```

4. Now, let's visualize it, as follows:

```
# Plot input data
plt.figure()
plt.scatter(X, y, s=40, c='k', facecolors='none')
plt.title('Input data')
```

5. We just generated some data and evaluated a continuous-valued function on all these points. Let's define a denser grid of points:

```
# Create the 1D grid with 10 times the density of the input data
x_values = np.linspace(-0.5*amplitude, 0.5*amplitude,
10*num_points)[:, np.newaxis]
```

We defined this denser grid because we want to evaluate our regressor on all of these points and look at how well it approximates our function.

6. Let's now define the number of nearest neighbors that we want to consider:

```
# Number of neighbors to consider
n_neighbors = 8
```

7. Let's initialize and train the k-nearest neighbors regressor using the parameters that we defined earlier:

```
# Define and train the regressor
knn_regressor = neighbors.KNeighborsRegressor(n_neighbors,
weights='distance')
y_values = knn_regressor.fit(X, y).predict(x_values)
```

8. Let's see how the regressor performs by overlapping the input and output data on top of each other:

```
plt.figure()
plt.scatter(X, y, s=40, c='k', facecolors='none', label='input
data')
plt.plot(x_values, y_values, c='k', linestyle='--',
label='predicted values')
plt.xlim(X.min() - 1, X.max() + 1)
plt.ylim(y.min() - 0.2, y.max() + 0.2)
plt.axis('tight')
plt.legend()
plt.title('K Nearest Neighbors Regressor')

plt.show()
```

9. If you run this code, the first diagram depicts the input datapoints:

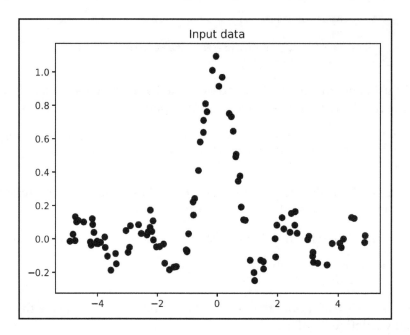

The second diagram depicts the values predicted by the regressor:

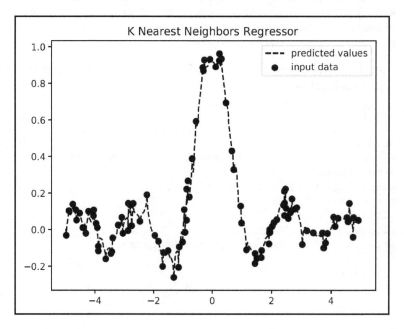

How it works...

The goal of a regressor is to predict continuous valued outputs. We don't have a fixed number of output categories in this case. We just have a set of real-valued output values, and we want our regressor to predict the output values for unknown datapoints. In this case, we used a `sinc` function to demonstrate the k-nearest neighbors regressor. This is also referred to as the **cardinal sine function**. A `sinc` function is defined by the following equation:

$$sinc(x) = \begin{cases} sin(x)/x & when\ x \neq 0 \\ 1 & when\ x = 0 \end{cases}$$

When x is 0, *sin(x)/x* takes the indeterminate form of *0/0*. Hence, we have to compute the limit of this function as x tends to be 0. We used a set of values for training, and we defined a denser grid for testing. As you can see in the preceding diagram, the output curve is close to the training outputs.

There's more...

The main advantages of this method are that it does not require learning or the construction of a model; it can adapt its decision boundaries in an arbitrary way, producing a representation of the most flexible model; and it also guarantees the possibility of increasing the training set. However, this algorithm also has many drawbacks, including being susceptible to data noise, being sensitive to the presence of irrelevant features, and requiring a similarity measure to evaluate proximity.

See also

- Refer to the official documentation of the `sklearn.neighbors.KNeighborsRegressor()` function: `https://scikit-learn.org/stable/modules/generated/sklearn.neighbors.KNeighborsRegressor.html`
- Refer to *Regression Analysis with R*, Giuseppe Ciaburro, Packt Publishing
- Refer to *Comparison of Linear Regression with K-Nearest Neighbors* (from Duke University): `http://www2.stat.duke.edu/~rcs46/lectures_2017/03-lr/03-knn.pdf`

Computing the Euclidean distance score

Now that we have sufficient background in machine learning pipelines and the nearest neighbors classifier, let's start the discussion on recommendation engines. In order to build a recommendation engine, we need to define a similarity metric so that we can find users in the database who are similar to a given user. The Euclidean distance score is one such metric that we can use to compute the distance between datapoints. We will shift the discussion toward movie recommendation engines.

Getting ready

In this recipe, we will see how to compute the Euclidean score between two users.

How to do it...

Let's see how to compute the Euclidean distance score:

1. Create a new Python file and import the following packages (the full code is in the `euclidean_score.py` file that's already provided for you):

```
import json
import numpy as np
```

2. We will now define a function to compute the Euclidean score between two users. The first step is to check whether the users are present in the database:

```
# Returns the Euclidean distance score between user1 and user2
def euclidean_score(dataset, user1, user2):
    if user1 not in dataset:
        raise TypeError('User ' + user1 + ' not present in the
dataset')

    if user2 not in dataset:
        raise TypeError('User ' + user2 + ' not present in the
dataset')
```

3. In order to compute the score, we need to extract the movies that both the users rated:

```
# Movies rated by both user1 and user2
rated_by_both = {}

for item in dataset[user1]:
```

```
        if item in dataset[user2]:
            rated_by_both[item] = 1
```

4. If there are no common movies, then there is no similarity between the users (or at least, we cannot compute it given the ratings in the database):

```
# If there are no common movies, the score is 0
if len(rated_by_both) == 0:
    return 0
```

5. For each of the common ratings, we just compute the square root of the sum of squared differences and normalize it, so that the score is between 0 and 1:

```
        squared_differences = []

        for item in dataset[user1]:
            if item in dataset[user2]:
    squared_differences.append(np.square(dataset[user1][item] -
    dataset[user2][item]))
            return 1 / (1 + np.sqrt(np.sum(squared_differences)))
```

If the ratings are similar, then the sum of squared differences will be very low. Hence, the score will become high, which is what we want from this metric.

6. We will use the `movie_ratings.json` file as our data file. Let's load it, as follows:

```
    if __name__=='__main__':
        data_file = 'movie_ratings.json'

        with open(data_file, 'r') as f:
            data = json.loads(f.read())
```

7. Let's consider two random users and compute the Euclidean distance score:

```
user1 = 'John Carson'
user2 = 'Michelle Peterson'

print("Euclidean score:")
print(euclidean_score(data, user1, user2))
```

8. When you run this code, you will see the following Euclidean distance score printed on the Terminal:

```
0.29429805508554946
```

How it works...

In most cases, the distance used in the nearest neighbors algorithm is defined as the Euclidean distance between two
points, calculated according to the following formula:

$$distance = \sqrt{\sum_{i=0}^{n}(x_i - y_i)^2}$$

On a bidimensional plane, the Euclidean distance represents the minimum distance between two points, hence the straight line connecting two points. This distance is calculated as the square root of the sum of the squared difference between the elements of two vectors, as indicated in the previous formula.

There's more...

There are other types of metrics for calculating distances. All of these types generally try to avoid the square roots, since they are expensive in computational terms, and are the source of several errors. Metrics include **Minkowski**, **Manhattan**, and the **cosine** distance.

See also

- Refer to *MATLAB for Machine Learning*, Giuseppe Ciaburro, Packt Publishing
- Refer to *Similarities, Distances, and Manifold Learning* (from The University of York): http://simbad-fp7.eu/images/tutorial/02-ECCV2012Tutorial.pdf
- Refer to *The Euclidean distance* (from Wikipedia): https://en.wikipedia.org/wiki/Euclidean_distance

Computing the Pearson correlation score

The Euclidean distance score is a good metric, but it has some shortcomings. Hence, the Pearson correlation score is frequently used in recommendation engines. The Pearson correlation score between two statistical variables is an index that expresses a possible linear relation between them. It measures the tendency of two numerical variables to vary simultaneously.

Getting ready

In this recipe, we will see how to compute the Pearson correlation score.

How to do it...

Let's take a look at how to compute the Pearson correlation score:

1. Create a new Python file and import the following packages (the full code is in the `pearson_score.py` file that's already provided for you):

```
import json
import numpy as np
```

2. We will define a function to compute the Pearson correlation score between two users in the database. Our first step is to confirm that these users exist in the database:

```
# Returns the Pearson correlation score between user1 and user2
def pearson_score(dataset, user1, user2):
    if user1 not in dataset:
        raise TypeError('User ' + user1 + ' not present in the
dataset')

    if user2 not in dataset:
        raise TypeError('User ' + user2 + ' not present in the
dataset')
```

3. The next step is to get the movies that both of these users rated:

```
# Movies rated by both user1 and user2
rated_by_both = {}

for item in dataset[user1]:
    if item in dataset[user2]:
        rated_by_both[item] = 1

num_ratings = len(rated_by_both)
```

4. If there are no common movies, then there is no discernible similarity between these users; hence, we return 0:

```
# If there are no common movies, the score is 0
if num_ratings == 0:
    return 0
```

5. We need to compute the sum of squared values of common movie ratings:

```
# Compute the sum of ratings of all the common preferences
user1_sum = np.sum([dataset[user1][item] for item in rated_by_both])
user2_sum = np.sum([dataset[user2][item] for item in rated_by_both])
```

6. Now, let's compute the sum of squared ratings of all the common movie ratings:

```
# Compute the sum of squared ratings of all the common
preferences
    user1_squared_sum = np.sum([np.square(dataset[user1][item]) for
item in rated_by_both])
    user2_squared_sum = np.sum([np.square(dataset[user2][item]) for
item in rated_by_both])
```

7. Let's now compute the sum of the products:

```
# Compute the sum of products of the common ratings
    product_sum = np.sum([dataset[user1][item] *
dataset[user2][item] for item in rated_by_both])
```

8. We are now ready to compute the various elements that we require to calculate the Pearson correlation score:

```
# Compute the Pearson correlation
Sxy = product_sum - (user1_sum * user2_sum / num_ratings)
Sxx = user1_squared_sum - np.square(user1_sum) / num_ratings
Syy = user2_squared_sum - np.square(user2_sum) / num_ratings
```

9. We need to take care of the case where the denominator becomes 0:

```
if Sxx * Syy == 0:
    return 0
```

10. If everything is good, we return the Pearson correlation score, as follows:

```
return Sxy / np.sqrt(Sxx * Syy)
```

11. Let's now define the main function and compute the Pearson correlation score between two users:

```
if __name__=='__main__':
    data_file = 'movie_ratings.json'

    with open(data_file, 'r') as f:
        data = json.loads(f.read())

    user1 = 'John Carson'
```

```
user2 = 'Michelle Peterson'

print("Pearson score:")
print(pearson_score(data, user1, user2))
```

12. If you run this code, you will see the following Pearson correlation score printed on the Terminal:

```
Pearson score:
0.39605901719066977
```

How it works...

The *r* correlation coefficient of Pearson measures the correlation between variables at intervals or equivalent ratios. It is given by the sum of the products of the standardized scores of the two variables ($z_x * z_y$) divided by the number of subjects (or observations), as follows:

$$r = \frac{\sum z_x * z_y}{N}$$

This coefficient can assume values ranging between -1.00 (between the two variables, there is a perfect negative correlation) and + 1.00 (between the two variables, there is a perfect positive correlation). A correlation of 0 indicates that there is no relationship between the two variables.

There's more...

It is necessary to remember that Pearson's formula is related to a linear relationship, and therefore, all the different forms of relationship can produce anomalous results.

See also

- Refer to *Regression Analysis with R*, Giuseppe Ciaburro, Packt Publishing
- Refer to *The Pearson Correlation* (from Ken State University): https://libguides.library.kent.edu/spss/pearsoncorr

Finding similar users in the dataset

One of the most important tasks in building a recommendation engine is finding users who are similar. This is useful in creating the recommendations that will be provided to these users.

Getting ready

In this recipe, we will see how to build a model to find users who are similar.

How to do it...

Let's take a look at how to find similar users in the dataset:

1. Create a new Python file and import the following packages (the full code is in the `find_similar_users.py` file that's already provided for you):

```
import json
import numpy as np

from pearson_score import pearson_score
```

2. Let's define a function to find users who are similar to the input user. It takes three input arguments: the database, the input user, and the number of similar users that we are looking for. Our first step is to check whether the user is present in the database. If the user exists, we need to compute the Pearson correlation score between this user and all the other users in the database:

```
# Finds a specified number of users who are similar to the input
user
def find_similar_users(dataset, user, num_users):
    if user not in dataset:
        raise TypeError('User ' + user + ' not present in the
dataset')

    # Compute Pearson scores for all the users
    scores = np.array([[x, pearson_score(dataset, user, x)] for x
in dataset if user != x])
```

3. The next step is to sort these scores in descending order:

```
# Sort the scores based on second column
scores_sorted = np.argsort(scores[:, 1])
```

```
# Sort the scores in decreasing order (highest score first)
scored_sorted_dec = scores_sorted[::-1]
```

4. Let's extract the *k* top scores and then return them:

```
# Extract top 'k' indices
top_k = scored_sorted_dec[0:num_users]

return scores[top_k]
```

5. Let's now define the main function and load the input database:

```
if __name__=='__main__':
    data_file = 'movie_ratings.json'

    with open(data_file, 'r') as f:
        data = json.loads(f.read())
```

6. We want to find three similar users to, `John Carson`, for example. We do this by using the following steps:

```
user = 'John Carson'
print("Users similar to " + user + ":\n")
similar_users = find_similar_users(data, user, 3)
print("User\t\t\tSimilarity score\n")
for item in similar_users:
    print(item[0], '\t\t', round(float(item[1]), 2))
```

7. If you run this code, you will see the following printed on your Terminal:

```
Users similar to John Carson:

User                Similarity score
Michael Henry             0.99
Alex Roberts              0.75
Melissa Jones             0.59
```

How it works...

In this recipe, we are looking for similar users to the input user. Given the database, the input user, and the number of similar users that we are looking for, we first check whether the user is present in the database. If the user exists, the Pearson correlation score between this user and all the other users in the database is computed.

There's more...

To calculate the Pearson correlation score, the `pearson_score()` function was used. This function was defined in the previous *Computing the Pearson correlation score* recipe.

See also

- Refer to *Pearson's Correlation Coefficient* (from the University of the West of England): `http://learntech.uwe.ac.uk/da/default.aspx?pageid=1442`
- Refer to *Pearson correlation coefficient* (from Wikipedia): `https://en.wikipedia.org/wiki/Pearson_correlation_coefficient`

Generating movie recommendations

In this recipe, we will generate movie recommendations.

Getting ready

In this recipe, we will use all the functionality that we built in the previous recipes to build a movie recommendation engine. Let's take a look at how to build it.

How to do it...

Let's take a look at how to generate movie recommendations:

1. Create a new Python file and import the following packages (the full code is in the `movie_recommendations.py` file that's already provided for you):

```
import json
import numpy as np

from pearson_score import pearson_score
```

2. We will define a function to generate movie recommendations for a given user. The first step is to check whether the user exists in the dataset:

```
# Generate recommendations for a given user
def generate_recommendations(dataset, user):
    if user not in dataset:
```

```
                raise TypeError('User ' + user + ' not present in the
        dataset')
```

3. Let's now compute the Pearson score of this user with all the other users in the dataset:

```
total_scores = {}
similarity_sums = {}

for u in [x for x in dataset if x != user]:
    similarity_score = pearson_score(dataset, user, u)

    if similarity_score <= 0:
        continue
```

4. We need to find the movies that haven't been rated by this user:

```
        for item in [x for x in dataset[u] if x not in
    dataset[user] or dataset[user][x] == 0]:
            total_scores.update({item: dataset[u][item] *
    similarity_score})
            similarity_sums.update({item: similarity_score})
```

5. If the user has watched every single movie in the database, then we cannot recommend anything to this user. Let's take care of this condition:

```
if len(total_scores) == 0:
    return ['No recommendations possible']
```

6. We now have a list of these scores. Let's create a normalized list of movie ranks:

```
# Create the normalized list
movie_ranks = np.array([[total/similarity_sums[item], item]
        for item, total in total_scores.items()])
```

7. We need to sort the list in descending order based on the score:

```
# Sort in decreasing order based on the first column
movie_ranks = movie_ranks[np.argsort(movie_ranks[:, 0])[::-1]]
```

8. We are finally ready to extract the movie recommendations:

```
# Extract the recommended movies
recommendations = [movie for _, movie in movie_ranks]

return recommendations
```

9. Now, let's define the `main` function and load the dataset:

```
if __name__=='__main__':
    data_file = 'movie_ratings.json'

    with open(data_file, 'r') as f:
        data = json.loads(f.read())
```

10. Let's now generate recommendations for `Michael Henry`, as follows:

```
user = 'Michael Henry'
print("Recommendations for " + user + ":")
movies = generate_recommendations(data, user)
for i, movie in enumerate(movies):
    print(str(i+1) + '. ' + movie)
```

11. The `John Carson` user has watched all the movies. Therefore, if we try to generate recommendations for him, it should display 0 recommendations. Let's see whether this happens, as follows:

```
user = 'John Carson'
print("Recommendations for " + user + ":")
movies = generate_recommendations(data, user)
for i, movie in enumerate(movies):
    print(str(i+1) + '. ' + movie)
```

12. If you run this code, you will see the following output on your Terminal:

```
Recommendations for Michael Henry:
1. Jerry Maguire
2. Inception
3. Anger Management
Recommendations for John Carson:
1. No recommendations possible
```

How it works...

In this recipe, we have built a movie recommendation engine. To generate recommendations for a given user, the following steps are performed:

1. First, we check whether the user is present in the database
2. Then, we calculate the Person correlation score
3. We then create the normalized list

4. Then, we sort this list in decreasing order based on the first column
5. Finally, we extract the recommended movies

There's more...

To build a movie recommendation engine, the `pearson_score()` function was used. This function was defined in the previous *Computing the Pearson correlation score* recipe.

See also

- Refer to *Introduction to Correlation and Regression Analysis* (from Boston University School of Public Health): `http://sphweb.bumc.bu.edu/otlt/mph-modules/bs/bs704_multivariable/bs704_multivariable5.html`
- Refer to *Pearson Correlation Coefficient r* (From Penn State University): `https://newonlinecourses.science.psu.edu/stat501/node/256/`
- Refer to *Correlation and Causation* (from the Australian Bureau of Statistics): `http://www.abs.gov.au/websitedbs/a3121120.nsf/home/statistical+language+-+correlation+and+causation`

Implementing ranking algorithms

Learning to rank (**LTR**) is a method that is used in the construction of classification models for information retrieval systems. The training data consists of lists of articles with an induced partial order that gives a numerical or ordinal score, or a binary judgment for each article. The purpose of the model is to order the elements into new lists according to the scores that take into account the judgments obtained from the articles.

Getting ready

In this recipe, we will use the `pyltr` package, which is a Python LTR toolkit with ranking models, evaluation metrics, and data-wrangling helpers.

How to do it...

Let's take a look at how to implement ranking algorithms:

1. Create a new Python file and import the following package (the full code is in the `LambdaMARTModel.py` file that's already provided for you):

   ```
   import pyltr
   ```

2. We will load the data contained in the Letor dataset that's already provided for you (`train.txt`, `vali.txt`, and `test.txt`):

   ```
   with open('train.txt') as trainfile, \
           open('vali.txt') as valifile, \
           open('test.txt') as testfile:
       TrainX, Trainy, Trainqids, _ =
   pyltr.data.letor.read_dataset(trainfile)
       ValX, Valy, Valqids, _ =
   pyltr.data.letor.read_dataset(valifile)
       TestX, Testy, Testqids, _ =
   pyltr.data.letor.read_dataset(testfile)
       metric = pyltr.metrics.NDCG(k=10)
   ```

3. Let's now perform a validation of the data:

   ```
   monitor = pyltr.models.monitors.ValidationMonitor(
           ValX, Valy, Valqids, metric=metric, stop_after=250)
   ```

4. We will build the model, as follows:

   ```
   model = pyltr.models.LambdaMART(
       metric=metric,
       n_estimators=1000,
       learning_rate=0.02,
       max_features=0.5,
       query_subsample=0.5,
       max_leaf_nodes=10,
       min_samples_leaf=64,
       verbose=1,
   )
   ```

5. Now, we can fit the model using the text data:

   ```
   model.fit(TestX, Testy, Testqids, monitor=monitor)
   ```

6. Next, we can predict the data, as follows:

   ```
   Testpred = model.predict(TestX)
   ```

7. Finally, we print the results, as follows:

```
print('Random ranking:', metric.calc_mean_random(Testqids, Testy))
print('Our model:', metric.calc_mean(Testqids, Testy, Testpred))
```

The following results are printed:

```
Early termination at iteration 480
Random ranking: 0.27258472902087394
Our model: 0.5487673789992693
```

How it works...

LambdaMART is the enhanced tree version of LambdaRank, which is, in turn, based on RankNet. RankNet, LambdaRank, and LambdaMART are algorithms that are used to solve classification problems in many contexts. RankNet, LambdaRank, and LambdaMART have been developed by Chris Burges and his group at Microsoft Research. RankNet was the first one to be developed, followed by LambdaRank, and then LambdaMART.

RankNet is based on the use of neural networks, but the underlying model is not limited to neural networks alone. The cost function for RankNet aims to minimize the number of reversals in the ranking. RankNet optimizes the cost function using the stochastic gradient descent.

The researchers found that during the RankNet training procedure, the costs are not required, only the gradients (λ) of the cost compared to the model score. You can think of these gradients as small arrows attached to each document in the classified list, indicating the direction in which we could move those documents. LambdaRank is based on this assumption.

There's more...

Finally, LambdaMART combines the methods contained in LambdaRank and those present in **multiple regression additive trees** (**MART**). While MART uses decision trees with enhanced gradient for forecasting, LambdaMART uses enhanced gradient decision trees using a cost function derived from LambdaRank to solve a ranking task. LambdaMART proved to be more efficient than LambdaRank and the original RankNet.

See also

- Refer to *Learning to Rank using Gradient Descent*: `https://www.microsoft.com/en-us/research/wp-content/uploads/2005/08/icml_ranking.pdf`
- Refer to the Python LTR toolkit: `https://github.com/jma127/pyltr`
- Refer to *LETOR: Learning to Rank for Information Retrieval*: `https://www.microsoft.com/en-us/research/project/letor-learning-rank-information-retrieval/?from=http%3A%2F%2Fresearch.microsoft.com%2Fen-us%2Fum%2Fbeijing%2Fprojects%2Fletor%2F`

Building a filtering model using TensorFlow

Collaborative filtering refers to a class of tools and mechanisms that allow the retrieval of predictive information regarding the interests of a given set of users starting from a large and yet undifferentiated mass of knowledge. Collaborative filtering is widely used in the context of recommendation systems. A well-known category of collaborative algorithms is matrix factorization.

The fundamental assumption behind the concept of collaborative filtering is that every single user who has shown a certain set of preferences will continue to show them in the future. A popular example of collaborative filtering can be a system of suggested movies starting from a set of basic knowledge of the tastes and preferences of a given user. It should be noted that although this information is referring to a single user, they derive this from the knowledge that has been processed throughout the whole system of users.

Getting ready

In this recipe, we will see how to build a collaborative filtering model for personalized recommendations using TensorFlow. We will use the MovieLens 1M dataset, which contains 1 million ratings from approximately 6,000 users for approximately 4,000 movies.

How to do it...

Let's take a look at how to build a filtering model using TensorFlow:

1. Create a new Python file and import the following packages (the full code is in the `TensorFilter.py` file that's already provided for you):

```
import numpy as np
import pandas as pd
import tensorflow as tf
```

2. We will load the data contained in the MovieLens 1M dataset that's already provided for you (`ratings.csv`):

```
Data = pd.read_csv('ratings.csv', sep=';', names=['user', 'item',
'rating', 'timestamp'], header=None)

Data = Data.iloc[:,0:3]

NumItems = Data.item.nunique()
NumUsers = Data.user.nunique()

print('Item: ', NumItems)
print('Users: ', NumUsers)
```

The following returns are returned:

```
Item: 3706
Users: 6040
```

3. Now, let's perform data scaling, as follows:

```
from sklearn.preprocessing import MinMaxScaler
scaler = MinMaxScaler()
Data['rating'] = Data['rating'].values.astype(float)
DataScaled =
pd.DataFrame(scaler.fit_transform(Data['rating'].values.reshape(-1,
1)))
Data['rating'] = DataScaled
```

4. We will build the user item matrix, as follows:

```
UserItemMatrix = Data.pivot(index='user', columns='item',
values='rating')
UserItemMatrix.fillna(0, inplace=True)

Users = UserItemMatrix.index.tolist()
Items = UserItemMatrix.columns.tolist()

UserItemMatrix = UserItemMatrix.as_matrix()
```

5. Now, we can set some network parameters, as follows:

```
NumInput = NumItems
NumHidden1 = 10
NumHidden2 = 5
```

6. Now, we will initialize the TensorFlow placeholder. Then, `weights` and `biases` are randomly initialized:

```
X = tf.placeholder(tf.float64, [None, NumInput])

weights = {
    'EncoderH1': tf.Variable(tf.random_normal([NumInput,
NumHidden1], dtype=tf.float64)),
    'EncoderH2': tf.Variable(tf.random_normal([NumHidden1,
NumHidden2], dtype=tf.float64)),
    'DecoderH1': tf.Variable(tf.random_normal([NumHidden2,
NumHidden1], dtype=tf.float64)),
    'DecoderH2': tf.Variable(tf.random_normal([NumHidden1,
NumInput], dtype=tf.float64)),
}

biases = {
    'EncoderB1': tf.Variable(tf.random_normal([NumHidden1],
dtype=tf.float64)),
    'EncoderB2': tf.Variable(tf.random_normal([NumHidden2],
dtype=tf.float64)),
    'DecoderB1': tf.Variable(tf.random_normal([NumHidden1],
dtype=tf.float64)),
    'DecoderB2': tf.Variable(tf.random_normal([NumInput],
dtype=tf.float64)),
}
```

7. Now, we can build the encoder and decoder model, as follows:

```
def encoder(x):
    Layer1 = tf.nn.sigmoid(tf.add(tf.matmul(x,
```

```
weights['EncoderH1']), biases['EncoderB1']))
    Layer2 = tf.nn.sigmoid(tf.add(tf.matmul(Layer1,
weights['EncoderH2']), biases['EncoderB2']))
    return Layer2

def decoder(x):
    Layer1 = tf.nn.sigmoid(tf.add(tf.matmul(x,
weights['DecoderH1']), biases['DecoderB1']))
    Layer2 = tf.nn.sigmoid(tf.add(tf.matmul(Layer1,
weights['DecoderH2']), biases['DecoderB2']))
    return Layer2
```

8. We will construct the model and predict the value, as follows:

```
EncoderOp = encoder(X)
DecoderOp = decoder(EncoderOp)

YPred = DecoderOp

YTrue = X
```

9. We will now define `loss` and `optimizer`, and minimize the squared error and the evaluation metrics:

```
loss = tf.losses.mean_squared_error(YTrue, YPred)
Optimizer = tf.train.RMSPropOptimizer(0.03).minimize(loss)
EvalX = tf.placeholder(tf.int32, )
EvalY = tf.placeholder(tf.int32, )
Pre, PreOp = tf.metrics.precision(labels=EvalX, predictions=EvalY)
```

10. Let's now initialize the variables, as follows:

```
Init = tf.global_variables_initializer()
LocalInit = tf.local_variables_initializer()
PredData = pd.DataFrame()
```

11. Finally, we can start to train our model:

```
with tf.Session() as session:
    Epochs = 120
    BatchSize = 200

    session.run(Init)
    session.run(LocalInit)

    NumBatches = int(UserItemMatrix.shape[0] / BatchSize)
    UserItemMatrix = np.array_split(UserItemMatrix, NumBatches)
    for i in range(Epochs):
```

```
        AvgCost = 0

        for batch in UserItemMatrix:
            _, l = session.run([Optimizer, loss], feed_dict={X:
batch})
            AvgCost += l

        AvgCost /= NumBatches

        print("Epoch: {} Loss: {}".format(i + 1, AvgCost))

    UserItemMatrix = np.concatenate(UserItemMatrix, axis=0)

    Preds = session.run(DecoderOp, feed_dict={X: UserItemMatrix})

    PredData = PredData.append(pd.DataFrame(Preds))

    PredData = PredData.stack().reset_index(name='rating')
    PredData.columns = ['user', 'item', 'rating']
    PredData['user'] = PredData['user'].map(lambda value:
Users[value])
    PredData['item'] = PredData['item'].map(lambda value:
Items[value])
    keys = ['user', 'item']
    Index1 = PredData.set_index(keys).index
    Index2 = Data.set_index(keys).index

    TopTenRanked = PredData[~Index1.isin(Index2)]
    TopTenRanked = TopTenRanked.sort_values(['user', 'rating'],
ascending=[True, False])
    TopTenRanked = TopTenRanked.groupby('user').head(10)
    print(TopTenRanked.head(n=10))
```

The following results are returned:

```
     user item rating
2651 1 2858 0.295800
1106 1 1196 0.278715
1120 1 1210 0.251717
2203 1 2396 0.227491
1108 1 1198 0.213989
579  1 593  0.201507
802  1 858  0.196411
2374 1 2571 0.195712
309  1 318  0.191919
2785 1 2997 0.188679
```

These are the top 10 results for the 1 user.

How it works...

The collaborative filter approach focuses on finding users who have made similar judgments to the same objects, thus creating a link between users, to whom will be suggested objects that one of the two has reviewed in a positive way, or simply with which they have interacted. In this way, we look for associations between users, and no longer between objects.

There's more...

The user item matrix represents a user's preferences for an object, but, if read by columns, highlights who a certain movie was liked or disliked by. In this way, you can see how a similarity between two objects can also be expressed without the object matrix, simply by observing that the films that are liked by the same people are probably similar in some way.

See also

- Refer to *Collaborative filtering* (from The University of Texas at Dallas): https://www.utdallas.edu/~nrr150130/cs6375/2015fa/lects/Lecture_23_CF.pdf
- Refer to *Matrix Factorization and Collaborative Filtering* (from Carnegie Mellon University): https://www.cs.cmu.edu/~mgormley/courses/10601-s17/slides/lecture25-mf.pdf
- Refer to the *TensorFlow Tutorial* (from Stanford University): https://cs224d.stanford.edu/lectures/CS224d-Lecture7.pdf

7
Analyzing Text Data

In this chapter, we will cover the following recipes:

- Preprocessing data using tokenization
- Stemming text data
- Converting text to its base form using lemmatization
- Dividing text using chunking
- Building a bag-of-words model
- Building a text classifier
- Identifying the gender of a name
- Analyzing the sentiment of a sentence
- Identifying patterns in text using topic modeling
- Parts of speech tagging with spaCy
- Word2Vec using gensim
- Shallow learning for spam detection

Technical requirements

To complete the recipes in this chapter, you will need the following files (available on GitHub):

- `tokenizer.py`
- `stemmer.py`
- `lemmatizer.py`
- `chunking.py`
- `bag_of_words.py`
- `tfidf.py`
- `gender_identification.py`

- `sentiment_analysis.py`
- `topic_modeling.py`
- `data_topic_modeling.txt`
- `PosTagging.py`
- `GensimWord2Vec.py`
- `LogiTextClassifier.py`
- `spam.csv`

Introduction

Text analysis and **natural language processing** (**NLP**) are an integral part of modern artificial intelligence systems. Computers are good at understanding rigidly structured data with limited variety. However, when we deal with unstructured, free-form text, things begin to get difficult. Developing NLP applications is challenging because computers have a hard time understanding the underlying concepts. There are also many subtle variations to the way that we communicate things. These can be in the form of dialects, context, slang, and so on.

In order to solve this problem, NLP applications are developed based on machine learning. These algorithms detect patterns in text data so that we can extract insights from them. Artificial intelligence companies make heavy use of NLP and text analysis in order to deliver relevant results. Some of the most common applications of NLP include search engines, sentiment analysis, topic modeling, part-of-speech tagging, and entity recognition. The goal of NLP is to develop a set of algorithms so that we can interact with computers in plain English. If we can achieve this, then we won't need programming languages to instruct computers on what they should do. In this chapter, we will look at a few recipes that focus on text analysis and how we can extract meaningful information from text data.

We will use a Python package called **Natural Language Toolkit** (**NLTK**) heavily in this chapter. Make sure that you install this before you proceed:

- You can find the installation steps at `http://www.nltk.org/install.html`.
- You will also need to install `NLTK Data`, which contains many corpora and trained models. This is an integral part of text analysis! You can find the installation steps at `http://www.nltk.org/data.html`.

Preprocessing data using tokenization

Tokenization is the process of dividing text into a set of meaningful pieces. These pieces are called **tokens**. For example, we can divide a chunk of text into words, or we can divide it into sentences. Depending on the task at hand, we can define our own conditions to divide the input text into meaningful tokens. Let's take a look at how to do this.

Getting ready

Tokenization is the first step in the computational analysis of the text and involves dividing the sequences of characters into minimal units of analysis called **tokens**. Tokens include various categories of text parts (words, punctuation, numbers, and so on), and can also be complex units (such as dates). In this recipe, we will illustrate how to divide a complex sentence into many tokens.

How to do it...

Let's look at how to preprocess data using tokenization:

1. Create a new Python file and add the following lines (the full code is in the `tokenizer.py` file that's already been provided to you). Let's `import` the package and corpora:

```
import nltk
nltk.download('punkt')
```

2. Let's define some sample `text` for analysis:

```
text = "Are you curious about tokenization? Let's see how it works!
We need to analyze a couple of sentences with punctuations to see
it in action."
```

3. Let's start with sentence tokenization. NLTK provides a sentence tokenizer, so let's `import` that:

```
# Sentence tokenization
from nltk.tokenize import sent_tokenize
```

4. Run the sentence tokenizer on the input `text` and extract the tokens:

```
sent_tokenize_list = sent_tokenize(text)
```

5. Print the list of sentences to see whether it works correctly:

```
print("Sentence tokenizer:")
print(sent_tokenize_list)
```

6. Word tokenization is very commonly used in NLP. NLTK comes with a couple of different word tokenizers. Let's start with the basic word tokenizer:

```
# Create a new word tokenizer
from nltk.tokenize import word_tokenize

print("Word tokenizer:")
print(word_tokenize(text))
```

7. If you want to split this punctuation into separate tokens, then you will need to use the `WordPunct` tokenizer:

```
# Create a new WordPunct tokenizer
from nltk.tokenize import WordPunctTokenizer

word_punct_tokenizer = WordPunctTokenizer()
print("Word punct tokenizer:")
print(word_punct_tokenizer.tokenize(text))
```

8. If you run this code, you will see the following output on your Terminal:

```
Sentence tokenizer:
['Are you curious about tokenization?', "Let's see how it works!", 'We need
to analyze a couple of sentences with punctuations to see it in action.']

Word tokenizer:
['Are', 'you', 'curious', 'about', 'tokenization', '?', 'Let', "'s", 'see',
'how', 'it', 'works', '!', 'We', 'need', 'to', 'analyze', 'a', 'couple',
'of', 'sentences', 'with', 'punctuations', 'to', 'see', 'it', 'in',
'action', '.']

Word punct tokenizer:
['Are', 'you', 'curious', 'about', 'tokenization', '?', 'Let', "'", 's',
'see', 'how', 'it', 'works', '!', 'We', 'need', 'to', 'analyze', 'a',
'couple', 'of', 'sentences', 'with', 'punctuations', 'to', 'see', 'it',
'in', 'action', '.']
```

How it works...

In this recipe, we illustrated how to divide a complex sentence into many tokens. To do this, three methods of the `nltk.tokenize` package were used—`sent_tokenize`, `word_tokenize`, and `WordPunctTokenizer`:

- `sent_tokenize` returns a sentence-tokenized copy of text, using NLTK's recommended sentence tokenizer.
- `word_tokenize` tokenizes a string to split off punctuation other than periods.
- `WordPunctTokenizer` tokenizes a text into a sequence of alphabetic and non-alphabetic characters, using the regexp `\w+|[^\w\s]+`.

There's more...

Tokenization is a procedure that, depending on the language that is analyzed, can be an extremely complex task. In English, for example, we could be content to consider taking sequences of characters that do not have spaces and the various punctuation marks. Languages such as Japanese or Chinese, in which words are not separated by spaces but the union of different symbols, can completely change the meaning, and the task is much more complex. But in general, even in languages with words separated by spaces, precise criteria must be defined, as punctuation is often ambiguous.

See also

- The official documentation of the `nltk.tokenize` package: `https://www.nltk.org/api/nltk.tokenize.html`
- *Tokenization* (from the Natural Language Processing Group at Stanford University): `https://nlp.stanford.edu/IR-book/html/htmledition/tokenization-1.html`

Stemming text data

When we deal with a text document, we encounter different forms of words. Consider the word **play.** This word can appear in various forms, such as play, plays, player, playing, and so on. These are basically families of words with similar meanings. During text analysis, it's useful to extract the base forms of these words. This will help us to extract some statistics to analyze the overall text. The goal of **stemming** is to reduce these different forms into a common base form. This uses a heuristic process to cut off the ends of words in order to extract the base form.

Getting ready

In this recipe, we will use the `nltk.stem` package that offers a processing interface for removing morphological affixes from words. Different stemmers are available for different languages. For the English language, we will use `PorterStemmer`, `LancasterStemmer`, and `SnowballStemmer`.

How to do it...

Let's look at how to stem text data:

1. Create a new Python file and import the following packages (the full code is in the `stemmer.py` file that's already been provided to you):

```
from nltk.stem.porter import PorterStemmer
from nltk.stem.lancaster import LancasterStemmer
from nltk.stem.snowball import SnowballStemmer
```

2. Let's define a few `words` to play with, as follows:

```
words = ['table', 'probably', 'wolves', 'playing', 'is',
         'dog', 'the', 'beaches', 'grounded', 'dreamt', 'envision']
```

3. We'll define a list of `stemmers` that we want to use:

```
# Compare different stemmers stemmers = ['PORTER', 'LANCASTER',
'SNOWBALL']
```

4. Initialize the required objects for all three stemmers:

```
stemmer_porter = PorterStemmer() stemmer_lancaster =
LancasterStemmer() stemmer_snowball = SnowballStemmer('english')
```

5. In order to print the output data in a neat tabular form, we need to format it in the correct way:

```
formatted_row = '{:>16}' * (len(stemmers) + 1)
print('\n', formatted_row.format('WORD', *stemmers), '\n')
```

6. Let's iterate through the list of `words` and stem them by using the three stemmers:

```
for word in words: stemmed_words = [stemmer_porter.stem(word),
stemmer_lancaster.stem(word), stemmer_snowball.stem(word)]
print(formatted_row.format(word, *stemmed_words))
```

7. If you run this code, you will see the following output in your Terminal. Observe how the **LANCASTER** stemmer behaves differently for a couple of words:

WORD	PORTER	LANCASTER	SNOWBALL
table	tabl	tabl	tabl
probably	probabl	prob	probabl
wolves	wolv	wolv	wolv
playing	play	play	play
is	is	is	is
dog	dog	dog	dog
the	the	the	the
beaches	beach	beach	beach
grounded	ground	ground	ground
dreamt	dreamt	dreamt	dreamt
envision	envis	envid	envis

How it works...

All three stemming algorithms basically aim at achieving the same thing. The difference between the three stemming algorithms is basically the level of strictness with which they operate. If you observe the output, you will see that the **LANCASTER** stemmer is stricter than the other two stemmers. The **PORTER** stemmer is the least in terms of strictness, and the **LANCASTER** is the strictest. The stemmed words that we get from the **LANCASTER** stemmer tend to get confusing and obfuscated. The algorithm is really fast, but it will reduce the words a lot. So, a good rule of thumb is to use the **SNOWBALL** stemmer.

There's more...

Stemming is the process of reducing the inflected form of a word to its root form, called the **stem**. The stem doesn't necessarily correspond to the morphological root (lemma) of the word: it's normally sufficient that the related words are mapped to the same stem, even if the latter isn't a valid root for the word. The creation of a stemming algorithm has been a prevalent issue in computer science. The stemming process is applied in search engines for query expansion, and in other natural language processing problems.

See also

- The official home page for distribution of the Porter Stemming Algorithm, written and maintained by its author, Martin Porter: https://tartarus.org/martin/PorterStemmer/
- The official documentation of the nltk.stem package: https://www.nltk.org/api/nltk.stem.html
- *Stemming* (from Wikipedia): https://en.wikipedia.org/wiki/Stemming

Converting text to its base form using lemmatization

The goal of lemmatization is also to reduce words to their base forms, but this is a more structured approach. In the previous recipe, you saw that the base words that we obtained using stemmers don't really make sense. For example, the word **wolves** was reduced to **wolv**, which is not a real word. Lemmatization solves this problem by doing things with a vocabulary and morphological analysis of words. It removes inflectional word endings, such as -ing or -ed, and returns the base form of a word. This base form is known as the lemma. If you lemmatize the word wolves, you will get wolf as the output. The output depends on whether the token is a verb or a noun.

Getting ready

In this recipe, we will use the nltk.stem package to reducing a word's inflected form to its canonical form, called a **lemma**.

How to do it...

Let's look at how to convert text to its base form using lemmatization:

1. Create a new Python file and import the following package (the full code is in the `lemmatizer.py` file that's already been provided to you):

```
import nltk
nltk.download('wordnet')
from nltk.stem import WordNetLemmatizer
```

2. Let's define the same set of words that we used during stemming:

```
words = ['table', 'probably', 'wolves', 'playing', 'is', 'dog',
'the', 'beaches', 'grounded', 'dreamt', 'envision']
```

3. We will compare two lemmatizers: the NOUN and VERB lemmatizers. Let's list them:

```
# Compare different lemmatizers
lemmatizers = ['NOUN LEMMATIZER', 'VERB LEMMATIZER']
```

4. Create the object based on the WordNet lemmatizer:

```
lemmatizer_wordnet = WordNetLemmatizer()
```

5. In order to print the output in a tabular form, we need to format it in the right way:

```
formatted_row = '{:>24}' * (len(lemmatizers) + 1)
print('\n', formatted_row.format('WORD', *lemmatizers), '\n')
```

6. Iterate through the words and lemmatize them:

```
for word in words:
    lemmatized_words = [lemmatizer_wordnet.lemmatize(word,
pos='n'),
            lemmatizer_wordnet.lemmatize(word, pos='v')]
    print(formatted_row.format(word, *lemmatized_words))
```

7. If you run this code, you will see the following output:

WORD	NOUN LEMMATIZER	VERB LEMMATIZER
table	table	table
probably	probably	probably
wolves	wolf	wolves
playing	playing	play
is	is	be
dog	dog	dog
the	the	the
beaches	beach	beach
grounded	grounded	ground
dreamt	dreamt	dream
envision	envision	envision

Observe how the NOUN and VERB lemmatizers differ when they lemmatize the word, as shown in the preceding screenshot

How it works...

Lemmatization is the process of reducing a word's inflected form to its canonical form, called a lemma. In the processing of natural language, lemmatization is the algorithmic process that automatically determines the word of a given word. The process may involve other language processing activities, such as morphological and grammatical analysis. In many languages, words appear in different inflected forms. The combination of the canonical form with its part of speech is called the **lexeme** of the word. A lexeme is, in structural lexicology, the minimum unit that constitutes the lexicon of a language. Hence, every lexicon of a language may correspond to its registration in a dictionary in the form of a lemma.

There's more...

In NLTK, for lemmatization, WordNet is available, but this resource is limited to the English language. It's a large lexical database of the English language. In this package, names, verbs, adjectives, and adverbs are grouped into sets of cognitive synonyms (**synsets**), each of which expresses a distinct concept. The synsets are interconnected by means of semantic and lexical conceptual relationships. The resulting network of significantly related words and concepts can be navigated with the browser. WordNet groups words according to their meanings, connecting not only word forms (strings of letters) but specific words. Hence, the words that are in close proximity to each other in the network are semantically disambiguated. In addition, WordNet labels the semantic relationships between words.

See also

- *Keras 2.x Projects* by Giuseppe Ciaburro, from Packt Publishing
- The official documentation of the `nltk.stem` package: `https://www.nltk.org/api/nltk.stem.html`
- *Lemmatisation* (from Wikipedia): `https://en.wikipedia.org/wiki/Lemmatisation`

Dividing text using chunking

Chunking refers to dividing the input text into pieces, which are based on any random condition. This is different from tokenization in the sense that there are no constraints, and the chunks do not need to be meaningful at all. This is used very frequently during text analysis. While dealing with large text documents, it's better to do it in chunks.

How to do it...

Let's look at how to divide text by using chunking:

1. Create a new Python file and import the following packages (the full code is in the `chunking.py` file that's already been provided to you):

```
import numpy as np
nltk.download('brown')
from nltk.corpus import brown
```

2. Let's define a function to `split` the text into chunks. The first step is to divide the text based on spaces:

```
# Split a text into chunks
def splitter(data, num_words):
    words = data.split(' ')
    output = []
```

3. Initialize a couple of required variables:

```
cur_count = 0
cur_words = []
```

4. Let's iterate through the `words`:

```
for word in words:
    cur_words.append(word)
    cur_count += 1
```

5. Once you have hit the required number of words, reset the variables:

```
if cur_count == num_words:
    output.append(' '.join(cur_words))
    cur_words = []
    cur_count = 0
```

6. Append the chunks to the `output` variable, and return it:

```
output.append(' '.join(cur_words) )

return output
```

7. We can now define the main function. Load the data from the `brown` corpus. We will use the first 10,000 words:

```
if __name__=='__main__':
    # Read the data from the Brown corpus
    data = ' '.join(brown.words()[:10000])
```

8. Define the number of words in each chunk:

```
# Number of words in each chunk
num_words = 1700
```

9. Initialize a couple of relevant variables:

```
chunks = []
counter = 0
```

10. Call the `splitter` function on this text `data` and `print` the output:

```
text_chunks = splitter(data, num_words)

print("Number of text chunks =", len(text_chunks))
```

11. If you run this code, you will see the number of chunks that were generated printed in the Terminal:

```
Number of text chunks = 6
```

How it works...

Chunking (also called **shallow parsing**) is the analysis of a proposition, which is formed in a simple form by a subject and a predicate. The subject is typically a noun phrase, while the predicate is a verbal phrase formed by a verb with zero or more complements and adverbs. A chunk is made up of one or more adjacent tokens.

There are numerous approaches to the problem of chunking. For example, in the assigned task, a chunk is represented as a group of words delimited by square brackets, for which a tag representing the type of chunk is indicated. The dataset that was used was derived from a given corpora by taking the part related to journal articles and extracting chunks of information from the syntactic trees of the corpora.

There's more...

The Brown University Standard Corpus of Present-Day American English (or simply, the brown corpus) is a corpus that was compiled in the 1960s by Henry Kucera and W. Nelson Francis at Brown University, Providence, Rhode Island. It contains 500 text extracts in English, obtained from works published in the United States of America in 1961, for a total of about one million words.

See also

- The official documentation of the nltk.corpus package: https://www.nltk.org/api/nltk.corpus.html
- *Basics of Natural Language Processing* (from the University of Zagreb): https://www.fer.unizg.hr/_download/repository/TAR-02-NLP.pdf

Building a bag-of-words model

When it comes to dealing with text documents that consist of millions of words, converting them into numerical representations is necessary. The reason for this is to make them usable for machine learning algorithms. These algorithms need numerical data so that they can analyze them and output meaningful information. This is where the **bag-of-words** approach comes into the picture. This is basically a model that learns a vocabulary from all of the words in all the documents. It models each document by building a histogram of all of the words in the document.

Getting ready

In this recipe, we will build a bag-of-words model to extract a document term matrix, using the `sklearn.feature_extraction.text` package.

How to do it...

Let's look at how to build a bag-of-words model, as follows:

1. Create a new Python file and import the following packages (the full code is in the `bag_of_words.py` file that's already been provided to you):

```
import numpy as np
from nltk.corpus import brown
from chunking import splitter
```

2. Let's define the `main` function. Load the input `data` from the `brown` corpus:

```
if __name__=='__main__':
    # Read the data from the Brown corpus
    data = ' '.join(brown.words()[:10000])
```

3. Divide the text data into five chunks:

```
# Number of words in each chunk
num_words = 2000

chunks = []
counter = 0

text_chunks = splitter(data, num_words)
```

4. Create a dictionary that is based on these text chunks:

```
for text in text_chunks:
    chunk = {'index': counter, 'text': text}
    chunks.append(chunk)
    counter += 1
```

5. The next step is to extract a document term matrix. This is basically a matrix that counts the number of occurrences of each word in the document. We will use `scikit-learn` to do this because it has better provisions, compared to NLTK, for this particular task. Import the following package:

```
# Extract document term matrix
from sklearn.feature_extraction.text import CountVectorizer
```

6. Define the object and extract the document term matrix:

```
vectorizer = CountVectorizer(min_df=5, max_df=.95)
doc_term_matrix = vectorizer.fit_transform([chunk['text'] for chunk in chunks])
```

7. Extract the vocabulary from the `vectorizer` object and print it:

```
vocab = np.array(vectorizer.get_feature_names())
print("Vocabulary:")
print(vocab)
```

8. Print the `Document term matrix`:

```
print("Document term matrix:")
chunk_names = ['Chunk-0', 'Chunk-1', 'Chunk-2', 'Chunk-3', 'Chunk-4']
```

9. To print it in a tabular form, you will need to format this, as follows:

```
formatted_row = '{:>12}' * (len(chunk_names) + 1)
print('\n', formatted_row.format('Word', *chunk_names), '\n')
```

10. Iterate through the words and print the number of times each word has occurred in different chunks:

```
for word, item in zip(vocab, doc_term_matrix.T):
    # 'item' is a 'csr_matrix' data structure
    output = [str(x) for x in item.data]
    print(formatted_row.format(word, *output))
```

11. If you run this code, you will see two main things printed in the Terminal. The first output is the vocabulary, as shown in the following screenshot:

```
Vocabulary:
['about' 'after' 'against' 'aid' 'all' 'also' 'an' 'and' 'are' 'as' 'at'
 'be' 'been' 'before' 'but' 'by' 'committee' 'congress' 'did' 'each'
 'education' 'first' 'for' 'from' 'general' 'had' 'has' 'have' 'he'
 'health' 'his' 'house' 'in' 'increase' 'is' 'it' 'last' 'made' 'make'
 'may' 'more' 'no' 'not' 'of' 'on' 'one' 'only' 'or' 'other' 'out' 'over'
 'pay' 'program' 'proposed' 'said' 'similar' 'state' 'such' 'take' 'than'
 'that' 'the' 'them' 'there' 'they' 'this' 'time' 'to' 'two' 'under' 'up'
 'was' 'were' 'what' 'which' 'who' 'will' 'with' 'would' 'year' 'years']
```

12. The second thing is the **Document term matrix**, which is pretty long. The first few lines will look like the following:

```
Document term matrix:
      Word      Chunk-0    Chunk-1    Chunk-2    Chunk-3    Chunk-4
      about        1          1          1          1          3
      after        2          3          2          1          3
    against        1          2          2          1          1
        aid        1          1          1          3          5
        all        2          2          5          2          1
       also        3          3          3          4          3
         an        5          7          5          7         10
        and       34         27         36         36         41
        are        5          3          6          3          2
         as       13          4         14         18          4
         at        5          7          9          3          6
         be       20         14          7         10         18
       been        7          1          6         15          5
     before        2          2          1          1          2
        but        3          3          2          9          5
         by        8         22         15         14         12
  committee        2         10          3          1          7
   congress        1          1          3          3          1
        did        2          1          1          2          2
```

How it works...

Consider the following sentences:

- **Sentence 1**: The brown dog is running.
- **Sentence 2**: The black dog is in the black room.
- **Sentence 3**: Running in the room is forbidden.

If you consider all three of these sentences, you will have the following nine unique words:

- the
- brown
- dog
- is
- running
- black
- in
- room
- forbidden

Now, let's convert each sentence into a histogram, using the count of words in each sentence. Each feature vector will be nine-dimensional, because we have nine unique words:

- **Sentence 1**: [1, 1, 1, 1, 1, 0, 0, 0, 0]
- **Sentence 2**: [2, 0, 1, 1, 0, 2, 1, 1, 0]
- **Sentence 3**: [0, 0, 0, 1, 1, 0, 1, 1, 1]

Once we have extracted these feature vectors, we can use machine learning algorithms to analyze them.

There's more...

The bag-of-words model is a method that's used in information retrieval and in the processing of the natural language in order to represent documents by ignoring the word order. In this model, each document is considered to contain words, similar to a stock exchange; this allows for the management of these words based on lists, where each stock contains certain words from a list.

See also

- The official documentation of
  the `sklearn.feature_extraction.text.CountVectorizer()` function:
  `https://scikit-learn.org/stable/modules/generated/sklearn.feature_extraction.text.CountVectorizer.html`
- The *Bag-of-Words Model* (from Wikipedia): `https://en.wikipedia.org/wiki/Bag-of-words_model`

Building a text classifier

The main aim of text classification is to sort text documents into different classes. This is a vital analysis technique in NLP. We will use a technique that is based on a statistic called **tf-idf**, which stands for **term frequency-inverse document frequency**. This is an analysis tool that helps us to understand how important a word is to a document in a set of documents. This serves as a feature vector that's used to categorize documents.

Getting ready

In this recipe, we will use the term frequency-inverse document frequency method to evaluate the importance of a word for a document in a collection or a corpus, and to build a text classifier.

How to do it...

Let's look at how to build a text classifier:

1. Create a new Python file and import the following package (the full code is in the `tfidf.py` file that's already been provided to you):

```
from sklearn.datasets import fetch_20newsgroups
```

2. Let's select a list of categories and name them using a dictionary mapping. These categories are available as a part of the news groups dataset that we just imported:

```
category_map = {'misc.forsale': 'Sales', 'rec.motorcycles':
'Motorcycles',
    'rec.sport.baseball': 'Baseball', 'sci.crypt': 'Cryptography',
    'sci.space': 'Space'}
```

3. Load the training data based on the categories that we just defined:

```
training_data = fetch_20newsgroups(subset='train',
        categories=category_map.keys(), shuffle=True,
random_state=7)
```

4. Import the feature extractor:

```
# Feature extraction
from sklearn.feature_extraction.text import CountVectorizer
```

5. Extract the features by using the training data:

```
vectorizer = CountVectorizer() X_train_termcounts =
vectorizer.fit_transform(training_data.data) print("Dimensions of
training data:", X_train_termcounts.shape)
```

6. We are now ready to train the classifier. We will use the multinomial Naive Bayes classifier:

```
# Training a classifier
from sklearn.naive_bayes import MultinomialNB
from sklearn.feature_extraction.text import TfidfTransformer
```

7. Define a couple of random input sentences:

```
input_data = [ "The curveballs of right handed pitchers tend to
curve to the left", "Caesar cipher is an ancient form of
encryption", "This two-wheeler is really good on slippery roads"
]
```

8. Define the `tfidf_transformer` object and train it:

```
# tf-idf transformer
tfidf_transformer = TfidfTransformer()
X_train_tfidf = tfidf_transformer.fit_transform(X_train_termcounts)
```

9. Once we have the feature vectors, train the multinomial Naive Bayes classifier using this data:

```
# Multinomial Naive Bayes classifier
classifier = MultinomialNB().fit(X_train_tfidf, training_data.target)
```

10. Transform the input data using the word counts:

```
X_input_termcounts = vectorizer.transform(input_data)
```

11. Transform the input data using the tfidf_transformer module:

```
X_input_tfidf = tfidf_transformer.transform(X_input_termcounts)
```

12. Predict the output categories of these input sentences by using the trained classifier:

```
# Predict the output categories
predicted_categories = classifier.predict(X_input_tfidf)
```

13. Print the output, as follows:

```
# Print the outputs
for sentence, category in zip(input_data, predicted_categories):
    print('\nInput:', sentence, '\nPredicted category:', \
            category_map[training_data.target_names[category]])
```

14. If you run this code, you will see the following output printed in your Terminal:

```
Dimensions of training data: (2968, 40605)

Input: The curveballs of right handed pitchers tend to curve to the left
Predicted category: Baseball

Input: Caesar cipher is an ancient form of encryption
Predicted category: Cryptography

Input: This two-wheeler is really good on slippery roads
Predicted category: Motorcycles
```

How it works...

The tf-idf technique is used frequently in information retrieval. The goal is to understand the importance of each word within a document. We want to identify words that occur many times in a document. At the same time, common words such as **is** and **be** don't really reflect the nature of the content. So, we need to extract the words that are true indicators. The importance of each word increases as the count increases. At the same time, as it appears a lot, the frequency of this word increases, too. These two things tend to balance each other out. We extract the term counts from each sentence. Once we have converted this to a feature vector, we can train the classifier to categorize these sentences.

The **term frequency** (**TF**) measures how frequently a word occurs in a given document. As multiple documents differ in length, the numbers in the histogram tend to vary a lot. So, we need to normalize this so that it becomes a level playing field. To achieve normalization, we can divide the term-frequency by the total number of words in a given document. The **inverse document frequency** (**IDF**) measures the importance of a given word. When we compute the TF, all words are considered to be equally important. To counterbalance the frequencies of commonly occurring words, we need to weigh them down and scale up the rare ones. We need to calculate the ratio of the number of documents with the given word and divide it by the total number of documents. The IDF is calculated by taking the negative algorithm of this ratio.

There's more...

Simple words, such as **is** or **the**, tend to appear a lot in various documents. However, this doesn't mean that we can characterize the document based on these words. At the same time, if a word appears a single time, that is not useful, either. So, we look for words that appear a number of times, but not so much that they become noisy. This is formulated in the tf-idf technique and is used to classify documents. Search engines frequently use this tool to order search results by relevance.

See also

- Refer to the official documentation of the `sklearn.feature_extraction.text.TfidfTransformer()` function: https://scikit-learn.org/stable/modules/generated/sklearn.feature_extraction.text.TfidfTransformer.html
- Refer to the following page: *What does tf-idf mean?*: http://www.tfidf.com/

Identifying the gender of a name

Identifying the gender of a name is an interesting task in NLP. We will use the heuristic that the last few characters in a name is its defining characteristic. For example, if the name ends with **la**, it's most likely a female name, such as Angela or Layla. On the other hand, if the name ends with **im**, it's most likely a male name, such as Tim or Jim. As we aren't sure of the exact number of characters to use, we will experiment with this.

Getting ready

In this recipe, we will use the names corpora to extract labeled names, and then we will classify the gender based on the final part of the name.

How to do it...

Let's look at how to identify the gender:

1. Create a new Python file and import the following packages (the full code is in the `gender_identification.py` file that's already been provided to you):

   ```
   import nltk
   nltk.download('names')

   import random from nltk.corpus import names from nltk import
   NaiveBayesClassifier from nltk.classify import accuracy as
   nltk_accuracy
   ```

2. We need to define a function to extract features from input words:

   ```
   # Extract features from the input word def gender_features(word,
   num_letters=2): return {'feature': word[-num_letters:].lower()}
   ```

3. Let's define the main function. We need some labeled training data:

   ```
   if __name__=='__main__':
       # Extract labeled names
       labeled_names = ([(name, 'male') for name in
   names.words('male.txt')] +
               [(name, 'female') for name in
   names.words('female.txt')])
   ```

4. Seed the random number generator and shuffle the training data:

```
random.seed(7)
random.shuffle(labeled_names)
```

5. Define some input names to play with:

```
input_names = ['Leonardo', 'Amy', 'Sam']
```

6. As we don't know how many ending characters we need to consider, we will sweep the parameter space from 1 to 5. Each time, we will extract the features, as follows:

```
# Sweeping the parameter space
for i in range(1, 5):
    print('\nNumber of letters:', i)
    featuresets = [(gender_features(n, i), gender) for (n,
gender) in labeled_names]
```

7. Divide this into train and test datasets:

```
train_set, test_set = featuresets[500:], featuresets[:500]
```

8. We will use the Naive Bayes classifier to do this:

```
classifier = NaiveBayesClassifier.train(train_set)
```

9. Evaluate the `classifier` model for each value in the parameter space:

```
# Print classifier accuracy
print('Accuracy ==>', str(100 * nltk_accuracy(classifier,
test_set)) + str('%'))

# Predict outputs for new inputs
    for name in input_names:
        print(name, '==>',
classifier.classify(gender_features(name, i)))
```

10. If you run this code, you will see the following output printed in your Terminal:

```
Number of letters: 1
Accuracy ==> 76.2%
Leonardo ==> male
Amy ==> female
Sam ==> male

Number of letters: 2
Accuracy ==> 78.6%
```

```
Leonardo ==> male
Amy ==> female
Sam ==> male

Number of letters: 3
Accuracy ==> 76.6%
Leonardo ==> male
Amy ==> female
Sam ==> female

Number of letters: 4
Accuracy ==> 70.8%
Leonardo ==> male
Amy ==> female
Sam ==> female
```

How it works...

In this recipe, we used the names corpus to extract labeled names, and then we classified the gender based on the final part of the name. A Naive Bayes classifier is a supervised learning classifier that uses Bayes' theorem to build the model. This topic was addressed in the *Building a Naive Bayes classifier* recipe in Chapter 2, *Constructing a Classifier*.

There's more...

The Bayesian classifier is called naive because it ingenuously assumes that the presence or absence of a particular characteristic in a given class of interest is not related to the presence or absence of other characteristics, greatly simplifying the calculation. Let's go ahead and build a Naive Bayes classifier.

See also

- Chapter 2, *Constructing a Classifier*
- *Keras 2.x Projects* by Giuseppe Ciaburro, from Packt Publishing
- The official documentation of the nltk.classify package: http://www.nltk.org/api/nltk.classify.html?highlight=naivebayesclassifier
- *Bayes' Theorem* (from Stanford Encyclopedia of Philosophy): https://plato.stanford.edu/entries/bayes-theorem/

Analyzing the sentiment of a sentence

Sentiment analysis is one of the most popular applications of NLP. Sentiment analysis refers to the process of determining whether a given piece of text is positive or negative. In some variations, we consider neutral as a third option. This technique is commonly used to discover how people feel about a particular topic. This is used to analyze the sentiments of users in various forms, such as marketing campaigns, social media, e-commerce, and so on.

Getting ready

In this recipe, we will analyze the sentiment of a sentence by using a Naive Bayes classifier, starting with the data contained in the movie_reviews corpus.

How to do it...

Let's look at how to analyze the sentiment of a sentence:

1. Create a new Python file and import the following packages (the full code is in the sentiment_analysis.py file that's already been provided to you):

```
import nltk.classify.util
from nltk.classify import NaiveBayesClassifier
from nltk.corpus import movie_reviews
```

2. Define a function to extract the features:

```
def extract_features(word_list):
    return dict([(word, True) for word in word_list])
```

3. We need training data for this, so we will use the movie reviews in NLTK:

```
if __name__=='__main__':
    # Load positive and negative reviews
    positive_fileids = movie_reviews.fileids('pos')
    negative_fileids = movie_reviews.fileids('neg')
```

4. Let's separate them into positive and negative reviews:

```
features_positive =
[(extract_features(movie_reviews.words(fileids=[f])),
          'Positive') for f in positive_fileids]
    features_negative =
[(extract_features(movie_reviews.words(fileids=[f])),
          'Negative') for f in negative_fileids]
```

5. Divide the data into train and test datasets:

```
# Split the data into train and test (80/20)
threshold_factor = 0.8
threshold_positive = int(threshold_factor *
len(features_positive))
threshold_negative = int(threshold_factor *
len(features_negative))
```

6. Extract the features:

```
features_train = features_positive[:threshold_positive] +
features_negative[:threshold_negative]
features_test = features_positive[threshold_positive:] +
features_negative[threshold_negative:]
print("Number of training datapoints:", len(features_train))
print("Number of test datapoints:", len(features_test))
```

7. We will use a `NaiveBayesClassifier`. Define the object and train it:

```
# Train a Naive Bayes classifier
classifier = NaiveBayesClassifier.train(features_train)
print("Accuracy of the classifier:",
nltk.classify.util.accuracy(classifier, features_test))
```

8. The `classifier` object contains the most informative words that it obtained during analysis. These words basically have a strong say in what's classified as a positive or a negative review. Let's print them out:

```
print("Top 10 most informative words:")
for item in classifier.most_informative_features()[:10]:
    print(item[0])
```

9. Create a couple of random input sentences:

```
# Sample input reviews
input_reviews = [
    "It is an amazing movie",
    "This is a dull movie. I would never recommend it to anyone.",
    "The cinematography is pretty great in this movie",
    "The direction was terrible and the story was all over the place"
]
```

10. Run the classifier on those input sentences and obtain the predictions:

```
print("Predictions:")
for review in input_reviews:
    print("Review:", review)
    probdist =
classifier.prob_classify(extract_features(review.split()))
    pred_sentiment = probdist.max()
```

11. Print the output:

```
    print("Predicted sentiment:", pred_sentiment)
    print("Probability:", round(probdist.prob(pred_sentiment), 2))
```

12. If you run this code, you will see three main things printed in the Terminal. The first is the accuracy, as shown in the following code snippet:

```
Number of training datapoints: 1600
Number of test datapoints: 400
Accuracy of the classifier: 0.735
```

13. The next item is a list of the most informative words:

```
Top 10 most informative words:

outstanding
insulting
vulnerable
ludicrous
uninvolving
astounding
avoids
fascination
seagal
anna
```

14. The last item is the list of predictions, which are based on the input sentences:

```
Predictions:

Review: It is an amazing movie
Predicted sentiment: Positive
Probability: 0.61

Review: This is a dull movie. I would never recommend it to anyone.
Predicted sentiment: Negative
Probability: 0.77

Review: The cinematography is pretty great in this movie
Predicted sentiment: Positive
Probability: 0.67

Review: The direction was terrible and the story was all over the place
Predicted sentiment: Negative
Probability: 0.63
```

How it works...

We used NLTK's Naive Bayes classifier for our task here. In the feature extractor function, we basically extracted all the unique words. However, the NLTK classifier needs the data to be arranged in the form of a dictionary. Hence, we arranged it in such a way that the NLTK `classifier` object can ingest it. Once we divided the data into training and testing datasets, we trained the classifier to categorize the sentences into positive and negative ones.

If you look at the top informative words, you can see that we have words such as **outstanding** to indicate positive reviews and words such as **insulting** to indicate negative reviews. This is interesting information, because it tells us what words are being used to indicate strong reactions.

There's more...

The term sentiment analysis refers to the use of NLP techniques, text analysis, and computational linguistics to find information in written or spoken text sources. If this subjective information is taken from large amounts of data, and therefore from the opinions of large groups of people, sentiment analysis can also be called **opinion mining**.

See also

- The official documentation of the `nltk.corpus` package: https://www.nltk.org/api/nltk.corpus.html
- The official documentation of the `nltk.classify` package: http://www.nltk.org/api/nltk.classify.html?highlight=naivebayesclassifier
- *Sentiment Analysis* (from Stanford University): https://web.stanford.edu/class/cs124/lec/sentiment.pdf

Identifying patterns in text using topic modeling

Topic modeling refers to the process of identifying hidden patterns in text data. The goal is to uncover a hidden thematic structure in a collection of documents. This will help us to organize our documents in a better way, so that we can use them for analysis. This is an active area of research in NLP.

Getting ready

In this recipe, we will use a library called `gensim` to identify patterns in text, using topic modeling.

How to do it...

Let's look at how to identify patterns in text by using topic modeling:

1. Create a new Python file and import the following packages (the full code is in the `topic_modeling.py` file that's already been provided to you):

```
from nltk.tokenize import RegexpTokenizer
from nltk.stem.snowball import SnowballStemmer
from gensim import models, corpora
from nltk.corpus import stopwords
```

2. Define a function to load the input data. We will use the
   `data_topic_modeling.txt` text file that has already been provided to you:

```
# Load input data
def load_data(input_file):
    data = []
    with open(input_file, 'r') as f:
        for line in f.readlines():
            data.append(line[:-1])

    return data
```

3. Let's define a `class` to preprocess the text. This preprocessor will take care of
   creating the required objects and extracting the relevant features from the input
   text:

```
# Class to preprocess text
class Preprocessor(object):
    # Initialize various operators
    def __init__(self):
        # Create a regular expression tokenizer
        self.tokenizer = RegexpTokenizer(r'\w+')
```

4. We need a list of stop words so that we can exclude them from analysis. These
   are common words, such as **in**, **the**, **is**, and so on:

```
# get the list of stop words
self.stop_words_english = stopwords.words('english')
```

5. Define the `SnowballStemmer` module:

```
# Create a Snowball stemmer
self.stemmer = SnowballStemmer('english')
```

6. Define a processor function that takes care of tokenization, stop word removal,
   and stemming:

```
# Tokenizing, stop word removal, and stemming
def process(self, input_text):
    # Tokenize the string
    tokens = self.tokenizer.tokenize(input_text.lower())
```

7. Remove the stop words from the text:

```
# Remove the stop words
tokens_stopwords = [x for x in tokens if not x in
self.stop_words_english]
```

8. Perform stemming on the tokens:

```
# Perform stemming on the tokens
tokens_stemmed = [self.stemmer.stem(x) for x in tokens_stopwords]
```

9. Return the processed tokens:

```
return tokens_stemmed
```

10. We are now ready to define the main function. Load the input data from the text file:

```
if __name__=='__main__':
    # File containing linewise input data
    input_file = 'data_topic_modeling.txt'

    # Load data
    data = load_data(input_file)
```

11. Define an object that is based on the class that we defined:

```
# Create a preprocessor object
preprocessor = Preprocessor()
```

12. We need to process the text in the file and extract the processed tokens:

```
# Create a list for processed documents
processed_tokens = [preprocessor.process(x) for x in data]
```

13. Create a dictionary that is based on tokenized documents so that it can be used for topic modeling:

```
# Create a dictionary based on the tokenized documents
dict_tokens = corpora.Dictionary(processed_tokens)
```

14. We need to create a document term matrix using the processed tokens, as follows:

```
# Create a document term matrix
corpus = [dict_tokens.doc2bow(text) for text in processed_tokens]
```

15. Let's suppose that we know that the text can be divided into two topics. We will use a technique called **latent Dirichlet allocation** (**LDA**) for topic modeling. Define the required parameters and initialize the `LdaModel` object:

```
# Generate the LDA model based on the corpus we just created
num_topics = 2
num_words = 4

ldamodel = models.ldamodel.LdaModel(corpus,
        num_topics=num_topics, id2word=dict_tokens, passes=25)
```

16. Once this has identified the two topics, we can see how it's separating these two topics by looking at the most contributed words:

```
print("Most contributing words to the topics:")
    for item in ldamodel.print_topics(num_topics=num_topics,
num_words=num_words):
        print ("Topic", item[0], "==>", item[1])
```

17. The full code is in the `topic_modeling.py` file. If you run this code, you will see the following printed in your Terminal:

```
Most contributing words to the topics:
Topic 0 ==> 0.057*"need" + 0.034*"order" + 0.034*"work" +
0.034*"modern"
Topic 1 ==> 0.057*"need" + 0.034*"train" + 0.034*"club" +
0.034*"develop"
```

How it works...

Topic modeling works by identifying the important words or themes in a document. These words tend to determine what the topic is about. We use a regular expression tokenizer, because we just want the words, without any punctuation or other kinds of tokens. Hence, we use this to extract the tokens. The stop word removal is another important step, because this helps us to eliminate the noise caused by words such as **is** or **the**. After that, we need to stem the words to get to their base forms. This entire thing is packaged as a preprocessing block in text analysis tools. That is what we are doing here, as well!

We use a technique called LDA to model the topics. LDA basically represents the documents as a mixture of different topics that tend to spit out words. These words are spat out with certain probabilities. The goal is to find these topics! This is a generative model that tries to find the set of topics that are responsible for the generation of the given set of documents.

There's more...

As you can see from the output, we have words such as **talent** and **train** to characterize the sports topic, whereas we have **encrypt** to characterize the cryptography topic. We are working with a really small text file, which is why some words might seem less relevant. Obviously, the accuracy will improve if you work with a larger dataset.

See also

- The official documentation of the `gensim` library: `https://radimrehurek.com/gensim/install.html`
- *Introduction to Latent Dirichlet Allocation* (from MIT): `http://blog.echen.me/2011/08/22/introduction-to-latent-dirichlet-allocation/`
- *Topic Modeling* (from Columbia University): `http://www.cs.columbia.edu/~blei/topicmodeling.html`

Parts of speech tagging with spaCy

Parts-of-speech tagging (**PoS tagging**) is the process of labeling the words that correspond to particular lexical categories. The common linguistic categories include nouns, verbs, adjectives, articles, pronouns, adverbs, conjunctions, and so on.

Getting ready

In this recipe, we will use a library called `spacy` to perform PoS tagging.

How to do it...

Let's look at how to perform PoS tagging using `spacy`:

1. Create a new Python file and import the following packages (the full code is in the `PosTagging.py` file that's already been provided to you):

   ```
   import spacy
   ```

2. Load the `en_core_web_sm` model:

   ```
   nlp = spacy.load('en_core_web_sm')
   ```

3. Let's define an input text:

```
Text = nlp(u'We catched fish, and talked, and we took a swim now
and then to keep off sleepiness')
```

As a source, I used a passage based on the novel *The Adventures of Huckleberry Finn* by Mark Twain.

4. Finally, we will perform a PoS tagging:

```
for token in Text:
    print(token.text, token.lemma_, token.pos_, token.tag_,
token.dep_,
          token.shape_, token.is_alpha, token.is_stop)
```

5. The following results are returned:

```
We -PRON- PRON PRP nsubj Xx True False
catched catch VERB VBD ROOT xxxx True False
fish fish NOUN NN dobj xxxx True False
, , PUNCT , punct , False False
and and CCONJ CC cc xxx True True
talked talk VERB VBD conj xxxx True False
, , PUNCT , punct , False False
and and CCONJ CC cc xxx True True
we -PRON- PRON PRP nsubj xx True True
took take VERB VBD conj xxxx True False
a a DET DT det x True True
swim swim NOUN NN dobj xxxx True False
now now ADV RB advmod xxx True True
and and CCONJ CC cc xxx True True
then then ADV RB advmod xxxx True True
to to PART TO aux xx True True
keep keep VERB VB conj xxxx True True
off off PART RP prt xxx True True
sleepiness sleepiness NOUN NN dobj xxxx True False
```

How it works...

PoS tagging involves assigning a tag to each word of a document/corpus. The choice of the tagset to use depends on the language. The input is a string of words and the tagset to be used, and the output is the association of the best tag with each word. There may be multiple tags compatible with a word (**ambiguity**). The task of the PoS tagger is to solve these ambiguities by choosing the most appropriate tags, based on the context in which the word is located.

There's more...

To perform a PoS tagging, we used the `spacy` library. This library extracts linguistic features, such as PoS tags, dependency labels, and named entities, customizing the tokenizer and working with the rule-based matcher.

To install the `en_core_web_sm` model, use the following code:

```
$ python -m spacy download en
```

See also

- The official documentation of the `spacy` library: `https://spacy.io/usage/linguistic-features`
- *Parts-of-Speech Tagging* (from New York University): `https://cs.nyu.edu/courses/fall16/CSCI-UA.0480-006/lecture4-hmm.pdf`

Word2Vec using gensim

Word embedding allows us to memorize both the semantic and syntactic information of words, starting with an unknown corpus and constructing a vector space in which the vectors of words are closer if the words occur in the same linguistic contexts, that is, if they are recognized as semantically similar. Word2Vec is a set of templates that are used to produce word embedding; the package was originally created in C by Tomas Mikolov, and was then implemented in Python and Java.

Getting ready

In this recipe, we will use the `gensim` library to build a Word2Vec model.

How to do it...

Let's look at how to perform word embedding by using `gensim`:

1. Create a new Python file and import the following packages (the full code is in the `GensimWord2Vec.py` file that's already been provided to you):

```
import gensim
from nltk.corpus import abc
```

2. Build a model based on the Word2Vec methodology:

```
model= gensim.models.Word2Vec(abc.sents())
```

3. Let's extract the vocabulary from the data and put it into a `list`:

```
X= list(model.wv.vocab)
```

4. Now, we will find similarities with the word `'science'`:

```
data=model.wv.most_similar('science')
```

5. Finally, we will `print` the `data`:

```
print(data)
```

The following results will be returned:

```
[('law', 0.938495397567749), ('general', 0.9232532382011414), ('policy',
0.9198083877563477), ('agriculture', 0.918685793876648), ('media',
0.9151924252510071), ('discussion', 0.9143469929695129), ('practice',
0.9138249754905701), ('reservoir', 0.9102856516838074), ('board',
0.9069126844406128), ('tight', 0.9067160487174988)]
```

How it works...

Word2Vec is a simple two-layer artificial neural network that was designed to process natural language; the algorithm requires a corpus in the input and returns a set of vectors that represent the semantic distributions of words in the text. For each word contained in the corpus, in a univocal way, a vector is constructed in order to represent it as a point in the created multidimensional space. In this space, the words will be closer if they are recognized as semantically more similar.

There's more...

In this recipe, we used the Australian National Corpus (abc), a great collection of language data, both text-based and digital. To use this corpus, you must download it with the following code:

```
import nltk
nltk.download('abc')
```

See also

- The official documentation of the gensim library: https://radimrehurek.com/gensim/
- *Word2vec* (from Wikipedia): https://en.wikipedia.org/wiki/Word2vec

Shallow learning for spam detection

Spamming means sending large amounts of unwanted messages (usually commercial). It can be implemented through any medium, but the most commonly used are email and SMS. The main purpose of spamming is advertising, from the most common commercial offers to proposals for the sale of illegal material, such as pirated software and drugs without a prescription, and from questionable financial projects to genuine attempts at fraud.

Getting ready

In this recipe, we will use a logistic regression model for spam detection. To do this, a collection of labeled SMS messages collected for mobile phone spam research will be used. This dataset comprises of 5,574 real English non-encoded messages, tagged according to whether they are legitimate (ham) or spamming (spam).

How to do it...

Let's look at how to perform shallow learning for spam detection:

1. Create a new Python file and import the following packages (the full code is in the `LogiTextClassifier.py` file that's already been provided to you):

```
import pandas as pd
from sklearn.feature_extraction.text import TfidfVectorizer
from sklearn.linear_model.logistic import LogisticRegression
from sklearn.model_selection import train_test_split
```

2. Load the `spam.csv` file that was provided to you:

```
df = pd.read_csv('spam.csv', sep=',',header=None,
encoding='latin-1')
```

3. Let's extract the data for training and testing:

```
X_train_raw, X_test_raw, y_train, y_test =
train_test_split(df[1],df[0])
```

4. We need to `vectorize` the text data contained in the DataFrame:

```
vectorizer = TfidfVectorizer()
X_train = vectorizer.fit_transform(X_train_raw)
```

5. We can now build the logistic regression model:

```
classifier = LogisticRegression(solver='lbfgs',
multi_class='multinomial')
classifier.fit(X_train, y_train)
```

6. Define two SMS messages as test data:

```
X_test = vectorizer.transform( ['Customer Loyalty Offer:The NEW
Nokia6650 Mobile from ONLY £10 at TXTAUCTION!', 'Hi Dear how long
have we not heard.'] )
```

7. Finally, we will perform a prediction by using the model:

```
predictions = classifier.predict(X_test)
print(predictions)
```

The following results will be returned:

```
['spam' 'ham']
```

These indicate that the first SMS was identified as `spam`, while the second SMS was identified as `ham`.

How it works...

Logistic regression analysis is a method for estimating the regression function that best links the probability of a dichotomous attribute with a set of explanatory variables. **Logistic assault** is a nonlinear regression model that's used when the dependent variable is dichotomous. The objective of the model is to establish the probability with which an observation can generate one or the other values of the dependent variable; it can also be used to classify the observations into two categories, according to their characteristics.

There's more...

In addition to the measurement scale of the dependent variable, logistic regression analysis is distinguished from linear regression because a normal distribution of y is assumed for this, whereas if y is dichotomous, its distribution is obviously binomial. Similarly, in linear regression analysis, the y estimate obtained from the regression varies from $-\infty$ to $+\infty$, while in logistic regression analysis, the y estimate varies between 0 and 1.

See also

- The official documentation of
  the `sklearn.linear_model.LogisticRegression()` function: `https://scikit-learn.org/stable/modules/generated/sklearn.linear_model.LogisticRegression.html`

- The official documentation of
  the `sklearn.feature_extraction.text.TfidfVectorizer()` function: `https://scikit-learn.org/stable/modules/generated/sklearn.feature_extraction.text.TfidfVectorizer.html`

- *Regression Analysis with R* by Giuseppe Ciaburro, from Packt Publishing

- *Logistic Regression* (from the University of Sheffield): `https://www.sheffield.ac.uk/polopoly_fs/1.233565!/file/logistic_regression_using_SPSS_level1_MASH.pdf`

Speech Recognition 8

In this chapter, we will cover the following recipes:

- Reading and plotting audio data
- Transforming audio signals into the frequency domain
- Generating audio signals with custom parameters
- Synthesizing music
- Extracting frequency domain features
- Building **hidden Markov models** (**HMMs**)
- Building a speech recognizer
- Building a **text-to-speech** (**TTS**) system

Technical requirements

To address the recipes in this chapter, you will need the following files (which are available on GitHub):

- `read_plot.py`
- `input_read.wav`
- `freq_transform.py`
- `input_freq.wav`
- `generate.py`
- `synthesize_music.py`
- `extract_freq_features.py`
- `input_freq.wav`
- `speech_recognizer.py`
- `tts.py`

Introducing speech recognition

Speech recognition refers to the process of recognizing and understanding spoken language. The input comes in the form of audio data, and the speech recognizers will process this data to extract meaningful information from it. This has a lot of practical uses, such as voice-controlled devices, the transcription of spoken language into words and security systems.

Speech signals are very versatile in nature. There are many variations of speech in the same language. There are different elements to speech, such as language, emotion, tone, noise, and accent. It's difficult to rigidly define a set of rules of what can constitute speech. Even with all these variations, humans are very good at understanding all of this with relative ease. Hence, we need machines to understand speech in the same way.

Over the last couple of decades, researchers have worked on various aspects of speech, such as identifying the speaker, understanding words, recognizing accents, and translating speech. Among all these tasks, automatic speech recognition has been the focal point for many researchers. In this chapter, we will learn how to build a **speech recognizer**.

Reading and plotting audio data

Let's take a look at how to read an audio file and visualize the signal. This will be a good starting point, and it will give us a good understanding of the basic structure of audio signals. Before we start, we need to understand that audio files are digitized versions of actual audio signals. Actual audio signals are complex, continuous-valued waves. In order to save a digital version, we sample the signal and convert it into numbers. For example, speech is commonly sampled at 44,100 Hz. This means that each second of the signal is broken down into 44,100 parts, and the values at these timestamps are stored. In other words, you store a value every 1/44,100 seconds. As the sampling rate is high, we feel that the signal is continuous when we listen to it on our media players.

Getting ready

In this recipe, we will use the `wavfile` package to read the audio file from a `.wav` input file. So, we will draw the signal with a diagram.

How to do it...

We will use the following steps to read and plot audio using the `wavfile` package:

1. Create a new Python file and import the following packages (the full code is in the `read_plot.py` file that's already provided for you):

   ```
   import numpy as np
   import matplotlib.pyplot as plt
   from scipy.io import wavfile
   ```

2. We will use the `wavfile` package to read the audio file from the `input_read.wav` input file that's already provided for you:

   ```
   # Read the input file
   sampling_freq, audio = wavfile.read('input_read.wav')
   ```

3. Let's print out the parameters of this signal:

   ```
   # Print the params
   print('Shape:', audio.shape)
   print('Datatype:', audio.dtype)
   print('Duration:', round(audio.shape[0] / float(sampling_freq), 3),
   'seconds')
   ```

4. The audio signal is stored as 16-bit signed integer data; we need to normalize these values:

   ```
   # Normalize the values
   audio = audio / (2.**15)
   ```

5. Now, let's extract the first 30 values to plot, as follows:

   ```
   # Extract first 30 values for plotting
   audio = audio[:30]
   ```

6. The *x* axis is the **time axis**. Let's build this axis, considering the fact that it should be scaled using the sampling frequency factor:

   ```
   # Build the time axis
   x_values = np.arange(0, len(audio), 1) / float(sampling_freq)
   ```

7. Convert the units to seconds, as follows:

   ```
   # Convert to seconds
   x_values *= 1000
   ```

8. Let's now plot this as follows:

```
# Plotting the chopped audio signal
plt.plot(x_values, audio, color='black')
plt.xlabel('Time (ms)')
plt.ylabel('Amplitude')
plt.title('Audio signal')
plt.show()
```

9. The full code is in the read_plot.py file. If you run this code, you will see the following signal:

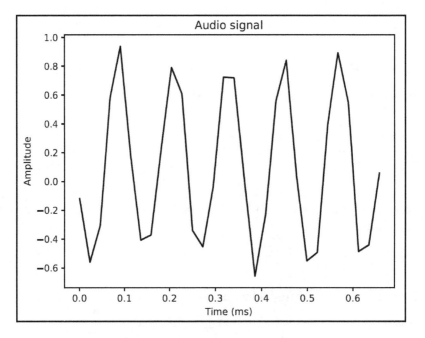

You will also see the following output printed on your Terminal:

```
Shape: (132300,)
Datatype: int16
Duration: 3.0 seconds
```

How it works...

Wave audio files are uncompressed files. The format was introduced with Windows 3.1 as a standard format for the sound used in multimedia applications. Its technical specifications and description can be found in the *Multimedia Programming Interface and Data Specifications 1.0* document (`https://www.aelius.com/njh/wavemetatools/doc/riffmci.pdf`). It is based on the **Resource Interchange File Format** (**RIFF**) specifications that were introduced in 1991, constituting a metaformat for multimedia files running in the Windows environment. The RIFF structure organizes blocks of data in sections called chunks, each of which describes a characteristic of the WAV file (such as the sample rate, the bit rate, and the number of audio channels), or contains the values of the samples (in this case, we are referring to chunk data). The chunks are 32 bit (with some exceptions).

There's more...

To read the WAV file, the `scipy.io.wavfile.read()` function was used. This function returns data from a WAV file along with the sample rate. The returned sample rate is a Python integer, and the data is returned as a NumPy array with a datatype that corresponds to the file.

See also

- Refer to the official documentation of the `scipy.io.wavfile.read()` function: `https://docs.scipy.org/doc/scipy-0.14.0/reference/generated/scipy.io.wavfile.read.html`
- Refer to *WAV* (from Wikipedia): `https://en.wikipedia.org/wiki/WAV`

Transforming audio signals into the frequency domain

Audio signals consist of a complex mixture of sine waves of different frequencies, amplitudes, and phases. Sine waves are also referred to as **sinusoids**. There is a lot of information that is hidden in the frequency content of an audio signal. In fact, an audio signal is heavily characterized by its frequency content. The whole world of speech and music is based on this fact. Before you proceed further, you will need some knowledge of **Fourier transforms**.

Getting ready

In this recipe, we will see how to transform an audio signal into the frequency domain. To do this, the `numpy.fft.fft()` function is used. This function computes the one-dimensional *n*-point **discrete Fourier transform** (**DFT**) with the efficient **fast Fourier transform** (**FFT**) algorithm.

How to do it...

Let's see how to transform audio signals into the frequency domain:

1. Create a new Python file and import the following package (the full code is in the `freq_transform.py` file that's already provided for you):

```
import numpy as np
from scipy.io import wavfile
import matplotlib.pyplot as plt
```

2. Read the `input_freq.wav` file that is already provided for you:

```
# Read the input file
sampling_freq, audio = wavfile.read('input_freq.wav')
```

3. Normalize the signal, as follows:

```
# Normalize the values
audio = audio / (2.**15)
```

4. The audio signal is just a NumPy array. So, you can extract the length using the following code:

```
# Extract length
len_audio = len(audio)
```

5. Let's apply the Fourier transform. The Fourier transform signal is mirrored along the center, so we just need to take the first half of the transformed signal. Our end goal is to extract the power signal, so we square the values in the signal in preparation for this:

```
# Apply Fourier transform
transformed_signal = np.fft.fft(audio)
half_length = np.ceil((len_audio + 1) / 2.0)
transformed_signal = abs(transformed_signal[0:int(half_length)])
transformed_signal /= float(len_audio)
transformed_signal **= 2
```

6. Extract the length of the signal, as follows:

```
# Extract length of transformed signal
len_ts = len(transformed_signal)
```

7. We need to double the signal according to the length of the signal:

```
# Take care of even/odd cases
if len_audio % 2:
    transformed_signal[1:len_ts] *= 2
else:
    transformed_signal[1:len_ts-1] *= 2
```

8. The power signal is extracted using the following formula:

```
# Extract power in dB
power = 10 * np.log10(transformed_signal)
```

9. The *x* axis is the time axis; we need to scale this according to the sampling frequency and then convert this into seconds:

```
# Build the time axis
x_values = np.arange(0, half_length, 1) * (sampling_freq /
len_audio) / 1000.0
```

10. Plot the signal, as follows:

```
# Plot the figure
plt.figure()
plt.plot(x_values, power, color='black')
plt.xlabel('Freq (in kHz)')
plt.ylabel('Power (in dB)')
plt.show()
```

11. If you run this code, you will see the following output:

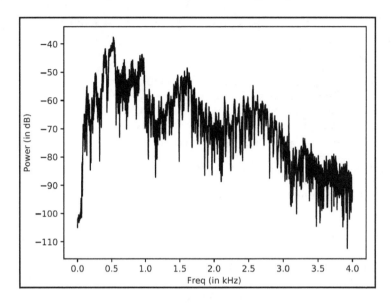

How it works...

The sound spectrum is a graphical representation of the sound level, normally in **decibels** (**dB**), depending on the frequency in Hz. If the sound to be analyzed is a so-called pure sound (signal at a single frequency constant over time), for example, a perfect sine wave, the signal spectrum will have a single component at the sine wave frequency, with a certain level in dB. In reality, any real signal consists of a large number of sinusoidal components of amplitude that are continuously variable over time. For these signals, it is impossible to analyze pure tones because there are always fractions of the signal energy that are difficult to represent with sinusoids. In fact, the representation of a signal as the sum of sinusoidal harmonic components, according to the Fourier transform theorem, is only valid for stationary signals, which often do not correspond to real sounds.

There's more...

The frequency analysis of the sounds is based on the Fourier transform theorem. That is, any periodic signal can be generated by summing together so many sinusoidal signals (called harmonics) having multiple whole frequencies of the frequency of the periodic signal (called fundamental frequency).

See also

- Refer to the official documentation of the `numpy.fft.fft()` function: `https://docs.scipy.org/doc/numpy-1.15.1/reference/generated/numpy.fft.fft.html`
- Refer to *The Fourier Transform*: `http://www.thefouriertransform.com/`
- Refer to *Time-frequency representations* (from Aalto University): `https://mycourses.aalto.fi/pluginfile.php/145214/mod_resource/content/3/slides_05_time-frequency_representations.pdf`

Generating audio signals with custom parameters

Sound is a particular type of wave in which a variation of pressure that is induced by a vibrating body (that is, a sound source) propagates in the surrounding medium (usually air). Some examples of sound sources include the following:

- Musical instruments in which the vibrating part can be a struck string (such as a guitar), or rubbed with a bow (such as the violin).
- Our vocal cords that are made to vibrate from the air that comes out of the lungs and give rise to the voice.
- Any phenomenon that causes a movement of air (such as the beating wings of a bird, an airplane that breaks down the supersonic barrier, a bomb that explodes, or a hammer beating on an anvil) having appropriate physical characteristics.

To reproduce sound through electronic equipment, it is necessary to transform it into an analogue sound that is an electric current that originates from the transformation by conversion of the mechanical energy of the sound wave into electrical energy. In order to be able to use the sound signals with the computer, it is necessary to transfigure the analogue in a digital signal originating from the transformation of the analog sound into an audio signal represented by a flow of 0 and 1 (bit).

Getting ready

In this recipe, we will use NumPy to generate audio signals. As we discussed earlier, audio signals are complex mixtures of sinusoids. So, we will bear this in mind when we generate our own audio signal.

How to do it...

Let's see how to generate audio signals with custom parameters:

1. Create a new Python file and import the following packages (the full code is in the `generate.py` file that's already provided for you):

```
import numpy as np
import matplotlib.pyplot as plt
from scipy.io.wavfile import write
```

2. We need to define the output file where the generated audio will be stored:

```
# File where the output will be saved
output_file = 'output_generated.wav'
```

3. Let's now specify the audio generation parameters. We want to generate a 3-second long signal with a sampling frequency of 44,100, and a tonal frequency of 587 Hz. The values on the time axis will go from $-2*pi$ to $2*pi$:

```
# Specify audio parameters
duration = 3   # seconds
sampling_freq = 44100   # Hz
tone_freq = 587
min_val = -2 * np.pi
max_val = 2 * np.pi
```

4. Let's generate the time axis and the audio signal. The audio signal is a simple sinusoid with the previously mentioned parameters:

```
# Generate audio
t = np.linspace(min_val, max_val, duration * sampling_freq)
audio = np.sin(2 * np.pi * tone_freq * t)
```

5. Now, let's add some noise to the signal:

```
# Add some noise
noise = 0.4 * np.random.rand(duration * sampling_freq)
audio += noise
```

6. We need to scale the values to 16-bit integers before we store them:

```
# Scale it to 16-bit integer values
scaling_factor = pow(2,15) - 1
audio_normalized = audio / np.max(np.abs(audio))
audio_scaled = np.int16(audio_normalized * scaling_factor)
```

7. Write this signal to the output file:

```
# Write to output file
write(output_file, sampling_freq, audio_scaled)
```

8. Plot the signal using the first 100 values:

```
# Extract first 100 values for plotting
audio = audio[:100]
```

9. Generate the time axis, as follows:

```
# Build the time axis
x_values = np.arange(0, len(audio), 1) / float(sampling_freq)
```

10. Convert the time axis into seconds:

```
# Convert to seconds
x_values *= 1000
```

11. Plot the signal, as follows:

```
# Plotting the chopped audio signal
plt.plot(x_values, audio, color='black')
plt.xlabel('Time (ms)')
plt.ylabel('Amplitude')
plt.title('Audio signal')
plt.show()
```

12. If you run this code, you will get the following output:

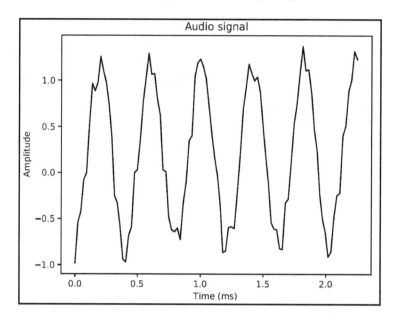

How it works...

In this recipe, we used the NumPy library to generate audio signals. We have seen that a digital sound is a sequence of numbers, so generating a sound will be enough to build an array that represents a musical tone. First, we set the filename to where the output will be saved. Then, we specified the audio parameters. Thus, we generated audio using a sine wave. We then added some noise, so we resized to 16-bit integer values. In the end, we wrote the signal on the output file.

There's more...

In the coding of a signal, each value assigned to the single sample is represented in bits. Each bit corresponds to a dynamic range of 6 dB. The higher the number of bits used, the higher the range of dB that can be represented by the single sample.

Some of the typical values are as follows:

- 8 bits per sample that correspond to 256 levels.
- 16 bits per sample (the number used for CDs) that correspond to 65,636 levels.

See also

- Refer to the official documentation of the NumPy library: http://www.numpy.org/
- Refer to *Sine wave* (from Wikipedia): https://en.wikipedia.org/wiki/Sine_wave

Synthesizing music

In traditional musical instruments, sound is produced by the vibration of mechanical parts. In synthetic instruments, vibration is described by functions over time, called signals, which express the variation in the time of the acoustic pressure. Sound synthesis is a process that allows you to generate the sound artificially. The parameters by which the timbre of the sound is determined differ according to the type of synthesis that is used for the generation, and can be provided directly by the composer, or with actions on appropriate input devices, or derived from the analysis of pre-existing sounds.

Getting ready

In this recipe, we will see how to synthesize some music. To do this, we will use various notes, such as *A*, *G*, and *D*, along with their corresponding frequencies, to generate some simple music.

How to do it...

Let's take a look at how to synthesize some music:

1. Create a new Python file and import the following packages (the full code is in the synthesize_music.py file that's already provided for you):

```
import json
import numpy as np
from scipy.io.wavfile import write
```

2. Define a function to synthesize a tone, based on input parameters:

```
# Synthesize tone
def synthesizer(freq, duration, amp=1.0, sampling_freq=44100):
```

3. Build the time axis values:

```
# Build the time axis
t = np.linspace(0, duration, round(duration * sampling_freq))
```

4. Construct the audio sample using the input arguments, such as amplitude and frequency:

```
# Construct the audio signal
audio = amp * np.sin(2 * np.pi * freq * t)

return audio.astype(np.int16)
```

5. Let's define the main function. You've been provided with a JSON file, called `tone_freq_map.json`, which contains some notes along with their frequencies:

```
if __name__=='__main__':
    tone_map_file = 'tone_freq_map.json'
```

6. Load that file, as follows:

```
# Read the frequency map
with open(tone_map_file, 'r') as f:
    tone_freq_map = json.loads(f.read())
```

7. Now, let's assume that we want to generate a G note for a duration of two seconds:

```
# Set input parameters to generate 'G' tone
input_tone = 'G'
duration = 2      # seconds
amplitude = 10000
sampling_freq = 44100     # Hz
```

8. Call the function with the following parameters:

```
# Generate the tone
synthesized_tone = synthesizer(tone_freq_map[input_tone], duration,
amplitude, sampling_freq)
```

9. Write the generated signal into the output file, as follows:

```
# Write to the output file
write('output_tone.wav', sampling_freq, synthesized_tone)
```

A single tone .wav file is generated (output_tone.wav). Open this file in a media player and listen to it. That's the G note!

10. Now, let's do something more interesting. Let's generate some notes in sequence to give it a musical feel. Define a note sequence along with their durations in seconds:

```
# Tone-duration sequence
tone_seq = [('D', 0.3), ('G', 0.6), ('C', 0.5), ('A', 0.3), ('Asharp',
0.7)]
```

11. Iterate through this list and call the synthesizer function for each of them:

```
# Construct the audio signal based on the chord sequence
output = np.array([])
for item in tone_seq:
    input_tone = item[0]
    duration = item[1]
    synthesized_tone = synthesizer(tone_freq_map[input_tone], duration,
amplitude, sampling_freq)
    output = np.append(output, synthesized_tone, axis=0)
output = output.astype(np.int16)
```

12. Write the signal to the output file:

```
# Write to the output file
write('output_tone_seq.wav', sampling_freq, output)
```

13. You can now open the output_tone_seq.wav file in your media player and listen to it. You can feel the music!

How it works...

Music is a work of ingenuity and creativity that is difficult to explain in a nutshell. Musicians read a piece of music recognizing the notes as they are placed on the stave. By analogy, we can regard the synthesis of sound as a sequence of the characteristic frequencies of the known ones. In this recipe, we have used this procedure to synthesize a short sequence of notes.

There's more...

To generate music artificially, the synthesizer is used. All synthesizers have the following basic components that work together to create a sound:

- An oscillator that generates the waveform and changes the tone
- A filter that cuts out some frequencies in the wave to change the timbre
- An amplifier that controls the volume of the signal
- A modulator to create effects

See also

- Refer to the official documentation of the NumPy library: http://www.numpy.org/
- Refer to the official documentation of the scipy.io.wavfile.write() function: https://docs.scipy.org/doc/scipy-0.14.0/reference/generated/scipy.io.wavfile.read.html
- Refer to *Frequencies of Musical Notes* (from Michigan Technological University): http://pages.mtu.edu/~suits/notefreqs.html
- Refer to *Principles of Sound Synthesis* (from the University of Salford): http://www.acoustics.salford.ac.uk/acoustics_info/sound_synthesis/

Extracting frequency domain features

In the *Transforming audio signals into the frequency domain* recipe, we discussed how to convert a signal into the frequency domain. In most modern speech recognition systems, people use frequency domain features. After you convert a signal into the frequency domain, you need to convert it into a usable form. **Mel Frequency Cepstral Coefficients** (**MFCC**) is a good way to do this. MFCC takes the power spectrum of a signal and then uses a combination of filter banks and **discrete cosine transform** (**DCT**) to extract the features.

Getting ready

In this recipe, we will see how to use the `python_speech_features` package to extract frequency domain features. You can find the installation instructions at `http://python-speech-features.readthedocs.org/en/latest`. So, let's take a look at how to extract MFCC features.

How to do it...

Let's see how to extract frequency domain features:

1. Create a new Python file and import the following packages (the full code is in the `extract_freq_features.py` file that's already provided for you):

```
import numpy as np
import matplotlib.pyplot as plt
from scipy.io import wavfile
from python_speech_features import mfcc, logfbank
```

2. Read the `input_freq.wav` input file that is already provided for you:

```
# Read input sound file
sampling_freq, audio = wavfile.read("input_freq.wav")
```

3. Extract the MFCC and filter bank features, as follows:

```
# Extract MFCC and Filter bank features
mfcc_features = mfcc(audio, sampling_freq)
filterbank_features = logfbank(audio, sampling_freq)
```

4. Print the parameters to see how many windows were generated:

```
# Print parameters
print('MFCC:\nNumber of windows =', mfcc_features.shape[0])
print('Length of each feature =', mfcc_features.shape[1])
print('\nFilter bank:\nNumber of windows =',
filterbank_features.shape[0])
print('Length of each feature =', filterbank_features.shape[1])
```

5. Let's now visualize the MFCC features. We need to transform the matrix so that the time domain is horizontal:

```
# Plot the features
mfcc_features = mfcc_features.T
plt.matshow(mfcc_features)
plt.title('MFCC')
```

6. Now, let's visualize the filter bank features. Again, we need to transform the matrix so that the time domain is horizontal:

```
filterbank_features = filterbank_features.T
plt.matshow(filterbank_features)
plt.title('Filter bank')
plt.show()
```

7. If you run this code, you will get the following output for MFCC features:

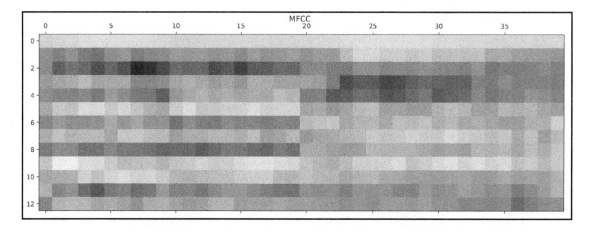

The filter bank features will look like the following output:

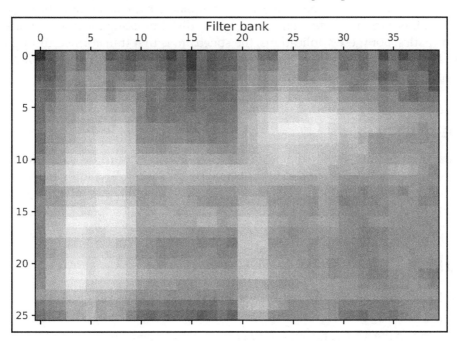

You will get the following output on your Terminal:

```
MFCC:
Number of windows = 40
Length of each feature = 13

Filter bank:
Number of windows = 40
Length of each feature = 26
```

How it works...

The **cepstrum** is the result of the Fourier transform applied to the dB spectrum of a signal. Its name is derived from the reversal of the first four letters of the word **spectrum**. It was defined in 1963 by Bogert et al. Thus, the cepstrum of a signal is the Fourier transform of the log value of the Fourier transform of the signal.

The graph of the cepstrum is used to analyze the rates of change of the spectral content of a signal. Originally, it was invented to analyze earthquakes, explosions, and the responses to radar signals. It is currently a very effective tool for discriminating the human voice in music informatics. For these applications, the spectrum is first transformed through the frequency bands of the Mel scale. The result is the spectral coefficient Mel, or MFCCs. It is used for voice identification and pitch detection algorithms.

There's more...

The cepstrum is used to separate the part of the signal that contains the excitation information from the transfer function performed by the larynx. The lifter action (filtering in the frequency domain) has as its objective the separation of the excitation signal from the transfer function.

See also

- Refer to the official documentation of the `python_speech_features` package: `https://python-speech-features.readthedocs.io/en/latest/`
- Refer to the MFCC tutorial: `http://practicalcryptography.com/miscellaneous/machine-learning/guide-mel-frequency-cepstral-coefficients-mfccs/`

Building HMMs

We are now ready to discuss speech recognition. We will use HMMs to perform speech recognition; HMMs are great at modeling time series data. As an audio signal is a time series signal, HMMs perfectly suit our needs. An HMM is a model that represents probability distributions over sequences of observations. We assume that the outputs are generated by hidden states. So, our goal is to find these hidden states so that we can model the signal.

Getting ready

In this recipe, we will see how to build an HMM using the `hmmlearn` package. Before you proceed, you will need to install the `hmmlearn` package. Let's take a look at how to build HMMs.

How to do it...

Let's see how to build HMMs:

1. Create a new Python file and define a class to model HMMs (the full code is in the speech_recognizer.py file that's already provided for you):

```
# Class to handle all HMM related processing
class HMMTrainer(object):
```

2. Let's initialize the class; we will use Gaussian HMMs to model our data. The n_components parameter defines the number of hidden states. cov_type defines the type of covariance in our transition matrix, and n_iter indicates the number of iterations it will go through before it stops training:

```
def __init__(self, model_name='GaussianHMM', n_components=4,
cov_type='diag', n_iter=1000):
```

The choice of the preceding parameters depends on the problem at hand. You need to have an understanding of your data in order to select these parameters in a smart way.

3. Initialize the variables, as follows:

```
self.model_name = model_name
self.n_components = n_components
self.cov_type = cov_type
self.n_iter = n_iter
self.models = []
```

4. Define the model with the following parameters:

```
if self.model_name == 'GaussianHMM':
    self.model = hmm.GaussianHMM(n_components=self.n_components,
            covariance_type=self.cov_type, n_iter=self.n_iter)
else:
    raise TypeError('Invalid model type')
```

5. The input data is a NumPy array, where each element is a feature vector consisting of *k* dimensions:

```
# X is a 2D numpy array where each row is 13D
def train(self, X):
    np.seterr(all='ignore')
    self.models.append(self.model.fit(X))
```

6. Define a method to extract the score, based on the model:

```
# Run the model on input data
def get_score(self, input_data):
    return self.model.score(input_data)
```

7. We built a class to handle HMM training and prediction, but we need some data to see it in action. We will use it in the next recipe to build a speech recognizer.

How it works...

HMM is a model where the system is assumed to be a Markov process with unobserved states. A stochastic process is called Markovian when, having chosen a certain instance of *t* for observation, the evolution of the process, starting with *t*, depends only on *t*, and does not depend in any way on the previous instances. Thus, a process is Markovian when, given the moment of observation, only a particular instance determines the future evolution of the process, and that evolution does not depend on the past.

There's more...

An HMM is, therefore, a Markov chain in which states are not directly observable. More precisely, it can be understood as follows:

- The chain has a number of states
- The states evolve according to a Markov chain
- Each state generates an event with a certain probability distribution that depends only on the state
- The event is observable, but the state is not

HMMs are particularly known for their applications in the recognition of the temporal pattern of spoken speeches, handwriting, texture recognition, and bioinformatics.

See also

- Refer to the official documentation of the hmmlearn package: https://hmmlearn.readthedocs.io/en/latest/
- Refer to *A Tutorial on Hidden Markov Models* (by Lawrence R. Rabiner): https://www.robots.ox.ac.uk/~vgg/rg/slides/hmm.pdf

Building a speech recognizer

Speech recognition is the process by which human oral language is recognized, and subsequently processed through a computer, or, more specifically, through a special speech recognition system. Speech recognition systems are used for automated voice applications in the context of telephone applications (such as automatic call centers) for dictation systems, which allow the dictation of speeches to the computer, for control systems of the navigation system satellite, or for a phone in a car via voice commands.

Getting ready

We need a database of speech files to build our speech recognizer. We will use the database available at https://code.google.com/archive/p/hmm-speech-recognition/downloads. This contains 7 different words, where each word has 15 audio files associated with it. Download the ZIP file and extract the folder that contains the Python file (rename the folder that contains the data as data). This is a small dataset, but it is sufficient in understanding how to build a speech recognizer that can recognize 7 different words. We need to build an HMM model for each class. When we want to identify the word in a new input file, we need to run all the models on this file and pick the one with the best score. We will use the HMM class that we built in the previous recipe.

How to do it...

Let's see how to build a speech recognizer:

1. Create a new Python file and import the following packages (the full code is in the speech_recognizer.py file that's already provided for you):

    ```python
    import os
    import argparse

    import numpy as np
    from scipy.io import wavfile
    from hmmlearn import hmm
    from python_speech_features import mfcc
    ```

2. Define a function to parse the input arguments in the command line:

    ```python
    # Function to parse input arguments
    def build_arg_parser():
        parser = argparse.ArgumentParser(description='Trains the HMM classifier')
    ```

```
        parser.add_argument("--input-folder", dest="input_folder",
required=True,
                help="Input folder containing the audio files in
subfolders")
        return parser
```

3. Let's use the `HMMTrainer` class defined in the previous *Building HMMs* recipe:

```
class HMMTrainer(object):
 def __init__(self, model_name='GaussianHMM', n_components=4,
cov_type='diag', n_iter=1000):
 self.model_name = model_name
 self.n_components = n_components
 self.cov_type = cov_type
 self.n_iter = n_iter
 self.models = []

if self.model_name == 'GaussianHMM':
 self.model = hmm.GaussianHMM(n_components=self.n_components,
 covariance_type=self.cov_type, n_iter=self.n_iter)
 else:
 raise TypeError('Invalid model type')

# X is a 2D numpy array where each row is 13D
 def train(self, X):
 np.seterr(all='ignore')
 self.models.append(self.model.fit(X))

# Run the model on input data
 def get_score(self, input_data):
 return self.model.score(input_data)
```

4. Define the main function, and parse the input arguments:

```
if __name__=='__main__':
    args = build_arg_parser().parse_args()
    input_folder = args.input_folder
```

5. Initiate the variable that will hold all the HMM models:

```
 hmm_models = []
```

6. Parse the input directory that contains all the database's audio files:

```
# Parse the input directory
for dirname in os.listdir(input_folder):
```

7. Extract the name of the subfolder:

```
# Get the name of the subfolder
subfolder = os.path.join(input_folder, dirname)

if not os.path.isdir(subfolder):
    continue
```

8. The name of the subfolder is the label of this class; extract it using the following code:

```
# Extract the label
label = subfolder[subfolder.rfind('/') + 1:]
```

9. Initialize the variables for training:

```
# Initialize variables
X = np.array([])
y_words = []
```

10. Iterate through the list of audio files in each subfolder:

```
# Iterate through the audio files (leaving 1 file for testing in
each class)
    for filename in [x for x in os.listdir(subfolder) if
x.endswith('.wav')][:-1]:
```

11. Read each audio file, as follows:

```
# Read the input file
filepath = os.path.join(subfolder, filename)
sampling_freq, audio = wavfile.read(filepath)
```

12. Extract the MFCC features, as follows:

```
# Extract MFCC features
mfcc_features = mfcc(audio, sampling_freq)
```

13. Keep appending this to the X variable, as follows:

```
# Append to the variable X
if len(X) == 0:
    X = mfcc_features
else:
    X = np.append(X, mfcc_features, axis=0)
```

14. Append the corresponding label too, as follows:

```
# Append the label
y_words.append(label)
```

15. Once you have extracted features from all the files in the current class, train and save the HMM model. As HMM is a generative model for unsupervised learning, we don't need labels to build HMM models for each class. We explicitly assume that separate HMM models will be built for each class:

```
# Train and save HMM model
hmm_trainer = HMMTrainer()
hmm_trainer.train(X)
hmm_models.append((hmm_trainer, label))
hmm_trainer = None
```

16. Get a list of test files that were not used for training:

```
# Test files
input_files = [
        'data/pineapple/pineapple15.wav',
        'data/orange/orange15.wav',
        'data/apple/apple15.wav',
        'data/kiwi/kiwi15.wav'
        ]
```

17. Parse the input files, as follows:

```
# Classify input data
for input_file in input_files:
```

18. Read in each audio file, as follows:

```
# Read input file
sampling_freq, audio = wavfile.read(input_file)
```

19. Extract the MFCC features, as follows:

```
# Extract MFCC features
mfcc_features = mfcc(audio, sampling_freq)
```

20. Define the variables to store the maximum score and the output label:

```
# Define variables
max_score = float('-inf')
output_label = None
```

21. Iterate through all the models and run the input file through each of them:

```
# Iterate through all HMM models and pick
# the one with the highest score
for item in hmm_models:
    hmm_model, label = item
```

22. Extract the score and store the maximum score:

```
score = hmm_model.get_score(mfcc_features)
if score > max_score:
    max_score = score
    output_label = label
```

23. Print the true and predicted labels:

```
# Print the output
print("True:",
input_file[input_file.find('/')+1:input_file.rfind('/')])
    print("Predicted:", output_label)
```

24. The full code is in the `speech_recognizer.py` file. Run this file using the following command:

```
$ python speech_recognizer.py --input-folder data
```

The following results are returned on your Terminal:

```
True: pineapple
Predicted: data\pineapple
True: orange
Predicted: data\orange
True: apple
Predicted: data\apple
True: kiwi
Predicted: data\kiwi
```

How it works...

In this recipe, we created a speech recognition system using an HMM. To do this, we first created a function to analyze input arguments. Then, a class was used to handle all HMM-related processing. Thus, we have classified the input data and then predicted the label of the test data. Finally, we printed the results.

There's more...

A voice recognition system is based on a comparison of the input audio, which is appropriately processed, with a database created during system training. In practice, the software application tries to identify the word spoken by the speaker, looking for a similar sound in the database, and checking which word corresponds. Naturally, it is a very complex operation. Moreover, it is not done on whole words, but on the phonemes that compose them.

See also

- Refer to the official documentation of the `hmmlearn` package: `https://hmmlearn.readthedocs.io/en/latest/`
- Refer to the official documentation of the `python_speech_features` package: `https://python-speech-features.readthedocs.io/en/latest/`
- Refer to the *Argparse Tutorial*: `https://docs.python.org/3/howto/argparse.html`
- Refer to *Fundamentals of Speech Recognition: A Short Course* (from Mississippi State University): `http://www.iitg.ac.in/samudravijaya/tutorials/fundamentalOfASR_picone96.pdf`

Building a TTS system

Speech synthesis is the technique that is used for the artificial reproduction of the human voice. A system used for this purpose is called a speech synthesizer and can be implemented by software or hardware. Speech synthesis systems are also known as TTS systems due to their ability to convert text into speech. There are also systems that convert phonetic symbols into speech.

Speech synthesis can be achieved by concatenating recordings of vocals stored in a database. The various systems of speech synthesis differ according to the size of the stored voice samples. That is, a system that stores single phonemes or double phonemes allows you to obtain the maximum number of combinations at the expense of overall clarity, while other systems which are designed for a specific use repeat themselves, to record whole words or entire sentences in order to achieve a high-quality result.

A synthesizer can create a completely synthetic voice using vocal traits and other human characteristics. The quality of a speech synthesizer is evaluated on the basis of both the resemblance to the human voice and its level of comprehensibility. A TTS conversion program with good performance can play an important role in accessibility; for example, by allowing people with impaired vision or dyslexia to listen to documents written on the computer. For this type of application (since the early 1980s), many operating systems have included speech synthesis functions.

Getting ready

In this recipe, we will introduce the Python library that allows us to create TTS systems. We will run the pyttsx cross-platform TTS wrapper library.

How to do it...

Let's see how to build a TTS system:

1. First, we must install pyttsx for the Python 3 library (offline TTS for Python 3) and its relative dependencies:

   ```
   $ pip install pyttsx3
   ```

2. To avoid possible errors, it is also necessary to install the pypiwin32 library:

   ```
   $ pip install pypiwin32
   ```

3. Create a new Python file and import the pyttsx3 package (the full code is in the tts.py file that's already provided for you):

   ```
   import pyttsx3;
   ```

4. We create an engine instance that will use the specified driver:

   ```
   engine = pyttsx3.init();
   ```

5. To change the speech rate, use the following commands:

   ```
   rate = engine.getProperty('rate')
   engine.setProperty('rate', rate-50)
   ```

6. To change the voice of the speaker, use the following commands:

```
voices = engine.getProperty('voices')
engine.setProperty('voice', 'TTS_MS_EN-US_ZIRA_11.0')
```

7. Now, we will use the `say` method to queue a command to speak an utterance. The speech is output according to the properties set before this command in the queue:

```
engine.say("You are reading the Python Machine Learning Cookbook");
engine.say("I hope you like it.");
```

8. Finally, we will invoke the `runAndWait()` method. This method blocks while processing all currently queued commands and invokes callbacks for engine notifications appropriately. It returns when all commands queued before this call are emptied from the queue:

```
engine.runAndWait();
```

At this point, a different voice will read the text supplied by us.

How it works...

A speech synthesis system or engine is composed of two parts: a frontend and a backend. The frontend part deals with the conversion of the text into phonetic symbols, while the backend part interprets the phonetic symbols and reads them, thus, transforming them into an artificial voice. The frontend has two key functions; first, it performs an analysis of the written text to convert all numbers, abbreviations, and abbreviations into words in full. This preprocessing step is referred to as tokenization. The second function consists of converting each word into its corresponding phonetic symbols and performing the linguistic analysis of the revised text, subdividing it into prosodic units, that is, into prepositions, sentences, and periods. The process of assigning phonetic transcription to words is called conversion from text to phoneme, or from grapheme to phoneme.

There's more...

An evolution of the classic TTS system is called `WaveNet`, and it seems to know how to speak, articulate accents, and pronounce a whole sentence fluently. WaveNet is a deep neural network that generates raw audio. It was created by researchers at the London-based artificial intelligence firm, DeepMind. WaveNet uses a deep generative model for sound waves that can imitate any human voice. The sentences pronounced by WaveNet sound 50% more similar to a human voice than the more advanced TTS. To demonstrate this, samples were created in English and Mandarin, and using the **Mean Opinion Scores (MOS)** system, which is now a standard in audio evaluation, samples of artificial intelligence were compared to those generated by normal TTS, parametric-TTS, and also with respect to the samples of real voices.

See also

- Refer to the official documentation of the `pyttsx3` package: `https://pyttsx3.readthedocs.io/en/latest/index.html`
- Refer to *Text to Speech: A Simple Tutorial* (by D. Sasirekha and E. Chandra): `https://pdfs.semanticscholar.org/e7ad/2a63458653ac965fe349fe375eb8e2b70b02.pdf`
- Refer to *WaveNet: A Generative Model for Raw Audio* (from Google DeepMind): `https://deepmind.com/blog/wavenet-generative-model-raw-audio/`

Dissecting Time Series and Sequential Data

9

In this chapter, we will cover the following recipes:

- Transforming data into a time series format
- Slicing time series data
- Operating on time series data
- Extracting statistics from time series data
- Building HMMs for sequential data
- Building CRFs for sequential text data
- Analyzing stock market data
- Using RNNs to predict time series data

Technical requirements

To address the recipes in this chapter, you need the following files (available on GitHub):

- `convert_to_timeseries.py`
- `data_timeseries.txt`
- `slicing_data.py`
- `operating_on_data.py`
- `extract_stats.py`
- `hmm.py`
- `data_hmm.txt`

- `crf.py`
- `AmazonStock.py`
- `AMZN.csv`
- `LSTMstock.py`

Introducing time series

Time series data is basically a sequence of measurements that are collected over time. These measurements are taken with respect to a predetermined variable and at regular time intervals. One of the main characteristics of time series data is that the ordering matters!

The list of observations that we collect is ordered on a timeline, and the order in which they appear says a lot about underlying patterns. If you change the order, this would totally change the meaning of the data. Sequential data is a generalized notion that encompasses any data that comes in a sequential form, including time series data.

Our objective here is to build a model that describes the pattern of the time series or any sequence in general. Such models are used to describe important features of the time series pattern. We can use these models to explain how the past might affect the future. We can also use them to see how two datasets can be correlated, to forecast future values, or to control a given variable that is based on some metric.

To visualize time series data, we tend to plot it using line charts or bar graphs. Time series data analysis is frequently used in finance, signal processing, weather prediction, trajectory forecasting, predicting earthquakes, or any field where we have to deal with temporal data. The models that we build in time series and sequential data analysis should take into account the ordering of data and extract the relationships among neighbors. Let's go ahead and check out a few recipes to analyze time series and sequential data in Python.

Transforming data into a time series format

A **time series** constitutes a sequence of observations of a phenomenon that's carried out in consecutive instants or time intervals that are usually, even if not necessarily, evenly spaced or of the same length. It follows that time is a fundamental parameter in the analysis of a time series. To start, we must therefore acquire a certain confidence in manipulating data that represents a long-term observation of a certain phenomenon.

Getting ready

We will start by understanding how to convert a sequence of observations into time series data and visualize it. We will use a library called `pandas` to analyze time series data. Make sure that you install `pandas` before you proceed further. You can find the installation instructions for `pandas` at the following link: `http://pandas.pydata.org/pandas-docs/stable/install.html`.

How to do it...

Let's see how we can transform data into a time series format:

1. Create a new Python file (the full code is given in the `convert_to_timeseries.py` file that is provided for you) and import the following packages:

   ```
   import numpy as np
   import pandas as pd
   import matplotlib.pyplot as plt
   ```

2. Let's define a function that reads an input file and converts sequential observations into time-indexed data:

   ```
   def convert_data_to_timeseries(input_file, column, verbose=False):
   ```

3. We will use a text file consisting of four columns. The first column denotes the year, the second column denotes the month, and the third and fourth columns denote data. Let's load this into a NumPy array:

   ```
   # Load the input file
   data = np.loadtxt(input_file, delimiter=',')
   ```

4. As this is arranged chronologically, the first row contains the start date and the last row contains the end date. Let's extract the start and end dates of this dataset:

   ```
   # Extract the start and end dates
   start_date = str(int(data[0,0])) + '-' + str(int(data[0,1]))
   end_date = str(int(data[-1,0] + 1)) + '-' + str(int(data[-1,1] % 12 + 1))
   ```

5. There is also a `verbose` mode for this function. So, if this is set to `true`, it will print a few things. Let's print out the start and end dates:

```
if verbose:
    print("Start date =", start_date)
    print("End date =", end_date)
```

6. Let's create a `pandas` variable, which contains the date sequence with monthly intervals:

```
# Create a date sequence with monthly intervals
dates = pd.date_range(start_date, end_date, freq='M')
```

7. Our next step is to convert the given column into time series data. You can access this data using the month and the year (as opposed to the index):

```
# Convert the data into time series data
data_timeseries = pd.Series(data[:,column], index=dates)
```

8. Use the `verbose` mode to print out the first 10 elements:

```
if verbose:
    print("Time series data:\n", data_timeseries[:10])
```

9. Return the time-indexed variable, as follows:

```
return data_timeseries
```

10. Define the main function, as follows:

```
if __name__=='__main__':
```

11. We will use the `data_timeseries.txt` file that is already provided to you:

```
# Input file containing data
input_file = 'data_timeseries.txt'
```

12. Load the third column from this text file and convert it into time series data:

```
# Load input data
column_num = 2
data_timeseries = convert_data_to_timeseries(input_file, column_num)
```

13. The `pandas` library provides a nice plotting function that you can run directly on the variable:

```
# Plot the time series data
data_timeseries.plot()
plt.title('Input data')

plt.show()
```

If you run the code, you will see the following output:

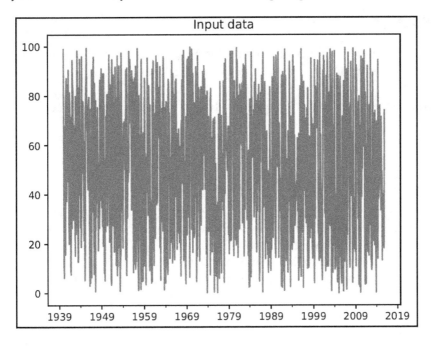

How it works...

In this recipe, we learned how to convert a sequence of observations into time series data and display it. To do this, we first loaded the input file in a `.txt` format, so we extracted the start and end dates. Then, we created a sequence of dates with monthly intervals and converted the data into time series data. Finally, we plotted the time series data.

There's more...

The `pandas` library is particularly suitable for working with time series data for all domains, thanks to the extensive capabilities and features it has. These features take advantage of the NumPy `datetime64` and `timedelta64` variables, and a large number of functionality from other Python libraries such as `scikits.timeseries`. These features have made `pandas` particularly efficient for manipulating time series data.

See also

- Refer to the official documentation of the `pandas` time series and date functionality: `https://pandas.pydata.org/pandas-docs/stable/user_guide/timeseries.html`
- *Time Series Basics* (from The Pennsylvania State University): `https://newonlinecourses.science.psu.edu/stat510/node/41/`

Slicing time series data

Slice and **dice** are two terms that refer to a dataset meaning to divide a large DataFrame into smaller parts or examine them from different points of view to understand it better. The term comes from culinary jargon and describes two types of knife skills that every chef has to master. To slice means to cut, while to dice means to cut food into very small and uniform sections, and the two actions are often performed in sequence. In data analysis, the term **slice and dice** generally involves a systematic reduction of a large dataset into smaller parts to extract more information.

Getting ready

In this recipe, we will learn how to slice time series data. This will help you extract information from various intervals in the time series data. We will learn how to use dates to handle subsets of our data.

How to do it...

Let's see how we can perform slicing time series data:

1. Create a new Python file and import the following packages (the full code is given in the `slicing_data.py` file that is provided for you):

```
import numpy as np
from convert_to_timeseries import convert_data_to_timeseries
```

Here, `convert_to_timeseries` is the function we defined in the previous recipe *Transforming data into a time series format*, that reads an input file and converts sequential observations into time-indexed data.

2. We will use the same text file that we used in the previous recipe (`data_timeseries.txt`) to slice and dice the data:

```
# Input file containing data
input_file = 'data_timeseries.txt'
```

3. We will extract only the third column:

```
# Load data
column_num = 2
data_timeseries = convert_data_to_timeseries(input_file,
column_num)
```

4. Let's assume that we want to extract the data between the given `start` and `end` years. Let's define these, as follows:

```
# Plot within a certain year range
start = '2000'
end = '2015'
```

5. Plot the data between the given year range:

```
plt.figure()
data_timeseries[start:end].plot()
plt.title('Data from ' + start + ' to ' + end)
```

6. We can also slice the data based on a certain range of months:

```
# Plot within a certain range of dates
start = '2008-1'
end = '2008-12'
```

7. Plot the data, as follows:

```
plt.figure()
data_timeseries[start:end].plot()
plt.title('Data from ' + start + ' to ' + end)
plt.show()
```

If you run the code, you will see the following screenshot:

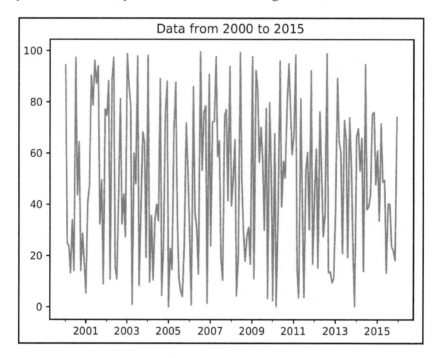

The following screenshot displays a smaller time frame; hence, it looks as if we have zoomed into it:

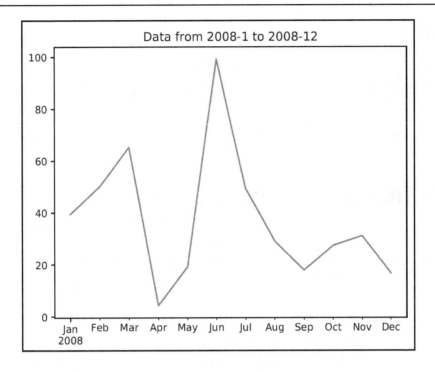

How it works...

In this recipe, we learned how to break up time series data. First, we imported the data contained in a .txt file. This data was transformed into a time series format using a function that we defined in the previous recipe. Thus, we have plotted the data, first within a certain period of years, and then within a certain range of dates.

There's more...

To transform data into a time series format, the pandas library was used. This library is particularly efficient for manipulating time series data.

See also

- Refer to the official documentation of the pandas time series and date functionality: `https://pandas.pydata.org/pandas-docs/stable/user_guide/timeseries.html`
- *Time Series* (by Prof Gesine Reinert, from the University of Oxford): `http://www.stats.ox.ac.uk/~reinert/time/notesht10short.pdf`

Operating on time series data

Now that we know how to slice data and extract various subsets, let's discuss how to operate on time series data. You can filter the data in many different ways. The `pandas` library allows you to operate on time series data in any way that you want.

Getting ready

In this recipe, we will use data contained in a `.txt` file and load it. Then, we will filter the data using a certain threshold to extract only a portion of the starting dataset that meets specific requirements.

How to do it...

Let's see how we can operate on time series data:

1. Create a new Python file and import the following packages (the full code is given in the `operating_on_data.py` file that is provided for you):

```
import pandas as pd
import matplotlib.pyplot as plt
from convert_to_timeseries import convert_data_to_timeseries
```

Here, `convert_to_timeseries` is the function we defined in the previous recipe, *Transforming data into a time series format*, that read an input file and converted sequential observations into time-indexed data.

2. We will use the same text file that we used in the previous recipes (data_timeseries.txt):

```
# Input file containing data
input_file = 'data_timeseries.txt'
```

3. We will use both the third and fourth columns in this .txt file (remember, Python lists the data starting from position 0, so the third and fourth columns have the indices 2 and 3):

```
# Load data
data1 = convert_data_to_timeseries(input_file, 2)
data2 = convert_data_to_timeseries(input_file, 3)
```

4. Convert the data into a pandas DataFrame:

```
dataframe = pd.DataFrame({'first': data1, 'second': data2})
```

5. Plot the data in the given year range:

```
# Plot data
dataframe['1952':'1955'].plot()
plt.title('Data overlapped on top of each other')
```

6. Let's assume that we want to plot the difference between the two columns that we just loaded in the given year range. We can do this using the following lines:

```
# Plot the difference
plt.figure()
difference = dataframe['1952':'1955']['first'] -
dataframe['1952':'1955']['second']
difference.plot()
plt.title('Difference (first - second)')
```

7. If we want to filter the data based on different conditions for the first and second columns, we can just specify these conditions and plot this:

```
# When 'first' is greater than a certain threshold
# and 'second' is smaller than a certain threshold
dataframe[(dataframe['first'] > 60) & (dataframe['second'] <
20)].plot(style='o')
plt.title('first > 60 and second < 20')

plt.show()
```

If you run the preceding code, the first output will look as follows:

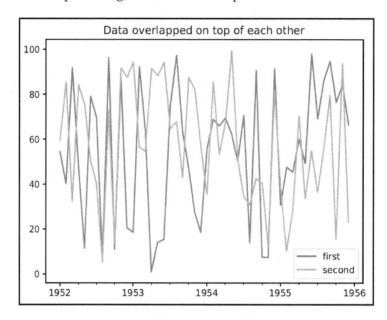

The second output screenshot denotes the difference, as follows:

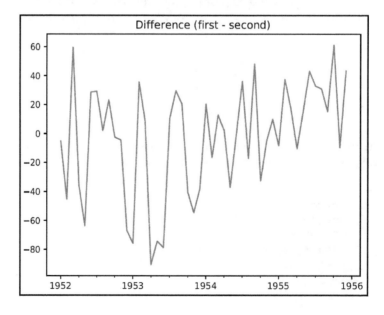

The third output screenshot denotes the filtered data, as follows:

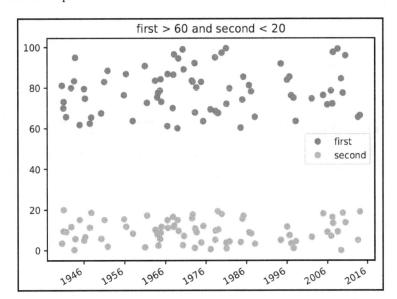

How it works...

In this recipe, we learned how to filter the data contained in a time series. First, we plotted the data between two years (from 1952 to 1955). Then, we plotted the difference between the data contained in two columns for a specific time interval (from 1952 to 1955). Finally, we plotted data using a certain threshold to extract only a portion of the starting dataset that meets specific requirements—in particular, when the first column is greater than 60 and when the second column is smaller than 20.

There's more...

To perform two-column filtering at the same time, the & operator was used. The & (and) operator is a logical operator (Boolean operator) of logical conjunction between two propositions. Given two propositions, A and B, the logical conjunction determines a third proposition, C, that manifests itself as true only when both propositions are true.

See also

- Refer to the *Fundamental concepts in Time Series Analysis* lecture, (from the University of Lausanne): `https://math.unice.fr/~frapetti/CorsoP/chapitre_1_part_1_IMEA_1.pdf`

Extracting statistics from time series data

One of the main reasons that we want to analyze time series data is to extract interesting statistics from it. This provides a lot of information regarding the nature of the data.

Getting ready

In this recipe, we will take a look at how to extract some statistics.

How to do it...

Let's see how we can extract statistics from time series data:

1. Create a new Python file and import the following packages (the full code is given in the `extract_stats.py` file that is provided for you):

   ```
   import pandas as pd
   import matplotlib.pyplot as plt
   from convert_to_timeseries import convert_data_to_timeseries
   ```

   The `convert_to_timeseries` function is the function we defined in the previous recipe, *Transforming data into a time series format,* that read an input file and converted sequential observations into time-indexed data.

2. We will use the same text file that we used in the previous recipes for analysis (`data_timeseries.txt`):

   ```
   # Input file containing data
   input_file = 'data_timeseries.txt'
   ```

3. Load both the data columns (third and fourth columns):

   ```
   # Load data
   data1 = convert_data_to_timeseries(input_file, 2)
   data2 = convert_data_to_timeseries(input_file, 3)
   ```

4. Create a `pandas` data structure to hold this data. This DataFrame is like a dictionary that has keys and values:

```
dataframe = pd.DataFrame({'first': data1, 'second': data2})
```

5. Let's start extracting some stats now. To extract the maximum and minimum values, use the following code:

```
# Print max and min
print('Maximum:\n', dataframe.max())
print('Minimum:\n', dataframe.min())
```

6. To print the mean values of your data or just the row-wise mean, use the following code:

```
# Print mean
print('Mean:\n', dataframe.mean())
print('Mean row-wise:\n', dataframe.mean(1)[:10])
```

7. The rolling mean is an important statistic that's used a lot in time series processing. One of the most famous applications is smoothing a signal to remove noise. *Rolling mean* refers to computing the mean of a signal in a window that keeps sliding on the time scale. Let's consider a window size of 24 and plot this, as follows:

```
# Plot rolling mean
DFMean = dataframe.rolling(window=24).mean()
plt.plot(DFMean)
```

8. Correlation coefficients are useful in understanding the nature of the data, as follows:

```
# Print correlation coefficients
print('Correlation coefficients:\n', dataframe.corr())
```

9. Let's plot this using a window size of 60:

```
# Plot rolling correlation
plt.figure()
DFCorr= dataframe.rolling(window=60).corr(pairwise=False)
plt.plot(DFCorr)
plt.show()
```

If you run the preceding code, the rolling mean will look as follows:

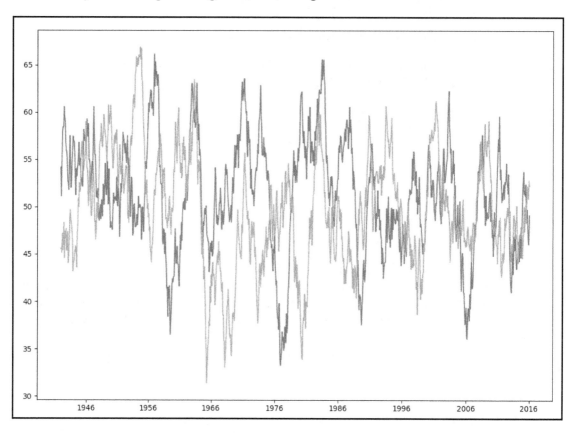

The second output indicates the rolling correlation (the following output is the result of a zoomed rectangle operation that was performed in the matplotlib window):

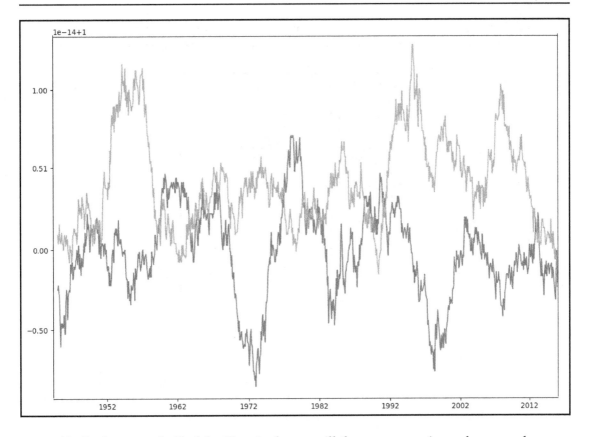

10. In the upper half of the Terminal, you will the see max, min, and mean values printed, as shown in the following output:

```
Maximum:
first      99.82
second     99.97
dtype: float64

Minimum:
first       0.07
second      0.00
dtype: float64

Mean:
first      51.264529
second     49.695417
dtype: float64
```

11. In the lower half of the terminal, you will see the row-wise mean stats and correlation coefficients printed, as shown in the following output:

```
Mean row-wise:
1940-01-31      81.885
1940-02-29      41.135
1940-03-31      10.305
1940-04-30      83.545
1940-05-31      18.395
1940-06-30      16.695
1940-07-31      86.875
1940-08-31      42.255
1940-09-30      55.880
1940-10-31      34.720
Freq: M, dtype: float64

Correlation coefficients:
               first      second
first      1.000000    0.077607
second     0.077607    1.000000
```

How it works...

In this recipe, we learned how to extract some statistics. We started by calculating the minimum, maximum, and mean of each of the two columns that were extracted from the dataset. Then, we calculated the mean for each row for the first 10 rows of the DataFrame. Finally, we performed a correlation analysis between the two features.

There's more...

To perform a correlation analysis, the `pandas.DataFrame.corr` function was used. This function computes a pairwise correlation of columns, excluding N/A or null values. The following methods are available:

- `pearson`: This is the standard correlation coefficient
- `kendall`: This is the **Kendall Tau** correlation coefficient
- `spearman`: This is the **Spearman rank** correlation coefficient

See also

- Refer to the official documentation of the `pandas.DataFrame.corr` function: `https://pandas.pydata.org/pandas-docs/stable/reference/api/pandas.DataFrame.corr.html`
- *Correlation* (from the SRM University): `http://www.srmuniv.ac.in/sites/default/files/downloads/CORRELATION.pdf`

Building HMMs for sequential data

Hidden Markov models (**HMMs**) are particularly suitable for sequential data analysis problems. They are widely used in fields such as speech analysis, finance, word sequencing, weather forecasting, and so on.

Any source of data that produces a sequence of outputs can produce patterns. Note that HMMs are generative models, which means that they can generate the data once they learn the underlying structure. HMMs cannot discriminate between classes in their base forms. This is in contrast to discriminative models that can learn to discriminate between classes but cannot generate data.

Getting ready

Let's say that we want to predict whether the weather will be sunny, chilly, or rainy tomorrow. To do this, we look at all the parameters, such as temperature, pressure, and so on, whereas the underlying state is hidden. Here, the underlying state refers to the three available options: sunny, chilly, or rainy.

How to do it...

Let's see how we can build HMMs for sequential data:

1. Create a new Python file and import the following packages (the full code is given in the `hmm.py` file that is provided for you):

```
import numpy as np
import matplotlib.pyplot as plt
from hmmlearn.hmm import GaussianHMM
```

2. We will use the data from a file named `data_hmm.txt` that is already provided to you. This file contains comma-separated lines. Each line contains three values: a year, a month, and a piece of floating-point data. Let's load this into a NumPy array:

```
# Load data from input file
input_file = 'data_hmm.txt'
data = np.loadtxt(input_file, delimiter=',')
```

3. Let's stack the data column-wise for analysis. We don't need to technically column-stack this because it's only one column. However, if you have more than one column to analyze, you can use the following structure:

```
# Arrange data for training
X = np.column_stack([data[:,2]])
```

4. Create and train the HMM using four components. The number of components is a hyperparameter that we have to choose. Here, by selecting four, we say that the data is being generated using four underlying states. We will see how the performance varies with this parameter:

```
# Create and train Gaussian HMM
print("Training HMM....")
num_components = 4
model = GaussianHMM(n_components=num_components,
covariance_type="diag", n_iter=1000)
model.fit(X)
```

5. Run the predictor to get the hidden states:

```
# Predict the hidden states of HMM
hidden_states = model.predict(X)
```

6. Compute the mean and variance of the hidden states:

```
print("Means and variances of hidden states:")
for i in range(model.n_components):
    print("Hidden state", i+1)
    print("Mean =", round(model.means_[i][0], 3))
    print("Variance =", round(np.diag(model.covars_[i])[0], 3))
```

7. As we discussed earlier, HMMs are generative models. So, let's generate, for example, `1000` samples and plot this:

```
# Generate data using model
num_samples = 1000
samples, _ = model.sample(num_samples)
plt.plot(np.arange(num_samples), samples[:,0], c='black')
plt.title('Number of components = ' + str(num_components))
plt.show()
```

The full code is given in the `hmm.py` file that is already provided to you. If you run the preceding code, you will see the following output:

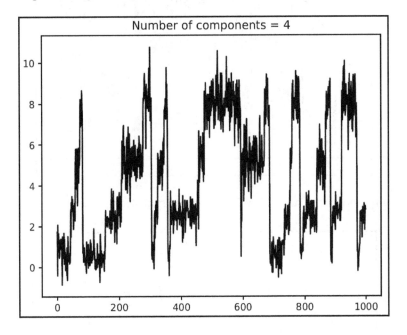

8. You can experiment with the `n_components` parameter to see how the curve gets nicer as you increase it. You can basically give it more freedom to train and customize by allowing a larger number of hidden states. If you increase it to 8, you will see the following output:

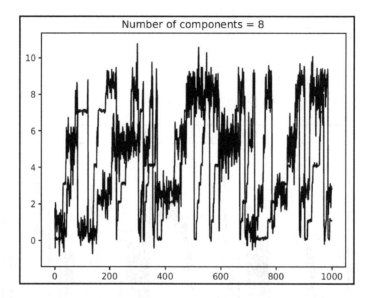

9. If you increase this to 12, it will get even smoother:

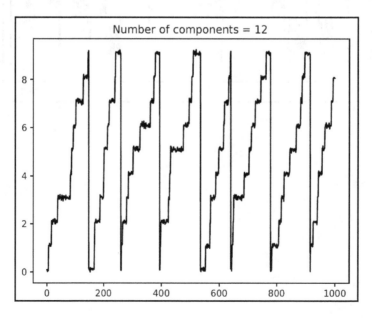

In the terminal, you will get the following output:

```
Training HMM....
Means and variances of hidden states:
Hidden state 1
Mean = 5.592
Variance = 0.253
Hidden state 2
Mean = 1.098
Variance = 0.004
Hidden state 3
Mean = 7.102
Variance = 0.003
Hidden state 4
Mean = 3.098
Variance = 0.003
Hidden state 5
Mean = 4.104
Variance = 0.003
```

How it works...

HMM is a model in which the system being modeled is assumed to be a Markov process with unobserved states. A stochastic process is called Markovian when, having chosen a certain instance of *t* for observation, the evolution of the process, starting with *t*, depends only on *t* and does not depend in any way on the previous instances. Thus, a process is Markovian when, given the moment of observation, only this instance determines the future evolution of the process, while this evolution does not depend on the past. In this recipe, we learned how to use HMMs to generate a time series.

There's more...

In this recipe, we used `hmmlearn` to build and train HMMs, which implements the HMMs. A HMM is a generative probabilistic model, wherein a sequence of observable variables is computed using a sequence of hidden internal states. Hidden states are not observed directly.

See also

- Refer to the official documentation of the `hmmlearn` library to find out more: `https://hmmlearn.readthedocs.io/en/latest/`
- *A Tutorial on Hidden Markov Models* (by Lawrence R Rabiner from Oxford University): `https://www.robots.ox.ac.uk/~vgg/rg/slides/hmm.pdf`

Building CRFs for sequential text data

Conditional random fields (**CRFs**) are probabilistic models that are used to analyze structured data. They are frequently used to label and segment sequential data. CRFs are discriminative models as opposed to HMMs, which are generative models. CRFs are used extensively to analyze sequences, stock, speech, words, and so on. In these models, given a particular labeled observation sequence, we define a conditional probability distribution over this sequence. This is in contrast to HMMs, where we define a joint distribution over the label and the observed sequence.

Getting ready

In this recipe, we will use a library called `pystruct` to build and train CRFs. Make sure that you install this before you proceed. You can find the installation instructions at `https://pystruct.github.io/installation.html`.

How to do it...

Let's see how we can build CRFs for sequential text data:

1. Create a new Python file and import the following packages (the full code is given in the `crf.py` file that is provided for you):

```
import argparse
import numpy as np
from pystruct.datasets import load_letters
from pystruct.models import ChainCRF
from pystruct.learners import FrankWolfeSSVM
```

2. Define an argument parser to take the `c` value as an input argument. Here, `c` is a hyperparameter that controls how specific you want your model to be without losing the power to generalize:

```
def build_arg_parser():
    parser = argparse.ArgumentParser(description='Trains the CRF
classifier')
    parser.add_argument("--c-value", dest="c_value",
required=False, type=float,
            default=1.0, help="The C value that will be used for
training")
    return parser
```

3. Define a `class` to handle all CRF-related processing:

```
class CRFTrainer(object):
```

4. Define an `init` function to initialize the values:

```
def __init__(self, c_value, classifier_name='ChainCRF'):
    self.c_value = c_value
    self.classifier_name = classifier_name
```

5. We will use `ChainCRF` to analyze the data. We need to add an error check to this, as follows:

```
if self.classifier_name == 'ChainCRF':
    model = ChainCRF()
```

6. Define the classifier that we will use with our CRF model. We will use a type of SVM to achieve this:

```
    self.clf = FrankWolfeSSVM(model=model, C=self.c_value,
max_iter=50)
        else:
            raise TypeError('Invalid classifier type')
```

7. Load the `letters` dataset. This dataset consists of segmented letters and their associated feature vectors. We will not analyze the images because we already have the feature vectors. The first letter from each word has been removed, so all we have are lowercase letters:

```
def load_data(self):
    letters = load_letters()
```

8. Load the data and labels into their respective variables:

```
X, y, folds = letters['data'], letters['labels'], letters['folds']
X, y = np.array(X), np.array(y)
return X, y, folds
```

9. Define a training method, as follows:

```
# X is a numpy array of samples where each sample
# has the shape (n_letters, n_features)
def train(self, X_train, y_train):
    self.clf.fit(X_train, y_train)
```

10. Define a method to evaluate the performance of the model:

```
def evaluate(self, X_test, y_test):
    return self.clf.score(X_test, y_test)
```

11. Define a method to classify new data:

```
# Run the classifier on input data
def classify(self, input_data):
    return self.clf.predict(input_data)[0]
```

12. The letters are indexed in a numbered array. To check the output and make it readable, we need to transform these numbers into alphabets. Define a function to do this:

```
def decoder(arr):
    alphabets = 'abcdefghijklmnopqrstuvwxyz'
    output = ''
    for i in arr:
        output += alphabets[i]

    return output
```

13. Define the main function and parse the input arguments:

```
if __name__=='__main__':
    args = build_arg_parser().parse_args()
    c_value = args.c_value
```

14. Initialize the variable with the class and the C value:

```
crf = CRFTrainer(c_value)
```

15. Load the `letters` data:

```
X, y, folds = crf.load_data()
```

16. Separate the data into training and testing datasets:

```
X_train, X_test = X[folds == 1], X[folds != 1]
y_train, y_test = y[folds == 1], y[folds != 1]
```

17. Train the CRF model, as follows:

```
print("Training the CRF model...")
crf.train(X_train, y_train)
```

18. Evaluate the performance of the CRF model:

```
score = crf.evaluate(X_test, y_test)
print("Accuracy score =", str(round(score*100, 2)) + '%')
```

19. Let's take a random test vector and predict the output using the model:

```
print("True label =", decoder(y_test[0]))
predicted_output = crf.classify([X_test[0]])
print("Predicted output =", decoder(predicted_output))
```

20. If you run the preceding code, you will get the following output on your terminal. As we can see, the word is supposed to be `commanding`. The CRF does a pretty good job of predicting all the letters:

```
Training the CRF model...
Accuracy score = 77.93%
True label = ommanding
Predicted output = ommanging
```

How it works...

HMMs assume that the current output is statistically independent of the previous outputs. This is needed by HMMs to ensure that the inference works in a robust way. However, this assumption doesn't always have to be true! The current output in a time series setup, more often than not, depends on previous outputs. One of the main advantages of CRFs over HMMs is that they are conditional by nature, which means that we are not assuming any independence between output observations. There are a few other advantages of using CRFs over HMMs. CRFs tend to outperform HMMs in a number of applications, such as linguistics, bioinformatics, speech analysis, and so on. In this recipe, we will learn how to use CRFs to analyze sequences of letters.

There's more...

PyStruct is a structured library of easy-to-use machine learning algorithms. It implements the max-margin and perceptron methods. Examples of learning algorithms that are implemented in PyStruct are CRFs, **maximum-margin Markov random fields (M3Ns)**, and structural SVMs.

See also

- Refer to the official documentation of the `pystruct` library for more information: https://pystruct.github.io/
- Look at the *Conditional Random Fields* lecture (from the University of Notre Dame): https://www3.nd.edu/~dchiang/teaching/nlp/2015/notes/chapter8v1.pdf

Analyzing stock market data

The stock market has always been a very popular topic; this is because stock market trends involve a truly impressive turnover. The interest that this topic arouses is clearly linked to the opportunity to get rich through good forecasting by a stock market title. A positive difference between the purchased stock price and that of the sold stock price entails a gain on the part of the investor. But, as we know, the performance of the stock market depends on multiple factors.

Getting ready

In this recipe, we'll look at how to analyze the stock price of a very popular company: I am referring to Amazon, the US e-commerce company, based in Seattle, Washington, which is the largest internet company in the world.

How to do it...

Let's see how we analyze stock market data:

1. Create a new Python file and import the following packages (the full code is given in the `AmazonStock.py` file that is provided for you):

```
import numpy as np
import pandas as pd
import matplotlib.pyplot as plt
from random import seed
```

2. Get the stock quotes from the `AMZN.csv` file that is provided for you:

```
seed(0)
Data = pd.read_csv('AMZN.csv',header=0, usecols=['Date',
'Close'],parse_dates=True,index_col='Date')
```

3. To extract preliminary information about the imported dataset, we can invoke the `info()` function:

```
print(Data.info())
```

The following results are returned:

```
<class 'pandas.core.frame.DataFrame'>
DatetimeIndex: 4529 entries, 2000-11-21 to 2018-11-21
Data columns (total 1 columns):
Close 4529 non-null float64
dtypes: float64(1)
memory usage: 70.8 KB
None
```

This function prints information about a DataFrame, including the index and the `dtypes` column, `non-null` values, and `memory usage`.

4. To display the first five rows of the imported DataFrame, we can use the `head()` function, as follows:

```
print(Data.head())
```

This function returns the first *n* rows for the object based on position. It is useful for quickly testing whether your object has the right type of data in it. By default, (if *n* is omitted), the first five rows are displayed. The following results are returned:

```
               Close
Date
2000-11-21  24.2500
2000-11-22  25.1875
2000-11-24  28.9375
2000-11-27  28.0000
2000-11-28  25.0312
```

5. To get a preview of the data contained in it, we can calculate a series of basic statistics. To do so, we will use the describe() function in the following way:

```
print(Data.describe())
```

The describe() function generates descriptive statistics that summarize the central tendency, the dispersion, and the form of the distribution of a dataset, excluding the NaN values. This function analyzes both numerical and object series, as well as the DataFrame column sets of mixed data types. The following results are returned:

```
               Close
count    4529.000000
mean      290.353723
std       407.211585
min         5.970000
25%        39.849998
50%       117.889999
75%       327.440002
max      2039.510010
```

6. Now, we are going to perform an initial visual exploratory analysis of the time series:

```
plt.figure(figsize=(10,5))
plt.plot(Data)
plt.show()
```

In the following graph, Amazon stock prices from 2000-11-21 to 2018-11-21 are shown:

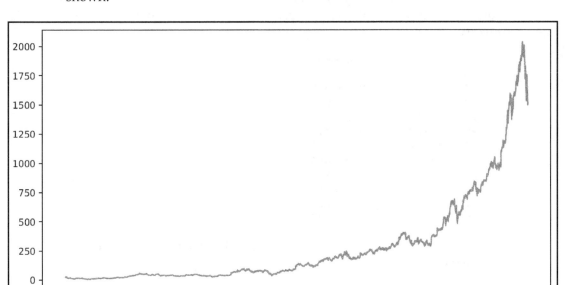

From the analysis of the previous graph, we can see that prices have increased considerably over time. In particular, starting from 2015, this increase has shown an exponential trend.

7. Now, let's try to obtain a deeper understanding of the change that Amazon stock has recorded over time. To calculate percentage changes in Python, we will use the `pct_change()` function. This function returns percentage changes over a given number of periods:

```
DataPCh = Data.pct_change()
```

What we have just calculated coincides with the concept of return.

8. To calculate the logarithm of returns, we will use the `log()` function from `numpy`:

```
LogReturns = np.log(1 + DataPCh)
print(LogReturns.tail(10))
```

The `tail()` function returns the last *n* rows from the object, based on position. It is useful for quickly verifying data—for example, after sorting or appending rows. The following values are returned (the last 10 rows of the `LogReturns` object):

```
                   Close
Date
2018-11-08      -0.000330
2018-11-09      -0.024504
2018-11-12      -0.045140
2018-11-13      -0.003476
2018-11-14      -0.019913
2018-11-15       0.012696
2018-11-16      -0.016204
2018-11-19      -0.052251
2018-11-20      -0.011191
2018-11-21       0.014123
```

9. Now, we will draw a diagram with the logarithm of the returns we have calculated:

```
plt.figure(figsize=(10,5))
plt.plot(LogReturns)
plt.show()
```

As we have done previously, we first set the dimensions of the graph, then we will plot the graph, and finally we will visualize it. The following graph shows the logarithm of the returns:

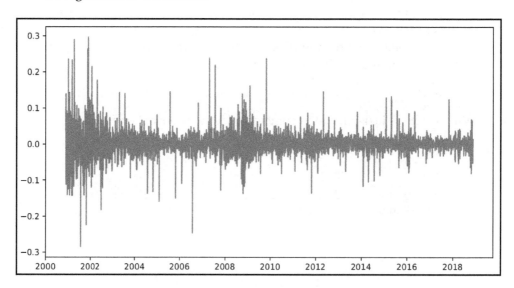

How it works...

To study the evolution of a phenomenon, a graph of its time series is not enough; we need to make comparisons between the intensity of the phenomenon at different times, that is, calculating the variations of intensity from one period to another. Furthermore, it can be interesting to analyze the trend of the variations of the phenomenon that occurred between adjoining periods of time. We indicate a time series with Y1,..., Yt,..., Yn. The time series is the chronological recording of experimental observations of a variable, such as price trends, stock market indices, spreads, and unemployment rates. It is therefore a succession of data that's been ordered over time from which we want to extract information for the characterization of the phenomenon under observation, and for the prediction of future values.

The variation that occurs between two different times (let's indicate them with t and $t + 1$) can be measured using the following ratio:

$$\frac{Y_{t+1} - Y_t}{Y_t}$$

This index is a percentage ratio and is called a **percentage change**. In particular, this is the percentage rate of variation of the phenomenon Y of the time $t + 1$, with respect to the previous time, t. This method gives a more detailed explanation about how the data has changed over a period of time. With this technique, we can track the prices of individual stocks and large market indices, as well as compare the values of different currencies.

There's more...

The advantage of using returns, compared to prices, lies in the normalization that allows us to measure all the variables in a comparable metric, thus allowing for the evaluation of analytical relationships between two or more variables.

See also

- Refer to the official documentation of the `pandas.DataFrame.pct_change` function: `https://pandas.pydata.org/pandas-docs/stable/reference/api/pandas.DataFrame.pct_change.html`

Using RNNs to predict time series data

Long short-term memory (**LSTM**) is a particular architecture of **recurrent neural networks** (**RNNs**). RNNs are based on the need to preserve the memory of past events; this behavior is not possible with normal networks, and that is why RNNs are used in areas where the classic networks do not produce results, such as the prediction of time series (weather, quotations, and so on) that refer to previous data.

An LSTM network consists of cells (LSTM blocks) that are linked together. Each cell is, in turn, composed of three types of ports: the input gate, output gate, and forget gate. They implement the write, read, and reset functions on the cell memory, respectively, so the LSTM modules are able to regulate what is stored and deleted. This is possible thanks to the presence of various elements called **gates**, which are composed of a sigmoid neural layer and a pointwise product. The output of each gate is in the range (0, 1), representing the percentage of information that flows inside it.

Getting ready

In this recipe, we'll look at how the LSTM model can be applied to predict the future stock price of a very popular company: I refer to Amazon, the US e-commerce company, based in Seattle, Washington, which is the largest internet company in the world.

How to do it...

Let's see how we can use RNNs to predict time series data:

1. Create a new Python file and import the following packages (the full code is given in the LSTMstock.py file that is provided for you). The first part of the file was tackled in the previous recipe, *Analyzing stock market data*. We report it only for the completeness of the algorithm:

```
import numpy as np
import pandas as pd
import matplotlib.pyplot as plt
from random import seed

seed(0)

Data = pd.read_csv('AMZN.csv',header=0, usecols=['Date',
'Close'],parse_dates=True,index_col='Date')
```

2. It is good practice to rescale the data before training an LSTM algorithm. With rescaling, data units are eliminated, allowing you to compare data from different locations easily. In this case, we will use the min-max method (usually called **feature scaling**) to get all the scaled data in the range [0, 1]. To perform feature scaling, we can use the preprocessing package that's available in the `sklearn` library:

```
from sklearn.preprocessing import MinMaxScaler
scaler = MinMaxScaler()
DataScaled = scaler.fit_transform(Data)
```

3. Now, let's split the data for the training and test model. Training and testing the model forms the basis for further usage of the model for prediction in predictive analytics. Given a dataset of 4,529 rows of data, we split it into a convenient ratio (say 70:30) and allocate 3,170 rows for training and 1,359 rows for testing:

```
np.random.seed(7)
TrainLen = int(len(DataScaled) * 0.70)
TestLen = len(DataScaled) - TrainLen
TrainData = DataScaled[0:TrainLen, :]
TestData = DataScaled[TrainLen:len(DataScaled), :]

print(len(TrainData), len(TestData))
```

The following results are returned:

```
3170 1359
```

4. Now, we need input and output to train and test our network. It is clear that the input is represented by the data that's present in the dataset. Therefore, we must construct our output; we will do so by supposing we want to predict the Amazon stock price at time $t + 1$ with respect to the value stored at time t. A recurrent network has memory, and this is maintained by fixing the so-called time step. The time step is all about how many steps back in time backpropagation uses when calculating gradients for weight updates during training. In this way, we set `TimeStep=1`. Then, we define a function that gives a dataset and a time step, which then returns the input and output data:

```
def DatasetCreation(dataset, TimeStep=1):
    DataX, DataY = [], []
    for i in range(len(dataset)-TimeStep-1):
        a = dataset[i:(i+TimeStep), 0]
        DataX.append(a)
        DataY.append(dataset[i + TimeStep, 0])
    return np.array(DataX), np.array(DataY)
```

In this function, `dataX =Input= data(t)` is the input variable and `DataY=output= data(t + 1)` is the predicted value at the next time period.

5. Let's use this function to set the train and test datasets that we will use in the next phase (network modeling):

```
TimeStep = 1
TrainX, TrainY = DatasetCreation(TrainData, TimeStep)
TestX, TestY = DatasetCreation(TestData, TimeStep)
```

In an LSTM/RNN network, the input for each LSTM layer must contain the following information:

*   **Observations**: Number of observations collected
*   **Time steps**: A time step is an observation point in the sample
*   **Features**: One feature for each step

Therefore, it is necessary to add a temporal dimension to those foreseen for a classical network. Thus, the input shape is as follows:

(Number of observations, number of time steps, number of features per steps)

In this way, the input for each LSTM layer becomes three-dimensional.

6. To transform the input datasets into 3D form, we will use the `np.reshape()` function, as follows:

```
TrainX = np.reshape(TrainX, (TrainX.shape[0], 1, TrainX.shape[1]))
TestX = np.reshape(TestX, (TestX.shape[0], 1, TestX.shape[1]))
```

7. Now that the data is in the right format, it's time to create the model. Let's start by importing the libraries:

```
from keras.models import Sequential
from keras.layers import LSTM
from keras.layers import Dense
```

8. We will use a `Sequential` model, that is, a linear stack of layers. To create a sequential model, we have to pass a list of layer instances to the constructor. We can also simply add layers via the `add()` method:

```
model = Sequential()
model.add(LSTM(256, input_shape=(1, TimeStep)))
model.add(Dense(1, activation='sigmoid'))
model.compile(loss='mean_squared_error',
```

```
optimizer='adam',metrics=['accuracy'])
model.fit(TrainX, TrainY, epochs=100, batch_size=1, verbose=1)
model.summary()
```

The following result is printed:

```
Layer (type)                    Output Shape                Param #
=================================================================
lstm_4 (LSTM)                   (None, 256)                 264192
_____
dense_4 (Dense)                 (None, 1)                   257
=================================================================
Total params: 264,449
Trainable params: 264,449
Non-trainable params: 0
```

9. To evaluate the performance of the model we have just adapted, we can use the `evaluate()` function, as follows:

```
score = model.evaluate(TrainX, TrainY, verbose=0)
print('Keras Model Loss = ',score[0])
print('Keras Model Accuracy = ',score[1])
```

The preceding function displays the loss value and metrics values for the model in the test mode. This is computed in batches. The following results are returned:

Keras Model Loss = 2.4628453362992094e-06
Keras Model Accuracy = 0.0003156565656565657

10. The model is now ready for use. We can therefore use it to execute our predictions:

```
TrainPred = model.predict(TrainX)
TestPred = model.predict(TestX)
```

11. The predictions must be reported in their original form so that they can be compared to the actual values:

```
TrainPred = scaler.inverse_transform(TrainPred)
TrainY = scaler.inverse_transform([TrainY])
TestPred = scaler.inverse_transform(TestPred)
TestY = scaler.inverse_transform([TestY])
```

12. To verify the correct prediction of data, we can now visualize the results by drawing an appropriate graph. To display the time series correctly, a prediction shift is required. This operation must be carried out both on the train set and the test set:

```
TrainPredictPlot = np.empty_like(DataScaled)
TrainPredictPlot[:, :] = np.nan
TrainPredictPlot[1:len(TrainPred)+1, :] = TrainPred
```

13. As we stated previously, the same operation must then be performed on the test set:

```
TestPredictPlot = np.empty_like(DataScaled)
TestPredictPlot[:, :] = np.nan
TestPredictPlot[len(TrainPred)+(1*2)+1:len(DataScaled)-1, :] =
TestPred
```

14. Finally, we have to plot the actual data and the predictions:

```
plt.figure(figsize=(10,5))
plt.plot(scaler.inverse_transform(DataScaled))
plt.plot(TrainPredictPlot)
plt.plot(TestPredictPlot)
plt.show()
```

The following screenshot shows the actual data and the predictions:

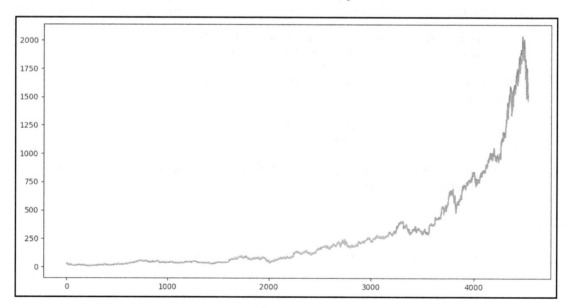

How it works...

At the beginning of this recipe, we said that the LSTM modules are able to regulate what is stored and deleted. This is possible thanks to the presence of various elements called gates, which are composed of a sigmoid neural layer and a pointwise product. The first part of the LSTM module decides what information is deleted from the cell. The gate takes the inputs and returns a value between 0 and 1 for each state of the cell. The gate output can take two values:

- 0: Complete reset of the cell status
- 1: Total storage of the cell value

Data storage is divided into two phases:

- The first is entrusted to one sigmoid layer called the **input gate layer**; it carries out an operation that establishes which values will need to be updated.
- The second phase is instead entrusted to a tanh layer that creates a vector of values, intended to be updated. To create an updated set of values, the outputs of the two layers are combined.

Finally, the result will be given by a sigmoid layer, which determines which parts of the cell will contribute to the output and from the current state of the cell, filtered through a tanh function to obtain a range from -1 to 1. The result of this operation is multiplied by the value of the sigmoid layer so that only the desired outputs are given.

There's more...

A RNN is a neural model in which a bidirectional flow of information is present. In other words, while the propagation of signals in feedforward networks takes place only in a continuous manner in one direction, from inputs to outputs, recurrent networks are different. In recurrent networks, this propagation can also occur from a neural layer following a previous one, between neurons belonging to the same layer, or even between a neuron and itself.

See also

- Refer to the official documentation of the Keras library: `https://keras.io/`
- Refer to *Recurrent Neural Networks* (from Yale University): `http://euler.stat.yale.edu/~tba3/stat665/lectures/lec21/lecture21.pdf`
- Refer to *Long Short-Term Memory* (from the University of Wisconsin, Madison): `http://pages.cs.wisc.edu/~shavlik/cs638/lectureNotes/Long%20Short-Term%20Memory%20Networks.pdf`

10
Analyzing Image Content

In this chapter, we will cover the following recipes:

- Operating on images using OpenCV-Python
- Detecting edges
- Histogram equalization
- Detecting corners
- Detecting SIFT feature points
- Building a Star feature detector
- Creating features using Visual Codebook and vector quantization
- Training an image classifier using Extremely Random Forests
- Building an object recognizer
- Using LightGBM for image classification

Technical requirements

To go through the recipes in this chapter, you need the following files (available on GitHub):

- operating_on_images.py
- capri.jpg
- edge_detector.py
- chair.jpg
- histogram_equalizer.py
- sunrise.jpg
- corner_detector.py
- box.png

- `feature_detector.py`
- `table.jpg`
- `star_detector.py`
- `trainer.py`
- `object_recognizer.py`
- `LightgbmClassifier.py`

Introducing computer vision

Computer vision is a field that studies how to process, analyze, and understand the contents of visual data. In image content analysis, we use a lot of computer vision algorithms to build our understanding of the objects in the image. Computer vision covers various aspects of image analysis, such as object recognition, shape analysis, pose estimation, 3D modeling, visual search, and so on. Humans are really good at identifying and recognizing things around them! The ultimate goal of computer vision is to accurately model the human vision system using computers.

Computer vision consists of various levels of analysis. In low-level vision, we deal with pixel-processing tasks, such as **edge detection**, **morphological processing**, and **optical flow**. In middle-level and high-level vision, we deal with things such as **object recognition**, **3D modeling**, **motion analysis**, and various other aspects of visual data. As we go higher, we tend to delve deeper into the conceptual aspects of our visual system and try to extract a description of visual data, based on activities and intentions. One thing to note is that higher levels tend to rely on the outputs of the lower levels for analysis.

One of the most common questions here is this: how is computer vision different than image processing? **Image processing** studies image transformations at the pixel level. Both the input and output of an image processing system are images. Some common examples are edge detection, **histogram equalization**, and **image compression**. Computer vision algorithms heavily rely on image processing algorithms to perform their duties. In computer vision, we deal with more complex things that include understanding the visual data at a conceptual level. The reason for this is that we want to construct meaningful descriptions of the objects in the images. The output of a computer vision system is an interpretation of the 3D scene in the given image. This interpretation can come in various forms, depending on the task at hand.

Operating on images using OpenCV-Python

In this chapter, we will use a library called **Open Source Computer Vision Library** (**OpenCV**), to analyze images. OpenCV is the world's most popular library for computer vision. As it has been highly optimized for many different platforms, it has become the de facto standard in the industry. Before you proceed, make sure that you install the library with Python support. You can download and install OpenCV at http://opencv.org. For detailed installation instructions on various operating systems, you can refer to the documentation section on the website.

Getting ready

In this recipe, we will take a look at how to operate on images using OpenCV-Python. In this recipe, we will look at how to load and display an image. We will also look at how to crop, resize, and save an image to an output file.

How to do it...

Let's see how we can operate on images using OpenCV-Python:

1. Create a new Python file and import the following packages (the full code is given in the operating_on_images.py file that is provided for you):

```
import sys
import cv2
```

2. Specify the input image as the first argument to the file, and read it using the image read function. We will use the forest.jpg file that is provided to you, as follows:

```
# Load and display an image -- 'forest.jpg'
input_file = sys.argv[1]
img = cv2.imread(input_file)
```

3. Display the input image, as follows:

```
cv2.imshow('Original', img)
```

4. We will now crop this image. Extract the height and width of the input image, and then specify the boundaries:

```
# Cropping an image
h, w = img.shape[:2]
start_row, end_row = int(0.21*h), int(0.73*h)
start_col, end_col= int(0.37*w), int(0.92*w)
```

5. Crop the image using NumPy-style slicing and display it:

```
img_cropped = img[start_row:end_row, start_col:end_col]
cv2.imshow('Cropped', img_cropped)
```

6. Resize the image to 1.3 times its original size and display it:

```
# Resizing an image
scaling_factor = 1.3
img_scaled = cv2.resize(img, None, fx=scaling_factor,
fy=scaling_factor,
interpolation=cv2.INTER_LINEAR)
cv2.imshow('Uniform resizing', img_scaled)
```

7. The previous method will uniformly scale the image on both dimensions. Let's assume that we want to skew the image based on specific output dimensions. We will use the following code:

```
img_scaled = cv2.resize(img, (250, 400),
interpolation=cv2.INTER_AREA)
cv2.imshow('Skewed resizing', img_scaled)
```

8. Save the image to an output file:

```
# Save an image
output_file = input_file[:-4] + '_cropped.jpg'
cv2.imwrite(output_file, img_cropped)

cv2.waitKey()
```

The `waitKey()` function displays the images until you hit a key on the keyboard.

9. We will run the code in a Terminal window:

```
$ python operating_on_images.py capri.jpg
```

You will see the following four images on the screen (*Capri's Faraglioni (Italy)*):

How it works...

In this recipe, we learned how to operate on images using the OpenCV-Python library. The following tasks were performed:

- Loading and displaying an image
- Cropping an image
- Resizing an image
- Saving an image

There's more...

OpenCV is a free software library that was originally developed by Intel and the Nizhny Novgorod research center in Russia. Later, it was maintained by Willow Garage and is now maintained by Itseez. The programming language that's mainly used to develop with this library is C ++, but it is also possible to interface through C, Python, and Java.

See also

- Refer to the official documentation of the OpenCV library at `http://opencv.org`
- Refer to the OpenCV tutorials at `https://docs.opencv.org/2.4/opencv_tutorials.pdf`

Detecting edges

Edge detection is one of the most popular techniques in computer vision. It is used as a preprocessing step in many applications. With edge detection, you can mark points in a digital image where light intensity suddenly changes. The sudden changes in the properties of an image want to highlight important events or changes in the physical world of which the images are representations. These changes identify, for example, surface orientation discontinuities, depth discontinuities, and so on.

Getting ready

In this recipe, we will learn how to use different edge detectors to detect edges in the input image.

How to do it...

Let's see how we can detect edges:

1. Create a new Python file and import the following packages (the full code is given in the `edge_detector.py` file that is provided for you):

```
import sys
import cv2
```

2. Load the input image. We will use `chair.jpg`:

```
# Load the input image -- 'chair.jpg'
# Convert it to grayscale
input_file = sys.argv[1]
img = cv2.imread(input_file, cv2.IMREAD_GRAYSCALE)
```

3. Extract the height and width of the image:

```
h, w = img.shape
```

4. The **Sobel filter** is a type of edge detector that uses a 3 x 3 kernel to detect horizontal and vertical edges separately:

```
sobel_horizontal = cv2.Sobel(img, cv2.CV_64F, 1, 0, ksize=5)
```

5. Run the vertical Sobel detector:

```
sobel_vertical = cv2.Sobel(img, cv2.CV_64F, 0, 1, ksize=5)
```

6. The **Laplacian edge detector** detects edges in both directions. We use it as follows:

```
laplacian = cv2.Laplacian(img, cv2.CV_64F)
```

7. Even though Laplacian addresses the shortcomings of Sobel, the output is still very noisy. The **Canny edge detector** outperforms all of them because of the way it treats the problem. It is a multistage process, and it uses hysteresis to come up with clean edges:

```
canny = cv2.Canny(img, 50, 240)
```

8. Display all the output images:

```
cv2.imshow('Original', img)
cv2.imshow('Sobel horizontal', sobel_horizontal)
cv2.imshow('Sobel vertical', sobel_vertical)
cv2.imshow('Laplacian', laplacian)
cv2.imshow('Canny', canny)

cv2.waitKey()
```

9. We will run the code in the terminal window using the following command:

```
$ python edge_detector.py siracusa.jpg
```

You will see the following five images on the screen (*The ancient theatre of Siracusa (Italy)*):

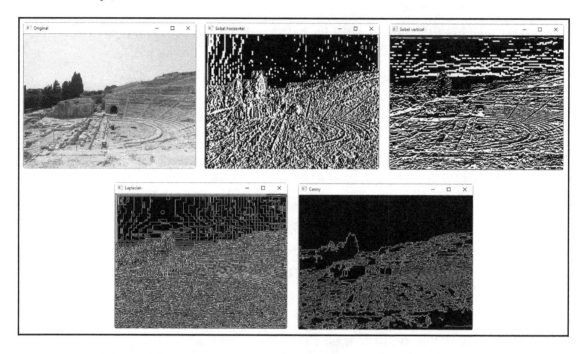

At the top of the screenshot is the original image, the horizontal Sobel edge detector output, and the vertical Sobel edge detector output. Note how the detected lines tend to be vertical. This is due to the fact that it's a horizontal edge detector, and it tends to detect changes in this direction. At the bottom of the screenshot is the Laplacian edge detector output and the Canny edge detector, which detects all the edges nicely.

How it works...

The Sobel operator is a differential operator, which calculates an approximate value of the gradient of a function that represents the brightness of the image. At each point in the image, the Sobel operator can correspond to the gradient vector or to the norm of that vector. The algorithm that's used by the Sobel operator is based on the convolution of the image with a filter, separated and of integer value, applied both in the vertical and horizontal direction, and is therefore economical in terms of the calculation power required.

The Laplacian edge detector is part of the zero-crossing methods that look for points where the second-order derivative goes through zero, which is usually the Laplacian function or a differential expression of a non-linear function.

There's more...

The Canny algorithm uses a multi-stage calculation method to find outlines of many of the types that are normally present in real images. To do this, the algorithm must identify and mark as many contours as possible in the image good location. Furthermore, the marked contours must be as close as possible to the real contours of the image. Finally, a given image contour must be marked only once, and if possible, the noise that's present in the image must not cause the detection of false contours.

See also

- *Sobel Operator*: http://www.tutorialspoint.com/dip/sobel_operator.htm
- *Laplacian edge detector*: http://homepages.inf.ed.ac.uk/rbf/HIPR2/log.htm
- *Canny edge detector*: http://homepages.inf.ed.ac.uk/rbf/HIPR2/canny.htm
- *Most Common Edge Detectors* (from the University of Minnesota): http://me.umn.edu/courses/me5286/vision/Notes/2015/ME5286-Lecture7.pdf

Histogram equalization

Histogram equalization is the process of modifying the intensities of the image pixels to enhance the image's contrast. The human eye likes contrast! This is the reason why almost all camera systems use histogram equalization to make images look nice.

Getting ready

The interesting thing is that the histogram equalization process is different for grayscale and color images. There's a catch when dealing with color images, and we'll see it in this recipe. Let's see how to do it.

How to do it...

Let's see how we can perform histogram equalization:

1. Create a new Python file and import the following packages (the full code is given in the `histogram_equalizer.py` file that is provided for you):

   ```
   import sys
   import cv2
   ```

2. Load the input image. We will use the `sunrise.jpg` image:

   ```
   # Load input image -- 'sunrise.jpg'
   input_file = sys.argv[1]
   img = cv2.imread(input_file)
   ```

3. Convert the image into `grayscale` and display it:

   ```
   # Convert it to grayscale
   img_gray = cv2.cvtColor(img, cv2.COLOR_BGR2GRAY)
   cv2.imshow('Input grayscale image', img_gray)
   ```

4. Equalize the histogram of the `grayscale` image and display it:

   ```
   # Equalize the histogram
   img_gray_histeq = cv2.equalizeHist(img_gray)
   cv2.imshow('Histogram equalized - grayscale', img_gray_histeq)
   ```

5. OpenCV loads images in the BGR format by default, so let's convert it from BGR into YUV first:

   ```
   # Histogram equalization of color images
   img_yuv = cv2.cvtColor(img, cv2.COLOR_BGR2YUV)
   ```

6. Equalize the Y channel, as follows:

   ```
   img_yuv[:,:,0] = cv2.equalizeHist(img_yuv[:,:,0])
   ```

7. Convert it back into BGR:

   ```
   img_histeq = cv2.cvtColor(img_yuv, cv2.COLOR_YUV2BGR)
   ```

8. Display the input and output images:

   ```
   cv2.imshow('Input color image', img)
   cv2.imshow('Histogram equalized - color', img_histeq)

   cv2.waitKey()
   ```

9. We will run the code in a terminal window:

```
$ python histogram_equalizer.py gubbio.jpg
```

You will see the following four images on the screen (*the medieval city of Gubbio (Italy)*):

How it works...

Histogram equalization is a digital image processing method with which you can calibrate the contrast using the image histogram. Histogram equalization increases the general contrast of many images, particularly when the usable image data is represented by very close intensity values. With this adaptation, intensities can be better distributed on the histogram. In this way, the areas with low local contrast obtain a greater contrast. The equalization of the histogram is achieved by spreading most of the values of frequent intensity.

There's more...

To equalize the histogram of the color images, we need to follow a different procedure. Histogram equalization only applies to the intensity channel. An RGB image consists of three color channels, and we cannot apply the histogram equalization process on these channels separately. We need to separate the intensity information from the color information before we do anything. So, we convert it into a YUV colorspace first, equalize the Y channel, and then convert it back into RGB to get the output.

See also

- *Contrast Enhancement* (from the Polytechnic University, Brooklyn): `http://eeweb.poly.edu/~yao/EL5123/lecture3_contrast_enhancement.pdf`
- *YUV Colorspace*: `http://softpixel.com/~cwright/programming/colorspace/yuv/`

Detecting corners

Corner detection is an important process in computer vision. It helps us identify the salient points in the image. This was one of the earliest feature extraction techniques that was used to develop image analysis systems.

Getting ready

In this recipe, we will learn how to detect the corner of a box by placing markers at the points that are identified.

How to do it...

Let's see how we can detect corners:

1. Create a new Python file and import the following packages (the full code is given in the `corner_detector.py` file that is provided for you):

```
import sys
import cv2
import numpy as np
```

2. Load the input image. We will use `box.png`:

```
# Load input image -- 'box.png'
input_file = sys.argv[1]
img = cv2.imread(input_file)
cv2.imshow('Input image', img)
```

3. Convert the image into `grayscale` and cast it to floating-point values. We need the floating-point values for the corner detector to work:

```
img_gray = cv2.cvtColor(img, cv2.COLOR_BGR2GRAY)
img_gray = np.float32(img_gray)
```

4. Run the `Harris corner detector` function on the `grayscale` image:

```
# Harris corner detector
img_harris = cv2.cornerHarris(img_gray, 7, 5, 0.04)
```

5. To mark the corners, we need to dilate the image, as follows:

```
# Resultant image is dilated to mark the corners
img_harris = cv2.dilate(img_harris, None)
```

6. Let's threshold the image to display the important points:

```
# Threshold the image
img[img_harris > 0.01 * img_harris.max()] = [0, 0, 0]
```

7. Display the output image:

```
cv2.imshow('Harris Corners', img)
cv2.waitKey()
```

8. We will run the code in a terminal window:

```
$ python corner_detector.py box.png
```

You will see the following two images on the screen:

How it works...

Corner detection is an approach that's used in computer vision to extract types of features and infer the contents of the image. It is often used in motion detection, image recording, video tracking, image mosaicization, image panoramas creation, 3D modeling, and object recognition. It is a topic similar to the detection of points of interest.

There's more...

Corner detection methods can be subdivided into two groups:

- Techniques based on the extraction of the contours and the subsequent identification of the points corresponding to the maximum curvature, or where the edge segments intersect
- Algorithms that search for corners directly from the intensity of the gray levels of the image pixels

See also

- *Harris Corner Detector* (from Penn State University): http://www.cse.psu.edu/~rtc12/CSE486/lecture06.pdf
- The official documentation of the Harris corner detector: https://docs.opencv.org/3.0-beta/doc/py_tutorials/py_feature2d/py_features_harris/py_features_harris.html

Detecting SIFT feature points

Scale invariant feature transform (**SIFT**) is one of the most popular features in the field of computer vision. David Lowe first proposed this in his seminal paper. It has since become one of the most effective features to use for image recognition and content analysis. It is robust against scale, orientation, intensity, and so on. This forms the basis of our object recognition system.

Getting ready

In this recipe, we will learn how to detect SIFT feature points.

How to do it...

Let's see how we can detect SIFT feature points:

1. Create a new Python file and import the following packages (the full code is given in the `feature_detector.py` file that is provided for you):

```
import sys
import cv2
import numpy as np
```

2. Load the input image. We will use `table.jpg`:

```
# Load input image -- 'table.jpg'
input_file = sys.argv[1]
img = cv2.imread(input_file)
```

3. Convert this image into grayscale:

```
img_gray = cv2.cvtColor(img, cv2.COLOR_BGR2GRAY)
```

4. Initialize the SIFT detector object and extract the keypoints:

```
sift = cv2.xfeatures2d.SIFT_create()
keypoints = sift.detect(img_gray, None)
```

5. The keypoints are the salient points, but they are not the features. This basically gives us the location of the salient points. SIFT also functions as a very effective feature extractor.

6. Draw the keypoints on top of the input image, as follows:

```
img_sift = np.copy(img)
cv2.drawKeypoints(img, keypoints, img_sift,
flags=cv2.DRAW_MATCHES_FLAGS_DRAW_RICH_KEYPOINTS)
```

7. Display the input and output images:

```
cv2.imshow('Input image', img)
cv2.imshow('SIFT features', img_sift)
cv2.waitKey()
```

8. We will run this in a terminal window:

$ python feature_detector.py flowers.jpg

You will see the following two images on the screen:

How it works...

For each object in an image, some interesting points are extracted to provide a description of the characteristics of the object. This feature, obtained from an image selected for training, is used to identify the object when trying to locate it in a test image that contains many other objects. To obtain a reliable recognition, the features that are extracted from the training image must be detectable, even with scale variations, noise, and lighting. These points are usually placed in high-contrast regions of the image, such as object contours.

There's more...

In Lowe's method, the key points of the SIFT objects are extracted from a set of reference images in the first phase and then they are stored in a database. The recognition of the object in a new image takes place by individually comparing each characteristic of the new image with the database that was obtained previously and looking for features based on the Euclidean distance of their feature vectors. From the complete set of matches in the new image, subsets of key points are identified that agree with the object and its position, scale, and orientation to filter the best matches.

See also

- *Introduction to SIFT (Scale-Invariant Feature Transform)*: `https://docs.opencv.org/3.4/d5/d3c/classcv_1_1xfeatures2d_1_1SIFT.html`
- The official documentation of the `OpenCV.xfeatures2d.SIFT` function: `https://docs.opencv.org/3.4/d5/d3c/classcv_1_1xfeatures2d_1_1SIFT.html`
- *Distinctive Image Features from Scale-Invariant Keypoints* (by David G Lowe from the University of British Columbia): `https://www.cs.ubc.ca/~lowe/papers/ijcv04.pdf`

Building a Star feature detector

The SIFT feature detector is good in many cases. However, when we build object recognition systems, we may want to use a different feature detector before we extract features using SIFT. This will give us the flexibility to cascade different blocks to get the best possible performance.

Getting ready

In this recipe, we will use the **Star feature detector** to detect features from an image.

How to do it...

Let's see how we can build a Star feature detector:

1. Create a new Python file and import the following packages (the full code is given in the `star_detector.py` file that is provided for you):

```
import sys
import cv2
```

2. Define a class to handle all the functions that are related to Star feature detection:

```
class StarFeatureDetector(object):
    def __init__(self):
        self.detector = cv2.xfeatures2d.StarDetector_create()
```

3. Define a function to run the detector on the input image:

```
def detect(self, img):
    return self.detector.detect(img)
```

4. Load the input image in the `main` function. We will use `table.jpg`:

```
if __name__=='__main__':
    # Load input image -- 'table.jpg'
    input_file = sys.argv[1]
    input_img = cv2.imread(input_file)
```

5. Convert the image into grayscale:

```
# Convert to grayscale
img_gray = cv2.cvtColor(input_img, cv2.COLOR_BGR2GRAY)
```

6. Detect features using the Star feature detector:

```
# Detect features using Star feature detector
keypoints = StarFeatureDetector().detect(input_img)
```

7. Draw keypoints on top of the input image:

```
cv2.drawKeypoints(input_img, keypoints, input_img,
        flags=cv2.DRAW_MATCHES_FLAGS_DRAW_RICH_KEYPOINTS)
```

8. Display the output image:

```
cv2.imshow('Star features', input_img)
cv2.waitKey()
```

9. We will run the code in a terminal window:

```
$ python star_detector.py table.jpg
```

You will see the following image on the screen:

How it works...

In this recipe, we learned how to use the OpenCV-Python library to build a Star feature detector. The following tasks were performed:

- Loading an image
- Converting to grayscale
- Detecting features using the Star feature detector
- Drawing keypoints and displaying the image

There's more...

The **Star function detector** is based on **CenSurE (Center Surrounded Extrema)**. The differences between the two detectors lie in the choice of polygons:

- CenSurE uses square, hexagons, and octagons as an alternative to the circle
- Star approximates the circle with two superimposed squares: one vertical and one rotated 45 degrees

See also

- The official documentation of OpenCV: `https://docs.opencv.org/2.4/ modules/features2d/doc/common_interfaces_of_feature_detectors.html? highlight= fast%20feature#StarFeatureDetector%20:%20public%20FeatureDetector`
- *CenSurE: Center Surround Extremas for Realtime Feature Detection and Matching*, in Computer Vision–ECCV 2008 (pp. 102-115). Springer Berlin Heidelberg: `http:// citeseerx.ist.psu.edu/viewdoc/download?doi=10.1.1.465.1117rep=rep1 type=pdf`

Creating features using Visual Codebook and vector quantization

To build an object recognition system, we need to extract feature vectors from each image. Each image needs to have a signature that can be used for matching. We use a concept called **Visual Codebook** to build image signatures. This codebook is basically the dictionary that we will use to come up with a representation for the images in our training data image signatures set. We use **vector quantization** to cluster many feature points and come up with **centroids**. These centroids will serve as the elements of our Visual Codebook.

Getting ready

In this recipe, we will create features using Visual Codebook and vector quantization. To build a robust object recognition system, you need tens of thousands of images. There is a dataset called `Caltech256` that's very popular in this field! It contains 256 classes of images, where each class contains thousands of samples.

How to do it...

Let's see how we can create features using Visual Codebook and vector quantization:

1. This is a lengthy recipe, so we will only look at the important functions. The full code is given in the `build_features.py` file that is already provided for you. Let's look at the class that's defined to extract features:

   ```
   class FeatureBuilder(object):
   ```

2. Define a method to extract features from the input image. We will use the Star detector to get the keypoints and then use SIFT to extract descriptors from these locations:

   ```
   def extract_ features(self, img):
       keypoints = StarFeatureDetector().detect(img)
       keypoints, feature_vectors = compute_sift_features(img, keypoints)
       return feature_vectors
   ```

3. We need to extract centroids from all the descriptors:

   ```
   def get_codewords(self, input_map, scaling_size, max_samples=12):
       keypoints_all = []
   ```

```
count = 0
cur_label = ''
```

4. Each image will give rise to a large number of descriptors. We will just use a small number of images because the centroids won't change much after this:

```
for item in input_map:
    if count >= max_samples:
        if cur_class != item['object_class']:
            count = 0
    else:
        continue

count += 1
```

5. The print progress is as follows:

```
if count == max_samples:
    print("Built centroids for", item['object_class'])
```

6. Extract the current label:

```
cur_class = item['object_class']
```

7. Read the image and resize it:

```
img = cv2.imread(item['image_path'])
img = resize_image(img, scaling_size)
```

8. Extract the features:

```
feature_vectors = self.extract_image_features(img)
keypoints_all.extend(feature_vectors)
```

9. Use vector quantization to quantize the feature points. Vector quantization is the *N*-dimensional version of rounding off:

```
kmeans, centroids = BagOfWords().cluster(keypoints_all)
return kmeans, centroids
```

10. Define the class to handle the bag-of-words model and vector quantization:

```
class BagOfWords(object):
    def __init__(self, num_clusters=32):
        self.num_dims = 128
        self.num_clusters = num_clusters
        self.num_retries = 10
```

11. Define a method to quantize the datapoints. We will use **k-means clustering** to achieve this:

```
def cluster(self, datapoints):
    kmeans = KMeans(self.num_clusters,
        n_init=max(self.num_retries, 1),
        max_iter=10, tol=1.0)
```

12. Extract the centroids, as follows:

```
res = kmeans.fit(datapoints)
centroids = res.cluster_centers_
return kmeans, centroids
```

13. Define a method to normalize the data:

```
def normalize(self, input_data):
    sum_input = np.sum(input_data)

    if sum_input > 0:
        return input_data / sum_input
    else:
        return input_data
```

14. Define a method to get the feature vector:

```
def construct_feature(self, img, kmeans, centroids):
    keypoints = StarFeatureDetector().detect(img)
    keypoints, feature_vectors = compute_sift_features(img,
keypoints)
    labels = kmeans.predict(feature_vectors)
    feature_vector = np.zeros(self.num_clusters)
```

15. Build a histogram and normalize it:

```
    for i, item in enumerate(feature_vectors):
        feature_vector[labels[i]] += 1

        feature_vector_img = np.reshape(feature_vector,
((1, feature_vector.shape[0])))
        return self.normalize(feature_vector_img)
```

16. Define a method, and then extract the SIFT features:

```
# Extract SIFT features
def compute_sift_features(img, keypoints):
    if img is None:
        raise TypeError('Invalid input image')
```

```
        img_gray = cv2.cvtColor(img, cv2.COLOR_BGR2GRAY)
        keypoints, descriptors =
    cv2.xfeatures2d.SIFT_create().compute(img_gray, keypoints)
        return keypoints, descriptors
```

As we mentioned earlier, please refer to build_features.py for the complete code. You should run the code in the following way:

```
$ python build_features.py --data-folder /path/to/training_images/
--codebook-file codebook.pkl --feature-map-file feature_map.pkl
```

This will generate two files called codebook.pkl and feature_map.pkl. We will use these files in the next recipe.

How it works...

In this recipe, we used a visual textbook as a dictionary, which we then used to create a representation for images in our image signatures, which are contained in the training set. So, we used vector quantization to group many characteristic points and create centroids. These centroids are served as elements of our visual textbook.

There's more...

We extract the features from various points in the image, counting the frequency of the values of the extracted features and classifying the image based on the frequency found, which is a technique that's similar to the representation of a document in a vector space. It is a vector quantization process with which I create a dictionary to discretize the possible values of the feature space.

See also

- *Visual Codebook* (by Tae-Kyun Kim, from Sidney Sussex College): http://mi.eng. cam.ac.uk/~cipolla/lectures/PartIB/old/IB-visualcodebook.pdf
- *Caltech-256 images repository* (from the California Institute of Technology): http:/ /www.vision.caltech.edu/Image_Datasets/Caltech256/

- *Vector Quantization Overview* (from Binghamton University): http://www.ws. binghamton.edu/fowler/fowler%20personal%20page/EE523_files/Ch_10_ 1%20VQ%20Description%20(PPT).pdf

Training an image classifier using Extremely Random Forests

An object recognition system uses an image classifier to classify the images into known categories. **Extremely Random Forests** (**ERFs**) are very popular in the field of machine learning because of their speed and accuracy. This algorithm is based on decision trees. Their differences compared to classical decision trees are in the choice of the points of division of the tree. The best division to separate the samples of a node into two groups is done by creating random subdivisions for each of the randomly selected features and choosing the best division between those.

Getting ready

In this recipe, we will use ERFs to train our image classifier. We basically construct decision trees based on our image signatures, and then train the forest to make the right decision.

How to do it...

Let's see how we can train an image classifier using ERFs:

1. Create a new Python file and import the following packages (the full code is given in the trainer.py file that is provided for you):

```
import argparse
import _pickle as pickle

import numpy as np
from sklearn.ensemble import ExtraTreesClassifier
from sklearn import preprocessing
```

2. Define an argument parser:

```
def build_arg_parser():
    parser = argparse.ArgumentParser(description='Trains the
classifier')
    parser.add_argument("--feature-map-file",
```

```
dest="feature_map_file", required=True,
            help="Input pickle file containing the feature map")
    parser.add_argument("--model-file", dest="model_file",
required=False,
            help="Output file where the trained model will be
stored")
    return parser
```

3. Define a class to handle ERF training. We will use a label encoder to encode our training labels:

```
class ERFTrainer(object):
    def __init__(self, X, label_words):
        self.le = preprocessing.LabelEncoder()
        self.clf = ExtraTreesClassifier(n_estimators=100,
                max_depth=16, random_state=0)
```

4. Encode the labels and train the classifier:

```
y = self.encode_labels(label_words)
self.clf.fit(np.asarray(X), y)
```

5. Define a function to encode the labels:

```
def encode_labels(self, label_words):
    self.le.fit(label_words)
    return np.array(self.le.transform(label_words),
dtype=np.float32)
```

6. Define a function to classify an unknown datapoint:

```
def classify(self, X):
    label_nums = self.clf.predict(np.asarray(X))
    label_words = self.le.inverse_transform([int(x) for x in
label_nums])
    return label_words
```

7. Define the main function and parse the input arguments:

```
if __name__=='__main__':
    args = build_arg_parser().parse_args()
    feature_map_file = args.feature_map_file
    model_file = args.model_file
```

8. Load the feature map that we created in the previous recipe:

```
# Load the feature map
with open(feature_map_file, 'rb') as f:
    feature_map = pickle.load(f)
```

9. Extract the feature vectors:

```
# Extract feature vectors and the labels
label_words = [x['object_class'] for x in feature_map]
dim_size = feature_map[0]['feature_vector'].shape[1]
X = [np.reshape(x['feature_vector'], (dim_size,)) for x in feature_map]
```

10. Train the ERF, which is based on the training data:

```
# Train the Extremely Random Forests classifier
erf = ERFTrainer(X, label_words)
```

11. Save the trained ERF model, as follows:

```
if args.model_file:
    with open(args.model_file, 'wb') as f:
        pickle.dump(erf, f)
```

12. Now, you should run the code in the Terminal:

```
$ python trainer.py --feature-map-file feature_map.pkl
--model-file erf.pkl
```

This will generate a file called `erf.pkl`. We will use this file in the next recipe.

How it works...

In this recipe, we used ERFs to train our image classifier. First, we defined an argument parser function and a class to handle ERF training. We used a label encoder to encode our training labels. Then, we loaded the feature map we obtained in the *Creating features using Visual Codebook and vector quantization* recipe. So, we extracted feature vectors and the labels, and finally we trained the ERF classifier.

There's more...

To train the image classifier, the `sklearn.ensemble.ExtraTreesClassifier` function was used. This function builds an extremely randomized tree classifier.

See also

- The official documentation of
  the `sklearn.ensemble.ExtraTreesClassifier` function: `https://scikit-learn.org/stable/modules/generated/sklearn.tree.ExtraTreeClassifier.html#sklearn.tree.ExtraTreeClassifier`
- *Random Forests* (by Leo Breiman and Adele Cutler, from the University of California, Berkeley): `https://www.stat.berkeley.edu/~breiman/RandomForests/cc_home.htm`
- *Extremely randomized trees* (by Pierre Geurts, Damien Ernst, and Louis Wehenkel, form *Machine learning Journal - Springer)*: `https://link.springer.com/content/pdf/10.1007/s10994-006-6226-1.pdf`

Building an object recognizer

In the previous recipe, *Training an image classifier using Extremely Random Forests*, we used ERFs to train our image classifier. Now that we have trained an ERF model, let's go ahead and build an object recognizer that can recognize the content of unknown images.

Getting ready

In this recipe, we will learn how to use a trained ERF model to recognize the content of unknown images.

How to do it...

Let's see how we can build an object recognizer:

1. Create a new Python file and import the following packages (the full code is given in the `object_recognizer.py` file that is provided for you):

```
import argparse
import _pickle as pickle

import cv2

import build_features as bf
from trainer import ERFTrainer
```

2. Define the argument parser:

```
def build_arg_parser():
    parser = argparse.ArgumentParser(description='Extracts features \
            from each line and classifies the data')
    parser.add_argument("--input-image", dest="input_image",
required=True,
            help="Input image to be classified")
    parser.add_argument("--model-file", dest="model_file",
required=True,
            help="Input file containing the trained model")
    parser.add_argument("--codebook-file", dest="codebook_file",
            required=True, help="Input file containing the
codebook")
    return parser
```

3. Define a class to handle the image tag extraction functions:

```
class ImageTagExtractor(object):
    def __init__(self, model_file, codebook_file):
        with open(model_file, 'rb') as f:
            self.erf = pickle.load(f)

        with open(codebook_file, 'rb') as f:
            self.kmeans, self.centroids = pickle.load(f)
```

4. Define a function to predict the output using the trained ERF model:

```
def predict(self, img, scaling_size):
    img = bf.resize_image(img, scaling_size)
    feature_vector = bf.BagOfWords().construct_feature(
            img, self.kmeans, self.centroids)
    image_tag = self.erf.classify(feature_vector)[0]
    return image_tag
```

5. Define the `main` function and load the input image:

```
if __name__=='__main__':
    args = build_arg_parser().parse_args()
    model_file = args.model_file
    codebook_file = args.codebook_file
    input_image = cv2.imread(args.input_image)
```

6. Scale the image appropriately, as follows:

```
scaling_size = 200
```

7. Print the output on the terminal:

```
print("Output:", ImageTagExtractor(model_file,
        codebook_file).predict(input_image, scaling_size))
```

8. Now, you should run the code in the following way:

```
$ python object_recognizer.py --input-image imagefile.jpg --model-
file erf.pkl --codebook-file codebook.pkl
```

How it works...

In this recipe, we used a trained ERF model to recognize the content of unknown images. To do this, the algorithms discussed in the two previous recipes were used, namely, *Creating features using Visual Codebook and vector quantization* and *Training an image classifier using Extremely Random Forests*.

There's more...

A **random forest** is an aggregate classifier that is made up of many decision trees and outputs the class that corresponds to the output of the individual tree classes. The algorithm for inducing a random forest was developed by Leo Breiman and Adele Cutler. It is based on the creation of a broad set of classifying trees, each of which is proposed to classify a single plant whose characteristics of any nature have been evaluated. Comparing the classification proposals provided by each tree in the forest shows the class to attribute the plant to it is the one that received the most indications or votes.

See also

- *Intro to random forest* (by Anthony Anh Quoc Doan, from California State University, Long Beach): https://web.csulb.edu/~tebert/teaching/lectures/551/random_forest.pdf

Using Light GBM for image classification

Gradient boosting is used in regression and classification problems to produce a predictive model in the form of a set of weak predictive models, typically decision trees. This methodology is similar to the boosting methods and generalizes them, allowing for the optimization of an arbitrary differentiable `loss` function.

The **Light Gradient Boosting Machine** (**LightGBM**) is a particular variation of gradient boosting, with some modifications that make it particularly advantageous. It is based on classification trees, but the choice of splitting the leaf at each step is done more effectively.

Getting ready

In this recipe, we will learn how to use LightGBM to classify handwritten digits. To do this, the **Modified National Institute of Standards and Technology** (**MNIST**) dataset will be used. This is a large database of handwritten digits. It has a set of 70,000 examples of data. It is a subset of NIST's larger dataset. The digits are of a 28 x 28 pixel resolution and are stored in a matrix of 70,000 rows and 785 columns; 784 columns form each pixel value from the 28 x 28 matrix, and one value is the actual digit. The digits have been size-normalized and centered in a fixed-size image.

How to do it...

Let's see how we can use LightGBM for image classification:

1. Create a new Python file and import the following packages (the full code is given in the `LightgbmClassifier.py` file that is provided for you):

```
import numpy as np
import lightgbm as lgb
from sklearn.metrics import mean_squared_error
from keras.datasets import mnist
from sklearn.metrics import confusion_matrix
from sklearn.metrics import accuracy_score
```

2. To import the `mnist` dataset, the following code must be used:

```
(XTrain, YTrain), (XTest, YTest) = mnist.load_data()
```

The following tuples are returned:

- XTrain, XTest: A uint8 array of grayscale image data with the (num_samples, 28, 28) shape
- YTrain, YTest: A uint8 array of digit labels (integers in the range 0-9) with the (num_samples) shape

3. So, each sample image consists of a 28 x 28 matrix. To reduce the dimensionality, we will flatten the 28 x 28 images into vectors of size 784:

```
XTrain = XTrain.reshape((len(XTrain), np.prod(XTrain.shape[1:])))
XTest = XTest.reshape((len(XTest), np.prod(XTest.shape[1:])))
```

4. Now, we will extract from the dataset that contains the digits from 0 to 9, but only the first two (0 and 1) because we want to build a binary classifier. To do this, we will use the numpy.where function:

```
TrainFilter = np.where((YTrain == 0 ) | (YTrain == 1))
TestFilter = np.where((YTest == 0) | (YTest == 1))

XTrain, YTrain = XTrain[TrainFilter], YTrain[TrainFilter]
XTest, YTest = XTest[TestFilter], YTest[TestFilter]
```

5. We create a dataset for lightgbm:

```
LgbTrain = lgb.Dataset(XTrain, YTrain)
LgbEval = lgb.Dataset(XTest, YTest, reference=LgbTrain)
```

6. Now, we have to specify the model parameters as a dictionary:

```
Parameters = {
        'boosting_type': 'gbdt',
        'objective': 'binary',
        'metric': 'binary_logloss',
        'num_leaves': 31,
        'learning_rate': 0.05,
        'feature_fraction': 0.9,
        'bagging_fraction': 0.8,
        'bagging_freq': 5,
        'verbose': 0
}
```

7. Let's train the model:

```
gbm = lgb.train(Parameters,
                LgbTrain,
                num_boost_round=10,
                valid_sets=LgbTrain)
```

8. Our model is now ready, so we can use it to classify the handwritten digits automatically. To do this, we will use the `predict()` method:

```
YPred = gbm.predict(XTest, num_iteration=gbm.best_iteration)
YPred = np.round(YPred)
YPred = YPred.astype(int)
```

9. Now, we can evaluate the model:

```
print('Rmse of the model is:', mean_squared_error(YTest, YPred) **
0.5)
```

The following result is returned:

Rmse of the model is: 0.05752992848417943

10. To analyze the errors that were made in the binary classification in more detail, we need to compute the confusion matrix:

```
ConfMatrix = confusion_matrix(YTest, YPred)
print(ConfMatrix)
```

The following results are returned:

[[978 2]
[5 1130]]

11. Finally, we will calculate the model's accuracy:

```
print(accuracy_score(YTest, YPred))
```

The following result is returned:

0.9966903073286052

The model is therefore able to classify images of handwritten digits with a high accuracy.

How it works...

In this recipe, we used LightGBM to classify handwritten digits. LightGBM is a particular variation of gradient boosting, with some modifications that make it particularly advantageous. It is based on classification trees, but the choice of splitting the leaf at each step is done more effectively.

While boosting operates a tree growth in depth, LightGBM makes this choice by combining two criteria:

- Optimization based on gradient descent
- To avoid overfitting problems, a limit for the maximum depth is set

This type of growth is called **leaf-wise**.

There's more...

Light GBM has many advantages:

- The procedure that's presented is, on average, an order of magnitude faster than similar algorithms. This is because it does not completely grow trees, and it also makes use of the binning of variables (a procedure that divides these into sub-groups, both to speed up the calculations and as a regularization method).
- More economical use of memory: the binning procedure involves less intensive use of memory.
- Better accuracy compared to the usual boosting algorithms: since it uses a leaf-wise procedure, the obtained trees are more complex. At the same time, to avoid overfitting, a limit is placed on the maximum depth.
- The algorithm is easily parallelizable.

See also

- The official documentation of the `LightGBM` library: `https://lightgbm.readthedocs.io/en/latest/`
- *A Gentle Introduction to Gradient Boosting* (from Northeastern University): `http://www.ccs.neu.edu/home/vip/teach/MLcourse/4_boosting/slides/gradient_boosting.pdf`
- *LightGBM: A Highly Efficient Gradient Boosting Decision Tree* (by Guolin Ke and others): `https://papers.nips.cc/paper/6907-lightgbm-a-highly-efficient-gradient-boosting-decision-tree.pdf`

Biometric Face Recognition

11

In this chapter, we will cover the following recipes:

- Capturing and processing video from a webcam
- Building a face detector using Haar cascades
- Building eye and nose detectors
- Performing principal component analysis
- Performing kernel principal component analysis
- Performing blind source separation
- Building a face recognizer using a local binary pattern histogram
- Recognizing faces using a HOG-based model
- Facial landmarks recognition
- User authentication by face recognition

Technical requirements

To address the recipes in this chapter, you need the following files (available on GitHub):

- video_capture.py
- face_detector.py
- eye_nose_detector.py
- pca.py
- kpca.py
- blind_source_separation.py
- mixture_of_signals.txt
- face_recognizer.py
- FaceRecognition.py

- `FaceLandmarks.py`
- `UserAuthentification.py`

Introduction

Face recognition refers to the task of identifying a person in a given image. This is different from face detection where we locate the face in a given image. During face detection, we don't care who the person is; we just identify the region of the image that contains the face. Therefore, in a typical biometric face recognition system, we need to determine the location of the face before we can recognize it.

Face recognition is very easy for humans. We seem to do it effortlessly, and we do it all the time! How do we get a machine to do the same thing? We need to understand what parts of the face we can use to uniquely identify a person. Our brain has an internal structure that seems to respond to specific features, such as edges, corners, motion, and so on. The human visual cortex combines all these features into a single coherent inference. If we want our machine to recognize faces with accuracy, we need to formulate the problem in a similar way. We need to extract features from the input image and convert them into a meaningful representation.

Capturing and processing video from a webcam

Webcams are certainly not an innovative technological innovation; their appearance dates back to the beginning of the 1990s and from then on, they gained increasing popularity thanks to the spread of video chat programs, street cams, and broadband internet connections. Currently, webcams are objects for everyone and are almost always integrated into the display frames of monitors, netbooks, and notebooks. The most common uses of a webcam are to transmit video streaming and record.

In the first case, webcams are used in video chat programs, television broadcasting, and street cams—cameras that film a fixed point of a given location. In the second case, webcams are used for creating photos and videos that you can then upload to the internet, for example, to YouTube or social networking sites. The advantage of these types of webcams is that they can replace the more classic uses of the camera, even if they are characterized by much poorer video quality.

Getting ready

In this recipe, we will use a webcam to capture video data. Let's see how we can capture video footage from a webcam using OpenCV-Python.

How to do it...

Let's see how we can capture and process video from a webcam by following these steps:

1. Create a new Python file and import the following packages (the full code is given in the `video_capture.py` file that is provided for you):

   ```
   import cv2
   ```

2. OpenCV provides a video capture object that we can use to capture images from the webcam. The 0 input argument specifies the ID of the webcam. If you connect a USB camera, then it will have a different ID:

   ```
   # Initialize video capture object
   cap = cv2.VideoCapture(0)
   ```

3. Define the scaling factor for frames that are captured using the webcam:

   ```
   scaling_factor = 0.5
   ```

4. Start an infinite loop and keep capturing frames until you press the *Esc* key. Read the frame from the webcam:

   ```
   # Loop until you hit the Esc key
   while True:
       # Capture the current frame
       ret, frame = cap.read()
   ```

5. Resizing the frame is optional but still a useful thing to have in your code:

   ```
   frame = cv2.resize(frame, None, fx=scaling_factor, fy=scaling_factor,
           interpolation=cv2.INTER_AREA)
   ```

6. Display the frame:

   ```
   cv2.imshow('Webcam', frame)
   ```

7. Wait for 1ms before capturing the next frame:

```
c = cv2.waitKey(1)
if c == 27:
    break
```

8. Release the video capture object:

```
cap.release()
```

9. Close all active windows before exiting the code:

```
cv2.destroyAllWindows()
```

If you run this code, you will see the video from the webcam.

How it works...

In this recipe, we used a webcam to capture video data via OpenCV-Python. To do this, the following operations have been performed:

1. Initialize video capture object.
2. Define the image size scaling factor.
3. Loop until you hit the *Esc* key:
    1. Capture the current frame.
    2. Resize the frame.
    3. Display the image.
    4. Detect whether the *Esc* key has been pressed.
4. Release the video capture object.
5. Close all active windows.

There's more...

OpenCV provides a very simple interface to capture live streaming with webcams. To capture a video, you need to create a `VideoCapture` object. Its argument can be the device index or the name of a video file. Then we can acquire them frame by frame. However, we must not forget to release the capture.

See also

- The official documentation of the OpenCV library: `https://docs.opencv.org/2.4/modules/highgui/doc/reading_and_writing_images_and_video.html`

Building a face detector using Haar cascades

As we discussed earlier, face detection is the process of determining the location of a face in an input image. In this recipe, we will use **Haar cascades** for face detection. This works by extracting many simple features from the image at multiple scales. These simple features are edge, line, and rectangle features that are very easy to compute. They are then trained by creating a cascade of simple classifiers.

Getting ready

In this recipe, we will learn how to determine the location of a face in the video frames that are captured by our webcam. The **adaptive boosting** technique is used to make this process robust.

How to do it...

Let's see how we can build a face detector using Haar cascades:

1. Create a new Python file and import the following packages (the full code is given in the `face_detector.py` file that is provided for you):

```
import cv2
import numpy as np
```

2. Load the face detector cascade file. This is a trained model that we can use as a detector:

```
face_cascade =
cv2.CascadeClassifier('cascade_files/haarcascade_frontalface_alt.xml')
```

3. Check whether the cascade file loaded properly:

```
if face_cascade.empty():
    raise IOError('Unable to load the face cascade classifier xml
file')
```

4. Create the video capture object:

```
cap = cv2.VideoCapture(0)
```

5. Define the scaling factor for image downsampling:

```
scaling_factor = 0.5
```

6. Keep looping until you hit the *Esc* key:

```
# Loop until you hit the Esc key
while True:
    # Capture the current frame and resize it
    ret, frame = cap.read()
```

7. Resize the frame:

```
frame = cv2.resize(frame, None, fx=scaling_factor, fy=scaling_factor,
        interpolation=cv2.INTER_AREA)
```

8. Convert the image to grayscale. We need grayscale images to run the face detector:

```
gray = cv2.cvtColor(frame, cv2.COLOR_BGR2GRAY)
```

9. Run the face detector on the grayscale image. The 1.3 parameter refers to the scale multiplier for each stage. The 5 parameter refers to the minimum number of neighbors that each candidate rectangle should have so that we can retain it. This candidate rectangle is basically a potential region where there is a chance of a face being detected:

```
face_rects = face_cascade.detectMultiScale(gray, 1.3, 5)
```

10. Draw a rectangle around each detected face region:

```
for (x,y,w,h) in face_rects:
    cv2.rectangle(frame, (x,y), (x+w,y+h), (0,255,0), 3)
```

11. Display the output image:

```
cv2.imshow('Face Detector', frame)
```

12. Wait for 1ms before going to the next iteration. If the user presses the Esc key, break out of the loop:

```
c = cv2.waitKey(1)
if c == 27:
    break
```

13. Release and destroy the objects before exiting the code:

```
cap.release()
cv2.destroyAllWindows()
```

If you run this code, you will see the face being detected in the webcam video.

How it works...

In this recipe, we learned how to determine the location of a face in video frames that were captured by the webcam. To do this, the following operations were performed:

1. Load the face cascade file.
2. Check whether the face cascade file has been loaded.
3. Initialize the video capture object.
4. Define the scaling factor.
5. Loop until you hit the *Esc* key:
    1. Capture the current frame and resize it.
    2. Convert into grayscale.
    3. Run the face detector on the grayscale image.
    4. Draw rectangles on the image.
    5. Display the image.
    6. Check if the *Esc* key has been pressed.
6. Release the video capture object and close all windows.

There's more...

Haar cascades is an approach, based on machine learning, in which a cascade function is trained by many positive and negative images. It is then used to detect objects in other images.

See also

- *Face Detection using Haar Cascades*: `https://docs.opencv.org/3.1.0/d7/d8b/tutorial_py_face_detection.html#gsc.tab=0`
- *Rapid Object Detection using a Boosted Cascade of Simple Features*: `https://www.cs.cmu.edu/~efros/courses/LBMV07/Papers/viola-cvpr-01.pdf`

Building eye and nose detectors

In the previous recipe, *Building a face detector using Haar cascades*, we used the Haar cascades method to detect the location of a face in video frames that were captured by a webcam. This method can be extended to detect all types of object. This is what we will be covering here.

Getting ready

In this recipe, we will see how we can use the Haar cascades method to detect the eyes and nose of a person in an input video.

How to do it...

Let's see how we can build eye and nose detectors:

1. Create a new Python file and import the following packages (the full code is given in the `eye_nose_detector.py` file that is provided for you):

```
import cv2
import numpy as np
```

2. Load the face, eyes, and nose cascade files:

```
# Load face, eye, and nose cascade files
face_cascade =
cv2.CascadeClassifier('cascade_files/haarcascade_frontalface_alt.xml')
eye_cascade =
cv2.CascadeClassifier('cascade_files/haarcascade_eye.xml')
nose_cascade =
cv2.CascadeClassifier('cascade_files/haarcascade_mcs_nose.xml')
```

3. Check whether the files have loaded correctly:

```
# Check if face cascade file has been loaded
if face_cascade.empty():
    raise IOError('Unable to load the face cascade classifier xml
file')

# Check if eye cascade file has been loaded
if eye_cascade.empty():
    raise IOError('Unable to load the eye cascade classifier xml
file')

# Check if nose cascade file has been loaded
if nose_cascade.empty():
    raise IOError('Unable to load the nose cascade classifier xml
file')
```

4. Initialize the video capture object:

```
# Initialize video capture object and define scaling factor
cap = cv2.VideoCapture(0)
```

5. Define the scaling factor:

```
scaling_factor = 0.5
```

6. Keep looping until the user presses the *Esc* key:

```
while True:
    # Read current frame, resize it, and convert it to grayscale
    ret, frame = cap.read()
```

7. Resize the frame:

```
    frame = cv2.resize(frame, None, fx=scaling_factor,
fy=scaling_factor,
            interpolation=cv2.INTER_AREA)
```

8. Convert the image into grayscale:

```
gray = cv2.cvtColor(frame, cv2.COLOR_BGR2GRAY)
```

9. Run the face detector on the grayscale image:

```
# Run face detector on the grayscale image
faces = face_cascade.detectMultiScale(gray, 1.3, 5)
```

10. Since we know that faces always have eyes and noses, we can run these detectors only in the face region:

```
# Run eye and nose detectors within each face rectangle
for (x,y,w,h) in faces:
```

11. Extract the face ROI:

```
# Grab the current ROI in both color and grayscale images
roi_gray = gray[y:y+h, x:x+w]
roi_color = frame[y:y+h, x:x+w]
```

12. Run the eye detector:

```
# Run eye detector in the grayscale ROI
eye_rects = eye_cascade.detectMultiScale(roi_gray)
```

13. Run the nose detector:

```
# Run nose detector in the grayscale ROI
nose_rects = nose_cascade.detectMultiScale(roi_gray, 1.3, 5)
```

14. Draw circles around the eyes:

```
# Draw green circles around the eyes
for (x_eye, y_eye, w_eye, h_eye) in eye_rects:
    center = (int(x_eye + 0.5*w_eye), int(y_eye + 0.5*h_eye))
    radius = int(0.3 * (w_eye + h_eye))
    color = (0, 255, 0)
    thickness = 3
    cv2.circle(roi_color, center, radius, color, thickness)
```

15. Draw a rectangle around the nose:

```
for (x_nose, y_nose, w_nose, h_nose) in nose_rects:
    cv2.rectangle(roi_color, (x_nose, y_nose), (x_nose+w_nose,
        y_nose+h_nose), (0,255,0), 3)
    break
```

16. Display the image:

```
# Display the image
cv2.imshow('Eye and nose detector', frame)
```

17. Wait for 1ms before going to the next iteration. If the user presses the *Esc* key, then break the loop:

```
# Check if Esc key has been pressed
c = cv2.waitKey(1)
if c == 27:
    break
```

18. Release and destroy the objects before exiting the code:

```
# Release video capture object and close all windows
cap.release()
cv2.destroyAllWindows()
```

If you run this code, you will see the eyes and nose of the person being detected in the webcam video.

How it works...

In this recipe, we learned how to detect the eyes and nose of a person in the input video. To do this, the following operations have been performed:

1. Load the face, eye, and nose cascade files.
2. Check whether the face, eye, and nose cascade files have been loaded.
3. Initialize a video capture object and define the scaling factor.
4. Loop on the frame:
    1. Read the current frame, resize it, and convert it into grayscale.
    2. Run the face detector on the grayscale image.
    3. Run the eye and nose detectors within each face rectangle.
    4. Display the image.
    5. Check whether the *Esc* key has been pressed.
5. Release the video capture object and close all windows.

There's more...

Identifying facial elements in a webcam can be useful for recognizing subjects. Both global visual information and local characteristics (eye and nose morphology) are fundamental in the perception and recognition of the face. In fact, studies on facial recognition document that men more easily identify faces with predominant elements such as aquiline nose, squinting eyes, and so on.

See also

- Classifier case study – *Viola-Jones Face Detector*: `http://www.cse.psu.edu/ ~rtc12/CSE586/lectures/violaJonesDetector.pdf`

Performing principal component analysis

Principal component analysis (**PCA**) is a dimensionality reduction technique that's used frequently in computer vision and machine learning. When we deal with features with large dimensionalities, training a machine learning system becomes prohibitively expensive. Therefore, we need to reduce the dimensionality of the data before we can train a system. However, when we reduce the dimensionality, we don't want to lose the information that's present in the data. This is where PCA comes into the picture! PCA identifies the important components of the data and arranges them in order of importance.

Getting ready

In this recipe, we will see how we can perform PCA on input data.

How to do it...

Let's see how we can perform a PCA on some input data:

1. Create a new Python file and import the following packages (the full code is given in the `pca.py` file that is provided for you):

```
import numpy as np
from sklearn import decomposition
```

2. Let's define five dimensions for our input data. The first two dimensions will be independent, but the next three dimensions will be dependent on the first two dimensions. This basically means that we can live without the last three dimensions because they do not give us any new information:

```
# Define individual features
x1 = np.random.normal(size=250)
x2 = np.random.normal(size=250)
x3 = 3*x1 + 2*x2
x4 = 6*x1 - 2*x2
x5 = 3*x3 + x4
```

3. Let's create a dataset with these features:

```
# Create dataset with the above features
X = np.c_[x1, x3, x2, x5, x4]
```

4. Create a PCA object:

```
# Perform Principal Component Analysis
pca = decomposition.PCA()
```

5. Fit a PCA model on the input data:

```
pca.fit(X)
```

6. Print the variances of the dimensions:

```
# Print variances
variances = pca.explained_variance_
print('Variances in decreasing order:\n', variances)
```

7. If a particular dimension is useful, then it will have a meaningful value for the variance. Let's set a threshold and identify the important dimensions:

```
# Find the number of useful dimensions
thresh_variance = 0.8
num_useful_dims = len(np.where(variances > thresh_variance)[0])
print('Number of useful dimensions:', num_useful_dims)
```

8. Just like we discussed earlier, PCA has identified that only two dimensions are important in this dataset:

```
# As we can see, only the 2 first components are useful
pca.n_components = num_useful_dims
```

9. Let's convert the dataset from a five-dimensional set into a two-dimensional set:

```
XNew = pca.fit_transform(X)
print('Shape before:', X.shape)
print('Shape after:', XNew.shape)
```

10. If you run this code, you will see the following on your Terminal:

```
Variances in decreasing order:
[2.77392134e+02 1.51557851e+01 9.54279881e-30 7.73588070e-32
9.89435444e-33]

Number of useful dimensions: 2
Shape before: (250, 5)
Shape after: (250, 2)
```

As we can see, the first two components contain all of the variance of the model.

How it works...

PCA generates a new set of variables, among which there are uncorrelated variables, also known as principal components. Each main component is a linear combination of the original variables. All principal components are orthogonal to each other, so there is no redundant information.

The principal components as a whole constitute an orthogonal basis for the data space. The goal of PCA is to explain the maximum amount of variance with the lowest number of principal components. PCA is a type of multidimensional scaling wherein the variables are linearly transformed into a lower dimensional space, thereby retaining the maximum amount of information possible about the variables. A principal component is therefore a combination of the original variables after a linear transformation.

There's more...

The variance measures how far a set of numbers are spread out from their mean. It represents the mean of the squares of deviations of individual values from their arithmetic mean.

See also

- Official documentation of the `sklearn.decomposition.PCA` function: `https://scikit-learn.org/stable/modules/generated/sklearn.decomposition.PCA.html`
- *Principal components analysis* (by Andrew Ng from Stanford University): `http://cs229.stanford.edu/notes/cs229-notes10.pdf`

- *Principle Component Analysis* (from Indiana University): `http://scholarwiki.` `indiana.edu/Z604/slides/week4-PCA.pdf`

Performing kernel principal component analysis

PCA is good at reducing the number of dimensions, but it works in a linear manner. If the data is not organized in a linear fashion, PCA fails to do the required job. This is where kernel PCA enters the picture.

Getting ready

In this recipe, we will see how we can perform a kernel PCA on the input data and compare the result to how PCA performs on the same data.

How to do it...

Let's see how we can perform a kernel PCA:

1. Create a new Python file and import the following packages (the full code is given in the `kpca.py` file that is provided for you):

```
import numpy as np
import matplotlib.pyplot as plt

from sklearn.decomposition import PCA, KernelPCA
from sklearn.datasets import make_circles
```

2. Define the `seed` value for the random number generator. This is needed to generate data samples for analysis:

```
# Set the seed for random number generator
np.random.seed(7)
```

3. Generate data that is distributed in concentric circles to demonstrate how PCA doesn't work in this case:

```
# Generate samples
X, y = make_circles(n_samples=500, factor=0.2, noise=0.04)
```

4. Perform PCA on this data:

```
# Perform PCA
pca = PCA()
X_pca = pca.fit_transform(X)
```

5. Perform kernel PCA on this data:

```
# Perform Kernel PCA
kernel_pca = KernelPCA(kernel="rbf", fit_inverse_transform=True,
gamma=10)
X_kernel_pca = kernel_pca.fit_transform(X)
X_inverse = kernel_pca.inverse_transform(X_kernel_pca)
```

6. Plot the original input data:

```
# Plot original data
class_0 = np.where(y == 0)
class_1 = np.where(y == 1)
plt.figure()
plt.title("Original data")
plt.plot(X[class_0, 0], X[class_0, 1], "ko", mfc='none')
plt.plot(X[class_1, 0], X[class_1, 1], "kx")
plt.xlabel("1st dimension")
plt.ylabel("2nd dimension")
```

7. Plot the PCA-transformed data:

```
# Plot PCA projection of the data
plt.figure()
plt.plot(X_pca[class_0, 0], X_pca[class_0, 1], "ko", mfc='none')
plt.plot(X_pca[class_1, 0], X_pca[class_1, 1], "kx")
plt.title("Data transformed using PCA")
plt.xlabel("1st principal component")
plt.ylabel("2nd principal component")
```

8. Plot the kernel PCA-transformed data:

```
# Plot Kernel PCA projection of the data
plt.figure()
plt.plot(X_kernel_pca[class_0, 0], X_kernel_pca[class_0, 1], "ko",
mfc='none')
plt.plot(X_kernel_pca[class_1, 0], X_kernel_pca[class_1, 1], "kx")
plt.title("Data transformed using Kernel PCA")
plt.xlabel("1st principal component")
plt.ylabel("2nd principal component")
```

9. Transform the data back to the original space using the Kernel method to show that the inverse is maintained:

```
# Transform the data back to original space
plt.figure()
plt.plot(X_inverse[class_0, 0], X_inverse[class_0, 1], "ko",
mfc='none')
plt.plot(X_inverse[class_1, 0], X_inverse[class_1, 1], "kx")
plt.title("Inverse transform")
plt.xlabel("1st dimension")
plt.ylabel("2nd dimension")

plt.show()
```

10. The full code is given in the kpca.py file that's already provided to you for reference. If you run this code, you will see four diagrams. The first diagram is the original data:

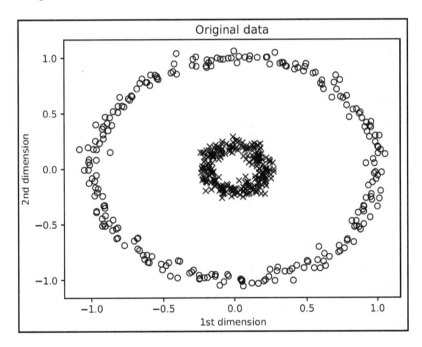

The second diagram depicts the data that was transformed using PCA:

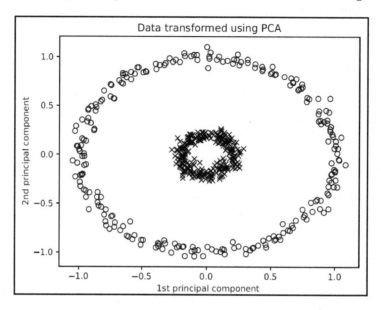

The third diagram depicts the data that was transformed using the kernel PCA. Note how the points are clustered on the right-hand side of the diagram:

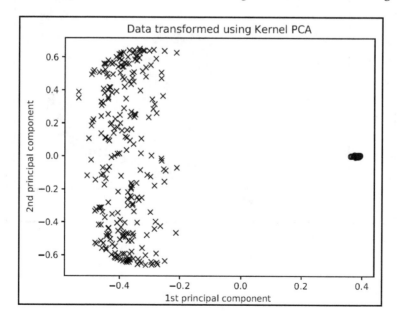

The fourth diagram depicts the inverse transform of the data back to the original space:

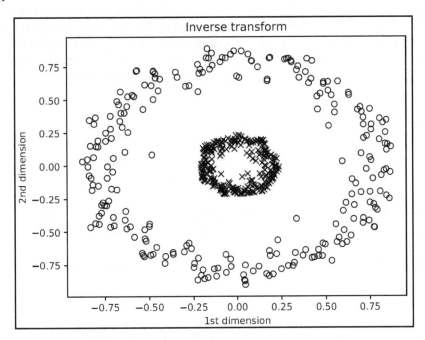

How it works...

Kernel principal component analysis (kernel PCA) is based on PCA while using the techniques of kernel methods. In PCA, the originally linear PCA operations are performed in a reproducing kernel Hilbert space.

Kernel methods are a class of algorithms used for the analysis of patterns and schemes, and whose most well-known element are SVMs. Kernel methods solve a problem by mapping data into a multidimensional feature space, and in this space each coordinate corresponds to a feature of the element's data, transforming the data into a set of Euclidean space points. Since the mapping can be general (for example, not necessarily linear), the relations that are found in this way are consequently very general.

There's more...

Kernel methods are named after kernel functions, which are used to operate on the characteristic space without calculating the data coordinates in space, but rather by calculating the internal product among the images of all copies of data in the function space. Kernel methods are often computationally cheaper than the explicit calculation of coordinates. The kernel trick refers to this approach as **problem resolution**.

See also

- Official documentation of the `sklearn.decomposition.KernelPCA` function: `https://scikit-learn.org/stable/modules/generated/sklearn.decomposition.KernelPCA.html`
- *Kernel Principal Components Analysis* (by Max Welling from the University of Toronto): `https://www.ics.uci.edu/~welling/classnotes/papers_class/Kernel-PCA.pdf`
- *KERNEL PCA* (by Rita Osadchy from Haifa University): `http://www.cs.haifa.ac.il/~rita/uml_course/lectures/KPCA.pdf`

Performing blind source separation

Blind source separation refers to the process of separating signals from a mixture. Let's say a bunch of different signal generators generate signals and a common receiver receives all of these signals. Now, our job is to separate these signals from this mixture using the properties of these signals. We will use **independent component analysis** (**ICA**) to achieve this.

Getting ready

In this recipe, we will use the data from a `.txt` file to separate the signals contained in it using **ICA**.

How to do it...

Let's see how we can perform a blind source separation:

1. Create a new Python file and import the following packages (the full code is given in the `blind_source_separation.py` file that is provided for you):

```
import numpy as np
import matplotlib.pyplot as plt
from sklearn.decomposition import PCA, FastICA
```

2. We will use data from the `mixture_of_signals.txt` file that's already provided for you. Let's load the data:

```
# Load data
input_file = 'mixture_of_signals.txt'
X = np.loadtxt(input_file)
```

3. Create the ICA object:

```
# Compute ICA
ica = FastICA(n_components=4)
```

4. Reconstruct the signals based on ICA:

```
# Reconstruct the signals
signals_ica = ica.fit_transform(X)
```

5. Extract the mixing matrix:

```
# Get estimated mixing matrix
mixing_mat = ica.mixing_
```

6. Perform PCA for comparison:

```
# Perform PCA
pca = PCA(n_components=4)
# Reconstruct signals based on orthogonal components
signals_pca = pca.fit_transform(X)
```

7. Define a list of signals to plot them:

```
# Specify parameters for output plots
models = [X, signals_ica, signals_pca]
```

8. Specify the colors of the plots:

```
colors = ['blue', 'red', 'black', 'green']
```

9. Plot the input signal:

```
# Plotting input signal
plt.figure()
plt.title('Input signal (mixture)')
for i, (sig, color) in enumerate(zip(X.T, colors), 1):
    plt.plot(sig, color=color)
```

10. Plot the ICA-separated signals:

```
# Plotting ICA signals
plt.figure()
plt.title('ICA separated signals')
plt.subplots_adjust(left=0.1, bottom=0.05, right=0.94,
        top=0.94, wspace=0.25, hspace=0.45)
```

11. Plot subplots with different colors:

```
for i, (sig, color) in enumerate(zip(signals_ica.T, colors), 1):
    plt.subplot(4, 1, i)
    plt.title('Signal ' + str(i))
    plt.plot(sig, color=color)
```

12. Plot the PCA-separated signals:

```
# Plotting PCA signals
plt.figure()
plt.title('PCA separated signals')
plt.subplots_adjust(left=0.1, bottom=0.05, right=0.94,
        top=0.94, wspace=0.25, hspace=0.45)
```

13. Use a different color in each subplot:

```
for i, (sig, color) in enumerate(zip(signals_pca.T, colors), 1):
    plt.subplot(4, 1, i)
    plt.title('Signal ' + str(i))
    plt.plot(sig, color=color)

plt.show()
```

If you run this code, you will see three diagrams. The first diagram depicts the input, which is a mixture of signals:

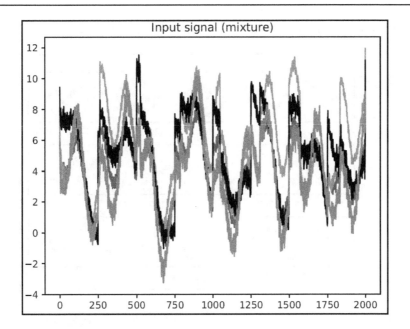

The second diagram depicts the signals, separated using ICA:

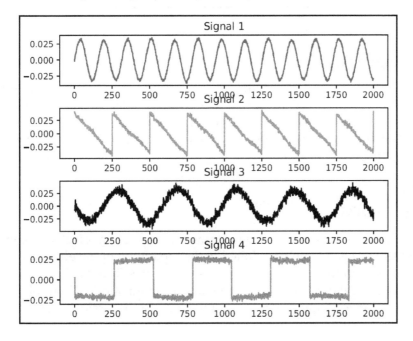

The third diagram depicts the signals, separated using PCA:

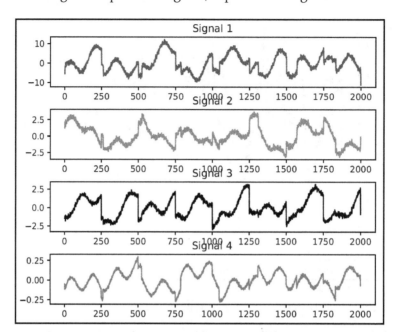

How it works...

ICA is a computational processing method that's used to separate a multivariant signal into its additive subcomponents, assuming that there is a mutual statistical independence of the source of non-Gaussian signals. This is a special case of blind source separation. This method finds the independent components, maximizing the statistical independence of the estimated components.

There's more...

An example of the application of ICA algorithms is in the field of **electroencephalography** (**EEG**), but it has also been widely exploited in the separation of the **electrocardiogram** (**ECG**) of the fetus from that of the `mother`. ICA techniques. This can be extended to the analysis of non-physical data that's either semantic or linguistic. For example, the ICA has been applied to make a computer understand the topic of discussion in a set of archives of news lists.

See also

- Official documentation of the `sklearn.decomposition.FastICA` function: `https://scikit-learn.org/stable/modules/generated/sklearn.decomposition.FastICA.html`
- *BLIND SOURCE SEPARATION: Principal and Independent Component Analysis* (from Massachusetts Institute of Technology): `http://www.mit.edu/~gari/teaching/6.555/LECTURE_NOTES/ch15_bss.pdf`

Building a face recognizer using a local binary patterns histogram

We are now ready to build a face recognizer. We need a face dataset for training, so we've provided you with a folder called `faces_dataset` that contains a small number of images that are sufficient for training. This dataset is a subset of the dataset that is available at `http://www.vision.caltech.edu/Image_Datasets/faces/faces.tar`. This dataset contains a good number of images that we can use to train a face recognition system.

We will use a **local binary patterns histogram** to build our face recognition system. In our dataset, you will see different people. Our job is to build a system that can learn to separate these people from one another. When we see an unknown image, our system will assign it to one of the existing classes.

Getting ready

In this recipe, we will see how we can build a face recognizer using a **local binary patterns histogram** and use a face dataset to train the model.

How to do it...

Let's see how we can build a face recognizer using a local binary patterns histogram:

1. Create a new Python file and import the following packages (the full code is given in the `face_recognizer.py` file that is provided for you):

    ```
    import os

    import cv2
    ```

```
import numpy as np
from sklearn import preprocessing
```

2. Let's define a class to handle all of the tasks that are related to label encoding for the classes:

```
# Class to handle tasks related to label encoding
class LabelEncoder(object):
```

3. Define a method to encode the labels. In the input training data, labels are represented by words. However, we need numbers to train our system. This method will define a preprocessor object that can convert words into numbers in an organized fashion by maintaining forward and backward mapping:

```
# Method to encode labels from words to numbers
def encode_labels(self, label_words):
    self.le = preprocessing.LabelEncoder()
    self.le.fit(label_words)
```

4. Define a method to convert a word into a number:

```
# Convert input label from word to number
def word_to_num(self, label_word):
    return int(self.le.transform([label_word])[0])
```

5. Define a method to convert the number back into the original word:

```
# Convert input label from number to word
def num_to_word(self, label_num):
    return self.le.inverse_transform([label_num])[0]
```

6. Define a method to extract the images and labels from the input folder:

```
# Extract images and labels from input path
def get_images_and_labels(input_path):
    label_words = []
```

7. Recursively iterate through the input folder and extract all of the image paths:

```
# Iterate through the input path and append files
for root, dirs, files in os.walk(input_path):
    for filename in (x for x in files if x.endswith('.jpg')):
        filepath = os.path.join(root, filename)
        label_words.append(filepath.split('/')[-2])
```

8. Initialize the variables:

```
# Initialize variables
images = []
le = LabelEncoder()
le.encode_labels(label_words)
labels = []
```

9. Parse the input directory for training:

```
# Parse the input directory
for root, dirs, files in os.walk(input_path):
    for filename in (x for x in files if x.endswith('.jpg')):
        filepath = os.path.join(root, filename)
```

10. Read the current image in grayscale format:

```
# Read the image in grayscale format
image = cv2.imread(filepath, 0)
```

11. Extract the label from the folder path:

```
# Extract the label
name = filepath.split('/')[-2]
```

12. Perform face detection on this image:

```
# Perform face detection
faces = faceCascade.detectMultiScale(image, 1.1, 2,
minSize=(100,100))
```

13. Extract the ROIs and return them, along with the label encoder:

```
# Iterate through face rectangles
for (x, y, w, h) in faces:
    images.append(image[y:y+h, x:x+w])
    labels.append(le.word_to_num(name))

return images, labels, le
```

14. Define the main function and the path to the face cascade file:

```
if __name__=='__main__':
    cascade_path = "cascade_files/haarcascade_frontalface_alt.xml"
    path_train = 'faces_dataset/train'
    path_test = 'faces_dataset/test'
```

15. Load the face cascade file:

```
# Load face cascade file
faceCascade = cv2.CascadeClassifier(cascade_path)
```

16. Create local binary patterns histogram for face recognizer objects:

```
# Initialize Local Binary Patterns Histogram face recognizer
recognizer = cv2.face.createLBPHFaceRecognizer()
```

17. Extract the images, labels, and label encoder for this input path:

```
# Extract images, labels, and label encoder from training dataset
images, labels, le = get_images_and_labels(path_train)
```

18. Train the face recognizer using the data that we extracted:

```
# Train the face recognizer
print "\nTraining..."
recognizer.train(images, np.array(labels))
```

19. Test the face recognizer on unknown data:

```
# Test the recognizer on unknown images
print '\nPerforming prediction on test images...'
stop_flag = False
for root, dirs, files in os.walk(path_test):
    for filename in (x for x in files if x.endswith('.jpg')):
        filepath = os.path.join(root, filename)
```

20. Load the image:

```
# Read the image
predict_image = cv2.imread(filepath, 0)
```

21. Determine the location of the face using the face detector:

```
# Detect faces
faces = faceCascade.detectMultiScale(predict_image, 1.1,
        2, minSize=(100,100))
```

22. For each face ROI, run the face recognizer:

```
# Iterate through face rectangles
for (x, y, w, h) in faces:
    # Predict the output
    predicted_index, conf = recognizer.predict(
            predict_image[y:y+h, x:x+w])
```

23. Convert the label into a word:

```
# Convert to word label
predicted_person = le.num_to_word(predicted_index)
```

24. Overlay the text on the output image and display it:

```
# Overlay text on the output image and display it
cv2.putText(predict_image, 'Prediction: ' +
predicted_person,
            (10,60), cv2.FONT_HERSHEY_SIMPLEX, 2,
(255,255,255), 6)
cv2.imshow("Recognizing face", predict_image)
```

25. Check whether the user pressed the *Esc* key. If so, break out of the loop:

```
c = cv2.waitKey(0)
if c == 27:
    stop_flag = True
    break

if stop_flag:
    break
```

If you run this code, you will get an output window that displays the predicted outputs for test images. You can press the *Space* button to keep looping. There are three different people in the test images.

How it works...

The Local Binary Patterns Histogram algorithm is based on a non-parametric operator that synthesizes the local structure of an image. At a particular pixel, the LBP operator associates an ordered binary sequence of color intensity comparisons between that pixel and the pixels belonging to the considered neighborhood. In particular, if the intensity of the central pixel is greater than or equal to the intensity of the adjacent pixel, then a value of 1 is assigned. Otherwise, 0 is assigned. Therefore, for a neighborhood of 8 pixels, for example, there will be 2^8 possible combinations.

There's more...

To apply this operator to the face recognition problem, the idea is to divide the image into m local regions and extract a histogram from each of them. The vector of the features to be extracted consists of the concatenation of these local histograms.

See also

- *Local Binary Patterns Histogram*: http://docs.opencv.org/2.4/modules/contrib/doc/facerec/facerec_tutorial.html#local-binary-patterns-histograms

Recognizing faces using the HOG-based model

By face recognition, we mean the process that returns the position of the faces that are present in an image. In the *Building a face detector using Haar cascades* recipe, we already addressed this topic. In this recipe, we will use the `face_recognition` library to perform a series of operations on these faces.

The focal objective of face recognition consists of detecting the characteristics of a face and ignoring everything else that surrounds it. This is a feature on multiple commercial devices, and it allows you to establish when and how to apply focus in an image so that you can capture it. In the world of computer vision, it is customary to divide the family of face detection algorithms into two major categories. What distinguishes these two categories is their different uses of information, derived from a priori knowledge of the structure and properties of the face:

- The first category includes methods based on the extraction of specification features
- The second category adopts a global approach to image analysis

Getting ready

In this recipe, we will see how we can use the `face_recognition` library to perform face recognition from a complex image. Before proceeding, install the `face_recognition` library. This library is based on the `dlib` library, which must be installed before we can go any further. `dlib` is a modern C++ toolkit that contains machine learning algorithms and tools for creating complex software in C++ to solve real-world problems. You can find information on installing the package at https://pypi.org/project/face_recognition/.

How to do it...

Let's see how we can recognize faces using a HOG-based model:

1. Create a new Python file and import the following packages (the full code is given in the `FaceRecognition.py` file that is provided for you):

```
from PIL import Image
import face_recognition
```

 The **Python Imaging Library** (**PIL**) is a free library for the Python programming language that adds support for opening, manipulating, and saving many different image file formats. `face_recognition` is a Python library that recognizes and manipulates faces from Python scripts or from the command line.

2. Let's load the `family.jpg` file into a NumPy array:

```
image = face_recognition.load_image_file("family.jpg")
```

3. We will now find all of the faces in the image using the default HOG-based model:

```
face_locations = face_recognition.face_locations(image)
```

4. Define a method to convert words into numbers:

```
print("Number {} face(s) recognized in this
image.".format(len(face_locations)))
```

5. Print the location of each face in this image:

```
for face_location in face_locations:

    top, right, bottom, left = face_location
    print("Face location Top: {}, Left: {}, Bottom: {}, Right:
{}".format(top, left, bottom, right))
```

6. Finally, we need to access the actual face itself:

```
face_image = image[top:bottom, left:right]
pil_image = Image.fromarray(face_image)
pil_image.show()
```

A thumbnail of each recognized face will be returned.

How it works...

Histogram of Oriented Gradients (**HOG**) is a feature descriptor that's used for object recognition. The algorithm counts the occurrences of the orientation of the gradient in localized portions of an image. It differs from other techniques that are used for the same purpose (scale-invariant feature transforms, edge orientation histograms, shape contexts) because it uses a dense grid of uniformly spaced cells and uses localized superimposed normalization to improve accuracy.

There's more...

The first to introduce this technology were Navneet Dalal and Bill Triggs (2005), researchers of the **Institut national de recherche en informatique et en automatique** (**INRIA**), while they were studying the problem of pedestrian detection in static images.

See also

- Official documentation of the `face_recognition` library: `https://github.com/ageitgey/face_recognition`
- *Histograms of Oriented Gradients for Human Detection* (by Navneet Dalal and Bill Triggs from INRIA): `https://lear.inrialpes.fr/people/triggs/pubs/Dalal-cvpr05.pdf`

Facial landmark recognition

Face recognition is also complicated because of its orientation. The same face, directed in different directions from that of the observer, can induce the algorithm to identify it as a different face. To solve this problem, we can use facial landmarks, which are specific points on the face such as eyes, eyebrows, lips, nose, and so on. By using this technique, you can identify as many as 68 points on any face.

Getting ready

In this recipe, we will see how we can extract facial features as facial landmarks.

How to do it...

Let's see how we can perform facial landmark recognition:

1. Create a new Python file and import the following packages (the full code is given in the `FaceLandmarks.py` file that is provided for you):

   ```
   from PIL import Image, ImageDraw
   import face_recognition
   ```

2. Let's load the `ciaburro.jpg` file into a NumPy array:

   ```
   image = face_recognition.load_image_file("ciaburro.jpg")
   ```

3. Let's find all facial features in all of the faces in the image:

   ```
   FaceLandmarksList = face_recognition.face_landmarks(image)
   ```

4. Print the number of faces that were recognized in the image:

   ```
   print("Number {} face(s) recognized in this
   image.".format(len(FaceLandmarksList)))
   ```

   The following result is returned:

   Number 1 face(s) recognized in this image

5. Create a PIL imagedraw object so that we can draw on the picture:

   ```
   PilImage = Image.fromarray(image)
   DrawPilImage = ImageDraw.Draw(PilImage)
   ```

6. At this point, we will insert a cycle that returns the position of the points for each facial feature that's included in the list and trace a line to the image:

   ```
   for face_landmarks in FaceLandmarksList:
   ```

7. First, we print the location of each facial feature in this image:

   ```
   for facial_feature in face_landmarks.keys():
       print("{} points: {}".format(facial_feature,
   face_landmarks[facial_feature]))
   ```

8. Then we trace out each facial feature in the image with a line:

   ```
   for facial_feature in face_landmarks.keys():
       DrawPilImage.line(face_landmarks[facial_feature], width=5)
   ```

9. Finally, we draw the image with the highlighted landmarks:

```
PilImage.show()
```

In the following image, we can see the input image and the image with highlighted landmarks:

In addition, the positions of the landmarks are printed as follows:

```
chin points: [(112, 236), (113, 271), (116, 305), (124, 338), (141, 367),
    (167, 389), (200, 407), (234, 423), (268, 428), (296, 422), (317, 405),
    (333, 383), (343, 356), (349, 328), (352, 300), (353, 273), (350, 248)]
left_eyebrow points: [(169, 212), (187, 199), (210, 193), (234, 197), (257, 204)]
right_eyebrow points: [(281, 207), (300, 203), (319, 202), (335, 207), (345, 219)]
nose_bridge points: [(272, 221), (274, 237), (277, 254), (279, 271)]
nose_tip points: [(248, 291), (259, 294), (272, 298), (282, 296), (290, 293)]
left_eye points: [(194, 225), (207, 218), (222, 217), (234, 225), (220, 228), (206, 228)]
right_eye points: [(290, 229), (303, 223), (317, 224), (326, 233), (315, 235), (302, 233)]
top_lip points: [(218, 342), (238, 330), (257, 325), (271, 328), (282, 326), (297, 333),
    (308, 346), (301, 346), (281, 339), (270, 340), (257, 338), (228, 342)]
bottom_lip points: [(308, 346), (297, 360), (283, 362), (272, 361), (258, 359), (239, 352),
    (218, 342), (228, 342), (259, 343), (273, 344), (283, 344), (301, 346)]
```

How it works...

In this recipe, we learned how to extract facial landmarks from an image and how to draw these points on the same image. The following landmarks were detected:

- chin
- left_eyebrow
- right_eyebrow
- nose_bridge
- nose_tip
- left_eye
- right_eye
- top_lip
- bottom_lip

For each feature that was detected, connecting lines of the detection points were drawn to show the contours.

There's more...

To extract facial landmarks, the face_recognition library was used. This library performed this task by using the method that was introduced by Vahid Kazemi and Josephine Sullivan in the following paper: *One Millisecond Face Alignment with an Ensemble of Regression Trees*. To estimate the face's landmark positions, an ensemble of regression trees was used.

See also

- Official documentation of the face_recognition library: https://github.com/ageitgey/face_recognition
- *One Millisecond Face Alignment with an Ensemble of Regression Trees* (by Vahid Kazemi and Josephine Sullivan): http://www.csc.kth.se/~vahidk/papers/KazemiCVPR14.pdf

User authentication by face recognition

Authentication technologies based on facial recognition have been a consolidated reality for several decades now. We no longer have to carry pocket cards, store it on the phone, or use mnemonics to remember a different one each time, if we are so considerate to change it often. What we need to do is authenticate that which we already had it with us. To do this, we just look at our webcam. An identification system based on facial recognition tries to identify a person by comparing the image of the face that was just acquired with those present in a database to find a possible correspondence. This leads to either allowing or prohibiting access.

Getting ready

In this recipe, we will see how we can build an identification system based on facial recognition using the `face_recognition` library.

How to do it...

Let's see how we can perform user authentication by using face recognition:

1. Create a new Python file and import the following packages (the full code is given in the `UserAuthentification.py` file that is provided for you):

   ```
   import face_recognition
   ```

2. Let's load all of the image files into NumPy arrays:

   ```
   Image1 = face_recognition.load_image_file("giuseppe.jpg")
   Image2 = face_recognition.load_image_file("tiziana.jpg")
   UnknownImage = face_recognition.load_image_file("tiziana2.jpg")
   ```

   Three images have been loaded: the first two images refer to the faces we've already seen, while the third is the image to be compared (`tiziana`).

3. Get the face encodings for each face in each image file:

   ```
   try:
       Image1Encoding = face_recognition.face_encodings(Image1)[0]
       Image2Encoding = face_recognition.face_encodings(Image2)[0]
       UnknownImageEncoding =
   face_recognition.face_encodings(UnknownImage)[0]
   except IndexError:
   ```

```
print("Any face was located. Check the image files..")
quit()
```

4. Let's define the known faces:

```
known_faces = [
    Image1Encoding,
    Image2Encoding
]
```

5. Let's compare the known faces with the unknown face we just loaded:

```
results = face_recognition.compare_faces(known_faces,
UnknownImageEncoding)
```

6. Finally, we will print the results of the comparison:

```
print("Is the unknown face a picture of Giuseppe?
{}".format(results[0]))
print("Is the unknown face a picture of Tiziana?
{}".format(results[1]))
print("Is the unknown face a new person that we've never seen
before? {}".format(not True in results))
```

The following results are returned:

```
Is the unknown face a picture of Giuseppe? False
Is the unknown face a picture of Tiziana? True
Is the unknown face a new person that we've never seen before?
False
```

As we can see, the authentication system recognized the user as Tiziana.

How it works...

In this recipe, we learned how to build an identification system based on facial recognition. To do this, we extracted some basic measures from every face in the known database. In doing so, we were able to compare these basic measures with the basic measures of other faces that require authentication.

These measurements were made using a deep convolutional neural network. The learning process works by analyzing three images simultaneously:

- An image that contains the face of a known person (anchor)
- Another image of the same known person (positive)
- An image of a completely different person (negative)

At this point, the algorithm examines the measures it is generating for each of these three images. Then it adjusts the weights of the neural network to make sure that the measurements that were generated for faces 1 and 2 are slightly closer, while the measures for faces 2 and 3 are slightly more distant. This technique is called `Triplet Loss`.

There's more...

So far, we have said that the secret to the success of an algorithm based on machine learning lies in the number of examples that are used in the learning phase. The greater the number, the greater the accuracy of the model. In the cases that we dealt with in this chapter, this cannot be considered valid. This is because, in the algorithms for facial recognition, the examples at our disposal were very limited.

Therefore, the construction and formation of a typical convolutional neural network will not work because it cannot learn the required functionality with the amount of data that's available. In these cases, we use a **one-shot learning** approach in which we construct a similarity function that compares two images and tells you if there is a match.

See also

- Official documentation of the `face_recognition` library: https://github.com/ageitgey/face_recognition
- *One-shot learning* (from Wikipedia): https://en.wikipedia.org/wiki/One-shot_learning
- *One-shot learning of simple visual concepts* (from MIT): https://web.mit.edu/jgross/Public/lake_etal_cogsci2011.pdf
- *Siamese/Triplet Networks* (from Virginia Tech University): https://filebox.ece.vt.edu/~jbhuang/teaching/ece6554/sp17/lectures/Lecture_08_Siamese_Triplet_Networks.pdf

12
Reinforcement Learning Techniques

In this chapter, we will cover the following recipes:

- Weather forecasting with MDP
- Optimizing a financial portfolio using DP
- Finding the shortest path
- Deciding the discount factor using Q-learning
- Implementing a deep Q-learning algorithm
- Developing an AI-based dynamic modeling system
- Deep reinforcement learning with Double Q-learning
- Deep Q-Network algorithm with dueling Q-learning

Technical requirements

To address the recipes in this chapter, you will need the following files (available on GitHub):

- MarkovChain.py
- KPDP.py
- DijkstraNX.py
- FrozenQlearning.py
- FrozenDeepQLearning.py
- dqn_cartpole.py
- DoubleDQNCartpole.py
- DuelingDQNCartpole.py

Introduction

Reinforcement learning represents a family of algorithms that are able to learn and adapt to environmental changes. It is based on the concept of receiving external stimuli based on the choices of the algorithm. A correct choice will result in a reward, while a wrong choice will lead to a penalty. The goal of the system is to achieve the best possible result.

In supervised learning, the correct output is clearly specified (learning with a teacher). But it is not always possible to do so. Often, we only have qualitative information. The information that's available is called a **reinforcement signal**. In these cases, the system does not provide any information on how to update the agent's behavior (for example, weights). You cannot define a cost function or a gradient. The goal of the system is to create the smart agents that are able to learn from their experience.

In the following screenshot, we can see a flowchart that displays the reinforcement learning interaction with the environment:

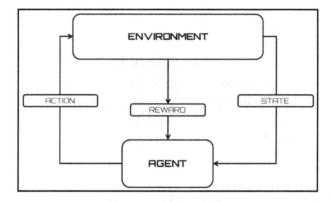

Here are the steps to follow to correctly apply a reinforcement learning algorithm:

1. Preparation of the agent
2. Observation of the environment
3. Selection of the optimal strategy
4. Execution of actions
5. Calculation of the corresponding reward (or penalty)
6. Development of updating strategies (if necessary)
7. Repetition of steps 2 to 5 iteratively until the agent learns the optimal strategies

Reinforcement learning tries to maximize the rewards that are received for the execution of the action or set of actions that allow a goal to be achieved.

Weather forecasting with MDP

To avoid load problems and computational difficulties, the agent-environment interaction is considered a **Markov decision process** (**MDP**). An MDP is a discrete time stochastic control process.

Stochastic processes are mathematical models that are used to study the evolution of phenomena following random or probabilistic laws. It is known that in all natural phenomena, both by their very nature and by observational errors, a random or accidental component is present.

This component causes the following: at every instance of *t*, the result of the observation of the phenomenon is a random number or random variable, *st*. It is not possible to predict with certainty what the result will be; you can only state that it will take one of several possible values, each of which has a given probability.

A stochastic process is called **Markovian** when, having chosen a certain instance of *t* for observation, the evolution of the process, starting with *t*, depends only on *t* and does not depend in any way on the previous instances. Thus, a process is Markovian when, given the moment of observation, only this instance determines the future evolution of the process, while this evolution does not depend on the past.

Getting ready

In this recipe, we want to build a statistical model to predict the weather. To simplify the model, we will assume that there are only two states: sunny and rainy. Let's further assume that we have made some calculations and discovered that tomorrow's time is somehow based on today's time.

How to do it...

Let's see how we can perform weather forecasting with MDP:

1. We will use the `MarkovChain.py` file that is already provided for you as a reference. To start, we import the `numpy`, `time`, and `matplotlib.pyplot` packages:

```
import numpy as np
import time
from matplotlib import pyplot
```

2. Let's set the seed of a random number generator and the state of the weather:

```
np.random.seed(1)
states = ["Sunny","Rainy"]
```

3. At this point, we have to define the possible transitions of weather conditions:

```
TransStates = [["SuSu","SuRa"],["RaRa","RaSu"]]
TransnMatrix = [[0.75,0.25],[0.30,0.70]]
```

4. Then, we insert the following check to verify that we did not make mistakes in defining the transition matrix:

```
if sum(TransnMatrix[0])+sum(TransnMatrix[1]) != 2:
    print("Warning! Probabilities MUST ADD TO 1. Wrong transition
matrix!!")
    raise ValueError("Probabilities MUST ADD TO 1")
```

5. Let's set the initial condition:

```
WT = list()
NumberDays = 200
WeatherToday = states[0]
print("Weather initial condition =",WeatherToday)
```

6. We can now predict the weather conditions for each of the days set by the `NumberDays` variable. To do this, we will use a `while` loop, as follows:

```
i = 0
while i < NumberDays:
    if WeatherToday == "Sunny":
    TransWeather =
np.random.choice(TransStates[0],replace=True,p=TransnMatrix[0])
        if TransWeather == "SuSu":
            pass
        else:
            WeatherToday = "Rainy"
    elif WeatherToday == "Rainy":
        TransWeather =
np.random.choice(TransStates[1],replace=True,p=TransnMatrix[1])
        if TransWeather == "RaRa":
            pass
        else:
            WeatherToday = "Sunny"
    print(WeatherToday)
    WT.append(WeatherToday)
    i += 1
    time.sleep(0.2)
```

It consists of a control condition and a loop body. At the entrance of the cycle and every time that all the instructions contained in the body are executed, the validity of the control condition is verified. The cycle ends when the condition, consisting of a Boolean expression, returns `false`.

7. At this point, we have generated forecasts for the next 200 days. Let's plot the chart using the following code:

    ```
    pyplot.plot(WT)
    pyplot.show()
    ```

    The following graph shows the weather conditions for the next 200 days, starting from the sunny condition:

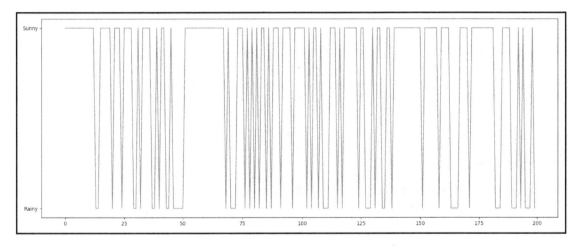

At first sight, it seems that sunny days prevail over the rainy ones.

How it works...

A Markov chain is a mathematical model of a random phenomenon that evolves over time in such a way that the past influences the future only through the present. In other words, a stochastic model describes a sequence of possible events where the probability of each event depends only on the state that was attained in the previous event. So, Markov chains have the property of memorylessness.

The structure of a Markov chain is therefore completely represented by the following transition matrix:

$$P = \begin{bmatrix} p_{11} & p_{12} & \cdots & p_{1n} \\ p_{21} & p_{22} & \cdots & p_{2n} \\ \cdots & \cdots & \cdots & \cdots \\ p_{n1} & p_{n2} & \cdots & p_{nn} \end{bmatrix}$$

The properties of transition probability matrices derive directly from the nature of the elements that compose them.

There's more...

A very intuitive alternative to the description of a Markov chain through a transition matrix is associating an oriented graph (transition diagram) to a Markov chain. The transition matrix and transition diagram provide the same information regarding the same Markov chain.

See also

- *Keras Reinforcement Learning Projects*, Giuseppe Ciaburro, Packt Publishing
- *INTRODUCTION TO MARKOV MODELS* (from Clemson University): http:// cecas.clemson.edu/~ahoover/ece854/refs/Ramos-Intro-HMM.pdf
- *Markov Decision Processes* (from Carnegie Mellon University): http://egon. cheme.cmu.edu/ewo/docs/SchaeferMDP.pdf

Optimizing a financial portfolio using DP

The management of financial portfolios is an activity that aims to combine financial products in a manner that best represents the investor's needs. This requires an overall assessment of various characteristics, such as risk appetite, expected returns, and investor consumption, as well as an estimate of future returns and risk. **Dynamic programming** (**DP**) represents a set of algorithms that can be used to calculate an optimal policy given a perfect model of the environment in the form of an MDP. The fundamental idea of DP, as well as reinforcement learning in general, is the use of state values and actions to look for good policies.

Getting ready

In this recipe, we will address the **knapsack problem**: a thief goes into a house and wants to steal valuables. They put them in their knapsack, but they are limited by the weight. Each object has its own value and weight. They must choose the objects that are of value, but that do not have excessive weight. The thief must not exceed the weight limit in the knapsack, but, at the same time, they must optimize their gain.

How to do it...

Let's see how we can optimize a financial portfolio using DP:

1. We will use the KPDP.py file that is already provided for you as a reference. This algorithm starts with the definition of a `KnapSackTable()` function that will choose the optimal combination of the objects respecting the two constraints imposed by the problem: the total weight of the objects equal to 10, and the maximum value of the chosen objects, as shown in the following code:

```
def KnapSackTable(weight, value, P, n):
T = [[0 for w in range(P + 1)]
for i in range(n + 1)]
```

2. Then, we set an iterative loop on all objects and on all weight values, as follows:

```
for i in range(n + 1):
    for w in range(P + 1):
        if i == 0 or w == 0:
            T[i][w] = 0
        elif weight[i - 1] <= w:
            T[i][w] = max(value[i - 1]
                + T[i - 1][w - weight[i - 1]],
                    T[i - 1][w])
        else:
            T[i][w] = T[i - 1][w]
```

3. Now, we can memorize the result that was obtained, which represents the maximum value of the objects that can be carried in the knapsack, as follows:

```
res = T[n][P]
print("Total value: " ,res)
```

4. The procedure we've followed so far does not indicate which subset provides the optimal solution. We must extract this information using a set procedure:

```
w = P
totweight=0
for i in range(n, 0, -1):
    if res <= 0:
        break
```

5. If the current element is the same as the previous one, we will move on to the next one, as follows:

```
if res == T[i - 1][w]:
    continue
```

6. If it is not the same, then the current object will be included in the knapsack, and this item will be printed, as follows:

```
else:
    print("Item selected: ",weight[i - 1],value[i - 1])
    totweight += weight[i - 1]
    res = res - value[i - 1]
    w = w - weight[i - 1]
```

7. Finally, the total included weight is printed, as follows:

```
print("Total weight: ",totweight)
```

In this way, we have defined the function that allows us to build the table.

8. Now, we have to define the input variables and pass them to the function, as follows:

```
objects = [(5, 18),(2, 9), (4, 12), (6,25)]
print("Items available: ",objects)
print("**********************************")
```

9. At this point, we need to extract the weight and variable values from the objects. We put them in a separate array to better understand the steps, as follows:

```
value = []
weight = []
for item in objects:
    weight.append(item[0])
    value.append(item[1])
```

10. Finally, the total weight that can be carried by the knapsack and the number of available items is set, as follows:

```
P = 10
n = len(value)
```

11. Finally, we print out the results:

```
KnapSackTable(weight, value, P, n)
The following results are returned:
Items available: [(5, 18), (2, 9), (4, 12), (6, 25)]
*******************************
Total value: 37
Item selected: 6 25
Item selected: 4 12
Total weight: 10
```

The DP algorithm allowed us to obtain the optimal solution, saving on computational costs.

How it works...

Consider, for example, the problem of finding the best path that joins two locations. The principle of optimality states that each sub path included in it, between any intermediate location and the final location, must in turn be optimal. Based on this principle, DP solves a problem by taking one decision at a time. At every step, the best policy for the future is determined, regardless of the past choices (it is a Markov process), assuming that the latter choices are also optimal.

There's more...

DP is a technique for solving recursive problems more efficiently. Why is this the case? Oftentimes, in recursive procedures, we solve sub problems repeatedly. In DP, this does not happen: we memorize the solution of these sub problems so that we do not have to solve them again. This is called **memoization**. If the value of a variable at a given step depends on the results of previous calculations, and if the same calculations are repeated over and over, then it is convenient to store the intermediate results so as to avoid repeating computationally expensive calculations.

See also

- Refer to *Keras Reinforcement Learning Projects*, Giuseppe Ciaburro, Packt Publishing
- Refer to *Dynamic Programming* (from Stanford University): `https://web.stanford.edu/class/cs97si/04-dynamic-programming.pdf`
- Refer to *The Knapsack Problem* (from Eindhoven University): `http://www.es.ele.tue.nl/education/5MC10/Solutions/knapsack.pdf`
- Refer to *Memoization* (from Radford University): `https://www.radford.edu/~nokie/classes/360/dp-memoized.html`

Finding the shortest path

Given a weighted graph and a designated vertex X, we will often need to find the path from X to each of the other vertices in the graph. Identifying a path connecting two or more nodes of a graph appears as a sub problem of many other problems of discrete optimization and has, in addition, numerous applications in the real world.

Getting ready

In this recipe, we will find the shortest path between two points using the **Dijkstra** algorithm. We will also use the `networkx` package to represent graphs in Python.

How to do it...

Let's see how we can find the shortest path:

1. We will use the `DijkstraNX.py` file that is already provided for you as a reference. First, we import the libraries we will use here:

```
import networkx as nx
import matplotlib.pyplot as plt
```

2. Then, a graph object is created and the vertices are added:

```
G = nx.Graph()
G.add_node(1)
G.add_node(2)
G.add_node(3)
G.add_node(4)
```

3. Subsequently, the weighted edges are added:

```
G.add_edge(1, 2, weight=2)
G.add_edge(2, 3, weight=2)
G.add_edge(3, 4, weight=3)
G.add_edge(1, 3, weight=5)
G.add_edge(2, 4, weight=6)
```

4. At this point, we have drawn the graph by adding labels to the edges with the indication of weight:

```
pos = nx.spring_layout(G, scale=3)
nx.draw(G, pos,with_labels=True, font_weight='bold')
edge_labels = nx.get_edge_attributes(G,'r')
nx.draw_networkx_edge_labels(G, pos, labels = edge_labels)
plt.show()
```

To do this, the `draw_networkx_edge_labels` function was used. The following diagram shows the results of this:

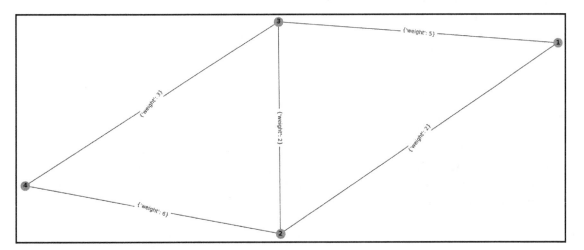

5. Finally, the shortest path from one to four nodes has been calculated:

```
print(nx.shortest_path(G,1,4,weight='weight'))
```

6. The `shortest_path` function computes the shortest paths and path lengths between nodes in the graph. The following are the results:

```
[1, 2, 3, 4]
```

7. Finally, the length of the shortest paths has been calculated:

```
print(nx.nx.shortest_path_length(G,1,4,weight='weight'))
```

The following is the result:

```
7
```

As we can verify, we have obtained the same result.

How it works...

The Dijkstra algorithm is able to solve the problem of finding the shortest path from the source, s, to all of the nodes. The algorithm maintains a label $d(i)$ to the nodes representing an upper bound on the length of the shortest path of the node i.

At each step, the algorithm partitions the nodes in V into two sets: the set of permanently labeled nodes and the set of nodes that are still temporarily labeled. The distance of permanently labeled nodes represents the shortest path distance from the source to these nodes, whereas the temporary labels contain a value that can be greater than or equal to the shortest path length.

There's more...

The basic idea of the algorithm is to start from the source and try to permanently label the successor nodes. At the beginning, the algorithm places the value of the source distance to zero and initializes the other distances to an arbitrarily high value (by convention, we will set the initial value of the distances: $d[i] = +\infty, \forall i \in V$).

At each iteration, the node label i is the value of the minimum distance along a path from the source that contains, apart from i, only permanently labeled nodes. The algorithm selects the node whose label has the lowest value among those labeled temporarily, labels it permanently, and updates all the labels of the nodes adjacent to it. The algorithm terminates when all the nodes have been permanently labeled.

See also

- Check out *Keras Reinforcement Learning Projects*, Giuseppe Ciaburro, Packt Publishing
- Check out *Solving Shortest Path Problem: Dijkstra's Algorithm* (from Illinois University): `http://www.ifp.illinois.edu/~angelia/ge330fall09_dijkstra_118.pdf`
- Check out *Graph Theory Tutorials* (from the University of Tennessee at Martin): `https://primes.utm.edu/graph/index.html`

Deciding the discount factor using Q-learning

Q-learning is one of the most used reinforcement learning algorithms. This is due to its ability to compare the expected utility of the available actions without requiring an environment model. Thanks to this technique, it is possible to find an optimal action for every given state in a finished MDP.

A general solution to the reinforcement learning problem is to estimate, thanks to the learning process, an evaluation function. This function must be able to evaluate, through the sum of the rewards, the convenience or otherwise of a particular policy. In fact, Q-learning tries to maximize the value of the Q function (the action-value function), which represents the maximum discounted future reward when we perform actions, a, in the state, s.

Getting ready

In this recipe, we will deal with the problem of controlling a character's movement in a grid world by offering a first solution based on Q-learning.

How to do it...

Let's see how we can decide on the discount factor using Q-learning:

1. We will use the `FrozenQlearning.py` file that is already provided for you as reference. Let's start by importing the libraries:

```
import gym
import numpy as np
```

2. Then, we will move on and create the environment by calling the `make` method:

```
env = gym.make('FrozenLake-v0')
```

This method creates the environment that our agent will run in.

3. Now, let's initialize the parameters, starting with `QTable`:

```
QTable = np.zeros([env.observation_space.n, env.action_space.n])
```

4. Let's define some parameters:

```
alpha = .80
gamma = .95
NumEpisodes = 2000
```

Here, `alpha` is the learning rate, `gamma` is the discount factor, and `NumEpisodes` is the number of episodes.

4. Now, we will create a list to contain the total rewards:

```
RewardsList = []
```

5. At this point, after setting the parameters, it is possible to start the Q-learning cycle:

```
for i in range(NumEpisodes):
    CState = env.reset()
    SumReward = 0
    d = False
    j = 0
    while j < 99:
        j+=1
        Action = np.argmax(QTable[CState,:] +
np.random.randn(1,env.action_space.n)*(1./(i+1)))
        NState,Rewards,d,_ = env.step(Action)
        QTable[CState,Action] = QTable[CState,Action] +
```

```
alpha*(Rewards + gamma*np.max(QTable[NState,:]) -
QTable[CState,Action])
        SumReward += Rewards
        CState = NState
        if d == True:
            break

    RewardsList.append(SumReward)
```

At the end of each episode, the list of rewards is enriched with a new value.

6. Finally, we print the results:

```
print ("Score: " +  str(sum(RewardsList)/NumEpisodes))
print ("Final Q-Table Values")
print (QTable)
```

The following screenshot shows the final Q-Table:

```
Score: 0.441
Final Q-Table Values
[[8.09790682e-02 9.69476193e-03 4.11286493e-03 3.72643060e-03]
 [1.28341407e-03 6.03882961e-04 8.06474557e-04 2.68672382e-01]
 [1.91967449e-03 1.92834234e-03 1.35171928e-03 1.44758358e-01]
 [7.17684420e-04 3.66341807e-07 1.37698057e-04 8.63455110e-02]
 [8.34610385e-02 4.22336752e-06 3.86592526e-05 1.25979894e-03]
 [0.00000000e+00 0.00000000e+00 0.00000000e+00 0.00000000e+00]
 [2.97743191e-04 1.84465934e-05 1.15548361e-01 7.03460389e-06]
 [0.00000000e+00 0.00000000e+00 0.00000000e+00 0.00000000e+00]
 [3.05085281e-05 8.22833888e-04 1.18894379e-03 9.85186767e-02]
 [5.88378899e-04 3.46691598e-01 3.80809242e-04 2.51803451e-04]
 [5.10025290e-01 1.83055349e-03 9.49003480e-04 2.15726641e-05]
 [0.00000000e+00 0.00000000e+00 0.00000000e+00 0.00000000e+00]
 [0.00000000e+00 0.00000000e+00 0.00000000e+00 0.00000000e+00]
 [0.00000000e+00 1.13547942e-03 7.02402188e-01 2.29674937e-04]
 [0.00000000e+00 0.00000000e+00 9.45161063e-01 0.00000000e+00]
 [0.00000000e+00 0.00000000e+00 0.00000000e+00 0.00000000e+00]]
```

To improve the result, the retuning of the configuration parameters is required.

How it works...

The `FrozenLake` environment is a 4 × 4 grid that contains four possible areas: **Safe (S)**, **Frozen (F)**, **Hole (H)**, and **Goal (G)**. The agent controls the movement of a character in a grid world, and moves around the grid until it reaches the goal or the hole. Some tiles of the grid are walkable, and others lead to the agent falling into the water. If it falls into the hole, it has to start from the beginning and is rewarded with the value 0. Additionally, the direction in which the agent will move is uncertain and only partially depends on the chosen direction. If the agent finds a walkable path to a goal tile, it is rewarded. The agent has four possible moves: up, down, left, and right. The process continues until it learns from every mistake and reaches the goal.

There's more...

Q-learning estimates the function value $q(s, a)$ incrementally, updating the value of the state-action pair at each step of the environment, following the logic of updating the general formula for estimating the values for the temporal difference methods. Q-learning has off-policy characteristics; that is, while the policy is improved according to the values estimated by $q(s, a)$, the value function updates the estimates following a strictly greedy secondary policy: given a state, the chosen action is always the one that maximizes the *max* $q(s, a)$ value. However, the π policy has an important role in estimating values, because through it the state-action pairs to be visited and updated are determined.

See also

- Check out *Keras Reinforcement Learning Projects*, Giuseppe Ciaburro, Packt Publishing
- Refer to *Reinforcement Learning: A Tutorial* (from University of Toronto): http://www.cs.toronto.edu/~zemel/documents/411/rltutorial.pdf
- Check out the official site of the `gym` library: https://gym.openai.com/
- Check out the *FrozenLake-v0* environment: https://gym.openai.com/envs/FrozenLake-v0/

Implementing the deep Q-learning algorithm

Deep Q-learning represents an evolution of the basic Q-learning method. The state-action is replaced by a neural network, with the aim of approximating the optimal value function. Compared to the Q-learning approaches, where it was used to structure the network in order to request both input and action and providing its expected return, deep Q-learning revolutionizes the structure to request only the state of the environment and supply as many status-action values as there are actions that can be performed in the environment.

Getting ready

In this recipe, we will use the deep Q-learning approaches to controls a character's movement in a grid world. In this recipe, the `keras-rl` library will be used; to learn about it further, refer to the *Developing AI-based dynamic modeling system* recipe.

How to do it...

Let's see how we can implement a deep Q-learning algorithm:

1. We will use the `FrozenDeepQLearning.py` file that is already provided for you as a reference. Let's start by importing the libraries:

```
import gym
import numpy as np
from keras.models import Sequential
from keras.layers.core import Dense, Reshape
from keras.layers.embeddings import Embedding
from keras.optimizers import Adam
from rl.agents.dqn import DQNAgent
from rl.policy import BoltzmannQPolicy
from rl.memory import SequentialMemory
```

2. Then, we will define the environment and set the seed:

```
ENV_NAME = 'FrozenLake-v0'
env = gym.make(ENV_NAME)
np.random.seed(1)
env.seed(1)
```

3. Now, we will extract the actions that are available to the agent:

```
Actions = env.action_space.n
```

The `Actions` variable now contains all the actions that are available in the selected environment. Gym will not always tell you the meaning of those actions, but only about which ones are available.

4. Now, we will build a simple neural network model using the `keras` library:

```
model = Sequential()
model.add(Embedding(16, 4, input_length=1))
model.add(Reshape((4,)))
print(model.summary())
```

Now, the neural network model is ready to use, so let's configure and compile our agent. One problem with using the DQN is that the neural network that was used in the algorithm tends to forget previous experiences because it overwrites them with new experiences.

5. So, we need a list of previous experiences and observations to reform the model with previous experiences. For this reason, a memory variable is defined that will contain the previous experiences, and a policy will be set:

```
memory = SequentialMemory(limit=10000, window_length=1)
policy = BoltzmannQPolicy()
```

6. We just have to define the agent:

```
Dqn = DQNAgent(model=model, nb_actions=Actions,
               memory=memory, nb_steps_warmup=500,
               target_model_update=1e-2, policy=policy,
               enable_double_dqn=False, batch_size=512
               )
```

7. Let's proceed to compile and fit the model:

```
Dqn.compile(Adam())
Dqn.fit(env, nb_steps=1e5, visualize=False, verbose=1,
log_interval=10000)
```

8. At the end of the training, it is necessary to save the obtained weights:

```
Dqn.save_weights('dqn_{}_weights.h5f'.format(ENV_NAME),
overwrite=True)
```

9. Finally, we will evaluate our algorithm for 20 episodes:

```
Dqn.test(env, nb_episodes=20, visualize=False)
```

Our agent is now able to identify the path that allows them to reach the goal.

How it works...

A general solution to the reinforcement learning problem is to estimate, thanks to the learning process, an evaluation function. This function must be able to evaluate, through the sum of the rewards, the convenience or otherwise of a particular policy. In fact, Q-learning tries to maximize the value of the Q function (action-value function), which represents the maximum discounted future reward when we perform actions, *a*, in the state, *s*. DQN represents an evolution of the basic Q-learning method, where the state-action is replaced by a neural network, with the aim of approximating the optimal value function.

There's more...

OpenAI Gym is a library that helps us implement algorithms based on reinforcement learning. It includes a growing collection of benchmark issues that expose a common interface, and a website where people can share their results and compare algorithm performance.

OpenAI Gym focuses on the episodic setting of reinforced learning. In other words, the agent's experience is divided into a series of episodes. The initial state of the agent is randomly sampled by a distribution, and the interaction proceeds until the environment reaches a terminal state. This procedure is repeated for each episode, with the aim of maximizing the total reward expectation per episode and achieving a high level of performance in the fewest possible episodes.

See also

- Refer to *Keras Reinforcement Learning Projects*, Giuseppe Ciaburro, Packt Publishing
- Refer to *Learning 2048 with Deep Reinforcement Learning* (from the University of Waterloo): https://cs.uwaterloo.ca/~mli/zalevine-dqn-2048.pdf
- Refer to *Deep RL with Q-Functions* (from UC Berkeley): http://rail.eecs.berkeley.edu/deeprlcourse/static/slides/lec-8.pdf

Developing an AI-based dynamic modeling system

A **Segway** is a personal transport device that exploits an innovative combination of computer science, electronics, and mechanics. It functions as an extension of the body; as with a partner in a dance, it is able to anticipate every move. The operating principle is based on the **reverse pendulum** system. The reverse pendulum system is an example that's commonly found in textbooks on control and research literature. Its popularity derives in part from the fact that it is unstable without control and has a non-linear dynamic, but, above all, because it has several practical applications, such as controlling a rocket's take-off or a Segway.

Getting ready

In this recipe, we will analyze the functioning of a physical system that's made by connecting a rigid rod to a cart, modeling the system using different approaches. The rod is connected through a pivot that's hinged on the carriage and is free to rotate around it. This mechanical system, which is called the reverse pendulum, is a classic problem in control theory.

How to do it...

Let's see how we can develop an AI-based dynamic modeling system:

1. We will use the dqn_cartpole.py file that is already provided for you as a reference. Let's start by importing the libraries:

```
import numpy as np
import gym
from keras.models import Sequential
from keras.layers import Dense, Activation, Flatten
from keras.optimizers import Adam
from rl.agents.dqn import DQNAgent
from rl.policy import BoltzmannQPolicy
from rl.memory import SequentialMemory
```

2. Now, we will define and load the environment:

```
ENV_NAME = 'CartPole-v0'
env = gym.make(ENV_NAME)
```

3. To set the `seed` value, the NumPy library's `random.seed()` function is used, as follows:

```
np.random.seed(123)
env.seed(123)
```

4. Now, we will extract the actions that are available to the agent:

```
nb_actions = env.action_space.n
```

5. We will build a simple neural network model using the `keras` library:

```
model = Sequential()
model.add(Flatten(input_shape=(1,) + env.observation_space.shape))
model.add(Dense(16))
model.add(Activation('relu'))
model.add(Dense(16))
model.add(Activation('relu'))
model.add(Dense(16))
model.add(Activation('relu'))
model.add(Dense(nb_actions))
model.add(Activation('linear'))
print(model.summary())
```

6. A `memory` variable and a `policy` will be set:

```
memory = SequentialMemory(limit=50000, window_length=1)
policy = BoltzmannQPolicy()
```

7. We just have to define the agent:

```
dqn = DQNAgent(model=model, nb_actions=nb_actions, memory=memory,
nb_steps_warmup=10,
            target_model_update=1e-2, policy=policy)
```

8. Let's move on to compile and fit the model:

```
dqn.compile(Adam(lr=1e-3), metrics=['mae'])
dqn.fit(env, nb_steps=1000, visualize=True, verbose=2)
```

9. At the end of the training, it is necessary to save the obtained weights:

```
dqn.save_weights('dqn_{}_weights.h5f'.format(ENV_NAME),
overwrite=True)
```

Saving the weight of a network or an entire structure takes place in an `HDF5` file, an efficient and flexible storage system that supports complex multidimensional datasets.

10. Finally, we will evaluate our algorithm for 10 episodes:

```
dqn.test(env, nb_episodes=5, visualize=True)
```

How it works...

In this recipe, we used the `keras-rl` package to develop an AI-based dynamic modeling system. This package implements some deep reinforcement learning algorithms in Python, and integrates seamlessly with Keras' in-depth learning library.

Furthermore, `keras-rl` works immediately with OpenAI Gym. OpenAI Gym includes a growing collection of benchmark issues that shows a common interface and a website where people can share their results and compare algorithm performance. This library will be adequately addressed in the next chapter—for now, we will limit ourselves to using it.

There's more...

These choices do not limit the use of the `keras-rl` package, in the sense that the uses of `keras-rl` can be easily adapted to our needs. You can use the built-in Keras callbacks and metrics, or define others. For this reason, it is easy to implement your own environments, and even algorithms, simply by extending some simple abstract classes.

See also

- Check out *Keras Reinforcement Learning Projects*, Giuseppe Ciaburro, Packt Publishing
- Check out *Tutorial: Deep Reinforcement Learning* (from Google DeepMind): `https://icml.cc/2016/tutorials/deep_rl_tutorial.pdf`
- Refer to *Deep Reinforcement Learning* (by Xu Wang): `https://pure.tue.nl/ws/files/46933213/844320-1.pdf`

Deep reinforcement learning with double Q-learning

In the Q-learning algorithm, the future maximum approximated action value is evaluated using the same Q function as the current stock selection policy. In some cases, this can overestimate the action values, slowing down learning. A variation called **Double Q-learning** was proposed by DeepMind researchers in the following paper: *Deep reinforcement learning with Double Q-learning*, H van Hasselt, A Guez, and D Silver, March, 2016, at the Thirtieth AAAI Conference on Artificial Intelligence. As a solution to this problem, the authors proposed to modify the Bellman update.

Getting ready

In this recipe, we will control an inverted pendulum system using the Double Q-learning algorithm.

How to do it...

Let's see how we can perform deep reinforcement learning with Double Q-learning:

1. We will use the `DoubleDQNCartpole.py` file that is already provided for you as a reference. Let's start by importing the libraries:

```
import numpy as np
import gym
from keras.models import Sequential
from keras.layers import Dense, Activation, Flatten
from keras.optimizers import Adam
from rl.agents.dqn import DQNAgent
from rl.policy import BoltzmannQPolicy
from rl.memory import SequentialMemory
```

2. Now, we will define and load the environment:

```
ENV_NAME = 'CartPole-v0'
env = gym.make(ENV_NAME)
```

3. To set the `seed` value, the NumPy library's `random.seed()` function is used, as follows:

```
np.random.seed(1)
env.seed(1)
```

4. Now, we will extract the actions that are available to the agent:

```
nb_actions = env.action_space.n
```

5. We will build a simple neural network model using the `keras` library:

```
model = Sequential()
model.add(Flatten(input_shape=(1,) + env.observation_space.shape))
model.add(Dense(16))
model.add(Activation('relu'))
model.add(Dense(16))
model.add(Activation('relu'))
model.add(Dense(16))
model.add(Activation('relu'))
model.add(Dense(nb_actions))
model.add(Activation('linear'))
print(model.summary())
```

6. A `memory` variable and a `policy` will be set:

```
memory = SequentialMemory(limit=50000, window_length=1)
policy = BoltzmannQPolicy()
```

7. We just have to define the agent:

```
dqn = DQNAgent(model=model, nb_actions=nb_actions, memory=memory,
               nb_steps_warmup=10, enable_double_dqn=True,
               target_model_update=1e-2,policy=policy)
```

To enable the double network, we have to set the `enable_double_dqn` option to `True`.

8. Let's move on to compile and fit the model:

```
dqn.compile(Adam(lr=1e-3), metrics=['mae'])
dqn.fit(env, nb_steps=1000, visualize=True, verbose=2)
```

9. At the end of the training, it is necessary to save the obtained weights:

```
dqn.save_weights('dqn_{}_weights.h5f'.format(ENV_NAME),
overwrite=True)
```

Saving the weight of a network or an entire structure takes place in an `HDF5` file, an efficient and flexible storage system that supports complex multidimensional datasets.

10. Finally, we will evaluate our algorithm for 10 episodes:

```
dqn.test(env, nb_episodes=5, visualize=True)
```

How it works...

The overestimation of the action value is due to the maximum operator that is used in the Bellman equation. The max operator uses the same value for both selecting and evaluating an action. Now, if we select the best action as the one that has the maximum value, we will end up selecting a sub-optimal action (which assumes the maximum value by mistake) instead of the optimal action. We can solve this problem by having two separate Q functions, each of which learns independently. A Q1 function is used to select an action, and the other Q2 function is used to evaluate an action. To do this, simply change the objective function.

There's more...

Essentially, the following two networks are used:

- The DQN network to select what is the best action to take for the next state (the action with the highest Q value)
- The target network, to calculate the target Q value of taking that action at the next state

See also

- Check out *Keras Reinforcement Learning Projects*, Giuseppe Ciaburro, Packt Publishing
- Refer to *Deep Reinforcement Learning with Double Q-learning*: https://www.aaai. org/ocs/index.php/AAAI/AAAI16/paper/download/12389/11847

Deep Q-network algorithm with dueling Q-learning

To improve convergence speed by making our network's architecture closer represent one of the last challenges of reinforcement learning, a definite improvement in the performance of a DQN model has been proposed by Wang and others in the following paper: *Dueling network architectures for deep reinforcement learning*, Z Wang, T Schaul, M Hessel, H van Hasselt, M Lanctot, and N de Freitas, 2015, arXiv preprint arXiv:1511.06581.

Getting ready

In this recipe, we will control an inverted pendulum system using the dueling Q-learning algorithm.

How to do it...

Let's see how we can perform deep Q-network algorithm with dueling Q-learning:

1. We will use the `DuelingDQNCartpole.py` file that is already provided for you as a reference. Let's start by importing the libraries:

```
import numpy as np
import gym
from keras.models import Sequential
from keras.layers import Dense, Activation, Flatten
from keras.optimizers import Adam
from rl.agents.dqn import DQNAgent
from rl.policy import BoltzmannQPolicy
from rl.memory import SequentialMemory
```

2. Now, we will define and load the environment:

```
ENV_NAME = 'CartPole-v0'
env = gym.make(ENV_NAME)
```

3. To set the `seed` value, the NumPy library's `random.seed()` function is used, as follows:

```
np.random.seed(2)
env.seed(2)
```

4. Now, we will extract the actions, available to the agent:

```
nb_actions = env.action_space.n
```

5. We will build a simple neural network model using the Keras library:

```
model = Sequential()
model.add(Flatten(input_shape=(1,) + env.observation_space.shape))
model.add(Dense(16))
model.add(Activation('relu'))
model.add(Dense(16))
model.add(Activation('relu'))
model.add(Dense(16))
model.add(Activation('relu'))
model.add(Dense(nb_actions))
model.add(Activation('linear'))
print(model.summary())
```

6. A `memory` variable and a `policy` will be set:

```
memory = SequentialMemory(limit=50000, window_length=1)
policy = BoltzmannQPolicy()
```

We just have to define the agent:

```
dqn = DQNAgent(model=model, nb_actions=nb_actions, memory=memory,
               nb_steps_warmup=10, enable_dueling_network=True,
               dueling_type='avg',target_model_update=1e-2,
               policy=policy)
```

To enable the dueling network, we have to specify the `dueling_type` to one of the following:`'avg'`, `'max'`, or `'naive'`.

8. Let's move on to compile and fit the model:

```
dqn.compile(Adam(lr=1e-3), metrics=['mae'])
dqn.fit(env, nb_steps=1000, visualize=True, verbose=2)
```

9. At the end of the training, it is necessary to save the obtained weights:

```
dqn.save_weights('dqn_{}_weights.h5f'.format(ENV_NAME),
overwrite=True)
```

Saving the weight of a network or an entire structure takes place in an HDF5 file, an efficient and flexible storage system that supports complex multidimensional datasets.

9. Finally, we will evaluate our algorithm for 10 episodes:

```
dqn.test(env, nb_episodes=5, visualize=True)
```

How it works...

In reinforcement learning, the function Q and the value function play a fundamental role:

- The Q function specifies how good an agent is to perform an action in the *s* state
- The value function specifies how good it is for an agent to be in a state, *s*

To introduce a further improvement in the performance of a DQN, we introduce a new function called an `advantage` function, which can be defined as the difference between the `value` function and the `benefit` function. The `benefit` function specifies how good an agent is at performing an action compared to other actions.

Therefore, the `value` function specifies the goodness of a state and the `advantage` function specifies the goodness of an action. Then, the combination of these two functions tells us how good it is for an agent to perform an action in a state that is actually our Q function. So, we can define our Q function as the sum of a `value` function and an `advantage` function.

The dueling DQN is essentially a DQN, in which the fully connected final layer is divided into two streams:

- One calculates the `value` function
- The other calculates the `advantage` function

Finally, the two streams are combined using the aggregate level for obtaining the Q function.

There's more...

The approximation of the `value` function via the neural network is anything but stable. To achieve convergence, the basic algorithm should be modified by introducing techniques to avoid oscillations and divergences.

The most important technique is called `experience replay`. During the episodes, at each step, the agent's experience is stored in a dataset, called `replay memory`. In the internal cycle of the algorithm, instead of performing the training on the network based on the only transition just performed, a subset of transitions is selected randomly from the replay memory, and the training takes place according to the loss calculated on the subset of transitions.

The experience of the `replay` technique, that is, randomly selecting transitions from `replay memory`, eliminates the problem of correlation between consecutive transitions and reduces variance among different updates.

See also

- Check out *Keras Reinforcement Learning Projects*, Giuseppe Ciaburro, Packt Publishing
- Refer to *Dueling Network Architectures for Deep Reinforcement Learning* for more information: `https://arxiv.org/abs/1511.06581`

13
Deep Neural Networks

In this chapter, we will cover the following recipes:

- Building a perceptron
- Building a single layer neural network
- Building a deep neural network
- Creating a vector quantizer
- Building a recurrent neural network for sequential data analysis
- Visualizing the characters in an OCR database
- Building an optical character recognizer using neural networks
- Implementing optimization algorithms in ANN

Technical requirements

To address the recipes in this chapter, you need the following files (available on GitHub):

- `perceptron.py`
- `single_layer.py`
- `data_single_layer.txt`
- `deep_neural_network.py`
- `vector_quantization.py`
- `data_vq.txt`
- `recurrent_network.py`
- `visualize_characters.py`
- `ocr.py`
- `IrisClassifier.py`

Introduction

Our brain is really good at identifying and recognizing things. We want machines to be able to do the same. A neural network is a framework that is modeled after the human brain to simulate our learning processes. Neural networks are designed to learn from data and recognize the underlying patterns. As with all learning algorithms, neural networks deal with numbers. Therefore, if we want to achieve any real-world task involving images, text, sensors, and so on, we have to convert them into a numerical format before we feed them into a neural network. We can use a neural network for classification, clustering, generation, and many other related tasks.

A neural network consists of layers of **neurons**. These neurons are modeled after the biological neurons in the human brain. Each layer is basically a set of independent neurons that are connected to the neurons on adjacent layers. The input layer corresponds to the input data that we provide, and the output layer consists of the output that we desire. All the layers in between are called **hidden layers**. If we design a neural network with more hidden layers, then we give it more freedom to train itself with higher accuracy.

Let's say that we want the neural network to classify data, based on our needs. For a neural network to work accordingly, we need to provide labeled training data. The neural network will then train itself by optimizing the `cost` function. This `cost` function is the error between actual labels and the predicted labels from the neural network. We keep iterating until the error goes below a certain threshold.

What exactly are *deep* neural networks? Deep neural networks are neural networks that consist of many hidden layers. In general, this falls under the realm of deep learning. This is a field that is dedicated to the study of these neural networks, composed of multiple layers that are used across many verticals.

Building a perceptron

Let's start our neural network adventure with a **perceptron**. A perceptron is a single neuron that performs all the computations. It is a very simple model, but it forms the basis of building up complex neural networks. The following is what it looks like:

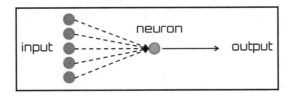

The neuron combines inputs using different weights, and it then adds a bias value to compute the output. It's a simple linear equation relating input values to the output of the perceptron.

Getting ready

In this recipe, we will use a library called `neurolab` to define a perceptron with two inputs. Before you proceed, make sure that you install it. You can find the installation instructions at `https://pythonhosted.org/neurolab/install.html`. Let's go ahead and look at how to design and develop this neural network.

How to do it...

Let's see how to build a perceptron:

1. Create a new Python file, and import the following packages (the full code is given in the `perceptron.py` file that is provided to you):

    ```
    import numpy as np
    import neurolab as nl
    import matplotlib.pyplot as plt
    ```

2. Define some input data and its corresponding labels:

    ```
    # Define input data
    data = np.array([[0.3, 0.2], [0.1, 0.4], [0.4, 0.6], [0.9, 0.5]])
    labels = np.array([[0], [0], [0], [1]])
    ```

3. Let's plot this data to see where the datapoints are located:

```
# Plot input data
plt.figure()
plt.scatter(data[:,0], data[:,1])
plt.xlabel('X-axis')
plt.ylabel('Y-axis')
plt.title('Input data')
```

4. Let's define a `perceptron` with two inputs. This function also needs us to specify the minimum and maximum values in the input data:

```
# Define a perceptron with 2 inputs;
# Each element of the list in the first argument
# specifies the min and max values of the inputs
perceptron = nl.net.newp([[0, 1],[0, 1]], 1)
```

5. Let's train the `perceptron` model:

```
# Train the perceptron
error = perceptron.train(data, labels, epochs=50, show=15, lr=0.01)
```

6. Let's plot the results, as follows:

```
# plot results
plt.figure()
plt.plot(error)
plt.xlabel('Number of epochs')
plt.ylabel('Training error')
plt.grid()
plt.title('Training error progress')

plt.show()
```

If you run this code, you will see two diagrams. The first diagram displays the input data, as follows:

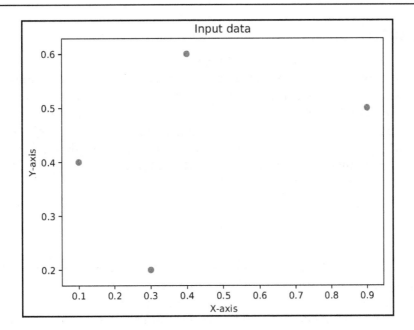

The second diagram displays the training error progress, as follows:

How it works...

In this recipe, we used a single neuron that performs all the computations. To train the `perceptron`, the following parameters are set. The number of epochs specifies the number of complete passes through our training dataset. The `show` parameter specifies how frequently we want to display the progress. The `lr` parameter specifies the learning rate of the `perceptron`. It is the step size for when the algorithm searches through the parameter space. If this is large, then the algorithm may move faster, but it might miss the optimum value. If this is small, then the algorithm will hit the optimum value, but it will be slow. So, it's a trade-off; hence, we choose a value of `0.01`.

There's more...

We can understand a `perceptron` concept as anything that takes multiple inputs and produces one output. This is the simplest form of a neural network. The `perceptron` concept was suggested by Frank Rosenblatt in 1958 as an object with an input and output layer and a learning rule targeted at minimizing errors. This learning function called **error backpropagation** changes connective weights (synapses) relying on the actual output of the network, with respect to a given input, as the difference between the actual output and the desired output.

See also

- Refer to the official documentation of the `neurolab` library: `https://pythonhosted.org/neurolab/`
- *Refer to A Basic Introduction to Neural Networks* (from the University of Wisconsin-Madison): `http://pages.cs.wisc.edu/~bolo/shipyard/neural/local.html`

Building a single layer neural network

In the previous recipe, *Building a perceptron*, we learned how to create a `perceptron`; now let's create a single layer neural network. A single layer neural network consists of multiple neurons in a single layer. Overall, we will have an input layer, a hidden layer, and an output layer, as shown in the following diagram:

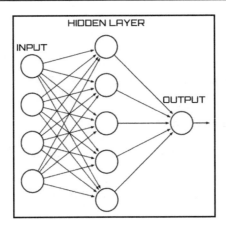

Getting ready

In this recipe, we will learn how to create a single layer neural network using the `neurolab` library.

How to do it...

Let's see how to build a single layer neural network:

1. Create a new Python file, and import the following packages (the full code is given in the `single_layer.py` file that is provided to you):

```
import numpy as np
import matplotlib.pyplot as plt
import neurolab as nl
```

2. We will use the data in the `data_single_layer.txt` file. Let's load this:

```
# Define input data
input_file = 'data_single_layer.txt'
input_text = np.loadtxt(input_file)
data = input_text[:, 0:2]
labels = input_text[:, 2:]
```

3. Let's plot the input data:

```
# Plot input data
plt.figure()
plt.scatter(data[:,0], data[:,1])
plt.xlabel('X-axis')
plt.ylabel('Y-axis')
plt.title('Input data')
```

4. Let's extract the minimum and maximum values:

```
# Min and max values for each dimension
x_min, x_max = data[:,0].min(), data[:,0].max()
y_min, y_max = data[:,1].min(), data[:,1].max()
```

5. Let's define a single layer neural network with two neurons in the hidden layer:

```
# Define a single-layer neural network with 2 neurons;
# Each element in the list (first argument) specifies the
# min and max values of the inputs
single_layer_net = nl.net.newp([[x_min, x_max], [y_min, y_max]], 2)
```

6. Train the neural network for 50 epochs:

```
# Train the neural network
error = single_layer_net.train(data, labels, epochs=50, show=20,
lr=0.01)
```

7. Plot the results, as follows:

```
# Plot results
plt.figure()
plt.plot(error)
plt.xlabel('Number of epochs')
plt.ylabel('Training error')
plt.title('Training error progress')
plt.grid()
plt.show()
```

8. Let's test the neural network on new test data:

```
print(single_layer_net.sim([[0.3, 4.5]]))
print(single_layer_net.sim([[4.5, 0.5]]))
print(single_layer_net.sim([[4.3, 8]]))
```

If you run this code, you will see two diagrams. The first diagram displays the input data, as follows:

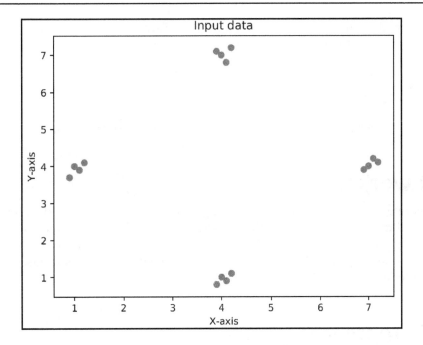

The second diagram displays the training error progress, as follows:

You will see the following printed on your Terminal, indicating where the input test points belong:

```
[[ 0.   0.]]
[[ 1.   0.]]
[[ 1.   1.]]
```

You can verify that the outputs are correct based on our labels.

How it works...

A single layer neural network has the following architecture: the inputs form the input layer, the middle layer that performs the processing is called the hidden layer, and the outputs form the output layer. The hidden layer can convert the input to the desired output. Understanding the hidden layer requires knowledge of weights, bias, and activation functions.

There's more...

Weights are vital to convert an input so it impacts the output; they are numerical parameters that monitor how all of the neurons affect the others. The related concept resembles the slope in linear regression, where a weight is multiplied to the input to add up and form the output.

Bias is similar to the intercept added to a linear equation. It is also an additional parameter that is used to regulate the output along with the weighted sum of the inputs to the neuron.

An activation function is a mathematical function that converts the input to an output and determines the total signal a neuron receives. Without activation functions, neural networks would behave like linear functions.

See also

- Refer to the official documentation of the neurolab library: https://pythonhosted.org/neurolab/
- *Refer to Introduction to Neural Networks* (from Yale University): http://euler.stat.yale.edu/~tba3/stat665/lectures/lec12/lecture12.pdf

Building a deep neural network

We are now ready to build a **deep neural network**. A deep neural network consists of an input layer, many hidden layers, and an output layer. This looks like the following:

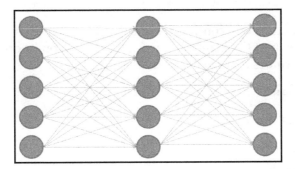

The preceding diagram depicts a multilayer neural network with one input layer, one hidden layer, and one output layer. In a deep neural network, there are many hidden layers between the input and output layers.

Getting ready

In this recipe, we will build a deep neural network. Deep learning forms an advanced neural network with numerous hidden layers. Deep learning is a vast subject and is an important concept in building AI. In this recipe, we will use generated training data and define a multilayer neural network with two hidden layers.

How to do it...

Let's see how to build a deep neural network:

1. Create a new Python file, and import the following packages (the full code is given in the deep_neural_network.py file that is provided to you):

```
import neurolab as nl
import numpy as np
import matplotlib.pyplot as plt
```

2. Let's define parameters to generate some training data:

```
# Generate training data
min_value = -12
max_value = 12
num_datapoints = 90
```

3. This training data will consist of a function we define that will transform the values. We expect the neural network to learn this on its own, based on the input and output values that we provide:

```
x = np.linspace(min_value, max_value, num_datapoints)
y = 2 * np.square(x) + 7
y /= np.linalg.norm(y)
```

4. Reshape the arrays:

```
data = x.reshape(num_datapoints, 1)
labels = y.reshape(num_datapoints, 1)
```

5. Plot the input data:

```
plt.figure()
plt.scatter(data, labels)
plt.xlabel('X-axis')
plt.ylabel('Y-axis')
plt.title('Input data')
```

6. Define a deep neural network with two hidden layers, where each hidden layer consists of 10 neurons and the output layer consists of one neuron:

```
multilayer_net = nl.net.newff([[min_value, max_value]], [10, 10, 1])
```

7. Set the training algorithm to gradient descent:

```
multilayer_net.trainf = nl.train.train_gd
```

8. Train the network:

```
error = multilayer_net.train(data, labels, epochs=800, show=100, goal=0.01)
```

9. Predict the output for the training inputs to see the performance:

```
predicted_output = multilayer_net.sim(data)
```

10. Plot the training error:

```
plt.figure()
plt.plot(error)
plt.xlabel('Number of epochs')
plt.ylabel('Error')
plt.title('Training error progress')
```

11. Let's create a set of new inputs and run the neural network on them to see how it performs:

```
x2 = np.linspace(min_value, max_value, num_datapoints * 2)
y2 = multilayer_net.sim(x2.reshape(x2.size,1)).reshape(x2.size)
y3 = predicted_output.reshape(num_datapoints)
```

12. Plot the outputs:

```
plt.figure()
plt.plot(x2, y2, '-', x, y, '.', x, y3, 'p')
plt.title('Ground truth vs predicted output')
plt.show()
```

If you run this code, you will see three diagrams. The first diagram displays the input data, as follows:

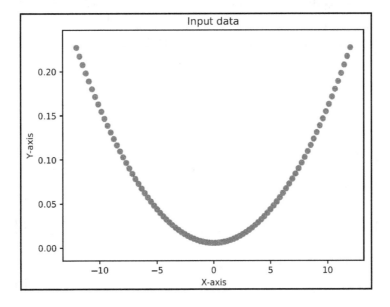

The second diagram displays the training error progress, as follows:

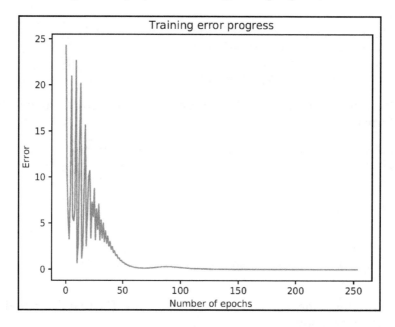

The third diagram displays the output of the neural network, as follows:

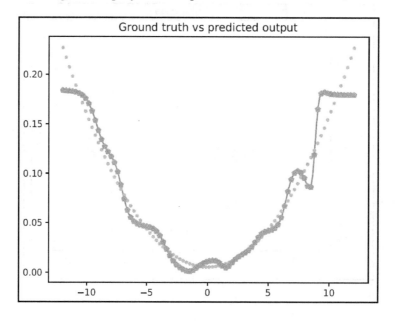

You will see the following on your Terminal:

```
Epoch: 100; Error: 4.634764957565494;
Epoch: 200; Error: 0.7675153737786798;
Epoch: 300; Error: 0.21543996465118723;
Epoch: 400; Error: 0.027738499953293118;
Epoch: 500; Error: 0.019145948877988192;
Epoch: 600; Error: 0.11296232736352653;
Epoch: 700; Error: 0.03446237629842832;
Epoch: 800; Error: 0.03022668735279662;
The maximum number of train epochs is reached
```

How it works...

In this recipe, we will use generated training data to train a multilayer deep neural network with two hidden layers. To train the model, the gradient descent algorithm was used. **Gradient descent** is an iterative approach used for error correction in any learning model. A gradient descent approach is the process of iterating updating weights and biases with the error times derivative of the activation function (backpropagation). In this approach, the steepest descent step size is substituted by a similar size from the previous step. Gradient is the slope of the curve, as it is the derivative of the activation function.

There's more...

The objective of finding the gradient descent at every step is to find the global cost minimum, where the error is the lowest. And this is where the model has a good fit for the data, and predictions are more accurate.

See also

- Refer to the official documentation of the `neurolab` library: `https://pythonhosted.org/neurolab/lib.html`
- Some notes on gradient descent (by Marc Toussaint from Stuttgart University): `https://ipvs.informatik.uni-stuttgart.de/mlr/marc/notes/gradientDescent.pdf`

Creating a vector quantizer

You can use neural networks for vector quantization as well. **Vector quantization** is the *N*-dimensional version of rounding off. This is very commonly used across multiple areas in computer vision, NLP, and machine learning in general.

Getting ready

In previous recipes, we have already addressed **vector quantization** concepts: *Compressing an image using vector quantization* and *Creating features using visual Codebook and vector quantization*. In this recipe, we will define a neural network with two layers—10 neurons in input layer and 4 neurons in the output layer. Then we will use this network to divide the space into four regions.

Before starting, you need to make a change to fix a library bug. You need to open the following file: `neurolab | net.py`. Then find the following:

```
inx = np.floor (cn0 * pc.cumsum ()). astype (int)
```

Replace the preceding line with the following:

```
inx = np.floor (cn0 * pc.cumsum ())
```

How to do it...

Let's see how to create a vector quantizer:

1. Create a new Python file and import the following packages (the full code is given in the `vector_quantization.py` file that is provided to you):

```
import numpy as np
import matplotlib.pyplot as plt
import neurolab as nl
```

2. Let's load the input data from the `data_vq.txt` file:

```
input_file = 'data_vq.txt'
input_text = np.loadtxt(input_file)
data = input_text[:, 0:2]
labels = input_text[:, 2:]
```

3. Define a **learning vector quantization** (**LVQ**) neural network with two layers. The array in the last parameter specifies the percentage weightage for each output (they should add up to 1):

```
net = nl.net.newlvq(nl.tool.minmax(data), 10, [0.25, 0.25, 0.25,
0.25])
```

4. Train the LVQ neural network:

```
error = net.train(data, labels, epochs=100, goal=-1)
```

5. Create a grid of values for testing and visualization:

```
xx, yy = np.meshgrid(np.arange(0, 8, 0.2), np.arange(0, 8, 0.2))
xx.shape = xx.size, 1
yy.shape = yy.size, 1
input_grid = np.concatenate((xx, yy), axis=1)
```

6. Evaluate the network on this grid:

```
output_grid = net.sim(input_grid)
```

7. Define the four classes in our data:

```
class1 = data[labels[:,0] == 1]
class2 = data[labels[:,1] == 1]
class3 = data[labels[:,2] == 1]
class4 = data[labels[:,3] == 1]
```

8. Define the grids for all these classes:

```
grid1 = input_grid[output_grid[:,0] == 1]
grid2 = input_grid[output_grid[:,1] == 1]
grid3 = input_grid[output_grid[:,2] == 1]
grid4 = input_grid[output_grid[:,3] == 1]
```

9. Plot the outputs:

```
plt.plot(class1[:,0], class1[:,1], 'ko', class2[:,0], class2[:,1],
'ko',
                class3[:,0], class3[:,1], 'ko', class4[:,0],
class4[:,1], 'ko')
plt.plot(grid1[:,0], grid1[:,1], 'b.', grid2[:,0], grid2[:,1],
'gx',
                grid3[:,0], grid3[:,1], 'cs', grid4[:,0],
grid4[:,1], 'ro')
plt.axis([0, 8, 0, 8])
plt.xlabel('X-axis')
```

```
plt.ylabel('Y-axis')
plt.title('Vector quantization using neural networks')
plt.show()
```

If you run this code, you will see the following diagram, where the space is divided into regions. Each region corresponds to a bucket in the list of vector-quantized regions in the space:

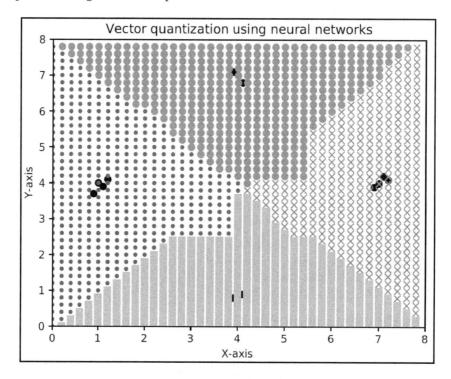

How it works...

In this recipe, we defined a neural network with two layers: 10 neurons in the input layer and 4 neurons in the output layer. This neural network was first trained and then used to divide the space into four regions. Each region corresponds to a bucket in the list of vector-quantized regions in the space.

There's more...

Vector quantization is based on the division of a large set of points (vectors) into groups that show the same number of points closer to them. Each group is identified by its centroid point, as is the case with most clustering algorithms.

See also

- Refer to the official documentation of the `neurolab` library: `https://pythonhosted.org/neurolab/`

Building a recurrent neural network for sequential data analysis

Recurrent neural networks are really good at analyzing sequential and time-series data. A **recurrent neural network** (**RNN**) is a neural model in which a bidirectional flow of information is present. In other words, while the propagation of signals in feedforward networks takes place only in a continuous manner, going from inputs to outputs, recurrent networks are different. In them, this propagation can also occur from a neural layer following a previous one, or between neurons belonging to the same layer, and even between a neuron and itself.

Getting ready

When we deal with sequential and time-series data, we cannot just extend generic models. The temporal dependencies in the data are really important, and we need to account for this in our models. Let's build a recurrent neural network using the `neurolab` library.

How to do it...

Let's see how to build a recurrent neural network for sequential data analysis:

1. Create a new Python file, and import the following packages (the full code is given in the `recurrent_network.py` file that is provided to you):

```
import numpy as np
import matplotlib.pyplot as plt
import neurolab as nl
```

2. Define a function to create a waveform, based on input parameters:

```
def create_waveform(num_points):
    # Create train samples
    data1 = 1 * np.cos(np.arange(0, num_points))
    data2 = 2 * np.cos(np.arange(0, num_points))
    data3 = 3 * np.cos(np.arange(0, num_points))
    data4 = 4 * np.cos(np.arange(0, num_points))
```

3. Create different amplitudes for each interval to create a random waveform:

```
    # Create varying amplitudes
    amp1 = np.ones(num_points)
    amp2 = 4 + np.zeros(num_points)
    amp3 = 2 * np.ones(num_points)
    amp4 = 0.5 + np.zeros(num_points)
```

4. Combine the arrays to create output arrays. This data corresponds to the input and the amplitude corresponds to the labels:

```
    data = np.array([data1, data2, data3,
data4]).reshape(num_points * 4, 1)
    amplitude = np.array([[amp1, amp2, amp3,
amp4]]).reshape(num_points * 4, 1)

    return data, amplitude
```

5. Define a function to draw the output after passing the data through the trained neural network:

```
# Draw the output using the network
def draw_output(net, num_points_test):
    data_test, amplitude_test = create_waveform(num_points_test)
    output_test = net.sim(data_test)
    plt.plot(amplitude_test.reshape(num_points_test * 4))
    plt.plot(output_test.reshape(num_points_test * 4))
```

6. Define the `main` function and start by creating sample data:

```
if __name__=='__main__':
    # Get data
    num_points = 30
    data, amplitude = create_waveform(num_points)
```

7. Create a recurrent neural network with two layers:

```
# Create network with 2 layers
net = nl.net.newelm([[-2, 2]], [10, 1], [nl.trans.TanSig(),
nl.trans.PureLin()])
```

8. Set the initialized functions for each layer:

```
# Set initialized functions and init
net.layers[0].initf = nl.init.InitRand([-0.1, 0.1], 'wb')
net.layers[1].initf= nl.init.InitRand([-0.1, 0.1], 'wb')
net.init()
```

9. Train the recurrent neural network:

```
# Training the recurrent neural network
error = net.train(data, amplitude, epochs=1000, show=100, goal=0.01)
```

10. Compute the output from the network for the training data:

```
# Compute output from network
output = net.sim(data)
```

11. Plot the training error:

```
# Plot training results
plt.subplot(211)
plt.plot(error)
plt.xlabel('Number of epochs')
plt.ylabel('Error (MSE)')
```

12. Plot the results:

```
plt.subplot(212)
plt.plot(amplitude.reshape(num_points * 4))
plt.plot(output.reshape(num_points * 4))
plt.legend(['Ground truth', 'Predicted output'])
```

13. Create a waveform of random length and see whether the network can predict it:

```
# Testing on unknown data at multiple scales
plt.figure()

plt.subplot(211)
draw_output(net, 74)
plt.xlim([0, 300])
```

14. Create another waveform with a shorter length and see whether the network can predict it:

```
plt.subplot(212)
draw_output(net, 54)
plt.xlim([0, 300])

plt.show()
```

If you run this code, you will see two diagrams. The first diagram displays training errors and the performance on the training data, as follows:

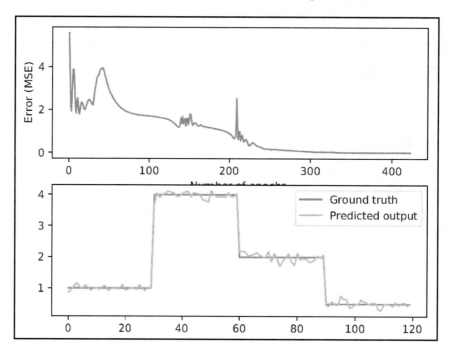

The second diagram displays how a trained recurrent neural net performs on sequences of arbitrary lengths, as follows:

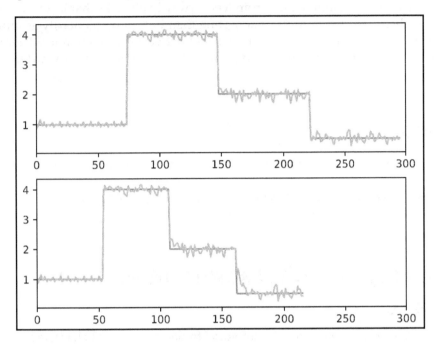

You will see the following on your Terminal:

```
Epoch: 100; Error: 1.2635865600014597;
Epoch: 200; Error: 0.4001584483592344;
Epoch: 300; Error: 0.06438997423142029;
Epoch: 400; Error: 0.03772354900253485;
Epoch: 500; Error: 0.031996105192696744;
Epoch: 600; Error: 0.011933337009068408;
Epoch: 700; Error: 0.012385370178600663;
Epoch: 800; Error: 0.01116995004102195;
Epoch: 900; Error: 0.011191016373572612;
Epoch: 1000; Error: 0.010584255803264013;
The maximum number of train epochs is reached
```

How it works...

In this recipe, first, we created an artificial signal with waveform characteristics, that is, a curve showing the shape of a wave at a given time. Then we built a recurrent neural network to see whether the network could predict a waveform of random length.

There's more...

Recurrent networks are distinguished from feedforward networks thanks to the feedback loop linked to their past decisions, thus accepting their output momentarily as inputs. This feature can be emphasized by saying that recurrent networks have memory. There is information in the sequence, and it is used perform the tasks that feedforward networks cannot.

See also

- Refer to the official documentation of `neurolab` library: `https://pythonhosted.org/neurolab/`
- Refer to *Recurrent Neural Networks* (from Yale University): `http://euler.stat.yale.edu/~tba3/stat665/lectures/lec21/lecture21.pdf`

Visualizing the characters in an OCR database

We will now look at how to use neural networks to perform **optical character recognition** (**OCR**). This refers to the process of identifying handwritten characters in images. We have always been particularly sensitive to the problem of the automatic recognition of writing in order to achieve a simpler interaction between humans and machines. Especially in the last few years, this problem has been subject to interesting developments and more and more efficient solutions thanks to a very strong economic interest and an ever-greater capacity to process data of modern computers. In particular, some countries, such as Japan, and Asian countries in general, are investing heavily, in terms of research and financial resources, to make state-of-the-art OCR.

Getting ready

In this recipe, we will display the handwritten digits contained in a dataset. We will use the dataset available at `http://ai.stanford.edu/~btaskar/ocr`. The default file name after downloading is `letter.data`. To start with, let's see how to interact with the data and visualize it.

How to do it...

Let's see how to visualize the characters in an OCR database:

1. Create a new Python file, and import the following packages (the full code is given in the `visualize_characters.py` file that is provided to you):

```
import cv2
import numpy as np
```

2. Define the input file name:

```
# Load input data
input_file = 'letter.data'
```

3. Define visualization parameters:

```
# Define visualization parameters
scaling_factor = 10
start_index = 6
end_index = -1
h, w = 16, 8
```

4. Keep looping through the file until the user presses the *Escape* key. Split the line into tab-separated characters:

```
# Loop until you encounter the Esc key
with open(input_file, 'r') as f:
    for line in f.readlines():
        data = np.array([255*float(x) for x in
line.split('\t')[start_index:end_index]])
```

5. Reshape the array into the required shape, resize it, and display it:

```
img = np.reshape(data, (h,w))
img_scaled = cv2.resize(img, None, fx=scaling_factor,
fy=scaling_factor)
cv2.imshow('Image', img_scaled)
```

6. If the user presses *Escape*, break the loop:

```
c = cv2.waitKey()
if c == 27:
    break
```

If you run this code, you will see a window displaying characters.

How it works...

In this recipe, we showed the handwritten figures contained in a dataset. To do this, the following tasks are performed:

- Load input data
- Define visualization parameters
- Loop until you encounter the *Escape* key

There's more...

Approaches to the OCR problem are basically of two types: one is based on pattern matching or on the comparison of a model and the other is based on structural analysis. Often, these two techniques are used in combination, and provide remarkable results in terms of recognition and speed.

See also

- Refer to the official documentation of the OpenCV library: https://opencv.org/

Building an optical character recognizer using neural networks

Now that we know how to interact with data, let's build a neural network-based OCR system. The operations of classification and indexing the images are based on the automatic analysis of the image content, which constitutes the main application field of the imaging analysis. The objective of an automatic image recognition system consists in the description, through mathematical models and computer implementations, the content of an image, all the while trying, as far as possible, to respect the principles of the human visual system.

Getting ready

In this recipe, we will build a neural network-based OCR system.

How to do it...

Let's see how to build an optical character recognizer using neural networks:

1. Create a new Python file, and import the following packages (the full code is given in the `ocr.py` file that is provided to you):

```
import numpy as np
import neurolab as nl
```

2. Define the input filename:

```
input_file = 'letter.data'
```

3. When we work with neural networks that deal with large amounts of data, it takes a lot of time to train. To demonstrate how to build this system, we will take only 20 datapoints:

```
num_datapoints = 20
```

4. If you look at the data, you will see that there are seven distinct characters in the first 20 lines. Let's define them:

```
orig_labels = 'omandig'
num_output = len(orig_labels)
```

5. We will use 90% of the data for training and the remaining 10% for testing. Define the training and testing parameters:

```
num_train = int(0.9 * num_datapoints)
num_test = num_datapoints - num_train
```

6. The starting and ending indices in each line of the dataset file are specified:

```
start_index = 6
end_index = -1
```

7. Create the dataset:

```
data = []
labels = []
with open(input_file, 'r') as f:
    for line in f.readlines():
        # Split the line tabwise
        list_vals = line.split('\t')
```

8. Add an error check to see whether the characters are in our list of labels (if the label is not in our ground truth labels, skip it):

```
if list_vals[1] not in orig_labels:
    continue
```

9. Extract the label, and append it to the main list:

```
label = np.zeros((num_output, 1))
label[orig_labels.index(list_vals[1])] = 1
labels.append(label)
```

10. Extract the character, and append it to the main list:

```
cur_char = np.array([float(x) for x in
list_vals[start_index:end_index]])
    data.append(cur_char)
```

11. Exit the loop once we have enough data:

```
if len(data) >= num_datapoints:
    break
```

12. Convert this data into NumPy arrays:

```
data = np.asfarray(data)
labels = np.array(labels).reshape(num_datapoints, num_output)
```

13. Extract the number of dimensions in our data:

```
num_dims = len(data[0])
```

14. Train the neural network until $10,000$ epochs:

```
net = nl.net.newff([[0, 1] for _ in range(len(data[0]))], [128, 16,
num_output])
net.trainf = nl.train.train_gd
error = net.train(data[:num_train, :], labels[:num_train, :],
epochs=10000,
        show=100, goal=0.01)
```

15. Predict the output for test inputs:

```
predicted_output = net.sim(data[num_train:, :])
print("Testing on unknown data:")
for i in range(num_test):
    print("Original:", orig_labels[np.argmax(labels[i])])
    print("Predicted:",
orig_labels[np.argmax(predicted_output[i])])
```

16. If you run this code, you will see the following on your Terminal at the end of training:

```
Epoch: 5000; Error: 0.032178530603536336;
Epoch: 5100; Error: 0.023122560947574727;
Epoch: 5200; Error: 0.040615342668364626;
Epoch: 5300; Error: 0.01686314983574041;
The goal of learning is reached
```

The output of the neural network is shown as follows:

```
Testing on unknown data:
Original: o
Predicted: o
Original: m
Predicted: m
```

How it works...

In this recipe, we used a neural network to recognize the handwritten digits. To do this, the following tasks are performed:

- Loading and manipulating input data
- Creating the dataset
- Converting data and labels into NumPy arrays
- Extracting the number of dimensions
- Creating and training the neural network
- Predicting the output for test inputs

There's more...

The term **handwriting recognition (HWR)** refers to the ability of a computer to receive and interpret as text intelligible handwritten input from sources such as paper documents, photographs, and touchscreens. Written text can be detected on a piece of paper via optical scanning (OCR) or **intelligent word recognition**.

See also

- Refer to the official documentation of the `neurolab` library: `https://pythonhosted.org/neurolab/`
- Refer to *Optical character recognition* (from Wikipedia): `https://en.wikipedia.org/wiki/Optical_character_recognition`
- Refer to *Handwriting recognition* (from Wikipedia): `https://en.wikipedia.org/wiki/Handwriting_recognition`

Implementing optimization algorithms in ANN

So far, we have built several neural networks and obtained satisfactory overall performances. We have evaluated the model's performance using the `loss` function, which is a mathematical way to measure how wrong our predictions are. To improve the performance of a model based on neural networks, during the training process, weights are modified to try to minimize the `loss` function and make our predictions as correct as possible. To do this, optimizers are used: they are algorithms that regulate the parameters of the model, updating it in relation to what is returned by the `loss` function. In practice, optimizers shape the model in its most accurate form possible by overcoming weights: The `loss` function tells the optimizer when it is moving in the right or wrong direction.

Getting ready

In this recipe, we will build a neural network using the Keras library and improve the performance of the model by adopting several optimizers. To do this, the `iris` dataset will be used. I'm referring to the **Iris flower dataset**, a multivariate dataset introduced by the British statistician and biologist Ronald Fisher in his 1936 paper: *The use of multiple measurements in taxonomic problems as an example of linear discriminant analysis.*

How to do it...

Let's see how to implement optimization algorithms in ANN:

1. Create a new Python file, and import the following packages (the full code is given in the `IrisClassifier.py` file that is provided to you):

```
from sklearn.datasets import load_iris
from sklearn.model_selection import train_test_split
from sklearn.preprocessing import OneHotEncoder
from keras.models import Sequential
from keras.layers import Dense
```

2. Import the data from the `sklearn` dataset:

```
IrisData = load_iris()
```

3. Divide the data into an input and target:

```
X = IrisData.data
Y = IrisData.target.reshape(-1, 1)
```

For the target, the data was converted to a single column.

4. Let's encode the class labels as One Hot Encode:

```
Encoder = OneHotEncoder(sparse=False)
YHE = Encoder.fit_transform(Y)
```

5. Split the data for training and testing:

```
XTrain, XTest, YTrain, YTest = train_test_split(X, YHE,
test_size=0.30)
```

6. Let's build the model:

```
model = Sequential()
```

7. Three layers will be added: an input layer, a hidden layer, and an output layer.

```
model.add(Dense(10, input_shape=(4,), activation='relu'))
model.add(Dense(10, activation='relu'))
model.add(Dense(3, activation='softmax'))
```

8. Let's compile the model:

```
model.compile(optimizer='SGD',loss='categorical_crossentropy',
metrics=['accuracy'])
```

The following three arguments are passed:

- `optimizer='SGD'`: Stochastic gradient descent optimizer. Includes support for momentum, learning rate decay, and Nesterov momentum.

- `loss='categorical_crossentropy'`: We have used the `categorical_crossentropy` argument here. When using `categorical_crossentropy`, your targets should be in categorical format (we have three classes; the target for each sample must be a three-dimensional vector that is all-zeros except for a 1 at the index corresponding to the class of the sample).

- `metrics=['accuracy']`: A `metric` is a function that is used to evaluate the performance of your model during training and testing.

9. Let's train the model:

```
model.fit(XTrain, YTrain, verbose=2, batch_size=5, epochs=200)
```

10. Finally, test the model using unseen data:

```
results = model.evaluate(XTest, YTest)
print('Final test set loss:' ,results[0])
print('Final test set accuracy:', results[1])
```

The following results are returned:

```
Final test set loss: 0.17724286781416998
Final test set accuracy: 0.9555555568801032
```

11. Now let's see what happens if we use a different optimizer. To do this, just change the optimizer parameter in the compile method, as follows:

```
model.compile(optimizer='adam',loss='categorical_crossentropy',
metrics=['accuracy'])
```

The `adam` optimizer is an algorithm for the first-order, gradient-based optimization of stochastic objective functions, based on adaptive estimates of lower-order moments.

The following results are returned:

```
Final test set loss: 0.0803464303414027
Final test set accuracy: 0.9777777777777777
```

How it works...

As we said in the *Building a deep neural network* recipe, gradient descent is an iterative approach used for error correction in any learning model. Gradient descent approach is the process of iterating the update of weights and biases with the error times derivative of the activation function (backpropagation). In this approach, the steepest descent step size is substituted by a similar size from the previous step. The gradient is the slope of the curve, as it is the derivative of the activation function. The SGD optimizer is based on this approach.

There's more...

Optimization problems are usually so complex that it is not possible to determine a solution analytically. Complexity is determined primarily by the number of variables and constraints, which define the size of the problem, and then by the possible presence of non-linear functions. An analytical solution is only possible in the case of a few variables and extremely simple functions. In practice, to solve an optimization problem, it is necessary to resort to an iterative algorithm, that is, to a calculation program that, given a current approximation of the solution, determines, with an appropriate sequence of operations, a new approximation. Starting from an initial approximation, a succession is thus determined.

See also

- Refer to the official documentation of the Keras optimizer: `https://keras.io/optimizers/`
- Refer to *Optimization for Deep Neural Networks* (from The University of Chicago): `https://ttic.uchicago.edu/~shubhendu/Pages/Files/Lecture6_pauses.pdf`

14
Unsupervised Representation Learning

In this chapter, we will cover the following recipes:

- Using denoising autoencoders to detect fraudulent transactions
- Generating word embeddings using CBOW or skipgram representations
- Visualizing the MNIST dataset using PCA and t-SNE
- Using word vectors for Twitter sentiment analysis
- Implementing LDA with scikit-learn
- Using LDA to classify text documents
- Preparing data for LDA

Technical requirements

To address the recipes in this chapter, you need the following files (available on GitHub):

- `CreditCardFraud.py`
- `creditcard.csv`
- `WordEmbeddings.py`
- `MnistTSNE.py`
- `TweetEmbeddings.py`
- `Tweets.csv`
- `LDA.py`
- `TopicModellingLDA.py`
- `PrepDataLDA.py`

Introduction

In Chapter 4, *Clustering with Unsupervised Learning*, we have already addressed unsupervised learning. We said that unsupervised learning is a paradigm in machine learning where we build models without relying on labeled training data. Why return to this topic? In this case, we will discuss the problem of learning representations for data such as images, video, and the corpus of natural language, in an unsupervised way.

Using denoising autoencoders to detect fraudulent transactions

In Chapter 4, *Clustering with Unsupervised Learning*, we dealt with the topic of **autoencoders**. In the *Autoencoders to reconstruct handwritten digit images* recipe, there is a neural network whose purpose is to code its input into small dimensions, and the result obtained, to be able to reconstruct the input itself. The purpose of autoencoders is not simply to perform a sort of compression of the input or look for an approximation of the identity function; there are also techniques that allow us to direct the model (starting from a hidden layer of reduced dimensions) to give greater importance to some data properties.

Getting ready

In this recipe, we will train an autoencoder in unsupervised mode to detect anomalies in credit card transaction data. To do this, the credit card fraud detection dataset will be used. This is a dataset containing the anonymized credit card transactions labeled as fraudulent or genuine. Transactions made by credit cards in September 2013 by European cardholders are listed. This dataset presents 492 transactions labeled as frauds out of 284,807 transactions. The dataset is highly unbalanced, as the positive class (frauds) accounts for 0.172% of all transactions. The dataset is available on Kabble at the following URL: https:/
/www.kaggle.com/mlg-ulb/creditcardfraud.

How to do it...

Let's see how to use denoising autoencoders to detect fraudulent transactions:

1. Create a new Python file, and import the following packages (the full code is in the `CreditCardFraud.py` file that's already provided to you):

```
import pandas as pd
import numpy as np
import matplotlib.pyplot as plt
from sklearn.model_selection import train_test_split
from keras.models import Model
from keras.layers import Input, Dense
from keras import regularizers
```

2. To make the experiment reproducible, in the sense that it provides the same results with each reproduction, it is necessary to set the seed:

```
SetSeed = 1
```

3. As already said, we will use the credit card fraud detection dataset (`creditcard.csv`) that is already provided to you:

```
CreditCardData = pd.read_csv("creditcard.csv")
```

4. Let's count the occurrences of the two classes (`fraud= 1`; `normal=0`):

```
CountClasses = pd.value_counts(CreditCardData['Class'], sort = True)
print(CountClasses)
```

The following results are returned:

```
0 284315
1 492
```

As anticipated, the dataset is highly unbalanced—the positive class (`frauds`) is 492 out of 284315.

5. Among the available variables, the amount of the transactions (`Amount`) is the most interesting one. Let's calculate some statistics:

```
print(CreditCardData.Amount.describe())
```

The following results are returned:

```
count  284807.000000
mean       88.349619
std       250.120109
min         0.000000
25%         5.600000
50%        22.000000
75%        77.165000
max     25691.160000
```

6. As we can see, the values are very different with a high standard deviation. It is advisable to perform a scaling of the data. Remember, it is a good practice to rescale the data before training a machine learning algorithm. With rescaling, data units are eliminated, allowing you to compare data from different locations easily. To do this, we will use the `sklearn StandardScaler()` function. This function removes the mean and scales the values to unit variance:

```
from sklearn.preprocessing import StandardScaler

Data = CreditCardData.drop(['Time'], axis=1)
Data['Amount'] =
StandardScaler().fit_transform(Data['Amount'].values.reshape(-1,
1))

print(Data.Amount.describe())
```

The following results are returned:

```
count    2.848070e+05
mean     2.913952e-17
std      1.000002e+00
min     -3.532294e-01
25%     -3.308401e-01
50%     -2.652715e-01
75%     -4.471707e-02
max      1.023622e+02
```

We have thus confirmed that now the data has `mean=0` and unit variance.

7. Now, we split the starting data into two sets: the training set (70%) and test set (30%). The training set will be used to train a classification model, and the test set will be used to test the model's performance:

```
XTrain, XTest = train_test_split(Data, test_size=0.3,
random_state=SetSeed)
XTrain = XTrain[XTrain.Class == 0]
```

```
XTrain = XTrain.drop(['Class'], axis=1)

YTest = XTest['Class']
XTest = XTest.drop(['Class'], axis=1)

XTrain = XTrain.values
XTest = XTest.values
```

8. We can build the Keras model as follows:

```
InputDim = XTrain.shape[1]

InputModel = Input(shape=(InputDim,))
EncodedLayer = Dense(16, activation='relu')(InputModel)
DecodedLayer = Dense(InputDim, activation='sigmoid')(EncodedLayer)
AutoencoderModel = Model(InputModel, DecodedLayer)
AutoencoderModel.summary()
```

The following shows the model architecture:

Layer (type)	Output Shape	Param #
input_11 (InputLayer)	(None, 29)	0
dense_27 (Dense)	(None, 16)	480
dense_28 (Dense)	(None, 29)	493

```
Total params: 973
Trainable params: 973
Non-trainable params: 0
```

9. So, we have to configure the model for training. To do this, we will use the `compile()` method, as follows:

```
NumEpoch = 100
BatchSize = 32
AutoencoderModel.compile(optimizer='adam',
                         loss='mean_squared_error',
                         metrics=['accuracy'])
```

10. At this point, we can train the model:

```
history = AutoencoderModel.fit(XTrain, XTrain,
                  epochs=NumEpoch,
                  batch_size=BatchSize,
                  shuffle=True,
                  validation_data=(XTest, XTest),
                  verbose=1,
                  ).history
```

11. Now, we can plot the loss history to evaluate the model convergence:

```
plt.plot(history['loss'])
plt.plot(history['val_loss'])
plt.title('model loss')
plt.ylabel('loss')
plt.xlabel('epoch')
plt.legend(['train', 'test'], loc='upper right');
```

12. At this point, we use the model to reconstruct the result of the transactions:

```
PredData = AutoencoderModel.predict(XTest)
mse = np.mean(np.power(XTest - PredData, 2), axis=1)
ErrorCreditCardData = pd.DataFrame({'Error': mse,
                        'TrueClass': YTest})
ErrorCreditCardData.describe()
```

To evaluate the quality of the prediction, we used the **mean squared error** (MSE) loss function. MSE measures the average of the squares of the errors—that is, the average squared difference between the estimated values and what is estimated. MSE is a measure of the quality of an estimator—it is always non-negative, and has values close to zero. So, we calculated some statistics related to the error and the real values. The following results were obtained:

```
          Error          TrueClass
count  85443.000000    85443.000000
mean       0.626414        0.001580
std        3.109587        0.039718
min        0.021684        0.000000
25%        0.182318        0.000000
50%        0.307632        0.000000
75%        0.513372        0.000000
max      250.801476        1.000000
```

13. Now, we can compare the results of the classification to the actual values. The best way to do this is to use a **confusion matrix**. In a confusion matrix, we compare our results to real data. What's good about a confusion matrix is that it identifies the nature of the classification errors, as well as their quantities. In this matrix, the diagonal cells show the number of cases that were correctly classified; all the other cells show the misclassified cases. To calculate the confusion matrix, we can use the `confusion_matrix()` function that's contained in the `sklearn.metrics` package as follows:

```
from sklearn.metrics import confusion_matrix

threshold = 3.
YPred = [1 if e > threshold else 0 for e in
ErrorCreditCardData.Error.values]
```

```
ConfMatrix = confusion_matrix(ErrorCreditCardData.TrueClass, YPred)
print(ConfMatrix)
```

The following confusion matrix is returned:

```
[[83641   1667]
 [   28    107]]
```

14. Finally, we will calculate the accuracy of the model:

```
from sklearn.metrics import accuracy_score

print(accuracy_score(ErrorCreditCardData.TrueClass, YPred))
```

The following accuracy is obtained:

```
0.9801622134054282
```

The result looks great, but unfortunately the input dataset is highly unbalanced. If we evaluate the accuracy of fraudulent transactions only, this data is significantly reduced.

How it works...

There are different types of autoencoders available:

- **Vanilla autoencoder**: It is the simplest form, characterized by a three-layer network, that is, a neural network with only one hidden layer. Input and output are the same.
- **Multilayer autoencoder**: If only one hidden layer is not enough, we can extend the autoencoder along the depth dimension. For example, three hidden layers are used, for better generalization, but we will also have to make the symmetric network using the intermediate layer.
- **Convolutional autoencoder**: Three-dimensional vectors are used instead of one-dimensional vectors. The input image is sampled to obtain a latent representation, that is, a dimensional reduction, thus forcing the autoencoder to learn from a compressed version of the image.
- **Regularized autoencoder**: Rather than limiting the model's capacity by maintaining a shallow encoder and decoder architecture, as well as a forced reduction, regularized autoencoders use a loss function to encourage the model to assume properties that go beyond the simple ability to copy the input to the output.

There's more...

In practice, we find two different types:

- **Sparse autoencoder**: This is usually used for classification. By training an autoencoder, the hidden units in the middle layer are activated too frequently. To avoid this, we need to lower their activation rate by limiting it to a fraction of the training data. This constraint is called a **sparsity constraint**, as each unit is activated only by a pre-defined type of input.
- **Denoising autoencoder**: Rather than adding a penalty to the `loss` function, we can make the object change, adding noise to the input image and making the autoencoder learn to remove it autonomously. This means that the network will extract only the most relevant information, and learn from a robust representation of the data.

See also

- Refer to the official documentation of the Keras library: `https://keras.io/`
- Refer to *Autoencoders* (from Stanford University): `http://ufldl.stanford.edu/tutorial/unsupervised/Autoencoders/`

Generating word embeddings using CBOW and skipgram representations

In `Chapter 7`, *Analyzing Text Data*, we already dealt with this topic. In the *Word2Vec using gensim* recipe, we used the `gensim` library to build a word2vec model. Now, we will deepen the topic. **Word embedding** allows the computer to memorize both semantic and syntactic information of words starting from an unknown corpus and constructs a vector space in which the vectors of words are closer if the words occur in the same linguistic contexts, that is, if they are recognized as semantically more similar. **Word2vec** is a set of templates that are used to produce word embedding.

Getting ready

In this recipe, we will use the `gensim` library to generate word embeddings. We will also analyze two techniques to do this: CBOW and skipgram representations.

How to do it...

Let's see how to generate word embeddings using CBOW and skipgram representations:

1. Create a new Python file, and import the following packages (the full code is in the `WordEmbeddings.py` file that's already provided to you):

```
import gensim
```

2. Let's define the training data:

```
sentences = [['my', 'first', 'book', 'with', 'Packt', 'is',
'on','Matlab'],
        ['my', 'second', 'book', 'with', 'Packt', 'is', 'on','R'],
        ['my', 'third', 'book', 'with', 'Packt', 'is',
'on','Python'],
        ['one', 'more', 'book'],
        ['is', 'on', 'Python', 'too']]
```

3. Now, we can train the first model:

```
Model1 = gensim.models.Word2Vec(sentences, min_count=1, sg=0)
```

Three arguments are used:

- `sentences`: The training data
- `min_count=1`: The minimum count of words to consider when training the model
- `sg=0`: The training algorithm, CBOW (0) or skip gram (1)

4. Let's print a summary of the model:

```
print(Model1)
```

The following result is returned:

Word2Vec(vocab=15, size=100, alpha=0.025)

5. Let's list and then print a summary of the vocabulary:

```
wordsM1 = list(Model1.wv.vocab)
print(wordsM1)
```

The following results are returned:

**['my', 'first', 'book', 'with', 'Packt', 'is', 'on', 'Matlab',
'second', 'R', 'third', 'Python', 'one', 'more', 'too']**

6. Finally, we will access the vector for one word (book):

```
print(Model1.wv['book'])
```

The following results are returned:

```
[ 2.9973486e-03 -2.1124829e-03  3.7657898e-03 -1.9050670e-03
 -5.5578595e-04  4.4527398e-03  3.5046584e-03 -1.1438223e-03
  6.0215552e-04 -4.7409125e-03  6.5806962e-04 -3.1985594e-03
  4.9693016e-03 -4.6585896e-03  3.9025352e-03  1.8993361e-03
 -3.1448407e-03 -3.9996076e-03 -8.3503849e-04  3.0914405e-03
  1.9336957e-03 -3.3351057e-03 -2.9735183e-03  2.7546713e-03
 -3.3761256e-03 -9.1228267e-04  3.2378505e-03  1.5043288e-03
  2.4148268e-03  2.5566125e-03  4.3902192e-03  2.9606789e-03
  3.2952502e-03  5.1441148e-04  4.9631284e-03  9.9989376e-04
  7.8822329e-04 -1.9999940e-03 -3.2441963e-03  3.4300482e-03
 -3.6022202e-03  1.4991680e-05 -2.6601211e-03  6.7162287e-04
 -3.7157589e-03  8.3351281e-04  4.1153287e-03  1.7590256e-03
  2.8772959e-03 -4.8740720e-03  4.2099557e-03 -3.3802991e-03
  6.6956610e-04 -6.9876245e-05  2.5645932e-03 -1.9160225e-03
  3.7302410e-03  4.5263176e-03  3.9929748e-03  2.4912667e-03
  1.7155730e-03  2.6570156e-03  4.7879852e-03 -2.6194321e-03
 -2.6944634e-03 -6.9214404e-04 -1.3537740e-03 -1.8741252e-04
  2.7855171e-03 -4.8087412e-03  4.6137013e-03  4.8322077e-03
 -4.5008543e-03  2.3164917e-03 -1.3799219e-03  3.4371777e-03
 -2.3554889e-03 -3.6085211e-03 -1.2845232e-03  3.0950166e-03
 -8.2744996e-04  1.9454588e-03 -3.5008623e-03  1.1105792e-03
  2.0449003e-03  1.3874291e-03 -2.0715776e-03  3.7589835e-03
  2.3339926e-03 -2.6291853e-03  7.2893663e-04 -3.3051639e-03
 -3.7970208e-04 -3.9213565e-03 -2.4992733e-03 -6.0153619e-04
  4.3616220e-03  4.7860332e-03 -2.0897989e-03 -5.8777170e-04]
```

7. To use the skipgram algorithm, we have to perform a similar procedure except we set the argument sg=1, as follows:

```
Model2 = gensim.models.Word2Vec(sentences, min_count=1, sg=1)
```

How it works...

Word2vec uses **continuous bag-of-words** (**CBOW**) and skipgram to word embeddings. In the CBOW algorithm, the model predicts the current word from a window of surrounding context words. Context word order does not influence prediction. In the skipgram algorithm, the model uses the current word to predict the surrounding window of context words.

There's more...

According to authors, CBOW is and skip-gram is but does a better job for infrequent words.

See also

- Refer to the official documentation of the `gensim` library: `https://radimrehurek.com/gensim/`
- Refer to *Efficient Estimation of Word Representations in Vector Space* (by Tomas Mikolov and others): `https://arxiv.org/abs/1301.3781`

Visualizing the MNIST dataset using PCA and t-SNE

In the case of datasets of important dimensions, the data is previously transformed into a reduced series of representation functions. This process of transforming the input data into a set of functionalities is called **features extraction**. This is because the extraction of the characteristics proceeds from an initial series of measured data and produces derived values that can keep the information contained in the original dataset, but discharged from the redundant data.

In this way, the subsequent learning and generalization phases will be facilitated and, in some cases, this will lead to better interpretations. It is a process of extracting new features from the original features, thereby reducing the cost of feature measurement, which boosts classifier efficiency. If the features are carefully chosen, it is assumed that the features set will run the desired task with the reduced representation, instead of the full-sized input.

Getting ready

In this recipe, we will use **principal component analysis (PCA)** and **t-distributed Stochastic Neighbor Embedding methods (t-SNE)** to perform a feature extraction procedure. In this way, we will be able to visualize how the different elements of a very large dataset, such as MNIST, are grouped together.

How to do it...

Let's see how to visualize the MNIST dataset using PCA and t-SNE:

1. Create a new Python file, and import the following packages (the full code is in the `MnistTSNE.py` file that's already provided to you):

   ```
   import numpy as np
   import matplotlib.pyplot as plt
   from keras.datasets import mnist
   ```

2. To import the `mnist` dataset, the following code must be used:

   ```
   (XTrain, YTrain), (XTest, YTest) = mnist.load_data()
   ```

   The following tuples are returned:

   - `XTrain`, `XTest`: A `uint8` array of grayscale image data with the (num_samples, 28, 28) shape
   - `YTrain`, `YTest`: A `uint8` array of digit labels (integers in the range 0-9) with the (num_samples) shape

3. To reduce the dimensionality, we will flatten the 28 x 28 images into vectors of size 784:

   ```
   XTrain = XTrain.reshape((len(XTrain), np.prod(XTrain.shape[1:])))
   XTest = XTest.reshape((len(XTest), np.prod(XTest.shape[1:])))
   ```

4. We extract only a part of the data from this large dataset to obtain a better visualization (only 1,000 records):

   ```
   from sklearn.utils import shuffle
   XTrain, YTrain = shuffle(XTrain, YTrain)
   XTrain, YTrain = XTrain[:1000], YTrain[:1000]
   ```

5. Let's perform a `pca` analysis:

   ```
   from sklearn.decomposition import PCA
   pca = PCA(n_components=2)
   XPCATransformed = pca.fit_transform(XTrain)
   ```

6. We display the data available in the new plan:

   ```
   fig, plot = plt.subplots()
   fig.set_size_inches(70, 50)
   plt.prism()
   plot.scatter(XPCATransformed[:, 0], XPCATransformed[:, 1],
   ```

```
c=YTrain)
plot.legend()
plot.set_xticks(())
plot.set_yticks(())
plt.tight_layout()
```

The following results are returned:

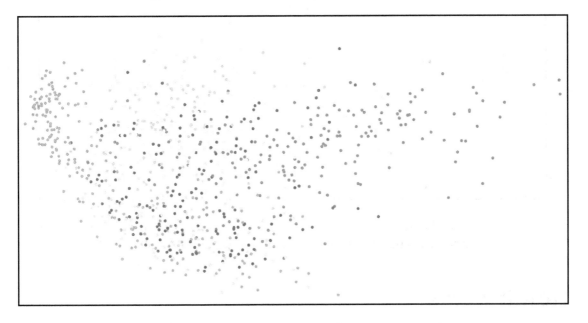

7. At this point, we will repeat the procedure using the t-SNE method:

```
from sklearn.manifold import TSNE
TSNEModel = TSNE(n_components=2)
XTSNETransformed = TSNEModel.fit_transform(XTrain)
```

8. We display the data available in the new plan:

```
fig, plot = plt.subplots()
fig.set_size_inches(70, 50)
plt.prism()
plot.scatter(XTSNETransformed[:, 0], XTSNETransformed[:, 1],
c=YTrain)
plot.set_xticks(())
plot.set_yticks(())
plt.tight_layout()
plt.show()
```

The following results are returned:

Comparing the two results obtained, it is clear that the second method allows us to identify the groups representing the different digits in more detail.

How it works...

PCA creates a new set of variables that are principal components. Each main component is a linear combination of the original variables. All principal components are orthogonal to one another, so there is no redundant information. The principal components as a whole constitute an orthogonal basis for the data space. The goal of PCA is to explain the maximum amount of variance with the least number of principal components. PCA is a form of multidimensional scaling. It transforms variables into a lower-dimensional space that retains the maximum details regarding the variables. A principal component is therefore a combination of the original variables after a linear transformation.

t-SNE is a dimensionality reduction algorithm developed by Geoffrey Hinton and Laurens van der Maaten, widely used as an automatic learning tool in many research fields. It is a non-linear dimension reduction technique that lends itself particularly to the embedding of high-dimensional datasets in a two- or three-dimensional space, in which they can be visualized by means of a dispersion plot. The algorithm models the points so that nearby objects in the original space are close together with reduced dimensionality, and distant objects are far away, trying to preserve the local structure.

There's more...

A t-SNE algorithm is divided into two main phases. In the first phase, a probability distribution is constructed so that each pair of points in the original high-dimensional space associates a high probability value if the two points are similar, and low if they are dissimilar. Then, a second analogous probability distribution is defined in the small-sized space. The algorithm then minimizes the divergence of Kullback–Leibler of the two distributions by descending the gradient, reorganizing the points in the small-sized space.

See also

- Refer to the official documentation of the `sklearn.decomposition.PCA` function: `https://scikit-learn.org/stable/modules/generated/sklearn.decomposition.PCA.html`
- Official documentation of the `sklearn.manifold.TSNE` function: `https://scikit-learn.org/stable/modules/generated/sklearn.manifold.TSNE.htm`

Using word embedding for Twitter sentiment analysis

In `Chapter 7`, *Analyzing Text Data*, we have already dealt with sentiment analysis. In *Analyzing the sentiment of a sentence* recipe, we have analyzed the sentiment of a sentence using a Naive Bayes classifier starting from the data contained in the `movie_reviews` corpus. On that occasion, we said that sentiment analysis is one of the most popular applications of NLP. *Sentiment analysis* refers to the process of determining whether a given piece of text is positive or negative. In some variations, we consider "neutral" as a third option.

Getting ready

In this recipe, we will use the word embedding method to analyze the sentiment of Twitter posts by customers of some US airlines. The Twitter data was classified based on the opinions of some contributors. They were asked to first classify positive, negative, and neutral tweets, followed by categorizing negative ones. The dataset is available at the following link: `https://www.kaggle.com/crowdflower/twitter-airline-sentiment.`

How to do it...

Let's see how to use word embedding for Twitter sentiment analysis:

1. Create a new Python file, and import the following packages (the full code is in the `TweetEmbeddings.py` file that's already provided to you):

```
import pandas as pd
import numpy as np
import matplotlib.pyplot as plt
from sklearn.model_selection import train_test_split
from keras.preprocessing.text import Tokenizer
from keras.preprocessing.sequence import pad_sequences
from keras.utils.np_utils import to_categorical
from sklearn.preprocessing import LabelEncoder
from keras import models
from keras import layers
```

2. To import the `Tweets` dataset (the `Tweets.csv` file that's already provided to you), the following code must be used:

```
TweetData = pd.read_csv('Tweets.csv')
TweetData =
TweetData.reindex(np.random.permutation(TweetData.index))
TweetData = TweetData[['text', 'airline_sentiment']]
```

Only two columns are extracted:

- `text`: Twitter posts
- `airline_sentiment`: Positive, neutral, or negative classification

3. Now, we split the starting data into two sets: the training set (70%) and test set (30%). The training set will be used to train a classification model, and the test set will be used to test the model's performance:

```
XTrain, XTest, YTrain, YTest = train_test_split(TweetData.text,
TweetData.airline_sentiment, test_size=0.3, random_state=11)
```

4. Now, we will convert words to numbers:

```
TkData = Tokenizer(num_words=1000,
                   filters='!"#$%&()*+,-
./:;<=>?@[\]^_`{"}~\t\n',lower=True, split=" ")
TkData.fit_on_texts(XTrain)
XTrainSeq = TkData.texts_to_sequences(XTrain)
XTestSeq = TkData.texts_to_sequences(XTest)
```

To do this and tokenize the `XTrain` dataset `Tokenizer`, the `fit_on_texts` and `texts_to_sequences` methods were used.

5. To transform the input data into a format compatible with Keras, `pad_sequences` models will be used. This method transforms a list of sequences (lists of scalars) into a 2D NumPy array, as follows:

```
XTrainSeqTrunc = pad_sequences(XTrainSeq, maxlen=24)
XTestSeqTrunc = pad_sequences(XTestSeq, maxlen=24)
```

6. So, we will convert the target classes to numbers:

```
LabelEnc = LabelEncoder()
YTrainLabelEnc = LabelEnc.fit_transform(YTrain)
YTestLabelEnc = LabelEnc.transform(YTest)
YTrainLabelEncCat = to_categorical(YTrainLabelEnc)
YTestLabelEncCat = to_categorical(YTestLabelEnc)
```

7. Now, we will build the Keras model:

```
EmbModel = models.Sequential()
EmbModel.add(layers.Embedding(1000, 8, input_length=24))
EmbModel.add(layers.Flatten())
EmbModel.add(layers.Dense(3, activation='softmax'))
```

The embedding layer takes as input a 2D tensor with shape (`batch_size`, `sequence_length`), where each entry is a sequence of integers. A 3D tensor with the shape (`batch_size`, `sequence_length`, and `output_dim`) is returned.

8. Now, we will compile and fit the model created:

```
EmbModel.compile(optimizer='rmsprop'
                , loss='categorical_crossentropy'
                , metrics=['accuracy'])

EmbHistory = EmbModel.fit(XTrainSeqTrunc
                , YTrainLabelEncCat
                , epochs=100
                , batch_size=512
                , validation_data=(XTestSeqTrunc,
YTestLabelEncCat)
                , verbose=1)
```

9. To evaluate the model's performance, let's print the accuracy:

```
print('Train Accuracy: ', EmbHistory.history['acc'][-1])
print('Validation Accuracy: ', EmbHistory.history['val_acc'][-1])
```

The following results are returned:

```
Train Accuracy: 0.9295472287275566
Validation Accuracy: 0.7625227688874486
```

10. Finally, we will plot the model history:

```
plt.plot(EmbHistory.history['acc'])
plt.plot(EmbHistory.history['val_acc'])
plt.title('model accuracy')
plt.ylabel('accuracy')
plt.xlabel('epoch')
plt.legend(['train', 'Validation'], loc='upper left')
plt.show()
```

The following diagram is returned:

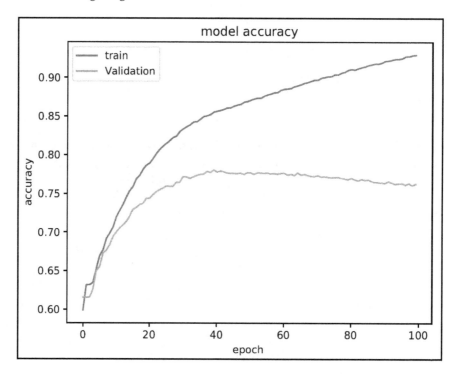

Analyzing the progress of the validation loss, we realize that the model is overfitting. To handle orverfitting, as we learned in the *Building a ridge regressor* recipe in `Chapter 1`, *The Realm of Supervised Learning*, we need to use a regularization method.

How it works...

The term **sentiment analysis** refers to the use of NLP techniques, text analysis, and computational linguistics to identify and extract subjective information in written or spoken text sources. Sentiment analysis can be tackled through different approaches. The most commonly used can be grouped into four macro-categories (*A Study and Comparison of Sentiment Analysis Methods for Reputation Evaluation* by Collomb A, Costea C, Joyeux D, Hasan O, and Brunie L, 2014):

- **Lexicon-based methods**: These detect emotional keywords, and assign arbitrary words affinity likely to represent particular emotions.
- **Rule-based methods**: These classify texts using emotional categories, based on the presence of unambiguous emotional words, such as *happy*, *sad*, and *bored*.
- **Statistical methods**: Here, we try to identify the owner of a sentiment, that is, who the subject is, and the objective, or the object to which the sentiment is felt. To measure opinion in context and find the characteristic that was judged, we check the grammatical relations between the words in the text. This is obtained through a thorough scan of the text.
- **Machine learning methods**: These use different learning algorithms to determine sentiment by having a dataset classified (supervised methods). The learning process is not immediate; in fact, models have to be built that associate a polarity to different types of comments and, if necessary, a topic for analysis purposes.

There's more...

The `regularization` methods involve modifying the performance function, normally selected as the sum of the squares of regression errors on the training set. When a large number of variables are available, the least square estimates of a linear model often have a low bias but a high variance with respect to models with fewer variables. Under these conditions, there is an overfitting problem. To improve precision prediction by allowing greater bias but a small variance, we can use variable selection methods and dimensionality reduction, but these methods may be unattractive for computational burdens in the first case, or provide a difficult interpretation in the other case.

See also

- Refer to the official documentation of the Keras library: `https://keras.io/`
- Refer to *Sentiment Analysis* (from Stanford University): `https://web.stanford.edu/class/cs124/lec/sentiment.pdf`

Implementing LDA with scikit-learn

Latent Dirichlet allocation (**LDA**) is a generative model, used in the study of natural language, which allows you to extract arguments from a set of source documents and provide a logical explanation on the similarity of individual parts of documents. Each document is considered as a set of words that, when combined, form one or more subsets of latent topics. Each topic is characterized by a particular distribution of terms.

Getting ready

In this recipe, we will use the `sklearn.decomposition.LatentDirichletAllocation` function to produce a feature matrix of token counts, similar to what the `CountVectorizer` function (just used in the *Building a bag-of-words model* recipe of `Chapter 7, Analyzing Text Data`) would produce on the text.

How to do it...

Let's see how to implement LDA with scikit-learn:

1. Create a new Python file, and import the following packages (the full code is in the `LDA.py` file that's already provided to you):

   ```
   from sklearn.decomposition import LatentDirichletAllocation
   from sklearn.datasets import make_multilabel_classification
   ```

2. To produce the input data, we will use the `sklearn.datasets.make_multilabel_classification` function. This function generates a random multilabel classification problem, as follows:

   ```
   X, Y = make_multilabel_classification(n_samples=100, n_features=20,
   n_classes=5, n_labels=2, random_state=1)
   ```

The following data is returned:

- X: The generated samples that is an array of shape [n_samples, n_features]
- Y: The label sets that is an array or sparse CSR matrix of shape [n_samples, n_classes]

In our case, the Y variable will not serve us, as we will use an unsupervised method that, as we know, does not require prior knowledge of the data label.

3. Now, we can build the LatentDirichletAllocation() model (with an online variational Bayes algorithm):

```
LDAModel = LatentDirichletAllocation(n_components=5,
random_state=1)
```

Only two parameters are passed:

- n_components=5: This is the number of topics, 5, because we used an input dataset built on the basis of five groups.
- random_state=1: This is the seed used by the random number generator.

4. Now, we will train the model for the data, X, with a variational Bayes method:

```
LDAModel.fit(X)
```

5. Finally, we will get topics for the last 10 samples of the X dataset:

```
print(LDAModel.transform(X[-10:]))
```

The following results are returned:

```
[[0.00446534 0.56017529 0.00444546 0.00448087 0.42643304]
 [0.00473608 0.23609134 0.00480174 0.11751968 0.63685116]
 [0.00465339 0.00467568 0.0046488  0.40054602 0.5854761 ]
 [0.0036422  0.00367292 0.00365825 0.00368085 0.98534578]
 [0.00391229 0.45669382 0.00393234 0.53151557 0.00394598]
 [0.49615403 0.49076604 0.00435414 0.00435434 0.00437146]
 [0.00371638 0.0824078  0.00375522 0.90637378 0.00374683]
 [0.00359108 0.41826357 0.00361352 0.00361033 0.57092149]
 [0.00475393 0.00476904 0.00473842 0.25953364 0.72620497]
 [0.00345123 0.98611337 0.0034578  0.00349065 0.00348694]]]
```

For each example provided as input, a sequence of five values is returned representing the probabilities that the topic belongs to that group. Obviously, the value closest to 1 represents the best probability.

How it works...

The generative process of the LDA algorithm is based on the analysis of the data contained in the text. Word combinations are considered random variables. The LDA algorithm can be executed in the following ways:

- A word distribution is associated with each topic
- Each document is found in a topic distribution
- For each word in the document, verify its attribution to a document topic and to a word distribution of the topic

There's more...

Depending on the type of inference, the LDA algorithm allows us to reach a certain level of effectiveness and cost (efficiency) in terms of temporal and spatial complexity. The LDA model was presented for the first time in 2003 in a paper published by David Blei, Andrew Ng, and Michael Jordan.

See also

- Refer to the official documentation of the `sklearn.decomposition.LatentDirichletAllocation` function: `https://scikit-learn.org/stable/modules/generated/sklearn.decomposition.LatentDirichletAllocation.html`
- Refer to *Latent Dirichlet Allocation* (by David Blei, Andrew Ng, and Michael Jordan): `http://www.jmlr.org/papers/volume3/blei03a/blei03a.pdf`
- Refer to `Chapter 7`, *Analyzing Text Data*

Using LDA to classify text documents

LDA is a natural language analysis model that allows to understand the semantic meaning of the text by analyzing the similarity between the distribution of the terms of the document with that of a specific topic (topic) or of an entity. More recently, LDA has gained notoriety even in semantic SEO as a possible ranking factor for the Google search engine.

Getting ready

In this recipe, we will use
the `sklearn.decomposition.LatentDirichletAllocation` function to perform a
topic modeling analysis.

How to do it...

Let's see how to use LDA to classify text documents:

1. Create a new Python file, and import the following packages (the full code is in
   the `TopicModellingLDA.py` file that's already provided to you):

   ```
   from sklearn.feature_extraction.text import CountVectorizer
   from sklearn.decomposition import LatentDirichletAllocation
   from sklearn.datasets import fetch_20newsgroups
   ```

2. To import the data, we will use the `fetch_20newsgroups` dataset from
   the `sklearn` library:

   ```
   NGData = fetch_20newsgroups(shuffle=True, random_state=7,
                               remove=('headers', 'footers',
   'quotes'))
   ```

   This is a collection of about 20,000 newsgroup documents, divided into 20
   different newsgroups. The dataset is particularly useful for dealing with text
   classification problems.

3. Now, we will print the name of the newsgroup available:

   ```
   print(list(NGData.target_names))
   ```

   The following results are returned:

   ```
   ['alt.atheism', 'comp.graphics', 'comp.os.ms-windows.misc',
   'comp.sys.ibm.pc.hardware', 'comp.sys.mac.hardware',
   'comp.windows.x', 'misc.forsale', 'rec.autos', 'rec.motorcycles',
   'rec.sport.baseball', 'rec.sport.hockey', 'sci.crypt',
   'sci.electronics', 'sci.med', 'sci.space',
   'soc.religion.christian', 'talk.politics.guns',
   'talk.politics.mideast', 'talk.politics.misc',
   'talk.religion.misc']
   ```

4. There are 11,314 samples in the data. We will extract only 2,000:

```
NGData = NGData.data[:2000]
```

5. Now, we will extract a document term matrix. This is basically a matrix that counts the number of occurrences of each word in the document. So, we will define the object, and extract the document term matrix:

```
NGDataVect = CountVectorizer(max_df=0.93, min_df=2,
                            max_features=1000,
                            stop_words='english')

NGDataVectModel = NGDataVect.fit_transform(NGData)
```

6. Now, we can build the LDA model (with an online variational Bayes algorithm):

```
LDAModel = LatentDirichletAllocation(n_components=10, max_iter=5,
                            learning_method='online',
                            learning_offset=50.,
                            random_state=0)
```

7. We will train the model for the data `NGDataVectModel` with a variational Bayes method:

```
LDAModel.fit(NGDataVectModel)
```

8. Finally, we will print the topic extracted:

```
NGDataVectModelFeatureNames = NGDataVect.get_feature_names()

for topic_idx, topic in enumerate(LDAModel.components_):
    message = "Topic #%d: " % topic_idx
    message += " ".join([NGDataVectModelFeatureNames[i]
    for i in topic.argsort()[:-20 - 1:-1]])
    print(message)
```

The following results are returned:

```
Topic 0: ax max b8f pl g9v 1d9 a86 34u 145 3t 0t 2tm wm 1t giz bhj 7ey sl bxn gk
Topic 1: key encryption chip keys des clipper security bit algorithm public law
         use used ripem number data escrow product enforcement cipher
Topic 2: people don just think god like does know say believe time good make way
         did said really right ve things
Topic 3: price 00 car sale new 50 excellent edu 20 condition shipping offer best
         asking old tape interested hard used send
Topic 4: cancer medical air hiv health research aids gun 800 care number center
         10 volume patients insurance page dr disease april
Topic 5: file use like edu program output windows thanks know available mail ftp
         does files need info don email help good
Topic 6: 55 10 18 11 17 40 14 12 24 15 16 period 34 pp 25 13 19 28 widget 20
Topic 7: new space people information university like time 1993 years available
         service know work public use center internet program technology nasa
Topic 8: drive card master slave mode video drives screen problem pin use driver
         16 bus jumper using disk apple scsi memory
Topic 9: game play team year games got season dod power bike second good like
         just right win great hit puck flyers
```

How it works...

Topic modeling refers to the process of identifying hidden patterns in text data. The goal is to uncover some hidden thematic structure in a collection of documents. This will help us organize our documents in a better way so that we can use them for analysis. This is an active area of research in NLP.

The LDA analysis automatically allows to go back to the topic of the phrases by the association of co-occurrences with a reference **knowledge base** (**KB**), without having to interpret the meaning of the sentences.

There's more...

Here, **de Finetti's theorem** establishes that any collection of changeable random variables is represented as a mixture of distributions, so if you want to have an exchangeable representation of words and documents, it is necessary to consider mixtures that capture the exchangeability of both. At the base of this methodology of thought lie the roots of the LDA model.

See also

- Refer to the official documentation of
  the `sklearn.decomposition.LatentDirichletAllocation` function: `https://scikit-learn.org/stable/modules/generated/sklearn.decomposition.LatentDirichletAllocation.html`
- Refer to `Chapter` 7, *Analyzing Text Data*
- Refer to *Exchangeability and de Finetti's Theorem* (from the University of Oxford): `http://www.stats.ox.ac.uk/~steffen/teaching/grad/definetti.pdf`

Preparing data for LDA

In the previous recipe, *Using LDA to classify text documents*, we have seen how to use the LDA algorithm for topic modeling. We have seen that, before constructing the algorithm, the dataset must be appropriately processed so as to prepare the data in a format compatible with the input provided by the LDA model. In this recipe, we will analyze in detail these procedures.

Getting ready

In this recipe, we will analyze the procedures necessary to transform the data contained in a specific dataset. This data will then be used as input for an algorithm based on the LDA method.

How to do it...

Let's see how to prepare data for LDA:

1. Create a new Python file, and import the following packages (the full code is in the `PrepDataLDA.py` file that's already provided to you):

```
from nltk.tokenize import RegexpTokenizer
from stop_words import get_stop_words
from nltk.stem.porter import PorterStemmer
from gensim import corpora, models
```

2. We define a series of sentences from which we want to extract the topics:

```
Doc1 = "Some doctors say that pizza is good for your health."
Doc2 = "The pizza is good to eat, my sister likes to eat a good
pizza, but not to my brother."
Doc3 = "Doctors suggest that walking can cause a decrease in blood
pressure."
Doc4 = "My brother likes to walk, but my sister don't like to
walk."
Doc5 = "When my sister is forced to walk for a long time she feels
an increase in blood pressure."
Doc6 = "When my brother eats pizza, he has health problems."
```

In the sentences we have just defined, there are topics that are repeated with different meanings. It is not easy to derive a link between them.

3. We insert these sentences into a list:

```
DocList = [Doc1, Doc2, Doc3, Doc4, Doc5, Doc6]
```

4. We set the elements that we will use in the transformation procedure:

```
Tokenizer = RegexpTokenizer(r'\w+')
EnStop = get_stop_words('en')
PStemmer = PorterStemmer()
Texts = []
```

5. To perform the transformation on all the phrases, it is necessary to set a loop that just goes through the list:

```
for i in DocList:
```

6. Now, we can start preparing the data. **Tokenization** is the process of dividing text into a set of meaningful pieces. These pieces are called **tokens**. For example, we can divide a chunk of text into words, or we can divide it into sentences. Let's start with sentence tokenization:

```
raw = i.lower()
Tokens = Tokenizer.tokenize(raw)
```

7. Let's move on to the removal of meaningless words. There are some words in typical English sentences that do not take on significant significance for the construction of a topic model. For example, conjunctions and articles do not help identify topics. These terms are called **stop words** and must be removed from our token list. These terms (stop words) change according to the context in which we operate. Let's remove the stop words:

```
StoppedTokens = [i for i in Tokens if not i in EnStop]
```

8. The last phase of data preparation concerns the stemming. The goal of stemming is to reduce these different forms into a common base form. This uses a heuristic process to cut off the ends of words to extract the base form. Let's make the stemming:

```
StemmedTokens = [PStemmer.stem(i) for i in StoppedTokens]
```

9. We just have to add the element obtained to the text list:

```
Texts.append(StemmedTokens)
```

10. At this point, we have to turn our token list into a dictionary:

```
Dictionary = corpora.Dictionary(Texts)
```

11. So, let's build a document term matrix using tokenized documents:

```
CorpusMat = [Dictionary.doc2bow(text) for text in Texts]
```

12. Finally, we build an LDA model and print the topics extracted:

```
LDAModel = models.ldamodel.LdaModel(CorpusMat, num_topics=3,
id2word = Dictionary, passes=20)
print(LDAModel.print_topics(num_topics=3, num_words=3))
```

The following results are returned:

```
[(0, '0.079*"walk" + 0.079*"blood" + 0.079*"pressur"'),
 (1, '0.120*"like" + 0.119*"eat" + 0.119*"brother"'),
 (2, '0.101*"doctor" + 0.099*"health" + 0.070*"pizza"')]
```

How it works...

Data preparation is essential for the creation of a topic model. The preparation of the data goes through the following procedures:

- **Tokenization**: The conversion of a document into its atomic elements
- **Stop words**: Removes meaningless words
- **Stemming**: The fusion of equivalent words in meaning

There's more...

Data preparation depends on the type of text we are processing. In some cases, it is necessary to carry out further operations before submitting the data to the LDA algorithm. For example, punctuation removal can be one of them, as well as the removal of special characters.

See also

- Refer to *Tokenization* (from the NLP group at Stanford University): `https://nlp.stanford.edu/IR-book/html/htmledition/tokenization-1.html`
- Refer to *Stemming and lemmatization* (from Stanford University): `https://nlp.stanford.edu/IR-book/html/htmledition/stemming-and-lemmatization-1.html`
- Refer to *Dropping common terms: stop words* (from Stanford University): `https://nlp.stanford.edu/IR-book/html/htmledition/dropping-common-terms-stop-words-1.html`

15
Automated Machine Learning and Transfer Learning

In this chapter, we will cover the following recipes:

- Working with Auto-WEKA
- Using AutoML to generate machine learning pipelines with TPOT
- Working with Auto-Keras
- Working with auto-sklearn
- Using MLBox for selection and leak detection
- Convolutional neural networks with transfer learning
- Transfer learning – pretrained image classifiers with ResNet-50
- Transfer learning – feature extraction with the VGG16 model
- Transfer learning with retrained GloVe embedding

Technical requirements

To address the recipes in this chapter, you will need the following files (available on GitHub):

- TPOTIrisClassifier.py
- AKClassifier.py
- MLBoxRegressor.py
- ASKLClassifier.py
- ImageTransferLearning.py
- PretrainedImageClassifier.py
- ExtractFeatures.py
- PTGloveEMB.py

Introduction

Automated machine learning (**AutoML**) refers to those applications that are able to automate the end-to-end process of applying machine learning to real-world problems. Generally, scientific analysts must process data through a series of preliminary procedures before submitting it to machine learning algorithms. In the previous chapters, you saw the necessary steps for performing a proper analysis of data through these algorithms. You saw how simple it is to build a model based on deep neural networks by using several libraries. In some cases, these skills are beyond those possessed by analysts, who must seek support from industry experts to solve the problem.

AutoML was born from a need to create an application that automated the whole machine learning process so that the user could take advantage of these services. Generally, machine learning experts must perform the following tasks:

- Data preparation
- Selecting features
- Selecting an appropriate model class
- Choosing and optimizing model hyperparameters
- Post-processing machine learning models
- Analyzing the results obtained

AutoML automates all of these operations. It offers the advantages of producing simpler and faster-to-create solutions that often outperform hand-designed models. There are a number of AutoML frameworks; in the following sections, we will look at some of them.

Working with Auto-WEKA

Weka is a software environment that's entirely written in Java. **Weka**, an acronym for **Waikato Environment for Knowledge Analysis**, is a machine learning software that was developed at the University of Waikato in New Zealand. It is open source and is distributed under the GNU General Public License. It is possible to build many models based on machine learning by using it.

However, each of the algorithms has its own hyperparameters, which can drastically change their performance. The task of the researcher is to find the right combination of these parameters that will maximize the performance of the model. Auto-WEKA automatically solves the problem of the selection of a learning algorithm and the setting of its hyperparameters.

Getting ready

In this recipe, you will learn how to use Auto-WEKA in only three main steps. To use this library, it is necessary to install it beforehand. For information on the system requirements and the installation procedure, refer to `https://www.cs.ubc.ca/labs/beta/Projects/autoweka/manual.pdf`.

How to do it...

Let's look at how to work with Auto-WEKA, as follows:

1. **Building the experiment definition and instantiating it**: In this step, you specify which dataset to use and which type of hyperparameter search will be performed. Then, the experiment is completely instantiated so that Auto-WEKA can identify the classifier to be used. In this phase, Auto-WEKA transforms all of the paths into absolute paths.
2. **Experiment execution**: Auto-WEKA uses multiple cores by running the same experiment with several random seeds; the only requirement is that all of the experiments have a similar filesystem.
3. **Analysis phase**: When Auto-WEKA uses a model-based optimization method, it produces a trajectory of hyperparameters that have identified by the optimization method as the best at a given time. The simplest form of analysis examines the best hyperparameters that have been found in all seeds and uses the trained model to make predictions about a new dataset.

How it works...

To select a learning algorithm and set its hyperparameters, Auto-WEKA uses a completely automated approach, taking advantage of recent innovations in Bayesian optimization.

There's more...

Auto-WEKA was the first library to use Bayesian optimization to automatically instantiate a highly parametric machine learning framework. Later, AutoML was also applied by other libraries.

See also

- Refer to the official Auto-WEKA website: `https://www.cs.ubc.ca/labs/beta/Projects/autoweka/`
- Refer to *Auto-WEKA 2.0: Automatic model selection and hyperparameter optimization in WEKA*: `https://www.cs.ubc.ca/labs/beta/Projects/autoweka/papers/16-599.pdf`
- Refer to *Auto-WEKA: Combined Selection and Hyperparameter Optimization of Classification Algorithms*: `https://www.cs.ubc.ca/labs/beta/Projects/autoweka/papers/autoweka.pdf`

Using AutoML to generate machine learning pipelines with TPOT

TPOT is a Python automated machine learning tool that optimizes machine learning pipelines by using genetic programming. In artificial intelligence, genetic algorithms are part of the class of evolutionary algorithms. A characteristic of the latter is finding solutions to problems by using techniques that are borrowed from natural evolution. The search for a solution to a problem is entrusted to an iterative process that selects and recombines more and more refined solutions until a criterion of optimality is reached. In a genetic algorithm, the population of solutions is pushed toward a given objective by evolutionary pressure.

Getting ready

In this recipe, you will learn how to build the best performing model to classify the iris species (setosa, virginica, and versicolor) from the `iris` dataset, using TPOT. To use this library, it is necessary to install it. For information on the system requirements and for the installation procedure, refer to `https://epistasislab.github.io/tpot/installing/`.

How to do it...

Let's look at how to use AutoML to generate machine learning pipelines with TPOT:

1. Create a new Python file and import the following packages (the full code is in the `TPOTIrisClassifier.py` file that's already been provided for you):

   ```
   from tpot import TPOTClassifier
   from sklearn.datasets import load_iris
   from sklearn.model_selection import train_test_split
   import numpy as np
   ```

2. Let's import the iris dataset, as follows:

   ```
   IrisData = load_iris()
   ```

3. Let's split the dataset, as follows:

   ```
   XTrain, XTest, YTrain, YTest =
   train_test_split(IrisData.data.astype(np.float64),
       IrisData.target.astype(np.float64), train_size=0.70,
   test_size=0.30)
   ```

4. Now, we can build the classifier:

   ```
   TpotCL = TPOTClassifier(generations=5, population_size=50,
   verbosity=2)
   ```

5. Then, we can train the model:

   ```
   TpotCL.fit(XTrain, YTrain)
   ```

6. Then, we will use the model with unseen data (`XTest`) to evaluate the performance:

   ```
   print(TpotCL.score(XTest, YTest))
   ```

7. Finally, we will export the model pipeline:

   ```
   TpotCL.export('TPOTIrisPipeline.py')
   ```

   If you run this code, a pipeline that achieves about 97% test accuracy will be returned.

How it works...

TPOT automates machine learning pipeline construction by combining a flexible representation of the pipeline expression tree with stochastic search algorithms, such as genetic programming. In this recipe, you learned how to use TPOT to search for the best pipeline to classify the iris species from the iris dataset.

There's more...

TPOT is built on the basis of `scikit-learn`, so all of the code that is generated will seem very familiar to us, given the extensive use of the `scikit-learn` libraries in the previous chapters. TPOT is a platform that's under active development, and it is therefore subject to continuous updates.

See also

- The official documentation of the TPOT tool: `https://epistasislab.github.io/tpot/`
- *Automating biomedical data science through tree-based pipeline optimization*, by Randal S. Olson, Ryan J. Urbanowicz, Peter C. Andrews, Nicole A. Lavender, La Creis Kidd, and Jason H. Moore (2016)

Working with Auto-Keras

Auto-Keras is an open source software library for AutoML that aims at providing easy access to deep learning models. Auto-Keras has a number of features that allow you to automatically set up the architecture and parameters of deep learning models. Its ease of use, simple installation, and numerous examples make it a very popular framework. Auto-Keras was developed by the DATA Lab at Texas A and M University and community contributors.

Getting ready

In this recipe, you will learn how to use the Auto-Keras library to classify handwritten digits. To install the Auto-Keras package, we can use the `pip` command, as follows:

```
$ pip install autokeras
```

At the time of writing this book, Auto-Keras was only compatible with Python 3.6. For the installation procedure, refer to the official website at `https://autokeras.com/`.

How to do it...

Let's look at how to work with Auto-Keras:

1. Create a new Python file and import the following packages (the full code is in the `AKClassifier.py` file that's already been provided for you):

```
from keras.datasets import mnist
import autokeras as ak
```

2. Let's import the `mnist` dataset, as follows:

```
(XTrain, YTrain), (XTest, YTest) = mnist.load_data()
```

3. Before defining a classifier, we must give a new form to the arrays containing the input data without changing its contents:

```
XTrain = XTrain.reshape(XTrain.shape + (1,))
XTest = XTest.reshape(XTest.shape + (1,))
```

4. Now, we can build the classifier:

```
AKClf = ak.ImageClassifier()
```

5. Then, we can train the model:

```
AKClf.fit(XTrain, YTrain)
```

6. Finally, we will use the model with unseen data (`XTest`):

```
Results = AKClf.predict(XTest)
```

How it works...

In this recipe, with a few lines of code, we have managed to construct a classifier which, by providing a series of images of handwritten digits, can correctly classify the digits.

There's more...

This is a package that allows us to automatically create an algorithm based on machine learning without worrying about the setting of the training parameters that, as you saw in previous chapters, are fundamental to the success of the model.

See also

- Refer to the official documentation of the Auto-Keras library: https://autokeras.com/
- Refer to *Auto-Keras: Efficient Neural Architecture Search with Network Morphism*, by Haifeng Jin, Qingquan Song, and Xia Hu (arXiv:1806.10282).

Working with auto-sklearn

Auto-sklearn works on the `scikit-learn` machine learning library. It represents a platform based on supervised machine learning that's ready for use. It automatically searches for the correct machine learning algorithm for a new dataset and optimizes its hyperparameters.

Getting ready

In this recipe, you will learn how to use auto-sklearn to build a classifier. To import the data, the `sklearn.datasets.load_digits` function will be used. This function loads and returns the digits dataset for classification problems. Each datapoint is an 8x8 image of a digit.

How to do it...

Let's look at how to work with auto-sklearn:

1. Create a new Python file and import the following packages (the full code is in the `ASKLClassifier.py` file that's already been provided for you):

```
import autosklearn.classification
import sklearn.model_selection
import sklearn.datasets
import sklearn.metrics
```

2. Let's import the `digits` dataset, as follows:

```
Input, Target = sklearn.datasets.load_digits()
```

3. Let's split the dataset, as follows:

```
XTrain, XTest, YTrain, YTest =
sklearn.model_selection.train_test_split(Input, Target,
random_state=3)
```

4. Now, we can build the classifier:

```
ASKModel = autosklearn.classification.AutoSklearnClassifier()
```

5. Then, we can train the model:

```
ASKModel.fit(XTrain, YTrain)
```

6. Finally, we will use the model with unseen data (`XTest`):

```
YPred = ASKModel.predict(XTest)
print("Accuracy score", sklearn.metrics.accuracy_score(YTest,
YPred))
```

How it works...

Auto-sklearn uses Bayesian optimization for hyperparameter tuning for traditional machine learning algorithms that are implemented within `scikit-learn`. The best machine learning algorithm and the parameters that are optimized are searched automatically.

There's more...

Auto-sklearn is a good choice to automate the process of selecting and optimizing an automatic learning model because it creates extremely precise machine learning models, avoiding the tedious tasks of selecting, training, and testing different models.

See also

- The official documentation of the `auto-sklearn` package: `https://automl.github.io/auto-sklearn/stable/`
- *Efficient and Robust Automated Machine Learning,* by Feurer, et al., in Advances in Neural Information Processing Systems

Using MLBox for selection and leak detection

MLBox is an automated library for machine learning. It supports distributed data processing, cleaning, formatting, and numerous algorithms for classification and regression. It allows for the extremely robust selection of functions and leak detection. It also provides stacking models, which means combining a set of model information to generate a new model that aims to perform better than the individual models.

Getting ready

To use this library, it is necessary to install it beforehand. For information on the system requirements and the installation procedure, refer to `https://mlbox.readthedocs.io/en/latest/installation.html`.

In this recipe, you will learn what's strictly necessary to set up a pipeline using MLBox. A regression problem will be addressed via the use of the Boston dataset that was already used in `Chapter 1`, *The Realm of Supervised Learning*.

How to do it...

Let's look at how to use MLBox for selection and leak detection:

1. Import the following packages (the full code is in the `MLBoxRegressor.py` file that's already been provided for you):

```
from mlbox.preprocessing import *
from mlbox.optimisation import *
from mlbox.prediction import *
```

2. Let's import the data, as follows:

```
paths = ["train.csv","test.csv"]
target_name = "SalePrice"
```

With this code, we have set up the list of paths to our datasets and the name of the target that we are trying to predict.

3. Now, we will read and preprocess these files:

```
data = Reader(sep=",").train_test_split(paths, target_name)
data = Drift_thresholder().fit_transform(data)
```

4. To evaluate the model, the following code will be used:

```
Optimiser().evaluate(None, data)
```

In this case, the default configuration was used.

5. Finally, to predict on the test set, use the following code:

```
Predictor().fit_predict(None, data)
```

If you want configure the pipeline (steps, parameters, and values), the following optional step must be used.

6. To test and optimize the whole pipeline, we will use the following code:

```
space = {

        'ne__numerical_strategy' : {"space" : [0, 'mean']},

        'ce__strategy' : {"space" : ["label_encoding",
"random_projection", "entity_embedding"]},

        'fs__strategy' : {"space" : ["variance",
"rf_feature_importance"]},
        'fs__threshold': {"search" : "choice", "space" : [0.1, 0.2,
0.3]},

        'est__strategy' : {"space" : ["XGBoost"]},
        'est__max_depth' : {"search" : "choice", "space" : [5,6]},
        'est__subsample' : {"search" : "uniform", "space" :
[0.6,0.9]}

        }

best = opt.optimise(space, data, max_evals = 5)
```

7. Finally, to predict on the test set, we will use the following code:

```
Predictor().fit_predict(best, data)
```

How it works...

MLBox builds the whole pipeline with the following three steps:

1. **Preprocessing**: All of the operations related to this phase make use of the `mlbox.preprocessing` sub-package. In this phase, we proceed to the reading and cleaning of the input file and then to the removal of the drift variables.

2. **Optimization**: All of the operations related to this phase make use of the sub-package `mlbox.mlbox.optimisation`. In this phase, the whole pipeline is optimized. The hyperparametric optimization method that's adopted uses the `hyperopt` library. This library creates a highly-dimensional space for the parameters to be optimized and chooses the best combination of parameters that lowers the validation score.

3. **Prediction**: All of the operations related to this phase make use of the `mlbox.prediction` sub-package. In this phase, we proceed to prediction by using the test dataset and the best hyperparameters that were identified in the previous phase.

There's more...

MLBox provides advanced algorithms and techniques, such as hyperparameter optimization, stacking, deep learning, leak detection, entity embedding, parallel processing, and more. The use of MLBox is currently limited to Linux only. MLBox was first developed using Python 2, and then it was extended to Python 3.

See also

- MLBox's official documentation: `https://mlbox.readthedocs.io/en/latest/`
- Installation guide: `https://mlbox.readthedocs.io/en/latest/installation.html`

Convolutional neural networks with transfer learning

Transfer learning is a methodology based on machine learning that exploits the memorization of the knowledge that's acquired during the resolution of a problem and the application of the same to different (but related) problems. The need to use transfer learning takes place when there is a limited supply of training data. This could be due to the fact that data is rare or expensive to collect or label, or inaccessible. With the growing presence of large amounts of data, the transfer learning option has become more frequently used.

Convolutional neural networks (**CNNs**) are essentially **artificial neural networks** (**ANNs**). In fact, just like the latter, CNNs are made up of neurons that are connected to one another by weighted branches (weight); the training parameters of the networks are once again the weight and the bias. In CNNs, the connection pattern between neurons is inspired by the structure of the visual cortex in the animal world. The individual neurons that are present in this part of the brain (the visual cortex) respond to certain stimuli in a narrow region of the observation, called the **receptive field**. The receptive fields of different neurons are partially overlapped to cover the entire field of vision. The response of a single neuron to stimuli taking place in its receptive field can be mathematically approximated by a convolution operation.

Getting ready

In this recipe, you will learn how to build an image recognition model by using transfer learning in Keras. To do this, the MobileNet model and Keras high-level neural networks API will be used to train the model images extracted from the `Caltech256` dataset that we already used in `Chapter 10`, *Image Content Analysis*. `Caltech256` is very popular in this field! It contains 256 classes of images, where each class contains thousands of samples.

How to do it...

Let's build an image recognition model by using transfer learning in Keras; in this section, we will explain the code step by step:

1. Create a new Python file and import the following packages (the full code is in the `ImageTransferLearning.py` file that's already been provided for you):

```
from keras.layers import Dense,GlobalAveragePooling2D
from keras.applications import MobileNet
from keras.applications.mobilenet import preprocess_input
from keras.preprocessing.image import ImageDataGenerator
from keras.models import Model
```

2. Let's import the `MobileNet` model and discard the last 1,000 neuron layers:

```
BasicModel=MobileNet(input_shape=(224, 224, 3),
weights='imagenet',include_top=False)
```

3. Let's define the Keras model architecture:

```
ModelLayers=BasicModel.output
ModelLayers=GlobalAveragePooling2D()(ModelLayers)
ModelLayers=Dense(1024,activation='relu')(ModelLayers)
ModelLayers=Dense(1024,activation='relu')(ModelLayers)
ModelLayers=Dense(512,activation='relu')(ModelLayers)
OutpModel=Dense(3,activation='softmax')(ModelLayers)
```

4. Now, we can build a model based on the architecture that was previously defined:

```
ConvModel=Model(inputs=BasicModel.input,outputs=OutpModel)
```

5. Now, we can move on to the training phase. Having adopted an approach based on transfer learning, it is not necessary to proceed with the training of the whole model. This is because MobileNet is already trained. Let's define the last dense levels as the trainable layer:

```
for layer in ConvModel.layers[:20]:
    layer.trainable=False
for layer in ConvModel.layers[20:]:
    layer.trainable=True
```

6. Let's load the training data into `ImageDataGenerator`:

```
TrainDataGen=ImageDataGenerator(preprocessing_function=preprocess_i
nput)
```

`ImageDataGenerator` is a built-in Keras class that creates groups of tensor image data with real-time data augmentation. The data will be wound over in groups.

7. Let's define some dependencies and a path for the training data:

```
TrainGenerator=TrainDataGen.flow_from_directory('training_images/',
#'train/'
target_size=(224,224),
                                        color_mode='rgb',
                                        batch_size=32,
class_mode='categorical',
                                        shuffle=True)
```

8. Let's compile the Keras model:

```
ConvModel.compile(optimizer='Adam',loss='categorical_crossentropy',
metrics=['accuracy'])
```

The following three arguments are passed:

- `optimizer='adam'`: An algorithm for first-order, gradient-based optimization of stochastic objective functions, based on adaptive estimates of lower-order moments.
- `loss='categorical_crossentropy'`: We have used the `categorical_crossentropy` argument here. When using `categorical_crossentropy`, your targets should be in a categorical format (we have 10 classes; the target for each sample must be a 10-dimensional vector that is all-zeros, except for a one at the index corresponding to the class of the sample).
- `metrics=['accuracy']`: A metric is a function that is used to evaluate the performance of your model during training and testing.

9. Finally, we will define the step size for training and fit the model, as follows:

```
StepSizeTrain=TrainGenerator.n//TrainGenerator.batch_size
ConvModel.fit_generator(generator=TrainGenerator,
 steps_per_epoch=StepSizeTrain,
 epochs=10)
```

The following results are printed:

```
Found 60 images belonging to 3 classes.
Epoch 1/10
1/1 [==============================] - 31s 31s/step - loss: 1.1935
- acc: 0.3125
Epoch 2/10
1/1 [==============================] - 21s 21s/step - loss: 2.7700
- acc: 0.5714
Epoch 3/10
1/1 [==============================] - 24s 24s/step - loss: 0.0639
- acc: 1.0000
Epoch 4/10
1/1 [==============================] - 21s 21s/step - loss: 0.2819
- acc: 0.7500
Epoch 5/10
1/1 [==============================] - 26s 26s/step - loss: 0.0012
- acc: 1.0000
Epoch 6/10
1/1 [==============================] - 21s 21s/step - loss: 0.0024
- acc: 1.0000
Epoch 7/10
1/1 [==============================] - 22s 22s/step - loss:
8.7767e-04 - acc: 1.0000
Epoch 8/10
1/1 [==============================] - 24s 24s/step - loss:
1.3191e-04 - acc: 1.0000
Epoch 9/10
1/1 [==============================] - 25s 25s/step - loss:
9.6636e-04 - acc: 1.0000
Epoch 10/10
1/1 [==============================] - 21s 21s/step - loss:
3.2019e-04 - acc: 1.0000
```

How it works...

In this recipe, you learned how to use transfer learning in an image recognition problem. Through transfer learning, a pretrained model can be used on a large and accessible dataset to find layers whose output have reusable features, which is done by using this output as input to train a smaller network that requires fewer parameters. This network will only need to know the relationships between the patterns that are obtained from the pretrained models and the specific problem to be solved. As a pretrained model, the MobileNet model was used.

`MobileNet` is an architecture that was proposed by Google and that is particularly suitable for vision-based applications. MobileNet uses deep separable convolutions that significantly reduce the number of parameters, compared to a network with normal convolutions with the same depth in the networks. Neural networks based on the MobileNet model are thus lighter. The normal convolution is replaced by a in-depth convolution, followed by a punctual convolution that is called **convolution separable in depth**.

The transfer learning procedure was then performed in two phases:

- First, almost all levels of the neural network were trained on a very large and generic dataset to allow for the acquisition of global notions
- Later, we used the specific dataset for the training of the remaining layers, deciding whether to propagate the errors through fine-tuning

There's more...

In this recipe, we used fine-tuning; in fact, we didn't simply replace the final level, but we also trained some of the previous levels. In the network that we used, the initial levels were used to acquire generic functionalities (exploiting the potential of the MobileNet trained network), while the subsequent ones were used to finalize the experience that was acquired on the specific activity in question. Using this procedure, we froze the first 20 layers while we traced the following layers to meet our needs. This methodology helps to achieve better performance with less training time.

Fine-tuning can be achieved through the following steps:

1. We start with a pretrained network trained on a similar problem and replace the output level with a new level of output by adjusting the number of classes.
2. The initial values of the weights are those of the pretrained net, except for the connections between successive layers whose weights are initialized randomly.
3. We perform new training iterations (SGD) for optimized weights with respect to the peculiarities of the new dataset (it does not need to be large).

In the fine-tuning process, the model parameters will be adjusted precisely to fit with certain observations.

See also

- Refer to Keras application models: `https://keras.io/applications/`
- Refer to *MobileNets: Efficient Convolutional Neural Networks for Mobile Vision Applications*: `https://arxiv.org/pdf/1704.04861.pdf`
- Refer to *Transfer Learning and Computer Vision* (from Yale University): `http://euler.stat.yale.edu/~tba3/stat665/lectures/lec18/lecture18.pdf`
- Refer to *A Survey on Transfer Learning*, S. J. Pan and Q. Yang, in IEEE Transactions on Knowledge and Data Engineering: `https://www.cse.ust.hk/~qyang/Docs/2009/tkde_transfer_learning.pdf`

Transfer learning with pretrained image classifiers using ResNet-50

The **residual network** (**ResNet**) represents an architecture that, through the use of new and innovative types of blocks (known as **residual blocks**) and the concept of residual learning, has allowed researchers to reach depths that were unthinkable with the classic feedforward model, due to the problem of the degradation of the gradient.

Pretrained models are trained on a large set of data, and so they allow us to obtain excellent performance. We can therefore adopt pretrained models for a problem similar to the one that we want to solve, to avoid the problem of a lack of data. Because of the computational costs of the formation of such models, they are available in ready-to-use formats. For example, the Keras library offers several models such as Xception, VGG16, VGG19, ResNet, ResNetV2, ResNeXt, InceptionV3, InceptionResNetV2, MobileNet, MobileNetV2, DenseNet, and NASNet.

Getting ready

In this recipe, you will learn how to use a pretrained model to predict the class of a single image. To do this, a ResNet-50 model will be used. This model is available from the `keras.applications` library.

How to do it...

Now, we will use a pretrained model to classify a single image; in this section, we will explain the code step by step:

1. Create a new Python file and import the following packages (the full code is in the `PretrainedImageClassifier.py` file that's already been provided for you):

   ```
   from keras.applications.resnet50 import ResNet50
   from keras.preprocessing import image
   from keras.applications.resnet50 import preprocess_input,
   decode_predictions
   import numpy as np
   ```

2. Let's define the pretrained model:

   ```
   PTModel = ResNet50(weights='imagenet')
   ```

3. Let's define the image to classify:

   ```
   ImgPath = 'airplane.jpg'
   Img = image.load_img(ImgPath, target_size=(224, 224))
   ```

4. Here, we will take an image instance and turn it into a numpy array with dtype float32:

   ```
   InputIMG = image.img_to_array(Img)
   ```

5. Now, we will expand the numpy array that's obtained in the shape that's required by the pretrained model:

   ```
   InputIMG = np.expand_dims(InputIMG, axis=0)
   ```

6. Then, we will preprocess the data:

   ```
   InputIMG = preprocess_input(InputIMG)
   ```

7. Finally, we will use the pretrained model to classify the input image:

   ```
   PredData = PTModel.predict(InputIMG)
   ```

8. To evaluate the model's performance, we will use the decode_predictions function, as follows:

   ```
   print('Predicted:', decode_predictions(PredData, top=3)[0])
   ```

The `keras.applications.resnet50.decode_predictions` function decodes the results into a list of tuples (class, description, and probability). The following results are printed:

```
Predicted: [('n02690373', 'airliner', 0.80847234), ('n04592741',
'wing', 0.17411195), ('n04552348', 'warplane', 0.008112171)]
```

The higher probability (0.80847234) tells us that it is an airliner; in fact, the following is the image that was provided as input:

How it works...

Instead of trying to estimate a function G that, given an x, returns G (x), ResNet learns the difference between the two values—a value called the **residual**. In the residual layer of the network, a classical convolution takes place and the input is added to the result. If the input and output are of different sizes, the input is transformed with another 1×1 filter convolution before being added to the output so that it has the same feature map number. The size of a feature map is preserved by padding. A benefit of this technique is that the L2 regularization, which tends the weights toward zero, does not make us forget what was learned previously, but simply preserves it.

There's more...

There are ResNet implementations with different depths; the deepest counts as many as 152 levels. There is also a prototype with 1,202 levels, but it achieved worse results due to overfitting. This architecture won ILSVRC 2015, with an error of 3.6%. To understand the value of this result, just consider that the error that's generally achieved by a human being is around 5-10%, based on their skills and knowledge. Thanks to these results, the ResNet model is currently state of the art in the field of computer vision.

See also

- The official documentation of the `keras.applications` models: `https://keras.io/applications/`
- *Deep Residual Learning for Image Recognition* (by Kaiming He, Xiangyu Zhang, Shaoqing Ren, and Jian Sun): `https://arxiv.org/abs/1512.03385`
- *Pretrained Models* (from Toronto University): `https://www.cs.toronto.edu/~frossard/tags/pre-trained-models/`

Transfer learning using feature extraction with the VGG16 model

As we stated in the *Visualizing the MNIST dataset using PCA and t-SNE* recipe of `Chapter 14`, *Unsupervised Representation Learning*, in the case of datasets of important dimensions, the data was transformed into a reduced series of representation functions. This process of transforming the input data into a set of functionalities is named **feature extraction**. This is because the extraction of the characteristics proceeds from an initial series of measured data and produces derived values that can keep the information contained in the original dataset, but excluded from the redundant data. In the case of images, feature extraction is aimed at obtaining information that can be identified by a computer.

Getting ready

In this recipe, you will learn how to extract features from a series of images. Then, we will use these features to classify the images by using the k-means algorithm. In this recipe, we will use the VGG16 pretrained model and the `klearn.cluster.KMeans` function.

How to do it...

Let's perform a feature extraction procedure by using the VGG16 model:

1. Create a new Python file and import the following packages (the full code is in the `ExtractFeatures.py` file that's already been provided for you):

```
from keras.applications.vgg16 import VGG16
from keras.preprocessing import image
from keras.applications.vgg16 import preprocess_input
import numpy as np
from sklearn.cluster import KMeans
```

2. Let's define the pretrained model:

```
model = VGG16(weights='imagenet', include_top=False)
```

3. Let's initialize the list of features that will be extracted:

```
VGG16FeatureList = []
```

4. For each image in the dataset, we have to proceed with the extraction of features:

```
import os
for path, subdirs, files in os.walk('training_images'):
    for name in files:
        img_path = os.path.join(path, name)
        print(img_path)
```

In this way, we have recovered the path of each image contained in the folder. The images that are used are contained in the `training_images` folder, which we already used in the *Convolutional neural networks with transfer learning* recipe. It is a series of images that was extracted from the `Caltech256` dataset.

5. Let's import the image, as follows:

```
img = image.load_img(img_path, target_size=(224, 224))
```

6. We will take an image instance and turn it into a NumPy array, with datatype as `float32`:

```
img_data = image.img_to_array(img)
```

7. Now, we will expand the NumPy array that's obtained in the shape that's required by the pretrained model:

```
img_data = np.expand_dims(img_data, axis=0)
```

8. Then, we will preprocess the data:

```
img_data = preprocess_input(img_data)
```

9. We will use the pretrained model to extract features from the input image:

```
VGG16Feature = model.predict(img_data)
```

10. At this point, we will create an array with the obtained features:

```
VGG16FeatureNp = np.array(VGG16Feature)
```

11. Now, we will add the array that was obtained, to the list of features that we are building (one element for each image):

```
VGG16FeatureList.append(VGG16FeatureNp.flatten())
```

12. We will transform the final list into an array:

```
VGG16FeatureListNp = np.array(VGG16FeatureList)
```

13. Now, we can use the features that was obtained from the images to group them by type. Remember that these are images from three categories: airplanes, cars, and motorbikes. So, we expect the images to be labeled with three different labels. To do this, we use the KMeans algorithm, as follows:

```
KmeansModel = KMeans(n_clusters=3, random_state=0)
```

14. After defining the model, we move on to training it:

```
KmeansModel.fit(VGG16FeatureListNp)
```

15. Finally, we print the labels of the images that are used:

```
print(KmeansModel.labels_)
```

The following results are printed:

```
[2 2 2 2 2 2 2 2 2 2 2 2 2 2 2 2 2 2 2 2
 0 0 0 0 0 0 0 0 0 0 0 0 0 0 0 0 0 0 0 0
 1 1 1 1 1 1 1 1 1 1 1 1 1 1 1 1 1 1 1 1]
```

As you can see, the 60 images have been correctly labeled in the three available categories.

How it works...

In this recipe, you learned how to extract features from a series of images. As we have a limited number of images available, we used a pretrained model (VGG16) to correctly extract the information that was needed for subsequent identification. This procedure is useful to understand how to proceed to perform automatic recognition of the images through an unsupervised model. After extracting the features, we used them to classify the images, using the KMeans algorithm.

There's more...

VGG16 is a convolutional neural network model that was presented by K. Simonyan and A. Zisserman, from the University of Oxford, in the paper *Very Deep Convolutional Networks for Large-Scale Image Recognition*. This model has achieved excellent results in image recognition (with 92.7% accuracy). The test was performed on the ImageNet dataset, with over 14 million images belonging to 1,000 classes.

See also

- Refer to the *Visualizing Mnist dataset using PCA and t-SNE* recipe in `Chapter 14,` *Unsupervised Representation Learning*
- Refer to *Very Deep Convolutional Networks for Large-Scale Image Recognition*: `https://arxiv.org/abs/1409.1556`

Transfer learning with pretrained GloVe embedding

GloVe is an unsupervised learning algorithm for obtaining vector representations of words. The training is performed on the aggregate global statistics on the co-occurrence of words that has been extracted from a body of text present in the code files. The resulting representations show interesting linear substructures in the vector space of words. In this recipe, you will learn how to use a pretrained GloVe embedding model to classify adjectives to describe a person in a positive or negative fashion.

Getting ready

To follow this recipe, you will need to download the `glove.6B.100d.txt` file. This file is available at `https://nlp.stanford.edu/projects/glove/`. There are several versions of the pretrained word vectors:

- **glove.6B**: 6B tokens, 400K vocab, uncased, 50d, 100d, 200d, and 300d vectors—822 MB
- **glove.42B.300d**: 42B tokens, 1.9M vocab, uncased, 300d vectors—1.75 GB
- **glove.840B.300d**: 840B tokens, 2.2M vocab, cased, 300d vectors—2.03 GB
- **Twitter**: 27B tokens, 1.2M vocab, uncased, 25d, 50d, 100d, and 200d vectors—1.42 GB

How to do it...

Let's classify the adjectives that are used to describe a person in a positive and negative fashion:

1. Create a new Python file and import the following packages (the full code is in the `PTGloveEMB.py` file that's already been provided for you):

```
from numpy import array
from numpy import zeros
from numpy import asarray
from keras.preprocessing.text import Tokenizer
from keras.preprocessing.sequence import pad_sequences
from keras.models import Sequential
from keras.layers import Dense
from keras.layers import Flatten
from keras.layers import Embedding
```

2. Let's define the 10 positive and 10 negative adjectives that are used to describe a person:

```
Adjectives = ['Wonderful',
        'Heroic',
        'Glamorous',
  'Valuable',
        'Excellent',
        'Optimistic',
        'Peaceful',
        'Romantic',
        'Loving',
```

```
                        'Faithful',
                        'Aggressive',
                        'Arrogant',
                        'Bossy',
                        'Boring',
                        'Careless',
                        'Selfish',
                        'Deceitful',
                        'Dishonest',
                        'Greedy',
                        'Impatient']
```

3. Let's define the labels of the adjectives that were defined previously (1 = positive, 0 = negative):

```
AdjLabels = array([1,1,1,1,1,1,1,1,1,1,0,0,0,0,0,0,0,0,0,0])
```

4. Let's tokenize the adjectives and prepare the vocabulary:

```
TKN = Tokenizer()
TKN.fit_on_texts(Adjectives)
VocabSize = len(TKN.word_index) + 1
```

5. Let's encode the adjectives into an integer sequence and transform a list of sequences into a two-dimensional NumPy array:

```
EncodedAdjectives = TKN.texts_to_sequences(Adjectives)
PaddedAdjectives = pad_sequences(EncodedAdjectives, maxlen=4,
padding='post')
```

6. Let's load the pretrained model:

```
EmbeddingsIndex = dict()
f = open('glove.6B.100d.txt',encoding="utf8")
for line in f:
  Values = line.split()
  Word = Values[0]
  Coefs = asarray(Values[1:], dtype='float32')
  EmbeddingsIndex[Word] = Coefs
f.close()
```

7. We will create a weight matrix for words in tokenized adjectives:

```
EmbeddingMatrix = zeros((VocabSize, 100))
for word, i in TKN.word_index.items():
  EmbeddingVector = EmbeddingsIndex.get(word)
  if EmbeddingVector is not None:
    EmbeddingMatrix[i] = EmbeddingVector
```

8. Now, we are ready to define the `keras` sequential model:

```
AdjModel = Sequential()
PTModel = Embedding(VocabSize, 100, weights=[EmbeddingMatrix],
input_length=4, trainable=False)
AdjModel.add(PTModel)
AdjModel.add(Flatten())
AdjModel.add(Dense(1, activation='sigmoid'))
print(AdjModel.summary())
```

The following summary is printed:

```
Layer (type) Output Shape Param #
=================================================================
embedding_13 (Embedding) (None, 4, 100) 2100
_____
flatten_10 (Flatten) (None, 400) 0
_____
dense_17 (Dense) (None, 1) 401
=================================================================
Total params: 2,501
Trainable params: 401
Non-trainable params: 2,100
```

As you can see, only part of the parameters have been trained.

9. Let's compile and fit the model:

```
AdjModel.compile(optimizer='adam', loss='binary_crossentropy',
metrics=['acc'])
AdjModel.fit(PaddedAdjectives, AdjLabels, epochs=50, verbose=1)
```

10. Finally, we will evaluate the model's performance:

```
loss, accuracy = AdjModel.evaluate(PaddedAdjectives, AdjLabels,
verbose=1)
print('Model Accuracy: %f' % (accuracy*100))
```

The following result is returned:

```
Model Accuracy: 100.000000
```

How it works...

To quantitatively capture the nuances that are necessary to distinguish a positive adjective from a negative adjective, a model has to associate more than a single number with word combinations. A simple method for a set of words is the vector difference between two vectors of words. GloVe is designed so that these vector differences capture the meanings specified by the juxtaposition of several words as closely as possible.

There's more...

In transfer learning, the weights of the network are adapted and transferred so that we can use this knowledge to pursue multiple different objectives. To obtain good performance from transfer learning, certain conditions must be met: the initial and final datasets must not be too different from each other, and they must share the same preprocessing operations.

So far, you have seen several examples of how the concepts of transfer learning can be applied to real cases. Actually, in practice, transfer learning takes on different types: `Inductive Transfer learning`, `Unsupervised Transfer Learning`, `Transductive Transfer Learning`, and `Instance Transfer`. We are trying to deepen those concepts.

To understand the differences between these methodologies, we will look at the terms—domains and tasks. By the term **domain**, we mean the type of data that's used by the network, while by the term **task**, we mean what the network intends to do. We will also use the terms **source** and **destination** to distinguish the network that's already trained on a large amount of data from the network that we intend to build.

Inductive transfer learning

One of the simplest forms of supervised machine learning is `inductive learning`. It is based solely on observation. Given an initial set of input-output examples, the agent elaborates on hypotheses to reconstruct the transfer function. The agent is designed to observe interactions with the outside world. In particular, the agent analyzes the feedback of its decisions. The perceptions of the artificial agent can be used as follows:

- To make decisions (reactive agent)
- To improve the agent's decision-making capacity (machine learning)

In `Inductive Transfer Learning` methods, the information that's processed by the two networks (the source and destination) is of the same type (images, sounds, and so on), while the tasks performed by the networks are different. In this case, the purpose of transfer learning is to use the `inductive-bias` that was recovered in the training of the source network to improve the performance of the destination network. By the term **inductive-bias**, we mean a series of hypotheses concerning the distribution of the data that the algorithm recovers in the training phase.

Unsupervised transfer learning

In unsupervised transfer learning, the information that's processed by the two networks (the source and destination) is of the same type (images, sounds, and so on), while the tasks that are performed by the networks are different, like in inductive transfer learning. The substantial difference between the two methods lies in the fact that no labeled data is available in unsupervised transfer learning.

Transductive transfer learning

In transductive transfer learning, the information that's processed by the two networks (the source and destination) is different, while the tasks that are performed by the networks are similar. This methodology is based on the concept of transductive inference, which brings the reasoning from specific (training) cases to specific cases (tests). Unlike induction, which requires the solution to a more general problem before solving a more specific problem, in transduction, we try to get the answer that we really need, but not a more general one.

Instance transfer learning

A scenario in which the domains of the origin and destination are perfectly similar is difficult to find. It is more possible to identify a part of data that is better approximating to those of destination but lies in the domain of origin which is of a much larger size than the destination one. In instance transfer learning, we look for the training samples in the origin domain that have a strong correlation with the destination domain. Once they are identified, they are reused in the learning phase of the target activity; in this way, the accuracy of the classification is improved.

See also

- Refer to *Global Vectors for Word Representation* (by Jeffrey Pennington, Richard Socher, and Christopher D. Manning): `https://www.aclweb.org/anthology/D14-1162`
- Refer to *A Review of Transfer Learning Algorithms* (by Mohsen Kaboli): `https://hal.archives-ouvertes.fr/hal-01575126/document`

16
Unlocking Production Issues

In this chapter, we will cover the following recipes:

- Handling unstructured data
- Deploying machine learning models
- Keeping track of changes into production
- Tracking accuracy to optimize model scaling

Technical requirements

To address the recipes in this chapter, you will need the following files (available on GitHub):

- UNData.py
- TextFile.txt

Introduction

In the previous chapters, we have extensively covered the main algorithms that are used in machine learning. We have seen how many and which tools the Python programmer has at their disposal to construct algorithms that are capable of predicting or classifying specific information. The next step is to create software that can be made available for production and subsequent marketing.

This is not a small challenge, given that making software available for marketing involves the resolution of considerable problems that include hardware and software aspects. In fact, we must first determine which types of devices will host the software and then select the programming platform that is most suitable for that type of technology.

Handling unstructured data

So far, we have highlighted the importance of input data in the creation of a model based on automatic learning. In particular, we have seen how important it is to adequately process this data before providing it in our algorithm. Another challenge that we must face before starting our production work is to learn how to deal with unstructured data. By unstructured data, we mean data that is stored without any scheme. An example is files containing text that has been produced by one of the most popular text editing software or a multimedia file, but this unstructured data could also take the form of emails, PDFs, and so on. Unstructured data differs from databases due to the fact that they may have irregularities that do not allow you to catalog or store them in a particular process.

Getting ready

As a source, I used a passage from the novel *The Adventures of Huckleberry Finn*, by Mark Twain, which can be viewed on GitHub.

As you can see, it is an unstructured text. We will handle this text and remove the unnecessary elements before saving the result in a structured form.

How to do it...

In this recipe, we will learn how to handle unstructured data. Follow these steps to begin:

1. Create a new Python file and import the following packages (the full code is in the `UNData.py` file already provided):

```
import re
```

2. Let's define the input filename:

```
input_file = 'TextFile.txt'
```

3. We need to initialize the dictionary that will contain the data:

```
data = {}
```

4. Now, we can load and print the data:

```
data['Twain'] = open(input_file,'r').read()
print(data['Twain'])
```

5. Let's convert the data into lowercase:

```
for k in data:
    data[k] = data[k].lower()
```

6. Let's remove any punctuation:

```
for k in data:
    data[k] = re.sub(r'[-./?!,":;()\']',' ',data[k])
```

7. Let's remove the numbers:

```
for k in data:
    data[k] = re.sub('[-|0-9]',' ',data[k])
```

8. Let's remove any extra blank spaces:

```
for k in data:
    data[k] = re.sub(' +',' ',data[k])
```

9. Finally, we will print and save the results in a .csv file:

```
print('#########################')
print(data['Twain'])

with open('Twain.csv', 'w') as f:
    for key in data.keys():
        f.write("%s,%s\n"%(key,data[key]))
    f.close()
```

The following screenshot shows the input file (left) and the results that were obtained (right):

```
Shaksperean Revival ! ! !                              shaksperean revival
Wonderful Attraction!                                  wonderful attraction
For One Night Only!                                    for one night only
The world renowned tragedians,                         the world renowned tragedians
David Garrick the Younger, of Drury Lane Theatre London,   david garrick the younger of drury lane theatre london
and                                                    and
Edmund Kean the elder, of the Royal Haymarket Theatre,  edmund kean the elder of the royal haymarket theatre
Whitechapel, Pudding Lane, Piccadilly, London, and the  whitechapel pudding lane piccadilly london and the
Royal Continental Theatres, in their sublime            royal continental theatres in their sublime
Shaksperean Spectacle entitled                          shaksperean spectacle entitled
The Balcony Scene                                       the balcony scene
in                                                      in
Romeo and Juliet ! ! !|                                 romeo and juliet
Romeo.................Mr. Garrick                        romeo mr garrick
Juliet.................Mr. Kean                          juliet mr kean
Assisted by the whole strength of the company!          assisted by the whole strength of the company
New costumes, new scenes, new appointments!             new costumes new scenes new appointments
Also:                                                   also
The thrilling, masterly, and blood-curdling             the thrilling masterly and blood curdling
Broad-sword conflict In Richard III. ! ! !              broad sword conflict in richard iii
Richard III............Mr. Garrick                      richard iii mr garrick
Richmond...............Mr. Kean                          richmond mr kean
Also:                                                   also
(by special request)                                    by special request
Hamlet's Immortal Soliloquy ! !                         hamlet's immortal soliloquy
By The Illustrious Kean!                                by the illustrious kean
Done by him 300 consecutive nights in Paris!            done by him consecutive nights in paris
For One Night Only, On account of imperative European engagements!   for one night only on account of imperative european engagements
Admission 25 cents; children and servants, 10 cents.    admission cents children and servants cents
```

How it works...

In this recipe, we learned how to handle unstructured data. To do this, a piece of text from Mark Twain's novel was used. After loaded the text, punctuation, numbers, and extra blank spaces were removed. Also, all of the text was transformed into lowercase. Finally, the results was stored in a `.csv` file.

There's more...

In this recipe, we have addressed the problem of text analysis, which represents the process of converting the unstructured text into meaningful data for a subsequent analysis phase. Several techniques can be used for text analysis, and we dealt with several in Chapter 7, *Analyzing Text Data*.

See also

- Refer to `Chapter 7`, *Analyzing Text Data*
- Refer to *Unstructured Data* (from Stanford University): `https://web.stanford.edu/class/cs102/lecturenotes/UnstructuredData.pdf`

Deploying machine learning models

Bringing into production a project based on machine learning isn't easy. In fact, there are only a few companies that have managed to do it, at least for large projects. The difficulties lie in the fact that artificial intelligence is not something that is produced with finished software. A starting platform is needed to implement its own software model encountering problems that are not analogous to those that the developers usually encounter. The classic approach of software engineering leads to abstraction so that you arrive at simple code that can be modified and improved. Unfortunately, it is difficult to pursue abstraction in machine learning applications, just as it is difficult to control the complexity of machine learning. The best thing to do is focus on a platform that has the functions you need and, at the same time, allows you to withdraw from the mathematical foundations of machine learning. In this recipe, we will present the Amazon SageMaker platform.

Getting ready

Amazon SageMaker is a paid service, but thanks to the AWS free usage plan, you can start using Amazon SageMaker for free for the first two months after registration. For further information on the available tariff plans, check out the following link: `https://aws.amazon.com`.

How to do it...

Let's see how we can make use of Amazon SageMaker:

1. First, you need to log in to the console:

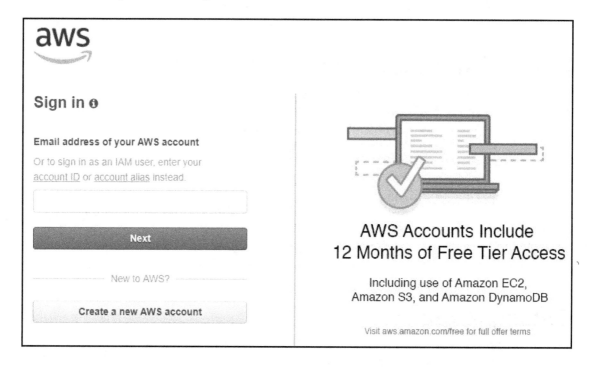

2. Launch a notebook instance with one of the example notebooks:

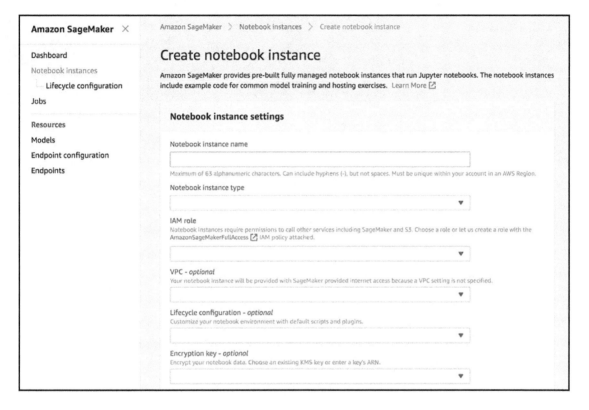

3. Change that instance by connecting to custom data sources.

4. Follow the examples to create, form, and validate the models:

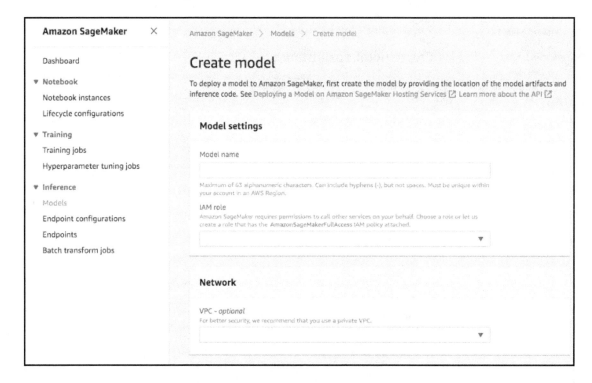

5. Finally, distribute the result in production by following the on-screen steps.

How it works...

Amazon SageMaker is a fully managed service for the creation, training, and distribution of models based on machine learning. Amazon SageMaker comes with three modules—**Build**, **Train**, and **Deploy**. The Build module allows us to work with data, experiment with algorithms, and view the output. The Train module trains the model and optimizes it on a large scale. Finally, there is the Deploy module, which allows us to easily test the inference of the model with low latency.

There's more...

Amazon SageMaker allows us to create machine learning models for use in intelligent and predictive apps. From a security standpoint, Amazon SageMaker encrypts all scripts based on machine learning. Requests to the API and the Amazon SageMaker console are forwarded via a **secure connection** (**SSL**). We can use AWS Identity and Access Management to automatically assign access permissions to training and distribution resources. We can also use Bucket S3, an Amazon SageMaker KMS key, to notebook training processes and endpoints to encrypt storage volumes.

See also

- Refer to the official documentation of Amazon SageMaker: `https://docs.aws.amazon.com/en_us/sagemaker/latest/dg/whatis.html`

Keeping track of changes into production

The distribution of the model is not the end—it's only the beginning. The real problems start from here. We have no control over the data in the real environment. Changes may occur and we must be ready to detect and update our model before it becomes obsolete. Monitoring is important to ensure the reliability, availability, and performance of our machine learning application. In this recipe, we will discuss some tools that we can use to keep track of changes that occur in the model.

How to do it...

The following tools are available to monitor an Amazon SageMaker application:

- **Amazon CloudWatch**: This tool, which is available in AWS, monitors the resources and applications that run in real time. Parameters can be collected and tracked, custom control panels can be created, and alerts can be set to notify or take action when a specified parameter reaches a specified threshold. The following screenshot shows an overview of Amazon CloudWatch:

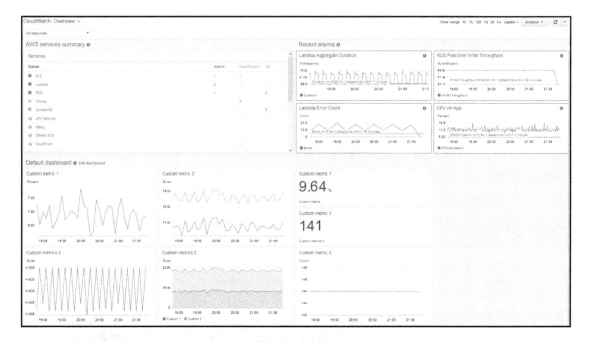

- **Amazon CloudWatch Logs**: This tool, which is available in AWS, allows you to monitor, store, and access log files from EC2, AWS CloudTrail instances, and other sources. The CloudWatch logs monitor information in the log files and allow us to send notifications when certain thresholds are reached.
- **AWS CloudTrail**: This tool, which is available in AWS, retrieves API calls and related events that are created by our account and returns a log file to a specified Amazon S3 bucket. We can also retrieve useful information about the users and accounts that have called the services, and we can trace the IP address from which the calls were made and when they occurred.

How it works...

To monitor Amazon SageMaker, we can use Amazon CloudWatch, which collects raw data and transforms it into readable parameters in real time. These statistics are kept for a period of 15 months so that you can access historical information and offer a better perspective on the performance of the service or web application. However, the Amazon CloudWatch console limits the search to the parameters that have been updated in the last two weeks. This limitation allows you to view the most up-to-date processes in the namespace. It is also possible to set alarms that control certain thresholds and send notifications or take action when these thresholds are reached.

There's more...

A machine learning model is based on a set of input training data with various attributes. Therefore, it is important to check whether the input data that the model was trained on still applies to the actual data in the real environment. The data change could be sudden, or it could change gradually over time. Therefore, it is essential to identify patterns of change and correct the model in advance. Once the model has been distributed in a production environment, it is necessary to follow the steps mentioned in the next recipe to keep our models healthy and useful for their end users.

See also

- Refer to the official documentation of Amazon CloudWatch: `https://docs.aws.amazon.com/cloudwatch/index.html`
- Refer to the official documentation of Amazon CloudWatch Logs: `https://docs.aws.amazon.com/en_us/AmazonCloudWatch/latest/logs/WhatIsCloudWatchLogs.html`
- Refer to the official documentation of Amazon CloudTrail: `https://docs.aws.amazon.com/cloudtrail/index.html`

Tracking accuracy to optimize model scaling

As we saw in `Chapter 15`, *Automated Machine Learning and Transfer Learning*, most machine learning algorithms employ a series of parameters that control the functionality of the underlying algorithm. These parameters are generally called hyperparameters; their values influence the quality of trained models. Automatic model optimization is the process of finding a set of hyperparameters of an algorithm that offer an optimal model. In this recipe, we will learn how to use the Amazon SageMaker tools to optimize our model automatically.

How to do it...

To perform an automatic optimization of our model, follow these steps:

1. Open the Amazon SageMaker console.
2. Select the **Endpoint** item in the navigation pane at the bottom-left.

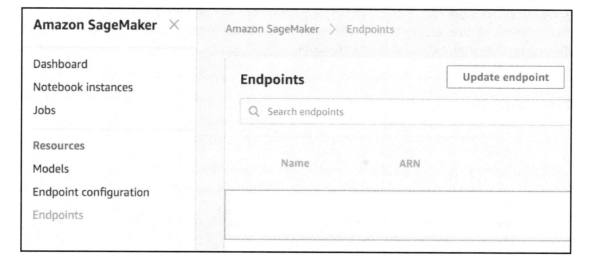

3. Select the endpoint you want to configure from those available.
4. Select the variant you want to configure and configure automatic scaling. Do this for the **Endpoint** runtime settings.
5. Enter the average number of invocations per instance, per minute for the variant. Do this for the target value.

6. Enter the number of seconds for each cooling period.
7. To prevent the scaling policy from deleting variant instances, select the **Disable scale** option.
8. Click **Save**.

How it works...

The hyperparameter optimization procedure represents a special case of regression. The problem can be framed as follows: a set of input features is available, and then this procedure optimizes a model for the adopted parameters. The choice of parameters is free as long as it is defined by the algorithm we are using. In the Amazon hyperparameter optimization procedure, SageMaker tries to find out what hyperparameter combinations are more likely to produce the best results, and tries to execute the training processes to test these attempts. To do this, the first set of values for those hyperparameters is tested, and then the procedure uses regression to choose the next set of values to be tested.

There's more...

When you choose the best hyperparameters for the next training process, hyperparameter optimization takes into consideration everything you know about the problem, up to the present time. In some cases, the hyperparameter optimization procedure can choose a point that produces an incremental improvement in the best result that's been found so far. In this way, the procedure uses already known results. In other cases, you can choose a set of hyperparameters far from those you have already tested. In this way, the procedure explores the space and searches for new areas that haven't been fully analyzed yet. The compromise between exploration and exploitation is common in many machine learning problems.

See also

- Refer to *Automatically Scale Amazon SageMaker Models*: `https://docs.aws.amazon.com/en_us/sagemaker/latest/dg/endpoint-auto-scaling.html`

Other Books You May Enjoy

If you enjoyed this book, you may be interested in these other books by Packt:

Building Machine Learning Systems with Python - Third Edition
Luis Pedro Coelho, Willi Richert, Matthieu Brucher

ISBN: 9781788623223

- Build a classification system that can be applied to text, images, and sound
- Employ Amazon Web Services (AWS) to run analysis on the cloud
- Solve problems related to regression using scikit-learn and TensorFlow
- Recommend products to users based on their past purchases
- Understand different ways to apply deep neural networks on structured data
- Address recent developments in the field of computer vision and reinforcement learning

Mastering Machine Learning Algorithms

Giuseppe Bonaccorso

ISBN: 9781788621113

- Explore how a ML model can be trained, optimized, and evaluated
- Understand how to create and learn static and dynamic probabilistic models
- Successfully cluster high-dimensional data and evaluate model accuracy
- Discover how artificial neural networks work and how to train, optimize, and validate them
- Work with Autoencoders and Generative Adversarial Networks
- Apply label spreading and propagation to large datasets
- Explore the most important Reinforcement Learning techniques

Leave a review - let other readers know what you think

Please share your thoughts on this book with others by leaving a review on the site that you bought it from. If you purchased the book from Amazon, please leave us an honest review on this book's Amazon page. This is vital so that other potential readers can see and use your unbiased opinion to make purchasing decisions, we can understand what our customers think about our products, and our authors can see your feedback on the title that they have worked with Packt to create. It will only take a few minutes of your time, but is valuable to other potential customers, our authors, and Packt. Thank you!

Index

CPSIA information can be obtained
at www.ICGtesting.com
Printed in the USA
BVHW010233120620
581397BV00007B/254